John W. R-Love M. D.
424-8300

C0-ASO-264

Clinical Psychiatry

CLINICAL PSYCHIATRY:
Issues and Challenges

Hans Oppenheimer, M.D.

Clinical Associate Professor of Psychiatry
State University of New York
Downstate Medical Center, Brooklyn, New York

MEDICAL DEPARTMENT
HARPER & ROW, PUBLISHERS
New York, Evanston, San Francisco, London

GRATEFUL ACKNOWLEDGEMENT IS MADE FOR PERMISSION TO REPRINT THE FOLLOWING:

Lines from "The Hollow Men" by T. S. Eliot in *Collected Poems 1909–1962* on pages 88 and 204. Reprinted by permission of Harcourt Brace Jovanovich, Inc.

Lines from "Sweeney Among the Nightingales" by T. S. Eliot in *Collected Poems 1909–1962* on page 277. Reprinted by permission of Harcourt Brace Jovanovich, Inc.

Figure 1, "Error on Green" by Paul Klee on page 280. Reprinted by permission of S.P.A.D.E.M. 1970, French Reproduction Rights, Inc.

Figure 2, "Psychotic Patient" in *Psychoanalytic Explorations in Art* by Ernst Kris on page 281. Reprinted by permission of International Universities Press, Inc. Copyright 1952 by International Universities Press, Inc.

Excerpts from *Dementia Praecox or The Group of Schizophrenias* by Eugen Bleuler. Reprinted by permission of International Universities Press, Inc. Copyright 1950 by International Universities Press, Inc.

CLINICAL PSYCHIATRY: Issues and Challenges

Copyright © 1971 by Harper & Row, Publishers, Inc. All rights reserved. No part of this book may be used or reproduced in any manner whatsoever without written permission except in the case of brief quotations embodied in critical articles and reviews. Printed in the United States of America. For information address Medical Department, Harper & Row, Publishers, Inc., 49 East 33rd Street, New York, N.Y. 10016.

First Edition

STANDARD BOOK NUMBER 06-141853-6
LIBRARY OF CONGRESS CATALOG CARD NUMBER: 77-134299

She has been the unspoken half of everything I ever wrote . . .

ROBERT FROST

Contents

Preface

This book is based on and evolved from lectures on clinical psychiatry that have been given by the author over a period of some years to residents and medical students as part of their psychiatric training. In its complete form, however, the book addresses itself to all students of clinical psychiatry who would share this author's belief, and pleasure, in the pursuit of disciplined inquisitive thought in this field.

Samuel Johnson is quoted as having remarked that he did not believe that lectures could do as much good as reading the books from which the lectures are taken. No teacher who likes his subject and aims toward increasing mastery of it could possibly disagree with Doctor Johnson's wise judgment. But if a teacher undertakes to write a book on his lectures, he may well ask himself whether reading such a book will do as much good as hearing the lectures. My conclusion—after careful consideration of this problem—has been that there are both advantages and disadvantages in such an endeavor. The precision of presentation and the need to forego the ease and informality of the spoken word may well make greater demands on the reader; his reward, on the other hand, will consist of the opportunity to study the text, reflect, and be encouraged to think independently.

In every lecture there is, in addition to the purely factual and didactic transmission of information, a subtle but significant element of personal contact between the teacher and the student. Much of this is nonverbal. But books contain only words. Therefore, the reader, it is hoped, will realize that on occasion modes of expression and even personal reflections were deliberately included in the text in order to maintain this personal contact, the teacher-student relationship.

Although this text deals with clinical psychiatry, it is not a textbook of clinical psychiatry, as such. The relationship of this book to a conventional textbook is not that of an alternative, but of a complement—a *supplementary text*. We have sought to find an equitable and profitable distribution between enumerative information, to present correlative knowledge in depth, and to pose significant but as yet unanswered questions. I have come to believe that these three pursuits constitute a natural and evolving process of maturation of the scientific mind, and I suppose that they do, or ought to, take place in the order in which I have just listed them. It would be unrealistic to attempt to do full justice to each of these goals. There are reference books to give us all the known facts; there are outstanding theoreticians whose papers and books we can consult. There is also the constant and independent flow of clinical observation which ought to help us in either confirming or correcting what we think is true.

In following the road I have chosen, I have tried to do justice to what, to the best of my knowledge, represents a reasonable and unbiased presentation of the material. The selection of the topics of the individual chapters was, of course, determined by their respective and particular relevance to clinical psychiatry. I might have been justified, and even expected, to add a few more. It seemed to me that each chapter, apart from its informative character, represented also an apposite central theme around which "correlative knowledge in depth" could be gathered.

Issues pertaining to therapy have not been included in any systematic way because this book does not address itself to this aspect of clinical psychiatry. There are many excellent books and articles available that deal with the various psychotherapies. In this connection I wish to comment upon well-motivated objections by psychiatrists who question the "practical" value of neurophysiological, phenomenological, theoretical, and so-called purely scientific expositions when the overriding problem, so they say, is to help the patient. The priority of therapy is, of course, beyond dispute. But what is at times overlooked is the fact that in psychotherapy (as in other forms of medical treatment) we do not offer, and the patient would not profit from, a *direct* and *unmodified* informative transmission of our knowledge of his pathology. Yet, such knowledge is prerequisite to the application of psychiatric treatment, from psychoanalysis to insulin shock treatment. Freud's lifework, at a level of unquestioned superiority, confirms that the theoretical yield is always ahead of the therapeutic one, or almost always.

In conclusion—and looking into a wider sphere of contemporary scientific thrust and fallout—I should like to say that a purely utilitarian (and in that sense materialistic) approach to the fruits and function of knowledge may entail hazards. Perhaps the bitter foretaste of these is already with us. Again, it is a matter of finding a wise balance. Knowledge for knowledge's sake at least will never enslave us. The reader of this book will recall T. S. Eliot's pensive question:

> *Where is the wisdom we have lost in*
> *knowledge?*
> *Where is the knowledge we have lost in*
> *information?*

> *Choruses from the Rock* (unpublished)

Brooklyn, New York

HANS OPPENHEIMER, M.D.

Acknowledgments

The author wishes to express his sincere thanks to Dr. Marvin Stein, Professor and Chairman, Department of Psychiatry, Downstate Medical Center, Brooklyn, N.Y.; Dr. Phillip Polatin, Professor of Clinical Psychiatry, College of Physicians and Surgeons, Columbia University, and Clinical Director of the New York Psychiatric Institute; and to Dr. Stanley M. Aronson, Professor of Medical Science, Brown University, Providence, R.I., for their interest and suggestions during the preparation of this book.

H.O.

1

The Scope of Clinical Psychiatry

In the long history of life on this planet the human brain is a late arrival, which evolution can proudly claim to be the latest exponent of "the survival of the fittest"—and we still hope to vindicate this promise. The human mind—with all its complexities, with all its power to adapt the environment to its needs, and with its aspirations and follies—has, of course, its precursors and simplified equivalents on the infrahuman level. I recall Karl Lashley's belief: "I am coming more and more to the conviction that . . . the rudiments of every human behavioral mechanism will be found far down on the evolutionary scale and also represented even in primitive activities of the nervous system."[1]

Similarly, the scientific study of the human mind and of its illnesses is a late arrival in the history of medicine. Because of its ineffable qualities and inescapable powers, man's mind has arrested the attention of mystics, philosophers, and poets long before it became the object of study by psychiatrists. Not only individual human existence but also all aspects of social human coexistence are made possible only as the result of mental processes. It therefore seems desirable to limit the concept of clinical psychiatry by defining it and, in so doing, confining it within its proper boundaries. Hughlings Jackson once said that a gardener and a botanist look at flowers from a different point of view. As physicians we must, of course, assume the attitude of the botanist.

It requires but little reflection to understand that only certain deviations in the mental life of man and only certain diseases of his brain fall within the scope of clinical psychiatry. We must attempt to define the boundaries that separate this field from clinical neurology on the one hand and on the other from that "no man's land" of everyday unhappiness that Freud once contrasted with "hysterical misery."[2] We shall also have something to say about the "never never land" called normality.

1

One can define the boundary between psychiatry and neurology in Jacksonian concepts, in terms of that pioneer's ideas concerning the evolution of the nervous system and the existence within it of lowest, intermediate, and highest levels. In the lowest and intermediate levels—such as the brainstem and certain cortical areas—there exists a rather close correspondence of localization and function (or "instrumentalities") such as Area 4 or 17 or the speech area; the farther downward we go, the closer will this correspondence be. By contrast, the highest levels are the material correlatives of states of consciousness and reactivity; they mediate the highest or mental functions. In disease, the amount of tissue lost more than the site of the lesion determines the nature and degree of pathology. Everything downward is, in Jackson's words, "re-re-represented"[3] at the highest levels. Jacksonian principles will be presented in the next chapter; for the moment we propose that psychiatry concerns itself with pathology of the highest levels, and neurology with that of the intermediate and lower levels.

This concept can be illustrated by presenting certain aspects of a case history. Toward the end of her illness this patient was reported occasionally to have run into objects as if she had not seen them. The optic discs were flat and the left disc was pale, suggesting possible blindness. The responsibility of the neurologist is that of dealing with this issue at lower and intermediate levels: with the regional localization of function. If the patient ran into objects, the neurologist should determine if this occurs only on her left side,—that is, if she has loss of left extrapersonal space, most likely associated with unawareness of the left side of her body. He could then conclude that she had a lesion in the right thalamoparietal bundle. Or he might conclude from the appearance of the discs that she had the Foster Kennedy syndrome, let us say secondary to an expanding lesion of the left prefrontal area. The psychiatrist would enter upon the scene if at the same time this patient denied her blindness. Denial of peripheral blindness in frontal lobe disease is a well-known phenomenon. Personality changes in disease of the prefrontal area include loss of normal concern (hence, euphoria) and affective as well as intellectual inability to project one's self into the future (hence, poor judgment and loss of anxiety, particularly social anxiety). Denial of blindness in such a case reflects a pathology of personality at the highest level.

There is another aspect of great practical significance to the difference between psychiatry and neurology, which is also rooted in the much greater complexity of the highest levels. Let us examine the difference between a neurological *diagnosis* and a psychiatric *interpretation*. As discussant at a Clinical Neuropathological Conference I remarked as follows.

I invite attention to the difference between causal and understandable connections. Nobody will deny that in the natural sciences only causal connections are valid. Their validity, even if expressed in abstract formulas, derives from the fact that ultimately phenomena can be reduced to an immediately given reality, such as, a perception. Thus in the field of neurology causal connections based on the more immediately given realities of neuroanatomy and neurophysiology permit us to establish an accurate correlation between a disease process and its clinical manifestations. The psychopathologist is at a distinct disadvantage; he requires a great deal of information, and time and favorable conditions to elicit it, before he can make causal connections. Unfortunately there is no Brodman area for the Oedipus complex or the meaning of a delusion. But the cause for a right homonymous hemianopsia is a lesion in the left visual pathways anywhere behind the chiasma. The hemianopsia is *diagnosed,* not *interpreted.* In psychopathology we use interpretations in order to establish connections . . . [But] the psychiatrist . . . will *not* make or accept an interpretation merely because it is understandable. Certain life experiences, past or current, may "understandably" lead to certain psychopathological phenomena; understandably, because one can feel oneself into the patient's reactions. This is one reason for error.[4]

Somewhat belatedly, psychiatry has caught up with the fact that "effects" are not mere consequences of single "causes," but reflect a complex set of altered relationships set into motion by a "cause." In this sense the "linear neurological diagnosis" had to be replaced by the multidimensional psychiatric interpretation. In psychiatry as well as in psychoanalysis the multitude of interacting factors necessitates a relativistic conception of etiology as well as of diagnosis. This is what is meant by interpretation.

A distinction should also be made between clinical psychiatry and psychoanalysis—a distinction, not a discrimination. The term *psychoanalysis* has, of course, many applications. It is a special method of psychotherapy; it is a theory of personality development and character formation; it has proven itself to be a highly successful model for understanding present-day behavior of a person in the light of his past experiences; it is the science of depth psychology; and it has been applied to the study of anthropology, wit, and religion, to name just a few of man's attempts to understand his past, his pastimes, and his passing existence. And then there is, finally, clinical psychoanalysis. It is, of course, with regard to the last application that a brief distinction from clinical psychiatry should be made. The distinction is inclusive, not exclusive. Within the broad field of clinical psychiatry, clinical psychoanalysis helps us most to understand a psychopathology which has resulted from *inter*personal, not *im*personal pathogenic causes—a psychopathology which is dynamic, not formal, functional, not organic. Thus, in any given patient, clinical psychoanalysis may have relevance in accordance with the prevalence of these suggested criteria.

In order to permit a comprehensive approach to clinical psychiatry, the use of descriptive psychiatry is of the greatest importance and benefit. In a paper entitled "Phenomenological and Descriptive Aspects of Psychiatry," H. C. Rümke proposes various frames of reference that he considers relevant to a complete description and thus to a holistic explanation and comprehension of each and every conceivable phenomenon within the scope of clinical psychiatry.[5] Each frame of reference may be of greater or lesser, or indeed of *decisive* significance in a given case; none is likely to be entirely extraneous in any given case. The holistic approach is not only scientifically sound because its structure takes cognizance of the composite totality of psychopathology, but it is also psychiatrically mature and protects us against the unwholesome consequences of parochial and sectarian adherence to only one ordained school of thought. John Morley's warning, "Where it is a duty to worship the sun it is pretty sure to be a crime to examine the laws of heat,"[6] should not go unheeded in our present context.

A brief comment about the term "descriptive psychiatry" is perhaps necessary. All psychiatry, including clinical psychoanalysis, is descriptive, although different things will be described in a phobia and in a case of epileptic automatism. The value of a description lies in the amount, depth, and validity of its content. Psychiatry has advanced far enough, together with its auxiliary sciences, since the era of Kraepelin to make the term "descriptive" scientifically respectable and responsible.

Some of Rümke's suggested frames of reference will now be presented. We shall have to include theoretical and academic issues, etiology, diagnosis, and therapy.

BIOLOGICAL CONSIDERATIONS

I do not wish to dwell here on the enormous amount of neurobiochemical and neuroelectrophysiological information which came to light when the psychological coin was turned on its other side. Instead, we will confine ourselves to the traditional distinction that is being made between organic and functional mental illnesses. What ought to be the meaning of these terms? A distinction is justified, but not in a manner which is still extant. It is true that demonstrable brain damage, gross or microscopic, is found in the so-called organic psychoses; but in dementia praecox, which is still described as a "functional psychosis," the most competent, modern, and convincing psychiatric opinion no longer doubts the decisive role of genetic and neurophysio-

logical abnormalities in making this disease possible. An idiopathic epileptic seizure is as fugitive and reversible as a fit of convulsive anger;
still, traditional psychiatry classifies the former as organic and the latter
as functional. There is little doubt that purely psychological influences
leave an as yet unrecognizable trace in the brain—but this fact, this
reasonable assumption of a "psychometabolism," is not the same as "organicity." I suggest that the apposite difference between "organic" and
functional lies in the area of etiology. If the brain becomes diseased
as a result of an *impersonal* defect—whether from injury, poison, or
vascular, neoplastic, and degenerative sickness, or a more elusive neuro-
metabolic abnormality—then the resulting condition is truly organic.
But the brain (and thus the mind) of a person can also be adversely
affected by prolonged, intense, and unhealthy influences originating from
other persons—particularly significant persons—and especially during
its time of least resistance (i.e., during childhood). This results not
in defects but in *conflicts* and in the consequences of unresolved conflicts
such as neurotic symptoms or character deformations. These are functional diseases that are intelligible and reducible to residues of the patient's life history, his ontogeny. This is what Freud meant when he
said that the hysteric suffers from memories. There is as little sense
to inquire about the patient's sexual or educational history in a case
of Pick's disease as there is in testing a patient's capacity for retention
and immediate recall of digits if he suffers from a sexual perversion,
or even from a hysterical amnesia. Psychiatric patients with organic
brain disease do, of course, quite often present signs and exaggeration
of functional abnormalities, resulting from and leading to interpersonal
difficulties. However, they are not of the essence, although they have
a place within the totality of the illness. This distinction between impersonal organicity and interpersonal functional disease on the basis
of etiology has also some relevance in regard to treatment. The physical
therapies (such as drugs or shock treatment) are "impersonal" in the
sense that they are applied to the brain; psychotherapy, by contrast,
appeals to the person and is "interpersonal" in a very special way.

SURFACE PHENOMENA

Surface phenomena are expressions of psychopathology which
either present themselves spontaneously or else can be elicited
most readily and by very simple methods of examination. In many cases,
their value—both for diagnosis and as a guide for our professional approach to the patient—can hardly be overstated. Surface phenomena
are not superficial manifestations.

Let me illustrate the application of this frame of reference with a few clinical examples. Suppose a patient is mute; one look at his face by an experienced examiner will usually suffice in deciding whether he is depressed or catatonic; or the patient's visible efforts to speak, accompanied by an obvious paralysis of the right side, permit a diagnosis of peripheral motor aphasia. Another patient resorts to a metonymic choice of a word, and our attention is immediately arrested; we suspect a schizophrenic thought and language pathology. A third patient *describes* an object shown him instead of *naming* it; he has retreated from the higher level of abstraction to the lower level of concreteness. There is really no reason why we should consider a Freudian slip to be more significant than a Jacksonian slump! Generally, surface phenomena tell us more about the *form* than the *content* of mental illness, but even with regard to content and its dynamics they may provide the experienced listener with hints pointing toward the depths. As an example, one may point out that an analyst readily appreciates the defensive significance of a *spontaneous* denial on the part of a patient.

DEPTH PHENOMENA

In order to elicit, understand, and deal with even a fragment of depth-psychopathology it should first be made clear what we mean by *depth*. The obvious implication is a general impression of remoteness; depth phenomena, although potent, may leave the surface appearance of the patient's behavior rather unruffled; rationalization is a case in point. Or else the remoteness may be purely temporal—distant but significant childhood experiences that are repressed and thus unknown to the patient may many years later determine his choice of a marriage partner in a futile attempt to realize an incestuous desire or to undo a childhood humiliation; the patient may remain unhappily undivorced, or he may divorce the spouse for the wrong reasons (rooted in the depths of an abnormal psychosexual development). There is a third quality of remoteness regarding depth phenomena: surface symptoms which are not immediately or easily accessible to comprehension, such as a phobia, an obsessive ritual, or a conversion symptom. An element of obscurity is added to the temporal distance between the symptom and its source. A great part of depth-psychology concerns itself with the derivatives of instinctual needs and of infantile fantasies; a host of mental mechanisms, such as displacement, desexualization, symbolization, isolation, or conversion, are at the disposal of the human mind to account for such coded present-day expressions of early, plain psychological experiences. This special form of psychological causality, which we call *motivation* in human beings, owes its obscurity to its complexity.

It is easy to see that the frame of reference of "depth" is desirable and indeed necessary for the understanding and treatment of functional disorders or, generally, of the neuroses. This approach also entails the kind of "history taking in depth" which we attempt through free association, dream interpretation, and observation of slips or symptomatic acts. The application of depth-psychology deals more with the mental content than the particular form through which psychopathology expresses itself. Thus indications for its use are largely determined by functional components of the illness, and its success in treatment may, in a given case, be less rewarding than its revelations; no patient recovers merely by being informed about the origin and meaning of his pathology. However, this is not the place to talk about indications for treatment in depth, but it may not be entirely amiss to caution against the tempting assumption that every aspect of behavior must be of profound significance merely because it derives from the depths.

LEVELS OF FUNCTIONING

We include in our total evaluation of psychopathology in a given patient an estimate of the kind and degree of pathological reduction—not of optimal, but of normal and expected capacities. We want to know at what level of functioning mentation and behavior take place. The leveling-off of function that concerns us here is never minute or isolated; it is substantial and broad. Against its background diagnosis, prognosis and treatment will become more accurate and effective.

Let us consider just three applications of this particular frame of reference: state of consciousness; dissolution as a Jacksonian term; and regression as conceived by Freud. It is obvious that the only common denominator of these three diverse psychological organismic states is what I referred to as "reduction."

Level of Consciousness. Lowering of the level of consciousness, for whatever reasons, is invariably accompanied by profound changes in mentation and behavior. For this reason psychiatric symptoms resulting from reduction of the state of consciousness are usually benign and often transient. Within the realm of fluctuations of alertness and wakefulness several examples may be mentioned. There is, above all, the phenomenon of the dream—a hallucination enigmatically composed of all the known ingredients of the primary process; possible, benign, and transient only because of the state of reduction of consciousness which accompanies the REM phase as it does the dreamless span of sleep. But even when the reduction of alertness is very slight—as in simple absent-mindedness—certain verbal or nonverbal *Fehlleistungen* (derailments) occur which differ fundamentally in origin and significance from the dynamically motivated parapraxes. In the field of psychopathology we consider hallucinations and certain delusions to be more malignant if they occur in a state of clear consciousness, as they do in almost all instances of schizophrenia. The same principle can be applied in a discriminating comparison of delirious disorientation and schizophrenic misidentification. In the former the inappropriate subjectivity revealed in the faulty orientation is rooted in remnants of the secondary process; in the latter it is the expression of autism, a much more malignant form of "subjectivity" and one that is closer, both dynamically and formally, to the primary process.

Dissolution.   This is a Jacksonian term denoting not only diffuse or circumscribed orderly retreat of mental capacities toward lower levels in case of disease, but which also represents Jackson's conception of the evolution and dissolution of the nervous system. It is clinically represented in the various syndromes seen in the organic dementias, in delirium, and in the paroxysmal or epileptic disorders. These are all conditions leading to a cognitive transformation of the personality.

Freud and Jackson were contemporaries. It is certain that Freud knew of Jackson's work because he mentions his name in his little-known monograph on aphasia. Both men advanced our understanding of the mind by taking a hard look backwards—Freud into ontogeny and Jackson into phylogeny. In dissolution more primitive layers or levels are set free; more automatic behavior replaces voluntary action; in less severe damage, in terms of Kurt Goldstein's concepts, concrete behavior has to substitute for the loss of abstract capacity; discrimination of differences is lost while comprehension of similarities is still retained; emotional language outlasts propositional use of words. There are, of course, some similarities in the cognitive limitations of the child and the state of dissolution of dementia; but it must not be overlooked that the speechless apoplectic adult as little reverts to "baby-talk" as the growing child "recovers from aphasia." Thus, when applying the frame of reference of dissolution, we find the developmental history of the patient of no particular help or importance.

Regression.   Psychoanalytic theory and practice have taught us that in the overall behavior of certain patients "earlier levels still persist along with . . . higher levels" and that "constitutional or experiential factors may cause this to become more transparent."[7] The "child" either persists in the adult because of a pathological fixation, or it returns under the stress of a difficult reality. There is a decisive balance and interaction among fixation, stress, and inherent ego strength, all of which factors decide the fact and degree of regressive and hence ineffectual (and even fateful) behavior. Regression has all the disadvantages of "the child within us," and none of its redeeming features. It is important, both for diagnosis and treatment—and particularly for the tactics of therapy—to recognize, tolerate, expose, and discourage the various kinds and depths of these inferior levels of functioning that are subsumed under the term "regression." Extreme degrees of regressive behavior, such as states of panic or of murderous rage, are easily recognized and require prompt and uncompromising attention. Less dramatic and more subtle but pervasive forms of regression, such as compulsive attitudes in their endless varieties, regressive forms of sexual behavior, or excessive claims and dependency cannot be met and opposed head-on. For a long time in the treatment of such patients we may be wise to respect the limits of what *can* be done instead of vainly trying to restore what *ought* to be.

The application of levels of functioning in terms of regression for purposes of diagnostic classification, as was done by Freud, is perhaps of greater academic than practical importance. No two patients with the same diagnosis are alike. Still, in the functional disorders, the discovery of the fact, area, depth, and tenacity of regression remains one of the several major objectives in the practice of clinical psychiatry.

There are many more levels of functioning that can only be mentioned here. They may include intelligence, capacity for sublimation, presence and availability of "inner resources," imagination, and capacity for fantasy—not the kind which is divorced from reality and at best sterile, but the sort which can make of reality more than meets the ordinary eye.

INTERPERSONAL ASPECTS

Man is a social animal that lives with, against, and for the members of his species in a society whose complexity matches the limitless inventiveness of his brain and whose demands, rewards, and punishments have to be reckoned with by him throughout his life (and even beyond his death). In the evolutionary process the anonymous contiguity of the flock has gradually been transformed into the togetherness of the family, the group, and the society—in accordance with the emergence of personality and individuality. This process has abruptly reached a position of ascendancy in man. He alone is subjected during his protracted childhood to influences by significant persons who form, or deform, his character. He alone can feel most keenly the differences between self and nonself; communicate across ego boundaries through language; bridge the gap through love; widen it by fear, hate, and suspicion; narrow it by identification—thus creating, for better or worse, what Erikson called *pseudo-speciation,* a variety of psychosocial groupings among and within his own species. Man alone receives, through his elders, his conscience and his ego-ideal—his morality. It is not always perfect, but it is always more than a built-in inhibitory mechanism. Tribal influences create the taboo; rational and lawful social order restrains and protects; true morality, based neither on the wand of the sorcerer nor the club of the policeman, remains the ultimate aspiration of man as a social and truly civilized creature.

The clinical psychiatrist is sensitive to the interpersonal frame of reference in several ways. Interpersonal influences are largely responsible for the etiology in the functional disorders; they are reactivated in the transference experience and are made use of in the psychotherapeutic process. These interpersonal influences are *intimate,* not only because of their frequent concern with sexuality and elimination and physical issues in general, but also in that they occur so frequently and decisively within the family, the innermost nucleus of our social relatedness. They are *intense* because they take place during our childhood, when we are most impressionable and most vulnerable. They are *intensive* because one single circumscribed area of our total experience is hit with overwhelming force, as in pregenital fixation resulting in character deformation or in the case of a childhood fear that leads to a phobia in adulthood.

It is difficult to find compelling reasons for the existence or establishment of boundaries of clinical psychiatry outside the realm of undisputed evidence of mental illness. The discovery and extensive investigation of the transference neuroses and the equally profound scrutiny of the more subtle and seemingly inconsequential "psychopathology of everyday life" were only the first step into an area to which I have referred as "no man's land." The entire question of whether and how to postulate and establish a distinction between the presence of psychological *illness* and the lack or lag of psychological *fitness* has become more urgent owing to the thrust and expansion of post-Freudian psychiatry. As the goals and standards of mental health were expanded, more and more areas and forms of human behavior were impounded as if they lay within the custody or even competence and power of psychological medicine. Enormity and simple ineffectiveness of behavior are equated, respectively, with malignancy and pathology. We rightly claim that *one* reliable and consistent criterion of mental illness—even in its mildest forms, as in the neurotic personality—is loss or impairment of reality testing. Reality, in this context, ranges from perception and the comprehension of causes and consequences to its more arbitrary, parentally and socially imposed aspects, such as right and wrong, good and evil, superior and inferior. I would agree with Kubie that the persistence in adult life of (unconsciously motivated) behavior patterns—which because of their ontogenetic but unrealistic origin become, in later life, not only obsolete but also unworkable sources of further complications and endless repetitions, as well as unyielding hindrances to autonomous and flexible adaptation—might fairly be considered to constitute the outermost outposts of psychopathology.[8] But I hasten to add that in our quest for a sensible delineation of psychopathology, a failure in reality testing must not be confused with the failure of social reality to supply the minimum requirements for individual psychological well-being, security, and satisfaction.

The criteria of psychological normality are relative and ambiguous. Several frames of reference can be as easily refuted as applied. There may be no psychological symptoms, but a psychological reason for failure to reach one's potential. There may be success, but at what cost in psychological health! There may be conformity at the expense of individuality, or adaptation dictated by guilt and fear rather than chosen by tolerance and mature sociality. There may be too much or too little access to the system Ucs—the former masquerading as spontaneity, the latter as control. It may perhaps be better not to attempt or insist on a definition of "normality." But it is to be hoped that the clinical psychiatrist will not be misled by any *pretense* of normality, either on the part of the patient or his culture and society. While we do not judge, we cannot avoid dealing with values, the pursuit of which is the *ultimate* effort on the road toward mental health.

REFERENCES

1. K. S. Lashley. *In:* L. A. Jeffress (ed.). *Cerebral Mechanisms in Behavior*, Hixon Symposium. New York, Wiley.
2. J. Breuer and S. Freud. *Studies in Hysteria*. Nervous and Mental Disease Monograph Series #61, New York, 1947, p. 232.
3. J. Taylor (ed.). *Selected Writings of John Hughlings Jackson*. New York, Basic Books, 1958, vol. 2.
4. Clinical Neuropathological Conference. *Diseases of the Nervous System*, vol. 24, #12, Dec. 1963.
5. H. C. Rümke, "Phenomenological and Descriptive Aspects of Psychiatry." *In: The Third World Congress of Psychiatry*. Montreal, Univer. of Toronto Press, 1961, vol. 1, pp. 17–25.

6. J. Morley. *In:* J. Bartlett, *Familiar Quotations,* 13th (centennial) ed. Boston, Little, Brown, 1955, p. 700a.

7. O. Fenichel. *The Psychoanalytic Theory of Neurosis.* New York, Norton, 1945, p. 53.

8. L. S. Kubie. "The Fundamental Nature of the Distinction between Normality and Neurosis." *Psychoanalytic Quarterly,* #23, 1954, pp. 167–204.

2

The Application of Hughlings Jackson's Principles

When Hughlings Jackson, almost one hundred years ago, delivered his famous lectures and addresses on the evolution and dissolution of the nervous system, he established and defined certain principles which significantly contributed toward making psychopathology caused by "organic" brain disease (both coarse and epileptic) intelligible. Chronologically, his lifespan places him between Darwin and Freud. The theme and impact of the idea of evolution was astir throughout the scientific world of the nineteenth century, and each of these three men, by confining himself to one particular aspect of the phenomenon, dealt with the subject differently.

It is therefore necessary to clarify at the outset Jackson's views on "evolution" as the term was applied by him in relation to the nervous system. He said that in this context evolution ". . . is not simply synonymous with Darwinism. . . . I have long thought that we shall be very much helped in our investigations of diseases of the nervous system by considering them as reversals of evolution, as dissolutions."[1] Thus Jackson introduced the principle of a close and significant correlation between "evolution" and "dissolution" within the nervous system—the former representing the normal development in the species, the latter, disease in the individual. Jackson, in contrast to Freud, investigated mental states resulting from structural or epileptic abnormalities of the brain, and thus of an "impersonal" etiology. Interpersonal or ontogenetically pathogenetic experiences of the patient were of no significance to his theme. Thus Jacksonian "dissolution" connotes a pathological reversal of a phylogenetic order, just as Freudian "regression" describes the neurotic adult's pathological sliding-back to infantile psychological

13

mentation and behavior. If, as has been said, scientific greatness and creativity reveal themselves in the mastery both of the larger design and of its more subtle expressions, Jackson and Freud were indeed exceptional in their respective fields by virtue of their remarkable capacity for combining astuteness of vision and scrutiny of minute detail. It is indeed a curious fact and also confirmation of this assessment to realize how much Jackson deduced from observing the twitching of the index finger at the start of an epileptic seizure, and Freud from the baby's obvious pleasure in sucking its thumb.

The most comprehensive exposition of Jackson's doctrine of the "evolution and dissolution" of the nervous system is contained in his Croonian Lectures. Of course, he elaborated and enlarged on his overall conception in most of his subsequent scientific papers and addresses. Jackson viewed the central nervous system in terms of an evolutionary hierarchy of interacting *levels*. This graded series of functional organizations reflected an evolutionary progression in phylogeny. Accordingly, Jackson conceived of the nervous system as being composed, in an ascending order, of lowest, intermediate, and highest levels. Jackson defined these levels in functional and physiological rather than in anatomical terms. Some broad topographic delineation was, of course, necessary—simply because it existed. Spinal-cord and the brain-stem structures represent the lowest levels in the cerebrum. The highest levels correspond to the anterior and posterior association areas, designations which are sufficiently vague to reflect the general limitations of an anatomical hierarchical parcellation. The intermediate levels are in, Jackson's view, represented by the motor region of Ferrier, the corresponding primary sensory cortical areas, and the several subcortical structures of the striatum—as well as by other subcortical gray masses. But, as already mentioned, Jackson's great contribution in his search for a better understanding of the "organ of the mind" lay in his discovery of, emphasis upon, and observation of functional designs and manifestations, both in health and disease. He was not, in his own words, a "localiser."

EVOLUTION AND DISSOLUTION IN THE NERVOUS SYSTEM

Lowest Levels

In functional terms the activities of these centers are the most automatic (least voluntary), the most fixed and organized, the least complex, and the most resistant to pathological influences affecting the brain in its entirety. Thus they are most likely to withstand progressive uniform "dissolution;" the most ancient representations of phylogenetic evolution; and the most completely and effectively evolved and operative at the time of the birth of the individual. For purposes of illustration one may, for instance, consider the functional qualities of the vital centers for respiration and circulation. These, and other similarly lowest-level structures represent what Jackson once called the "certainties" at birth: "the inherited experiences . . . [which] require scarcely any education."[2] By being the most fixed and organized they would not be easily (or inherently) responsive to further "education." Nor is there any need for further evolution, "learning," and alternative action within these centers. They are quite perfectly evolved for the purposes they serve; their being the "most automatic" guarantees the kind of stability and inflexible but reliable quality to which Lord Adrian once applied the analogy of "a silent and obedient regiment."[3] Jackson put it this way: "The becoming more automatic [of the lowest levels] is not dissolution . . . but is, on the contrary, evolution becoming complete."[4] In other words, for the tasks required of the lower centers, evolution had reached the point of optimal termination and in this sense its destination. But for the evolution of nervous structures which were to support a mental life, which was to be man's biological destiny, different neuronal arrangements, the "highest levels" in Jackson's conceptualization, were necessary.

Highest Levels

As might be expected, the functional qualities of processes engaging the highest levels will not only be distinctly different from but also superior to those of the lower centers. There is, at the highest levels, "something more than . . . a localisation of superiority." It is not only the fact that the highest evolved parts of the body (such as the hand and finger) are more extensively ("superiorly") represented at the cortical level. It is also that the functional superiority of the neuronal arrangements within the highest levels is, in Jackson's view, reflected in the following of their qualities: They are "least fixed and organised," and yet "most complex." This combination of attributes is not only compatible with but also prerequisite to highest-level ("mental") performance. As a neurophysiological hypothesis "least fixed and organized" means also least committed to *one*, or only a few, special and predetermined functions. Thus it could be assumed that such neuronal circuits are open rather than closed; modifiable rather than immutable; and capable of forming innumerable associational patterns, each of which may in turn become a part within a still larger whole. This is what is meant by "complexity." Such neurobiological potential could account for the observable complexities of mentation, particularly including the capacity for learning and growth. Jackson believed that the highest centers, because of the assumed features just referred to, were capable of producing and destined to produce those enormous and conspicuous changes which distinguish the mental life of the infant from that of the adult. He called this process "internal evolution," a term equivalent to mental and psychophysical maturation. "The highest centres are the most complexly evolving, but are also the least perfectly evolved [at birth]. In other words, the highest centres are 'the ravelled end.' "[5]

The fact that the highest centers have an evolutionary future within the life of the individual permits us to look at them, at the time of birth, as anlagen, not as finished products as is the case at the lowest levels. In his Huntarian Oration ("The Physiological Aspects of Education") Jackson remarks on this issue in the following words, using language as an example. "No child would ever talk unless he were taught; and no child could be taught unless he already possessed, by inheritance, a particular series of nervous arrangements ready for training."[6] The Jacksonian conceptions of the highest levels as being least fixed and organized, capable of internal evolution, and in fact requiring "elaborate education" are, while true, a mere fraction of the immense scope of normal and abnormal mental development. It is, for instance, not only a question of being taught to talk but also of learning and relearning and unlearning of much that had been said. It may also be pointed out in this context that, while all human beings are capable of "memory," this highest-level anlage is of different quality of perfection among individuals. But the greatest individual differences exist in regard to "memories." The significance of this fact is obvious to the clinical psychiatrist and particularly to the psychotherapist.

Jackson viewed evolution within the nervous system as a progression or "a passage from the most automatic to the most voluntary."[7] Accordingly, the highest centers function in a manner which Jackson liked to describe as "least automatic-most voluntary"—and he carefully avoided assigning to the concept "voluntary" any kind of philosophical connotation. Jackson's use of the terminology "least automatic-most voluntary" was entirely clinically oriented. If a patient suffering from moderate expressive aphasia was incapable of saying anything upon demand (i.e., propositionally), but could use the identical word or sequence of words as part of an automatic phrase, or during emotional excitement as part of some execration, then his highest-level function of speech had, in Jacksonian terms, suffered a dissolution from a previously more voluntary to a presently more automatic level.

Several features in the psychopathology of the brain-damaged patients who (in Kurt Goldstein's terms) have been forced to retreat from abstract to concrete performances and behavior seem to reflect a loss of voluntary capacity. This change may be evidenced by the patients' inability to initiate a mental process, their failures in word-finding tests, and their difficulties in shifting voluntarily from one aspect of a situation to another. Voluntary mental processes—ranging from the most simple to the most complex and indeed sublime—are never accomplished without what has at times been referred to as a subjective awareness of *effort*. Thus in the area of goal-directed thought, which is one of many highest-level functions, Jackson's deceptively simple formulations do not seem to have been contradicted by the most modern methods applied to investigation of these issues. The cognitive transformation of the personality in dementia and the cerebral insufficiency of delirium present a clinical picture much of which can be rendered intelligible by the application of Jackson's hypotheses. (All this will be presented in greater detail in the next two chapters.)

From his observations of patients suffering from structural, toxic, and epileptic disease of the nervous system, Jackson discovered another principle inherent in the evolution and dissolution of the nervous system. This principle, which is also known as Jackson's law, states that in the event of uniform or local dissolution (disease), functional impairment or loss proceed in a predictable order. The highest levels, which seem to be least resistant to pathogenic influences, will be affected first; they are the most vulnerable components of the nervous system. If the disease process progresses there will be a "peeling-off" of functional layers. Intermediate levels will remain operative—often in an exaggerated manner—after the highest levels have undergone dissolution. If dissolution should extend as far "downward" as the lowest levels, death would ensue. Thus dissolution ("organicity") reverses the hierarchical phylogenetic order of evolution. We will present clinical illustrations of this principle and its manifestations later in this chapter.

Intermediate Levels

The functional qualities of the intermediate levels fall between the lowest and the highest centers. Thus they may be considered to be more fixed, organized, and automatic than the highest centers, but not quite so automatic, fixed, and simple as the lowest ones. The designation "centers" should not mislead us into assuming that we are dealing with essentially anatomical determinations. Jackson said that "dissolution may be local in several senses."[8] He chose the example of "progressive muscular atrophy," a disease which affects the nervous system at the *anatomically* lowest level, the spinal cord. Nevertheless, he contends, the generally valid Law of Sequence holds in that the highest-evolved functions are affected first in this condition. "We see here that atrophy begins in the most voluntary limb, the arm; it affects first . . . the hand and, first of all, the most voluntary part of the hand; it then spreads to the trunk, in general to the more automatic parts."[9] Local dissolution at the intermediate level occurs for instance in so-called motor aphasia. Speech, as a skilled motor performance, may be regarded as an intermediate-level function similar to other circumscribed cortical functional representations. But speech as a particular expression of organized, orderly, and creative thought—"propositional speech" as Jackson called it—is a highest-level function. There are, as will be shown later in this chapter, significantly different "levels" of speech. There is, for instance, voluntary and involuntary speech, just as there is voluntary and involuntary movement. Involuntary speech, such as emotional and automatic utterances, are of a lower order than voluntary or propositional speech. Thus the former is often retained in mild motor aphasia while the patient has already lost the capacity for propositional speech—that is, for speech in the service of *ideation.*

Because organic brain disease may affect the brain diffusely (e.g., in toxic delirium and cerebral arteriosclerosis) or else be limited either to certain levels or to certain parts within the same level, Jackson discriminated between uniform and local dissolutions. Examples of local dissolutions are lesions affecting speech, motility, and certain forms and phases of epilepsy—such as temporal lobe seizures and preictal phenomena. When one considers preictal or aural phenomena, it may be well to recall Jackson's statement: "One of the most important questions we can ask an epileptic patient is, 'How does the fit begin?' "[10] In accordance with the Law of Sequence, Jacksonian motor seizures would begin with a twitching movement either of the index-thumb combination or at the angle of the mouth. These areas are the most voluntary motor parts of the body—they represent the highest echelon within the intermediate (motor) level; they are most prominently represented, spatially, in Penfield's homunculus schema; they are highest in "the order of 'intelligence,' so to speak," as Jackson put it.[11] Uniform dissolution denoting extensive or global disease affecting the brain as a whole will invariably be manifested by abnormalities of the highest representations or faculties—those faculties we tend to call "mental."

The conception that organic brain disease represents a general or local retreat from higher to lower levels (and thus from higher to lower performance) led Jackson to formulate his doctrine of the *duality of the symptom.* Since dissolution is a reversal of the path of evolution, any symptom or disease reveals *two* aspects: it shows the extent of evolution or capacity which the patient has lost (the *negative* symptom), but it also shows the extent of evolution or capacity still remaining (the *positive* symptom). An inferior or reduced performance caused by dissolution dominates the clinical picture in the form of a pathological ascendancy of levels which are normally in partial or total eclipse. In cases of dissolution, the activity of these levels is in fact often unusually intense, a phenomenon known as "Anstie's principle." As a simple illustration of the duality of the symptom in organic brain disease we may consider the inability of such patients, at times, to name familiar objects on demand. Instead, they "circumlocute," describing perhaps the physical qualities or the utility of the objects shown. They have lost the abstract capacity for finding the noun that categorizes the object; this is the negative symptom. They substitute the more concrete performance of commenting on the object; this is the positive symptom. As clinicians we may at times be inclined to pay more attention to the positive symptom, not only because it clamors louder but also because it may speak in a strange language. Yet the patient may be more incapacitated by the negative symptom, the loss of faculties which have been muted or silenced. Another illustration of the principle of the duality of the symptom is disorientation, which will be discussed in greater detail in a later chapter. The fact that disoriented patients cannot accurately identify their temporal, physical, or personal environment constitutes the negative symptom; but the substitutions which they offer instead are the positive symptom.

EVOLUTION AND DISSOLUTION OF HIGHEST-LEVELS INDEPENDENCE

In healthy adult man the division of labor among the various CNS levels is such as to assure the best possible adaptation of the organism to whatever task may be required of it at the moment. Broadly speaking, this aim is accomplished by relegating automatic or routine functions to the lower and intermediate centers in order to free the highest levels to perform the most complex functions of mentation, those of which they alone are capable. Thus normal thought is "silent;" it is neither heard nor articulated. In other circumstances the performance of highest-level functions is accompanied by activity of the lower levels. One need only think of a performing pianist who uses his feet, fingers, and eyes as well as his musicianship, or of a scientist peering comprehendingly into a miscroscope while at the same time adjusting accommodation of his eyes and the lenses of his instrument. Nevertheless, there exists a significant and substantial independence of the highest levels that is not yet attained by the child; it is slowly and laboriously acquired in the course of maturation into adulthood, and lost again, to various degrees, in the wake of pathology or dissolution.

While engaged in highest-level mentation—such as the concentrated study of a difficult text or the writing of it—a person may accomplish and reveal the relative independence of the highest levels in several ways. He is usually quite motionless. He is indifferent to the perceptual opportunities of his surroundings and intolerant of perceptual intrusions. Should he pace the floor while deep in silent thought, his movements are not only automatic but also totally divorced from any ideational or conative goal or purpose. He may in fact run into an object or endanger himself in other ways. He is said to be absent-minded. Nothing could be further from the truth—he is not "absent-minded," but "single-minded;" only his highest levels are engaged at the moment.

"As evolution progresses the highest centers not only gradually develop but also become more and more detached from, and more independent of, the lower centres out of which they have evolved."[12] Without this development we would indeed become, or remain, prisoners of the immediately present stimulus—that is, prisoners of the present. We would be deprived of the uniquely human expansion of consciousness which encompasses in a meaningful manner our past as well as our future, and through which silent thought may become a prudent rehearsal for action or, at times, a still wiser substitute for it.

Quoting Herbert Spencer, Jackson notes: "mind . . . means more especially a comparatively intricate co-ordination in *time*—the consciousness of a creature 'looking before and after,' and using past experiences to regulate future conduct."[13] The relevance of this statement to clinical psychiatry, from neurophysiology to psychoanalysis, can hardly be overstated. To use the terminology of contemporary semanticists man, and only man, is a *time-binding* organism.

In the course of a simple perception of an object or a sound it must be assumed that lowest, intermediate, and highest levels will be successively engaged. The qualities of such a perception account for the subjective experience of vividness, immediacy, and projection of the source of the percept outside ourselves. Jackson referred to this perceptual experience as a "strong image." On the other hand, in the absence of an external perceptual stimulus (and without Penfield's electrode) no strong images can be evoked under normal conditions. Instead, after some time these strong images lose their original vividness and become faint images on their way toward verbal coding, filing, and "hibernation." They can, however, be evoked as faint images by an act of will or in response to associative facilitation. It would seem inconceivable for man to deal with even minor and circumscribed adaptive tasks without the independence of the highest levels. Only then can the faint images of his perceptual microcosm serve as a reliable backdrop and guide whenever he looks at or listens to the macrocosm around him. It has been suggested that in hallucinations and in schizophrenic auditorization of thought faint images change into strong ones and that these phenomena are indicative of a loss of independence of the highest levels. One may also seriously consider the possibility that the well-known schizophrenic prominence and even ascendancy of literalness, pictorial representation, and desymbolization of the word, all of which constitute lower-level cognitive and semantic functions, represents, in its own way, the impairment or loss of highest-level conceptual independence or autonomy which characterizes normal thought and language processes.

Normal thought, verbal or otherwise, is silent thought. In children of a certain age, and before the highest levels have attained independence from the lower articulatory mechanisms, thinking tends to be accompanied by speaking—by thinking aloud. Max Levin quotes Russel Brain reporting on a little girl, who, when admonished to think before speaking, replied, "But how can I know what I think till I hear what I say?"[14] Even adults while in deep thought may at times be aware of the merest traces of sensations of articulation of the words they think. Agitated patients simply can no longer maintain independence of the highest levels and can be observed "talking" their thoughts, while pacing the floor, without the slightest intent or opportunity of communicating them to others.

CLINICAL ILLUSTRATIONS

In this section Jacksonian principles and ideas will be applied to explain or to study certain features of psychopathology, especially in coarse brain disease, delirium, and epilepsy. The recent revival of interest in Jackson's ideas, particularly by Henri Ey, Max Levin, and others, should be noted. Ey, who introduced the term and theme of an "organo-dynamic concept of psychiatry,"[15] may be considered the most prominent, vocal, and ambitious proponent of "neo-Jacksonian" psychiatry. However, it was "old Jackson" himself who elevated perceptive description to the level of explanation and thus of intelligibility. Whenever he departed on rare occasions from minute clinical observation and permitted himself to be lured into generalizations concerning the nature of "insanity," he paid the price for overextending himself. Even to this day not all the facts are in. Thus I do not think that one can speak of, and still less believe in, any "school of thought" with any sense or claim of finality. If so-called schools of thought become sanctuaries—sheltering those inside and excluding everyone else—there is a real danger of an occasional scholar with a better idea being either expelled as an iconoclast or ignored as an ignoramus.

Organodynamic Interpretation of Local Dissolution

The orderly and predictable dissolution of function (the de-differentiation of Kurt Goldstein) is particularly evident in the aphasias. Speech is more than the mere utterance of words and of sequences of words. It has a distinct ontogenetic evolution resulting in a hierarchical representation in the adult. Speech at its highest (Jacksonian) level is "propositional;" it is most voluntary and least automatic; it is in the service of formulation and expression of thought; it is speech in response to speech, i.e., speech on demand. For speech to be propositional it is not necessary that its vocabulary be rich and colorful, or that its content be complex. At the opposite end, the lowest Jacksonian level, is "emotional" speech. It is perhaps best defined as ejaculatory speech—in which slang, curses, or obscenities are uttered to express a strong and sudden upsurge of emotion; this "speech" is least voluntary and most automatic, almost reflex in character. It is the verbal equivalent of crude emotional states, usually of an unpleasant quality. Every clinician has had the experience of an aphasic, speechless patient's reacting with a well-articulated angry curse when he suddenly feels the pain of a needle during an injection. This kind of emotional-ejaculatory speech is, of course, not the speech of poetry or oratory; it lacks the blending of thought and feeling, each of a significant caliber, which ennobles the language of the artist. Shakespeare unwittingly but superbly described emotional-ejaculatory speech when he wrote: "He knew not what to say, and therefore swore."

Between these extremes of propositional and emotional speech lies a broad and somewhat indistinct spectrum of levels of speech, ranging from "small talk" to automatic phrases such as "How do you do?" when one is being formally introduced to a person. In that case nobody in his right mind would take the question seriously—that is, "propositionally;" in other words, such a question does not call for a reply.

Dissolution of speech proceeds in accordance with Jackson's law: given a mild or moderate impairment of the corresponding site within the speech area, propositional speech will be lost first and most extensively. At the same time emotional-ejaculatory speech may be entirely preserved. Some nearly speechless patients have retained fragments of automatic phrases (the positive symptom). Concerning this fact Jackson observed: "Some of these utterances have elaborate propositional structure, but no propositional value."[16] Jackson reported a totally speechless patient who could only say "yes" or "no." He could use these two words—which are the most basic and automatic expressions of consent and dissent, of wanting and not wanting—spontaneously or in reply to simple questions; but he could not produce them upon demand, that is to say, propositionally. Failure to do so represents the negative symptom.

Dissolution within the speech area may also be viewed as an expression of a reduction of voluntary to involuntary "movement" or function. Quoting Spencer, Jackson observed: "The difference between an involuntary movement of the leg and a voluntary one is, that whereas the involuntary takes place without any previous consciousness of the movement to be made [without any previous propositional formulation of thought], the voluntary takes place only *after it has been represented in consciousness* [after propositional formulation of thought]." Jackson then adds: "there is a subjective reproduction prior to objective reproduction."[17] In other words, in automatic—and even more so in ejaculatory—speech there is little or no subjective reproduction or ideational thought preceeding the utterance of the objective production.

In cases of moderately severe hemiplegia, it can be noted that (in accordance with Jackson's law) motility and skill suffer first, most, and longest within the most voluntary, most complex, and phylogenetically the most recent organizations of the affected side of the body. Thus the upper extremity tends to be more paralyzed than the leg; the hand more than the arm; the fingers more than the rest of the hand; and within the ranks of evolutionary eminence of the fingers, the index finger occupies the number-one spot. It is, in fact, the only finger that is "naturally" capable of conveying meaningful propositional gestures such as threatening, pointing, or beckoning. Jackson considered the index finger the most voluntary part of the entire body. Many years later Penfield mapped the cortical location and the extent of cortical spatial representation of the motor and sensory functions of body territories. The resulting composition showed a grotesquely disproportionate size of fingers, mouth, and tongue. It has been dubbed "homunculus," a somewhat misleading term. Penfield's homunculus is truly representative of *homo sapiens* if it is realized that in its appearance quality is represented by quantity. It is furthermore well known that patients with minor, subclinical strokes but without noticeable paralysis show drooping of the angle of the mouth; this area—which is highly susceptible to damage at the site of its cerebral representation—is high on the list of Jacksonian levels and of considerable size on Penfield's map.

Local dissolution in the epileptic disorders is necessarily confined to focal epileptic phenomena. The latter may occur either as preictal (aural) local dissolutions, or the entire paroxysm may be, and remain, focal. Both generalized and lateralized (Jacksonian) seizures are usually ushered in by preictal twitching of the most voluntary, most complex, and most extensively represented muscle groups of the body: the thumb-index combination, the perioral muscles, and the muscles affecting the big toe. Jackson referred to these three body areas as the "leading parts," as far as movement is concerned. The evidently low threshold of excitability within these parts represents, under ordinary circumstances, a highest-level quality. As epilepsy is a "discharging" lesion it would follow that grand mal and Jacksonian seizures will affect first and foremost the leading parts, just as the paralyzing lesion of hemiplegia does. These twitchings are not punctate; they are of a more comprehensive character and pattern. This is to be expected in a cortical paroxysm because, in Jackson's words, the cortex knows nothing of muscles, only of movements.

Two organodynamic interpretations of symptoms arising from focal discharge within the temporal lobe may be mentioned. Temporal-lobe seizures are often accompanied by short-lasting perceptual abnormalities known as illusions, which are characterized by alterations of the various parameters of the percept: there may be a subjective impression of changes of physical qualities, of distance, or of familiarity of objects or sounds, but without failure in recognition of identity. In other words, there is no agnosia. The negative symptom consists of the inability to establish a correspondence with the existing memory traces of the various perceptual qualities of the percept; the positive symptom is the illusion itself.

Kubie reported a particularly illuminating and relevant observation which illustrates the process of rapid evolution following rapid experimental focal dissolution, although he applied its significance to a different issue. The patient in question suffered from temporal-lobe seizures and underwent surgical intervention at the hands of Penfield. The following is the pertinent paragraph in Kubie's report.

> Shortly after exposure of the temporoparietal areas, a series of pictures were presented to the patient. . . . Dr. Penfield stimulated the area in the lobe which caused an arrest of speech. This occurred just as she had been shown the drawing of a human hand. . . . Then as the current was turned off she began first to make mouthing movements and then slowly and hesitatingly said in sequence: "five, five . . . five horses . . . five horses . . . five pigs . . . five fingers . . . hand."[18]

Here is a rare illustration of an evolutionary principle during the birth of a verbal symbol. It is generally recognized that evolution of functional integration proceeds from general and indistinct antecedent elements toward specific and precise configurations—that is, from diffusion toward specificity. It seems that this principle is reflected in the experiment by the progression from the diffuse and generalized idea and representation of "five" toward the precise and compact verbal symbol of "hand." The last step in this progression, from "five fingers" to "hand," is also of great interest. It confirms an evolutionary formulation which Jackson expressed in these words: "I believe that the most fundamental law of developmental education of the mind is the continuous reduction of successions to co-existences. . . . Operations occupying many separate units of time come to occur in fewer or in a single unit of time."[19] "Five fingers" represents a succession of separate units, as contrasted to "hand," which represents a coexistence. A pathological reversal of this sequence "successions-coexistences" may be inferred from the particular way in which brain-damaged patients fail when asked to name familiar objects. Instead of designating the presented object by the noun—a single word that would categorize such an object—they circumlocute by using many words to describe, let us say, the physical qualities or uses of the object shown. Another broad illustration of this principle is the evolution of concepts from a large and variegated mass of antecedent percepts and concrete memories.

Organodynamic Interpretation of Uniform Dissolution

In uniform dissolution, as Jackson defined the term, "the whole nervous system is under the same conditions or evil influence."[20] In more clinical language, there exists either a state of dementia or of delirium. In either case a cognitive reduction of the patient's personality and faculties ensues. In dementia this reduction tends to be chronic and irreversible owing to the death of a large number of cortical, highest-level cells, while in delirium the psychopathology is more acute and usually reversible. In both dementia and delirium the evolutionary order within the "mental brain" is rather evenly and uniformly reversed. The sequence of this reversal reflects the principle laid down in Jackson's law: the highest centers or levels suffer first (negative symptoms) and the lower or "now-highest" levels gain a pathological and usually exaggerated ascendancy (positive symptoms).

As special chapters will be devoted to a detailed presentation of the psychopathology of dementia and delirium, it will be sufficient for the present to confine ourselves to a general discourse of the applications of Jacksonian principles to these forms of organic psychopathology. Goldstein's conception of de-differentiation of function in organicity, of the loss of abstract or categorical capacity, and the concomitant emergence of concrete behavior represents essentially a truly Jacksonian interpretation of uniform (and local) dissolution. The orderly peeling-off process inherent in Jackson's concept of functional dissolution is reflected in the characteristic retreat from abstract to concrete performance in the brain-damaged patient. The pathology consists not merely in the fact that the patient performs concretely but also that, in sharp contrast to the normal person, he is incapable of acting abstractly when such behavior should be required or demanded. The various Jacksonian criteria of highest-level function are clearly compromised in the various manifestations of loss of abstract capacity. Some clinical illustrations of these failures have already been mentioned in this chapter. Some more may be briefly added. In such patients performance and behavior lose much of their voluntary quality and character—not only in isolated tests but also in the broad, global realm of the patients' total interaction with their environment and their inner mental life. There is a general poverty of spontaneous thought; while automatic responses to simple questions and in ordinary conversation may still be forthcoming, there will be noticeable dearth of elaborative thought and of initiative of thought. It is a well-known fact that patients with dementia encounter great and even unsurmountable difficulties if called upon to deal with novel, unaccustomed, or unfamiliar situations or surroundings. In such contingencies the lower-level habitual and automatic responses would be obsolete; the only effective alternative would be the capacity to initiate "voluntarily" a shift in mental attitude appropriate to the demands of the novel situation. Goldstein notes the great need of brain-damaged patients for "orderliness" in their surroundings, and the likelihood of catastrophic reactions if the unfamiliar and unexpected is encountered. The need for orderliness in dementia is quite different from the compulsive and perfectionistic orderliness in the neurotic patient. Neurotic orderliness is usually interpreted as a reaction formation against, or a sublimation of, so-called anal-erotic drives. In either case, neurotic orderliness is in the service of what may be broadly referred to as superego demands. In the brain-damaged patient orderliness is required by the reduced capacities of the conflict-free ego. The neurotic takes pride in his orderliness; the organic patient finds safety in it.

The cognitive or intellectual reduction of the personality seen in dementia reflects the dissolution of still another feature of highest-level capacities, which Jackson saw in their being "least organised and most complex." The meaning of these terms has already been explained. Some broad clinical illustrations may be given. Complex intellectual tasks which would require for their solution the fullest utilization of the potential for new neuronal combinations which the quality of "least organized" has to offer can no longer be solved. Comprehension suffers. The "merely possible," as Goldstein called it, can no longer be imagined or utilized in problem-solving. If it is true that within the "most-organized" lower centers the formation of new or alternative neuronal combinations—that is to say, the capacity for learning—is neither possible nor required, we may reasonably suspect the existence of some correlation between the learning process and the quality "least organized" or functionally "least committed" that distinguishes the highest centers of the nervous system. Their dissolution in dementia (and their insufficient evolution in mental retardation) would in part account for the conspicuous diminution of the efficiency of the learning process noted in these patients.

The characteristic memory disorder seen in dementia consists in impairment of immediate recall; the patient fails conspicuously if he is required to form immediate although temporary memory traces of data which are usually presented to him verbally, such as a series of words or a sequence of digits. The degree of failure corresponds to the complexity of the material presented for immediate retention and recall. In this context, "complexity" refers to the several characteristics of abstract qualities—such as abstract words (concepts) versus concrete ones, unrelated words or digits versus automatic series of related words or patterned numerical sequences, and the unfamiliar versus the already familiar. Modern hypotheses about the formation of memory traces, as reported by neurophysiologists, suggest that immediate recall may be represented by the formation of reverberating circuits, while remote and well-established memory traces (which are far less affected in dementia) are most likely deposited in the form of structural alterations in neurons concerned with these "most-organized" memory traces. The latter represent what is in clinical terms referred to as "remote" memory. The hypothesis suggests that after the initial establishment of reverberating circuits (representing a "less-organized" memory trace) a more permanent storage of information is accompanied and perhaps represented by an accumulation of ribonucleic acid (RNA) with enhanced protein synthesis. In Jacksonian terms, these latter neuronal alterations could be considered to be "fixed" or "more organized" and hence less susceptible to dissolution. Such an inference appears to be plausible, both in clinical and neurophysiological terms—even if we must admit that in regard to the latter the precise nature of the more permanent and organized alterations remains somewhat uncertain.

Other Jacksonian Ideas

For this section I have chosen only a few of the many examples of profound insight into psychopathology which distinguishes the ideas and clinical observations of Hughlings Jackson. Despite the fact that his work was almost entirely restricted to the study of mental states accompanying coarse brain disease and paroxysmal disorders, many of his general pronouncements appear astonishingly relevant to the broader issues concerning mental illness that confront modern clinical psychiatry.

In the best tradition of the great scientist that he was, Jackson recognized the need for the search of unifying principles, common denominators, and superior generalizations among an endless multitude and variety of seemingly disparate clinical phenomena. Even for his time, the statement that "we have multitudes of facts, but we require, as they accumulate, organisations of them into higher knowledge"[21] seems to me to be most signally relevant to one of the problems with which modern clinical psychiatry, and perhaps modern science at large, is being confronted. Jackson formulated the issue in these words: 'May I say that it is the classification of things which are for the most part very different by some fundamental peculiarity each of them has?"[22] Although Jackson restricted himself essentially to the psychopathology of organic dissolution, the relevance of his point of view to the search for an "essential nature" of the neurotic or schizophrenic process is quite obvious.

In order to illustrate his point Jackson invites us to consider the following clinical phenomena. (1) A patient's arm was blown off by an explosion and his subsequent phantom hand was and remained in the exact position it had been held at the time of the accident. (2) An aphasic patient will utter the same word or phrase in response to whatever may be said to him; that word or phrase he had said, or was about to say, at the moment when he suffered the stroke. (3) An epileptic had his first fit when, as a soldier, he was "numbering off;" subsequently he would start counting before regaining consciousness after his fits. To these examples we may add the many instances of perseverative thoughts and actions of patients who had been suddenly rendered unconscious by severe cerebral concussion; several of such instances were reported by Max Levin. The general principle which unites and explains all these diverse clinical phenomena is best presented in Jackson's own words:

These illustrations will appear incoherently grouped to those who do not see that the intention in stating them is not to deal with stumps, aphasia, epilepsy . . . , but to make the basis for the discovery of the reason why there is a fixation of states which are normally temporary, upon the sudden occurrence of lesions of the nervous system.[23]

In the course of one of his many references and reflections on the subject of speech and the aphasias, Jackson made certain observations the validity of which, surprisingly, has been sustained by the views of contemporary clinical psychiatrists concerning an understanding of certain features of schizophrenic dementia. The reader will find a detailed description and discussion of the psychopathology of schizophrenic dementia in a later chapter of this book; at this point I wish only to show how some of Jackson's statements on speech and thought could be applied to some aspects of the formal thought disorder of dementia praecox—a condition that is not even listed in the index of Jackson's writings. He says that "a proposition . . . consists of two names [meaning 'words'] each of which . . . modifies the meaning of the other."[24] Normally, the intended meaning of a multivalent word, such as "bar," is determined by, among other possibilities, its semantic context. In schizophrenic dementia this "negative feedback" mechanism often fails, and an unmodified and therefore false meaning is attributed to the polyvalent word. This phenomenon has been called a "semantic shift." The patient who considered the admitting office of the hospital a place to "admit one's sins or crimes" would be an example; he "knew" the other meaning of "admitting office" quite well, thus exemplifying what Jackson in his observations called the "doubleness of mental processes."

In the same paragraph Jackson seems to describe a phenomenon somewhat akin to what in modern terminology may be called the antecedents of thought—the insufficient screening and exclusion that contributes to the loosening and asyndetic quality of schizophrenic language.

It is not enough to say that speech consists of words. It consists of words referring to one another in a particular manner; and without a proper interrelation of its parts a verbal utterance would be a mere succession of names embodying no proposition. . . . All the names in a random succession of words may . . . excite perceptions in us, but not perceptions in any relation to one another deserving the name of thought. . . . We are *told* nothing by a mere sequence of names, although our organisation is stirred up by each of them.[25]

The particular manner in which words as carriers of thought are normally interrelated is largely the result of the application of causal links and of the elimination of tangential or irrelevant material, even if a word would, or potentially could, "excite perceptions in us" in our preconscious "organization." But in certain forms of schizophrenic thought and language pathology, such as in "sham language," the normal and proper interrelation of words is reduced to "a mere succession of names [words or short sequences of words] embodying no proposition"[25] at all; enumerative or antithetical irrelevancies replace organized and goal-directed thought; and schizophrenic incoherence and/or irrelevance of language and thought are further compounded by the characteristic overinclusion of tangential content and the interpenetration of psychodynamic mental content—all of which may be the result of a pathological excitation of "perceptions" within the mind of the patient, "but not [of] perceptions deserving the name of thought."[25] It is indeed astonishing how accurately and astutely Jackson described an organismic state which he observed in aphasia, a condition which he understood so well. It is likewise astounding that his observations proved to be even more applicable and vindicated with respect to another organismic state the identity and intricacies of which were practically unknown in his time.

Like Freud, Jackson had the prescience to tap what were then unlikely sources of knowledge in order to gain more insight into the mental life of man. Of course, he did so on a much lesser scale than Freud. Yet he was aware of the fact that the psychology of certain normal mental states—such as the dream and the phenomena of puns, wit, and humor—could profitably be compared with abnormal mental states by tracing resemblances as well as differences. In "An Address on the Psychology of Joking"[26] Jackson, among other investigations, undertakes a psychological analysis of punning. As was true of Freud (in his monumental book *Wit and Its Relation to the Unconscious*), Jackson considered punning to be the lowest or least sophisticated form of joking. The relevance of Jackson's comments for the clinical psychiatrist derives from the fact that puns vaguely resemble, but decisively differ from, certain pathological word uses and word experience seen in schizophrenic dementia. We occasionally derive a very slight sense of the faintly jocular—perhaps more properly called the ridiculous—when a schizophrenic patient resorts to desymbolization or reduction-to-literalness of a word, and, also, when in the course of a "semantic shift" he attributes a meaning to a word incongruous with the context in which it is used. As an illustration Jackson quotes a pun of especially inferior quality: "When is a little girl not a little girl?" Answer: "When she is a little horse (hoarse)." The jocular effect of this pun rests on the desymbolization to the sound level of the words "horse" and "hoarse." Jackson comments: "We have the sensation of complete resemblance with the sense of vast difference."[27] The difference is indeed vast, but not significant. As an example of a superior pun I like to quote President Kennedy who, at a $100-a-plate party dinner told the audience: "I could say I am deeply touched, but not as deeply touched as you have been in coming."[28] He could, of course, have omitted the second "touched" in this pun, which is so humorously based on a "semantic shift." The difference of meaning in this play on words is of considerable social significance.

In his address on joking, Jackson said: "If I had time I could, I think, show . . . that what has been said applies closely to the study of 'mental symptoms' in serious diseases."[29] He did not, it is true, ever mention schizophrenia. We do not even know whether he had reference to schizophrenic thought and language pathology, instances of which, it can be assumed, must have come to his clinical attention. One of my patients with a mild schizophrenic dementia once remarked about his "shortcomings and longcomings," meaning his liabilities and assets. When I confronted him with the unconventionality of expression resulting from the desymbolization of "shortcomings" and the corresponding neologism "longcomings," he disclaimed any intent to "be funny." "Long" was the opposite of "short," he said; he was not a punster. Nor was the patient of Bleuler's who referred to herself as "an apartment," a person who was always *apart,* different from others. Jackson said that "punning is playing at being foolish; it is only morbid in that slender sense."[30] He apparently referred to the slender similarities of *means* in punning and schizophrenia. But what about the differences? By a mere caricature of punning the schizophrenic who succumbs to desymbolization of the word or to the "semantic shift" does not use either as a means toward a significant *end.* While in superior punning a significant difference is allusively contained in the insignificant semantic similarity, the schizophrenic semantic pathology, however similar in form, does not allude to anything worthy of being considered significant.

REFERENCES

1. J. Taylor (ed.). *Selected Writings of John Hughlings Jackson.* New York, Basic Books, 1958, vol. 2, p. 45.
2. *Ibid.,* p. 267.
3. E. D. Adrian. "The Mental and Physical Origins of Behavior." *International Journal of Psychoanalysis,* vol. 27, 1946, pp. 1–6.
4. J. Taylor (ed.). *Op. cit.,*[1] p. 68, footnote #1.
5. *Ibid.*
6. *Ibid.,* p. 267.
7. *Ibid.,* p. 46.
8. *Ibid.,* p. 47.
9. *Ibid.,* p. 48.
10. *Ibid.,* p. 217.
11. *Ibid.,* p. 216.
12. J. Taylor (ed.). *Op. cit.,*[1] vol. 1, p. 375.
13. *Ibid.,* vol. 2, p. 217.
14. M. Levin. "The Levels of the Nervous System and their Capacity to Function Independently of Each Other." *The Journal of Nervous and Mental Diseases,* vol. 132, 1961, p. 75.
15. H. Ey. "Hughlings Jackson's Principles and the Organo-dynamic Concept of Psychiatry." *The American Journal of Psychiatry,* vol. 118, 1962, p. 673.
16. J. Taylor (ed.). *Op. cit.,*[1] vol. 2, p. 49.
17. *Ibid.,* p. 226.

18. L. S. Kubie. "Some Implications for Psychoanalysis of Modern Concepts of the Organization of the Brain." *Psychoanalytic Quarterly,* vol. 22, 1953, p. 43.

19. J. Taylor (ed.). *Op. cit.*,[1] vol. 2, p. 138, footnote #1.

20. *Ibid.,* p. 47.

21. *Ibid.,* p. 393.

22. *Ibid.*

23. *Ibid.,* p. 394.

24. *Ibid.,* p. 227.

25. *Ibid.*

26. *Ibid.,* pp. 359–364.

27. *Ibid.,* p. 359.

28. H. Farber. *The Kennedy Years.* New York, Viking, 1964, p. 221.

29. J. Taylor (ed.). *Op. cit.*,[1] vol. 2, p. 362.

30. *Ibid.,* p. 359.

3

The Cognitive Transformation
of the Personality
in Organic Dementia

Traditional psychiatry still distinguishes between "functional" and "organic" psychoses despite the obvious fact that function and structure are inseparable. Every psychological function requires a structural substratum; in many instances the latter has been identified, at least in the form of "suborgans" of the mental brain that occupy vast areas in the case of the more complex or highest-level functions, and smaller ones at the lower levels. The most modern concepts in neurophysiology suggest (and neurophysiologists are about to demonstrate) molecular and microstructural alterations within the neuron and its synapses that correlate with such functions as memory, learning, and even concept formation. While it may be said that there is no Brodmann area for the Oedipus complex or the meaning of a delusion, Ralph Gerard is equally right in having once remarked that for each twisted thought there is a twisted molecule.[1] No doubt, he meant this to be a statement of principle and was well aware of the innumerable molecules involved in the thought psychopathology of schizophrenia. On the other hand, structure within the mental brain (or anywhere else) has not been placed there for decoration. Thus, as "every symptom is both functional and organic,"[2] we may raise the question whether these terms can still be considered to carry meaningful implications. The answer would depend on the criteria which one uses in an attempt to justify the dichotomy.

By applying Webster's definition of *functional* as something "affecting functions but not structure," any mental disease or abnormality unaccompanied by structural changes must be functional. In view of the fact that no significant, let alone pathognomonic, alterations of brain structure have yet been found in schizophrenia, this psychosis is still classified as a functional disorder. On the other hand, idiopathic epilepsy is described as an organic condition despite the fact that no demonstrable structural abnormalities of the brain exist in this variety of paroxysmal disorders. Nor has the indisputably structural basis of genetic factors pertaining to incidence and predisposition in schizophrenia led to a general acceptance of an essentially organic basis for the disorder. This may be understandable in view of the prominent and even abundant psychodynamic coloring of many but by no means all forms and individual cases of this disease. But the question of why psychodynamic content is expressed through, say, neologisms, asyndetic language, or in the form of hallucinations is still unanswered and is not usually pressed with the urgency it deserves. Perhaps it is easier to speculate about purposes than to discover causes. Traditional psychiatry seems to imply that organic diseases are essentially irreversible whereas the prognosis of functional disorders is better. Yet most patients with delirium (an organic illness) recover, whereas those who have paranoia or hebephrenia, which are listed among functional psychoses, are generally considered to be incurable. Arieti believes that the term "functional" has not been "maintained merely through semantic inertia."[3] However, after acknowledging, as I do, the inherent contradictions in the use of the term he concludes, "The functional point of view focuses on the fact that, no matter what the complex causality of the disorder may be, it is the particular form of functioning (or of operating) with its content that constitutes the predominant and primary . . . essence of the disorder and leads to secondary sequels, both organic and functional."[4] It is difficult to see in this definition a clear, or at least plausible, distinction between "functional" and "organic" psychopathology.

ETIOLOGIC CRITERIA

I now propose that we turn to the criterion of *etiology*. As discussant in a clinical neuropathological conference I said:

The organic psychiatric symptomatology is the result of a *defect,* not a *conflict.* In this sense, organicity is "impersonal;" it is not intelligible in the light of the patient's life history, his interpersonal relations, his drives, and their developmental vicissitudes. The issues of good and evil, of instinct and conscience, of seeking pleasure and avoiding pain, of force and counterforce, of symbolic representation or distortion, are not of the essence. The roots of organicity are in the cognitive, not instinctual sphere of the personality. . . . Perhaps we could say, using Heinz Hartmann's term, that organicity affects the "conflict-free sphere" of the ego. . . . In accordance with our holistic views, affective and interpersonal disturbance may contribute to the clinical picture in organicity, but only in a subordinate role.[5]

To the above I would add that the term "conflict" is meant to denote the entire compass of pathogenic life experiences resulting from inter-personal interaction, particularly during childhood, and resulting in symptomatic and/or characterological expression and/or conditioning. Thus the neuroses are the most typical of all functional disorders. To the degree to which a mental illness is functional, remedial interpersonal interaction—that is to say, psychotherapy—will reverse the abnormal development; the appeal is to the *person,* through the skill and influence of another person. And to the degree to which mental illness is the result of impersonal affections of the mental brain, remedial action may restore the defect through "impersonal" (but humanely administered) therapeutic measures aimed at the *soma.* It may be recalled that Freud anticipated a future in which interpersonal ills would be responsive to impersonal "pills." We do not know the sentiments with which the discoverer and champion of the functional disorders pondered this pros-pect. The fact that we at times use "impersonal" drugs in functional disorders and supportive psychotherapy in certain patients with organic mental illnesses should not in any sense invalidate the etiologic distinc-tion between these two major categories of mental and emotional sickness.

The cognitive impairment in patients with organic dementia can be described, in general terms, as a reduction in efficiency. This reduction is uniform in the sense of a general retreat from previously occupied positions of capability. In Jacksonian terms the patient has suffered a uniform dissolution of highest-level functions (negative symptoms), and his present performance represents the best of what he is still capable (positive symptoms). Kurt Goldstein designated the essence of this cog-nitive impairment as a loss or diminution of the abstract attitude, which in turn, and by necessity, is replaced by the inferior quality of concrete-ness in the various fields of performance.

Abstract attitude is a compound faculty—as is intelligence, memory, or judgment. It seems impossible to isolate and define a common, single, and characteristic denominator. Its loss may be noted in failures as different as the inability to name familiar objects and to recognize simple geometric patterns. Goldstein himself lists a diverse series of capacities which are representative of the abstract attitude—such as assuming a mental set voluntarily, beginning a performance on demand, shifting from one aspect of a situation to another, keeping various aspects of a situation simultaneously in mind, grasping the essential of a given

whole, abstracting common properties, thinking or performing symbolically, detaching the ego from the outer world.[6] The meaning of these
capacities as well as the features of failure in patients who no longer
possess them is perhaps best conveyed by a presentation and interpretation of clinical tests and examples. However, it is necessary to remind
ourselves that we are testing brain-damaged patients who previously
had normal cognitive capacities. We are not testing intelligence.

The ascendancy of voluntary over automatic behavior, or at least the
capacity for the former, is one of the most far-reaching results of evolution within the central nervous system. Even ontogenetically, recent
and enlightened psychoanalytic conceptions stress the preponderance
of voluntary (conscious-preconscious) over automatic (unconscious)
determinants in motivation as reliable criteria of healthy, non-neurotic
behavior. In the present context, however, the contrast between voluntary
and automatic will be restricted to much simpler and isolated performances and also to the special connotation of "abstract versus concrete."

DIAGNOSTIC PROCEDURES

A patient is requested to recite a well known series; for example, the days of the week, the months of the year, or the
alphabet. He cannot do it, although he knows the words and the letters.
His difficulty is his inability to start—that is, to *initiate* a performance.
If we do it for him (e.g., by saying "Monday, Tuesday") he is likely
to complete the series, which in the course of anybody's life has become
automatic speech. For this very reason he will probably not be able
to recite such a series backwards, even if we started this task for him.
Another illustration of the relatively abstract nature of the task of initiating a mental performance is the well-known inability of brain-damaged
patients to recall a memory trace upon demand; they are still capable,
however, of *recognition* of its concrete representation. Thus, they
may have lost the ability of immediate recall of a word, but will recognize that word, if it is repeated, and often reject falsely inserted words.

The task of word-finding is a very instructive method to determine
the presence and degree of impairment of the abstract capacity to mobilize mental processes. It is, of course, understood that the patient's failure
is not in any way related to aphasia. Suppose we make this task as
easy as possible by asking for the words of "things that are used in
the kitchen." Why is this particular test for word-finding easy? The
patient in his search for the appropriate words is aided by a certain
degree of concreteness inherent in this task: to find words for *familiar
objects.* He can draw on well-established memories of objects and verbal

engrams; no special or repeated mental initiation is required. A brain-damaged patient will quite on his own resort to the same process of concretization if we ask him to say "just any five words that come to your mind."* He will then frequently produce words denoting objects around him, or perhaps some words closely associated with the use of these objects. This also reflects what Goldstein means by the inability of detaching the ego from the outer world—the outer world of immediately present perceptual stimuli. At its most demanding, the word-finding task is that of finding, without effort or delay, a specified number of "concepts" or other abstract words that are all unrelated to each other; in such a task separate initiating efforts are required for each word without resort to any concrete or perceptual prop.

Some brain-damaged patients cannot, on demand, name familiar objects shown them by the examiner. Instead, they may describe at great length the physical attributes or uses of these objects ("circumlocution") and even handle them correctly. It would appear that these patients give us more than we asked for, yet the opposite is true. The capacity to name a familiar object requires the availability of the requested noun—which in turn connotes that *category* of which the object is one of several possible representations. It is the use of the noun in a categorical sense which constitutes abstract behavior in this particular task. Circumlocution, being closer to the "perceptual" end of things, is for this reason more concrete. The difference between "this pen" and "a pen" may serve as a succinct illustration of the difference between describing and categorizing objects. Failure to do the latter is called anomia and must not be confused with agnosia and simple forgetting. The agnosic patient, if he is in possession of the capacity for abstraction, will name the object correctly by its noun if identification takes place through sensory modalities other than that in which he is agnosic. In the case of forgetting, the patient will not be able to recall and use the word during his circumlocutions; the patient with anomia, however, will do just that. Max Levin reported a patient who could not on demand name the physician's profession and when pressed replied, "But I don't know your profession, Doctor!"

The abstracting capacity for keeping various aspects of a situation simultaneously in mind is, of course, indispensable to the faculty of thinking—from its simplest to its most complex and exceptional varieties of reasoning, planning, or comprehending. In examining the brain-damaged individual, we shall again confine ourselves to performance levels which had been at the patient's disposal before he became ill. A good

* This is a special, although minor application of the well known "gift" of forcing freedom of choice upon a person, a gift which is a burden to the brain-damaged patient.

question to ask is: "To what number on the dial of a watch does the big hand point at twenty minutes after the hour?" A brain-damaged patient who is still able to read time may fail the test because in this situation he must keep in mind that "twenty" is represented on the dial by "four" when it is "after" the hour, and by "eight" if it is "before" the hour.

Another example of impairment of abstract capacity is what Goldstein called the loss of the abstract space scheme. He devised a simple but instructive test of this faculty, the "stick test."[7] Before the administration of and rationale for this test are described, it should be stated that the abstract-space scheme is totally different from the body-image concept, including the latter's directional components; nor is it related to the organization of extrapersonal space, itself an extension of the body image proper (see Chapter 11). In the stick test geometrical patterns are presented to the patient. From one to about eight sticks may be used; the number bears little or no relationship to the inherent complexity of the pattern and thus to the difficulty a patient will have. The task is first to copy a pattern and later to reproduce it from memory after looking at it for perhaps 30 seconds. The substance and clinical value of this test is best conveyed by a brief description of possible successes and failures by brain-damaged patients. I will omit comment on patients' copying performance except to mention that failure to copy the pattern indicates severe impairment, and that successful copying in no way represents intact function. Copying is obviously much closer to concreteness than reproduction from memory; yet the real significance of the test does not rest upon a simple act of memory.

1. The patient correctly reproduces the pattern □. Inquiry may reveal that it looked to him like a window or a box, both familiar objects. He may have succeeded only because the pattern lent itself to a concrete representation. At the abstract level, this pattern is a square. But suppose we now give our patient a configuration such as this ⌐. He may fail completely or perhaps make something like this ⌐⌐. His total failure must be regarded as indicative of loss of the abstract-space scheme, revealed by his inability to apprehend a geometric pattern which cannot easily be concretized—that is, which "doesn't look like anything." Or, if he comes up with the incorrect reproduction, he may do so because the original represented to him "something that was open."

2. Another patient could reproduce this figure ∧, but failed when it was presented to him inverted (∨). He explained that the first pattern was "a roof" but that the second "meant nothing." It is fair to consider both figures variations on the same abstract geometric theme; but this is what the brain-damaged patient cannot grasp.

3. The complexity of the test increases the more the patterns represent mere "abstract" spatial relationships. Thus, ╱ is as complex as ─|╱. Again, the number of sticks used has no real bearing on the outcome of the test. Just as a three-letter "nonsense word" is harder to retain than a ten-letter familiar one, a three-stick nonobjective pattern is, in this context, more demanding and of a higher order than a "house of ten sticks."

In a more literal sense, the capacity for abstraction denotes the ability to recognize, comprehend, and "extract" a pattern, an identity, idea, or "figure"—in other words, an *essence* which is contained (or even concealed) in a mass of detail or component parts. This capacity can be tested by nonverbal as well as verbal material. But as the complexity of configurations increases, the task of abstraction more and more assumes the character of an intelligence test rather than a test for brain damage; the tests, therefore, must be simple.

Even a normal simple act of apperception requires the ability to extract the pith of meaning from a multitude of detail, to recognize the relevant common denominator despite numerous but irrelevant singularities. How, for instance, may the compact idea "dog" be evoked in any brain in response to a myriad of different stimuli? How does the brain abstract the universal oneness? One may see a live dog of any conceivable size, shape, and color pattern; or it may be the picture or statue of a dog; the written or spoken word "dog" will do, despite the obvious differences of handwriting, print, or tone of voice. Even hearing a bark leads to the same recognition of an essence. If we examine this process of extracting a common essence from a mass of heterogeneous perceptual stimuli, we may be reminded of one of the gestaltist laws: namely, that the whole is more than the sum of its parts. But "more" in what sense? For sheer "brevity" (semantic, spatial, temporal) abstraction, like a valuable chemical extract, is always *less* than its mother substance or source—yet it is neither its fragment nor its abbreviation. It is "more" because it represents the sum of the parts at a higher cognitive level, the level of the hierarchies of *comprehension*. The assumed mental mechanisms which enable us to abstract the same identity from its manifold possible representations, thus leading to recognition and comprehension, were in fact given the name "universals."[8]

Brain-damaged patients may find it impossible to continue a simple graphic series, such as, ○ ○ ── ── ○ ○ ── ── ○ ○. They fail to abstract the geometric pattern of alternating pairs of circles and dashes. Still less will they be able to comprehend the meaning of the question whether the examiner "made a mistake" in drawing the series. In answer to this question organic patients occasionally point to differences in the length of the dashes or to unevenness in the outline of the circles—thus indicating that their comprehension does not reach beyond irrelevant singularities. A schizophrenic patient may do the same, but for entirely different reasons; in so doing he will reverse figure and ground by endowing such a singularity with special, autistic significance.

Another illustration of failure to abstract simple patterns is the Shipley-Hartford Test. The patterns consist of numbers or letters. No effort beyond the recognition of the pattern is required or intended. The following are three easy representative examples:

1. tot tot   bard drab   537 – – –

The task is to recognize the pattern of inverted order in each pair and to apply this principle to the sequence of numbers (735), thus shifting to a different set in the application of the pattern.

2. 1 2 3 2 1   2 3 4 3 2   3 4 5 4 3   4 5 6 – –

The task is to recognize the pattern of an evenly increasing and decreasing series of numbers, each new pattern beginning with the next highest number (5 4).

3. escape   scape   cape   – – –

The task is to recognize the pattern of omitting the first letter and to keep on doing just that, thus creating four words with entirely different meanings but containing in their sequence the same letter pattern (ape).

The ability to think and perform symbolically is most commonly applied to the use of words in language. All words are sound symbols, connoting and denoting any conceivable mental content. Thus the word may represent the symbolic process at various levels of complexity and sophistication. Concrete words signify the objects and their qualities in the world of perception; abstract words stand for conceptualization, relationships, ideas. Verbal symbolism reaches its ascendancy in that doubly indirect representation known as metaphor. We will again confine ourselves to simple words when testing this aspect of the capacity for abstraction in brain-damaged patients.

Definitions. Suppose we ask a patient, "What is a cat?" We expect him to give us the meaning of the word "cat" and *not* a comment about "a cat." If he can do the former he may say that a cat is an animal; he has responded abstractly by naming the principal category of which "cat" is a representative example. If, however, his capacity is reduced to concreteness, he will respond with a *sentence* about a cat—for example, "A cat catches mice," or "I once had a cat." One of my patients replied, "A cat is a cat." It may be of interest to compare this answer with one given by a schizophrenic, as reported by Eugen Bleuler, "A cat is a mouse." What are the respective pathological processes which account for these specific and characteristic failures? In the case of the brain-damaged patient the retreat to concreteness is so complete and the ability to mobilize thought so reduced that he can only produce the verbal equivalent of a memory trace evoked by the question about a very familiar object. The schizophrenic answer derives from entirely different processes. The question, "What is a cat?" mobilizes antecedent or preconscious, tangential ideas; furthermore, enumeration of opposites often replaces meaningful thought construction in dementia praecox. There is, after all, the proverbial antagonism of the "cat-and-mouse game." And so, with characteristic schizophrenic semantic expansion and diffusion, an incomprehensible *condensation* results, defining the predator in terms of his victim.

Similarities.   Two words with seemingly quite different meanings—such as "fire" and "flood"—are given to the patient, who is then asked to tell us what these two words have in common (i.e., in which way they describe or refer to the same thing). "Seemingly quite different" is, of course, true only in a limited sense—namely, if we assume a concrete attitude toward the words. In order to apply the capacity for abstraction to solve the task it is necessary that the patient find the supraordinate concept or idea which fits the test words—in this case, the concept "catastrophe," or at least the idea of danger to life. To accomplish this goal it would be necessary for the individual to imagine, under the stimulus of the two words, "the merely possible" and in general to be able to mobilize thought. The failures of brain-damaged patients are, as in most aspects of their psychopathology, trite and pedestrian; if they answer at all in terms of the required task they will do so con- cretely—perhaps "You can have a fire and you can have a flood." Fre- quently they will produce a brief concrete comment about either of the words, missing the point altogether. Their cognitive and conceptual shrinkage will become quite obvious in these tasks. By contrast, the responses of a schizophrenic tend not only to be overinclusive but may also be startling because of the admixture and interpenetration of formal and psychodynamic psychopathology provoked by the test words.

Differences.   The patient is given two words which suggest similar qual- ities or applications in one area, but which actually point to a difference of overriding significance. Samples are "fee and fine" or "child and midget." It will be noted that the insignificant similarities are within the scope of concrete attributes; in the first example "money," in the second "height." The differences, on the other hand, pertain to more complex or "abstract" connotations—such as the circumstances which would determine whether money is received for services rendered or is to be paid as penalty for an infraction of law. Another aspect of the abstract nature of the task is the need to shift from a more obvious to a less tangible frame of reference or mental set against which the implications of the two words must be judged. This process leads a normal person to recognize that a midget, while not taller than a small child, is nevertheless an adult, with adult behavior, responsibilities, and privileges. It is easy to see why brain-damaged patients fail to cope with the exacting demands of discrimination between two selected concepts, but the nature of their failure is also relevant. In order to define the differences in the manner just suggested it would be necessary to overcome the temptation of concreteness inherent in the irrelevant similarities; to mobilize thought and thus to create the merely possible situation and context appropriate to each of the contrasted words; and finally to abstract from this expanded mental image the significant difference. Again, the brain-damaged patient will either fail altogether or give an insufficient answer within his remaining concrete capacity. In contrast to the schizophrenic his response will be reduced, but not distorted or bizarre. His view of the conceptual world is myopic, not astigmatic.

Proverbs. The interpretation of proverbs and phrases is a useful test of the thought processes of patients, provided the examiner is fully conversant with the psychological implications of the task and the evaluation of the results. When we use this method of investigation we are much more interested in the psychopathology of form than of content, just as in the Rorschach test. The interpretation of proverbs requires a number of steps of mentation. Normal people sucessfully take these steps automatically, without instruction. First, the situation or idea contained in the proverb has to be comprehended and abstracted from the particular and usually concrete setting in which it is being presented. Thereafter, the meaning or moral thus extracted by a process Benjamin called "desymbolization"[9] has to be reformulated in such a manner as to fit, broadly speaking, the human situation. For instance, in the proverb "When the cat's away, the mice will play," desymbolization has been accomplished in an acceptable manner if the subject grasps the idea that with the departure of the powerful cat the mice will with impunity indulge in activities otherwise forbidden or dangerous because of the threat of "punishment" by the cat. The final step calls for a formulation, in reasonably abstract terms, of this same idea; a normal answer may be, "Without supervision discipline breaks down and effort slackens."

Failures in the task of interpreting proverbs occur in any of the major varieties of formal thought pathology: mental defect, organic dementia, and dementia praecox. The particular features of thought disorder in these three conditions are, of course, reflected in the responses of the patient. Brain-damaged patients resort by necessity to concrete "interpretations" in the form of literalness, remaining within the context of the words and activities described in the proverb and failing to apply the idea through a shift of their mental set to the human situation. At best they may produce a generalization within the domain of the given situation. A similar kind of response may be expected of high-grade mental defectives. Schizophrenics, on the other hand, show a number of abnormal responses in a manner so free of diagnostic ambiguity that this test may justly be considered ideal for the detection of such thought disorder. I will here only summarize the possibilities. (1) The schizophrenic, despite good or even superior native intelligence, may only be capable of literalness or generalization derived from literalness. (2) He may fail in the process of desymbolization, and his train of thought may be derailed into an irrelevant or false translation of the symbolism contained in the proverb. (3) He may "oversymbolize," probably because of an admixture of emerging dynamic and autistic material and —perhaps in conjunction with other verbal or associational thought pathology—produce a totally incomprehensible and overinclusive response. Here again lies an example of the contrast between the trite impoverishment of the brain-damaged patient and the esoteric and teeming drivel of schizophrenics.

We have emphasized the impaired or lost capacity for abstraction in organic dementia because reduction to concreteness best reflects the cognitive transformation of the personality in brain damage. In the following an attempt will be made to round out the presentation of the remaining general symptomatology.

GENERAL SYMPTOMS

There is a general reduction of expression of goal-directed activity that resembles apathy and indifference. Goldstein believes that this apparent lack of affective display under conditions of nonstress is the result of the patient's inability to imagine the "merely possible" and to transport himself mentally and emotionally into situations other than the immediate here and now. In this sense the apathetic behavior could be understood as another aspect of loss of the capacity for abstraction. The patient remains "stimulus-bound," a captive of the moment and of his present surroundings. The future is less despaired of than ignored; other places and people are not forgotten, but neither are they summoned into awareness. Goldstein cites as an example a patient who, while in the hospital, never spoke or thought of his family, but who during visits home behaved in every respect like an understanding and loving husband.[10] It may be added that the general reduction of executive mechanisms which are normally in the service of goal achievement very likely imposes upon the patient a drastic limitation of goal-directed activity—not so much as a result of conscious resignation but rather as an expression of a biological protective mechanism; in this way "catastrophic reaction" (see below) is prevented or at least minimized.

The greatest loss of adaptive capacity in dementia is within the broad field of those components of the conflict-free ego sphere which are normally needed for goal achievement. One may refer to them as adaptive mechanisms or instrumentalities. The various forms of abstract behavior which were explored and explained in the preceding paragraphs comprise a very substantial part of the faculties that are compromised. But there are others; some of these—such as memory and orientation—will be discussed in subsequent chapters; others are of concern to us now.

Patients with advanced cortical loss usually show a noticeable reduction in associational capability. This reduction or "cognitive shrinkage" is not the result of inhibiting or retarding affective influences, as it would be in certain forms of catatonia or depression. Therefore, one can not refer to the drastic reduction in associational and verbal output of demented patients by the term "mutism." The difficulty in initiating mental activity (to which reference was made earlier), may in part owe to the fact that, as Goldstein concluded, "All direct damage causes a rise of the threshold and a retardation of excitation."[11] This cognitive and conative impoverishment is, for instance, particularly pronounced in the so-called hypokinetic variety of Pick's disease, but it is also frequently seen in patients with ordinary cerebral senility. The reduction of the capacity for imagination and introspection is especially severe in coarse brain disease that affects the frontal lobes. These lobes, comprising almost one-half of the total neocortex, may in this respect be viewed both as a substantial portion of the entire cognitive apparatus and as a suborgan of the brain because of their close functional relation to the dorsomedial nucleus of the thalamus (see also Chapter 8). Thus frontal-lobe dementia will lead to a marked reduction in the capacity for fantasy and "inner life" in the form of "successful derivative creation."[12] The "short-circuiting" of cognitive (and affective) processes in such lesions may also account for (or contribute to) that arid and barren mental landscape in which, to use a psychoanalytic term, the preconscious potential—with all its enriching or at least augmenting potentialities—has been largely destroyed.

Brain-damaged patients show impaired capacity to maintain organization during stress and to recover from it promptly. It should be noted that the nature of the stress consists of situations which tax or surpass the patient's reduced capacities of cognitive adaptation, not his tolerance to deal with conflictual problems. I remember a patient suffering from the early stages of Alzheimer's disease who first showed symptoms of intense anxiety and confusion when confronted with the need in his civil-service job to cope with revised forms in the course of otherwise routine performances. He showed what Kurt Goldstein called "catastrophic reaction," which occurs in brain-damaged patients if they themselves become aware of their failures. They experience intense anxiety and rapid dissolution of their remaining faculties, from both of which they recover only very slowly. In the catastrophic state they are unable to perform tasks which would have been well within their power while in the "ordered state" of dementia without "catastrophe."

Perseveration is a special feature of the organic symptomatology. For example, having answered a simple question correctly the patient will repeat the same answer when asked the next question. Thus the patient who just responded with "John Brown" when we asked him for his name will again say "John Brown" when we ask him where he lives. Such perseveration is an abnormal reaction to a stimulus and not a spontaneous process. Similarly, perseveration of grasp (tonic innervation) in patients with frontal-lobe lesions and in normal infants whose frontal lobes have, of course, not as yet become functional (or myelinated) occurs in response to stroking movements on the palm. But we also encounter spontaneous perseverations in patients with coarse brain disease, both in the area of language and ideation as well as in motility. It is a common observation that some patients with expressive aphasia persist in uttering the very word, or parts of the word, which they were about to utter when striken by a cerebral hemorrhage. Max Levin reported patients who could not shake off a thought which they had at the moment they suffered a serious brain injury, or who continued the activity they had been engaged in at the moment they sustained a cerebral concussion. Levin mentions the case of a child who had been playing ball when she was hit; when about to emerge from a post-traumatic delirium, she tossed everything within reach off her bed. Oculogyric crises are at times accompanied by perseveration of meaningless (nondynamic) thoughts which cease as soon as the ocular tonic perseveration relaxes. It is still a matter of dispute how one can best explain the mechanism of perseveration, and whether the phenomenon can be assigned to a common pathophysiological cause. In stressing the effect of isolation of affected brain tissue from the rest of the neuronic environment, Goldstein notes that "When excitation takes place . . . it spreads abnormally and remains effective an excessively long time."[13] He further comments that "Many parts which formerly were background, now become figure."[14] The perseverating patient who responds to the second question by repeating his answer to the first one may indeed be said to have elevated an obsolete past (background) to a position of pathological ascendancy (figure) because of his inability to deactivate an innervation and thus to make room for a present stimulus. Whatever the explanation may be, it is certain that the repetitiveness of organic perseveration is not motivated or the result of a predominantly unconscious dynamic source. The fact of its occurrence—not its content or context—is its distinguishing mark. Organic perseveration in the Rorschach test occurs regardless of the differences among the individual cards, whereas in perseveration by schizophrenics the patient, "having a fixed idea, utilizes the actual form of the card more frequently and attempts to mold the perseveration to the card."[15] As the "fixed idea" may fairly be considered to be the expression of parasymbolically distorted content—emerging in a context which, however tenuously, lends itself to its release—the impersonal nature of organic perseveration becomes rather obvious, confirming the fundamental nature of the organic symptomatology.

By designating the essential psychopathology of organic dementia as a cognitive transformation of the personality, I meant to set the stage for a more far-reaching exposition and explanation of principle. I have briefly commented on the absence (or at least the very subordinate role of) instinctual, affective, interpersonal, and parasymbolic issues in organic "defect pathology" and on the irrelevance of conflict in pathogenesis as well as in clinical manifestations. The explanatory description and characterization of these signs clearly show the particular reduction in ego functions common to this form of mental illness. At this juncture it seems that we could profitably pursue the concept of the "conflict-free sphere" of the ego to gain further understanding of the essential unity of psychopathology in brain-damaged persons.

The concept "ego" was originally an integral part of Freud's topographic design of the mental apparatus. Initially, the ego was derived from the interaction of the id with the outer world; it was meant to conquer not so much the latter as it was the former. "Where id was there shall ego be" was Freud's hope, and indeed command. In *The Ego and the Id* he came "to the conclusion that the character of the ego is a precipitate of abandoned object-cathexes and that it contains a record of past object-choices."[16] Only much later (in "Analysis Terminable and Interminable") did Freud venture a speculative thought: "Our next question will be whether all ego modification . . . is acquired during the defensive conflicts of early childhood."[17] I think that we can now be more definite and comprehensive in the area of ego-psychology. The ego is not only a battlefield, strewn with "abandoned object-cathexes" or studded with defense mechanisms, but also a staging area and arena for wholesome and necessary expeditions into an external environment—challenging but not threatening, inanimate rather than personified. Toward this end the ego supplies, not logistics, but *tools* (although not of equal sharpness and utility amongst men) in the form of *adaptive* mechanisms. It is this part or function of the ego which Heinz Hartmann designated as the "conflict-free ego sphere."[18] There is, to be sure, interaction between the conflict-ridden and the conflict-free ego; a delicate and still largely unknown interaction may enhance or hinder both the solution of conflicts and the cognitive and conative mastering of the external world. "We must recognize that though the ego grows on conflicts, these conflicts are not the only sources of ego development."[19] It is perhaps best to quote and then to elaborate on some relevant statements made by Hartmann. "The core of what is later the conflict-free sphere are the pre-formed tools of adaptation. . . . It follows that human adaptation has two facets: pre-formed tools (endowment, special talents, general apparatuses, such as memory, perception, etc.) and actions directed by the ego (such as defenses, syntheses, problem solving, etc.)."[20] There is a difference between solving *problems,* for which task nature has given us preformed tools, and solving *conflicts,* which significant people in their unwisdom and at the time of our greatest psychological weakness have inflicted upon us and against which nature has given us only options of inferior adaptive value, such as, the compromise of symptom formation or the avoidance of the outer world—a world which we would otherwise be able to master to the limits of the preserved potential of our conflict-free ego strength. The difference between problem-solving and conflict-solving affords another illustration of the statement Freud once made, although in a different context, namely: "how the intellectual function is . . . distinct from the affective process."[21] In the cognitive transformation of dementia, adaptation is impaired because of dissolution of the "reality ego," not as a result of disappointment of the "pleasure ego." Thus problem-solving in the area of memory (or, rather, of immediate recall) is hampered by the *complexity* of the task; in the conflict situation of hysterical amnesia the inability to recall is determined by the *painfulness* of the elusive event. It is now quite clear what Hartmann meant when he said, "I propose that we adopt the provisional concept of conflict-free ego sphere for functions . . . insofar as they exert their actual effect outside of the realm of psychic conflict."[22] Hartmann specified these functions by referring "to the conflict-free development of perception, intention, object comprehension, thinking, language, recall phenomena and productivity; to that of the well-known phases of motor development . . . and to the maturation and learning processes implicit in all these . . . ."[23] All of these functions require only the gift of a normal brain and the opportunity of learning in order to mature and to effect adaptation, as well as enjoyment, in the world of cognition, conation, and thought. The organic symptomatology consists in characteristic pathology of these functions, inflicted in an impersonal manner; and while dementia will lead to wrong performances in the present and future, it cannot be attributed to wrongs done to the patient in the past.

REFERENCES

1. R. W. Gerard. "The Biological Roots of Psychiatry." *The American Journal of Psychiatry*, vol. 112, #1, 1955.
2. S. Cobb. *Borderland of Psychiatry*. Cambridge, Mass., Harvard Univer. Press, 1943.
3. S. Arieti. "Manic Depressive Psychosis." *In:* S. Arieti (ed.). *American Handbook of Psychiatry*. New York, Basic Books, 1959, vol. 1, p. 420.
4. *Ibid.*
5. Clinical Neuropathological Conference. *Diseases of the Nervous System*, vol. 23, #2, 1962.
6. K. Goldstein. "Functional Disturbances in Brain Damage." *In:* S. Arieti (ed.). *Op. cit.*, p. 774.
7. K. Goldstein. *Language and Language Disturbances*. New York, Grune & Stratton, 1948, p. 155 ff.
8. M. A. B. Brazier. "Expanding Concepts in Neurophysiology." *Archives of Neurology and Psychiatry*, #67, 1952, pp. 545–549.
9. J. D. Benjamin. "A Method for Distinguishing and Evaluating Formal Thinking Disorder in Schizophrenia." *In:* J. S. Kasanin (ed.). *Language and Thought in Schizophrenia*. Berkeley, Univer. of California Press, 1944, p. 65.
10. K. Goldstein. "Functional Disturbances." *In:* S. Arieti (ed.). *Op. cit.*, p. 791.
11. *Ibid.*, p. 781.
12. M. Ostow. "A Psychoanalytic Contribution to the Study of Brain Function: I. The Frontal Lobes." *Psychoanalytic Quarterly*. #23, 1954, p. 332.
13. K. Goldstein. "Functional Disturbances." *In:* S. Arieti (ed.). *Op. cit.*, p. 781.
14. K. Goldstein. *The Organism*. New York, American Book, 1939, p. 140.
15. B. Klopfer and D. M. Kelley. *The Rorschach Technique*. Yonkers, World Book, 1942, p. 333.
16. S. Freud. *The Ego and the Id*. London, Hogarth, 1947, p. 36.
17. S. Freud. "Analysis Terminable and Interminable." *In: Collected Papers*. London, Hogarth, 1950, vol. 5, pp. 394–95.

18. H. Hartman. "Ego Psychology and the Problem of Adaptation." *In:* D. Rapaport. *Oganization and Pathology of Thought: Selected Sources.* New York, Columbia Univer. Press, 1951, p. 362.

19. *Ibid.,* p. 364.

20. *Ibid.,* footnote #39, pp. 374–75.

21. S. Freud. "Negation." *In: Collected Papers.* London, Hogarth, 1950, vol. 5, p. 182.

22. H. Hartmann. *Op. cit.,* [18] p. 366.

23. *Ibid.,* p. 365.

4

The Psychopathology
of Disorientation
and of Delirium

A patient is said to be disoriented if he is unable to recognize the identity of his surroundings—both in regard to place and person—and to realize the relationship of the present to the ever-changing flow of time. Some degree of disorientation invariably accompanies delirium; it is also a feature of the various forms of dementia, in which it may occur either episodically or as a permanent and irreversible symptom if the cell death of dementia has reached sufficiently extensive proportions. In both the acute and the chronic brain syndromes the degree of disorientation is a measure of the severity of the cognitive insufficiency that is the hallmark of so-called organic syndromes. The perceptual or cognitive failure in disorientation is always substantial and comprehensive and, in contrast to agnosia, is not confined to a single sensory modality. A patient suffering from visual agnosia may still recognize the identity of an object through nonvisual pathways, such as touch; no such alternatives are available to the disoriented patient. Disorientation may also be differentiated from illusional perception; in the latter the identity of the percept is never in doubt, but some of its attributes appear to be altered—such as shape, distance, vividness, or feeling of familiarity. Finally, disorientation in regard to one's surroundings as an expression of a cognitive insufficiency must be distinguished from misidentification resulting from delusional (and therefore essentially affectively determined) misinterpretation. This phenomenon may occur in schizophrenia and, in its more subtle forms, in nonschizophrenic psychotic states.

The term "disorientation" may convey the wrong impression: that is, that the patient has no orientation at all. This is not so. He has an orientation, but not the right one. The Jacksonian doctrine of the duality of the symptom—that is, of the coexistence of its "negative" and "positive" components—is of great help in making the nature and expressions of disorientation intelligible. In each instance of disorientation we must consider these three questions:

1. What has the patient lost in terms of highest-level function? What constitutes the "negative" symptom?

2. What has the patient substituted for this loss in terms of a lower-level function? In what form does the "positive" symptom express itself?

3. What determines the choice and nature of the substitution?

Disorientation, following the laws of general, uniform dissolution, occurs in orderly steps and patterns. Those aspects of the spatial-temporal environment the comprehension and identification of which ordinarily require more complex adaptive efforts will be the first ones to be affected. Accordingly, disorientation in time precedes disorientation in regard to physical surroundings and persons; unfamiliar surroundings are misidentified by a patient who could still orient himself in familiar ones. Time is a rather intangible and indirect perceptual experience, except in the instance of direct awareness of day or night on the basis of light and darkness of the sky. Cultural conventions designate time (in larger and smaller amounts) by the names of days and months and by numbers as dates and years. Our many recollections, activities, and anticipations normally help us to orient ourselves in regard to time. This articulated awareness of the continuity of our experiences controls our abstract time scheme, although different frames of reference guide our orientation for time of day, date, month, or year. It is, therefore, easy to see how orientation in time represents a high-level function of considerable complexity. In accordance with "Jackson's law," highest-level functions are most vulnerable to dissolution and it is a fact that disorientation in time is one of the earliest expressions of cognitive insufficiency.

Identification of unfamiliar surroundings requires the initiation and successful completion of a large number of perceptual processes and combinations in order to accomplish the differentiation of the "new" from the more concrete, familiar and automatic "old."

The disoriented patient attempts to come to terms with the cognitive challenge of his temporal and physical relatedness by a regressive reorganization of experience which is rooted in *subjectivity*. It is a distinct type of subjectivity, reflected in his wrong answers to questions pertaining to orientation. It differs in principle from other forms of pathological subjectivity, such as autism. In fact, it is possible to hypothesize that, whereas the subjectivity of autism draws upon our innate potential of the primary process, the subjectivity in disorientation essentially represents residuals of the secondary process, usually in the form of acquired but presently ill-fitting mental content. This subjectivity determines, in the brain-damaged, disoriented patient, the substitution—that is, the "positive" symptom. A simple example may serve to illustrate the issue. A Catholic patient who on a Wednesday believes it is Friday because he is served fish for supper is disoriented; his substitution "Friday" is the "ill-fitting residual" of his secondary process. But a schizophrenic who entertains the delusion that he is Christ will for this reason declare that for him *any* day is Friday, the day of the crucifixion. He has falsified the temporal reality by imposing upon it a more malignant and affectively determined subjectivity which we would have to consider to be an expression of autism. Subjectivity, by imposing itself beyond a certain point upon the objective outer world, will lead us to false conclusions and falsifications of judgment. Depending on the nature of psychological mechanisms which may be operative in a given case the resulting falsifications will differ, both in character and in malignancy. The subjectivity in disorientation is essentially a result of cognitive dissolution; it is not motivated by affective needs and is not representative of the primary process.

It may be useful to recall here a distinction which Sapir made in regard to certain aspects of symbolism in language. He distinguishes and elaborates two main types of symbolism: the *referential* and the *experiential* or *condensation* symbolism.[1] The former represents, at least in theory, objective reality to the complete exclusion of any possible trace of subjective coloring or contamination. Such symbols are therefore unambiguous, unemotional and truly representative of the thing they symbolize. "The less emotionalized a symbolism becomes, the more it takes on the character of true reference."[1] To the mathematician the Greek letter π is a referential symbol, and to the average person in our society the letters "A.M." and "P.M." are equally unequivocal. The Morse code is another example. By contrast, Sapir's experiential (or condensation) symbolism is "a highly condensed form of substitutive behavior . . . , allowing for the ready release of emotional tension."[1] He cites the hand-washing ritual of the compulsion neurosis as a pure sample of condensation symbolism, adding that the "richness of meaning grows with increased dissociation."[1] Another illustration, in the relatively simple area of semantic symbolism, would be to compare the respective meaning of "walking" and "strutting"—the former is referential and the latter is experiential, condensing postures, movements, facial expression, and character traits, as well as the emotional reactions of the observer or listener to the word. The significant difference between these two forms of symbolisms lies, in Sapir's words, in the nature of the psychological forces and mechanisms which determine in a given instance either of these forms of representation.

While the referential symbol grows with formal elaboration in the conscious, . . . the condensation symbol strikes deeper and deeper roots in the unconscious and diffuses its emotional quality to types of behavior or situations apparently far removed from the original meaning of the symbol. . . . Delusional misidentification of time, place and person certainly reflects the just quoted qualities of the "condensation symbol."[1]

In disorientation owing to cognitive insufficiency, on the other hand, the patient—while steering clear of the condensation symbol—nevertheless fails to grasp the appropriate referential designation, replacing it with an inaccurate one. It is in this sense that I suggested that the substitution in disorientation derives from the remnants of the secondary process.

CLINICAL MATERIAL

The preceding theoretical presentation will help to make the psychopathology of disorientation intelligible. We can now record and interpret the reasons which patients advance in support and explanation of their substitutions. Retaining the actual sequence of delamination of function in disorientation, we will first discuss failures to maintain orientation in the area of time.

The various referential aspects of experiencing time are not of equal clinical significance. However, any normal person is expected to know approximately the time of day; errors which have obliterated the awareness of the usual meal times are significant. Apart from the elementary clues of light and darkness we judge the time of day largely against the background and feedback of the succession of our daily activities; we form memory traces of these elements, both of the events themselves and their approximate duration. These reverberating and interacting memory traces, while usually temporary, nevertheless contribute significantly to make our biological clock run on time and thus tell us the time.

The following illustrations are chosen partly from clinical material reported by E. A. Weinstein and R. L. Kahn,[2] and partly from my own observations. In reply to the question "What time do you think it is now?" disoriented patients have responded in various ways. One patient invariably said that it was 7 p.m. "because that's when my daughter comes to see me." This repetitive, familiar, and thus "concrete" event of his daughter's visit at an hour known to the patient had withstood the process of dissolution, and it constituted the "positive" symptom. One of my patients, on a cloudy, dusky morning, said that it was 6 o'clock in the evening "because it is getting dark." Many patients when awakening from a nap any time during the day, will persist in stating that it is morning; even normal persons, under such circumstances, may for a moment—but *only* for a moment—have the same impression, since a minimum of time is required for the normal dissolution of sleepiness to be dissipated.

The reasons which patients give for their misidentifications of the day of the week are of great interest. One patient observed by me thought it was Sunday because he had been praying all day, and another gave the same false day because he had seen a minister who was visiting patients on the ward. The familiar correlation between Sunday and religious activities or perceptions was quite obviously the determining factor in the patients' responses. None of these patients would feel that it was within their power to make any day into Sunday by the "magic" of praying; such a mechanism would be autistic, not organic.

A somewhat different mechanism seems to have been operative in a patient who said on a Wednesday that it was Monday. When I asked him what made him think so, he replied, "Yesterday was Sunday," and to my question why he thought that, he said, "because before that it was Saturday," and so on in serial fashion. Here the automatic and familiar sequence of the days of the week took the place of the more demanding and actual reality, although in the somewhat unusual reverse direction. Still, this was perhaps less demanding of his remaining cognitive resources than the effort required to identify the day. Another patient insisted on one occasion that it was Tuesday, and when I inquired into her reasons she said, with an embarrassed smile, that she had said "Tuesday" because she liked the sound of that word. This kind of subjectivity,—most likely the expression of embarrassment as is so often seen in mildly demented or delirious patients—is certainly quite different from the autistic subjectivity of a schizophrenic patient who replied to my question "What day is today?" with "Yesterday." He explained that "everything moves backward." This same patient, when asked for the month, replied "October" when it was actually March; October was, he explained, the third month "backward moving," while March is the third month in the normal forward order. (It may be added that in some subcultures the month is referred to by number rather than by name.)

Disorientation in regard to the month indicates considerable cognitive deficit, particularly if the falsification extends into the span of the seasons. Disoriented patients tend to give the wrong year more frequently in retrograde than in forward order, and in mild cases the mistake is restricted to *one* wrong digit, the last or penultimate number usually being misidentified.

Patients who are disoriented with regard to their physical surroundings seem to resort to two types of substitutions. They either believe themselves to be in a place which is, for whatever reason, familiar to them, or they arrive at a false designation by weaving the correct name into a memory trace which contains a semantic similarity. A patient at Kings County Hospital told me that he was now at "the Kings County County Clerk's Office." Another patient called it "Kingsbridge Hospital," the name of a local Veterans Administration hospital with which he was apparently familiar, at least to the extent of knowing its name. It is easy to see from these two examples that the patients probably had some dim awareness of the correct name of the hospital ("Kings County") which in turn supplied the semantic contribution to the substitution. In other instances the patient will name a hospital with an entirely different name, but to which he is cognitively linked by a previous experience of one kind or another. Such substitutive places are often, and in more ways than one, closer to home. Weinstein and Kahn[3] report a case which is most instructive because the restitution to normal orientation can be traced on the basis of day-to-day observation. This patient was at Walter Reed Hospital in Washington, D.C., but when he was first examined he believed himself to be at what he called the "Coolidge Memorial Hospital." This designation turned out to be a verbal condensation derived from two sources, both of which were familiar to the patient, namely, Cooley-Dickinson Hospital and Coolidge Memorial Bridge, places near his home in Georgia. At this point the true referential symbol had undergone complete dissolution. "Coolidge Memorial" was gradually located closer to Washington by him, via North Carolina and Virginia. The next step in the patient's recovery of his orientation was evident when he combined the true and the substitutive referential symbols, speaking of a "Walter Reed Memorial Hospital." Thereafter the true reference appeared as an ego-alien "pseudo-orientation," the patient remarking, "They say it's Walter Reed." Even after he had recovered his orientation he had the feeling "that there must be a Coolidge Hospital somewhere." This last statement may be considered to be an example or analogue of organic perseveration.

In severe disorientation the substitutions of the patients no longer include any trace of the lost referential symbol. Such patients may believe themselves to be at home or at other familiar places; they think and act as if they were engaged in their usual activities, as in the past. The purely descriptive term "occupational delirium" was meant to denote this substantial state of cognitive dissolution. Such patients are not delusional, but merely corroborate the validity of our theoretical premise in regard to the essential nature of disorientation. The subjectivity of familiarity differs from the subjectivity of autism as a memory differs from a fantasy. And it was Hughlings Jackson who said: "What is delirium except the *disorderly* revival of sensory-motor processes received in the past?"[4]

Disorientation in regard to the person exists if the patient mistakes an unfamiliar person for a familiar one. Thus the nurse is mistaken for the wife or another female relative; similarly, the physician or other male persons are mistaken for men whom the patient knows well, usually one of his relatives. The substitution never has the character of danger, suspicion, or eccentricity, as does schizophrenic or paranoid misidentification. This difference exists because—to repeat—the disorientation results from a dissolution of cognitive capacity.

Delusional misidentification is, by definition, rooted in affectivity. Patients with paranoid delusions will suspect or believe that the physician is an agent of the F.B.I. or a lawyer with ulterior motives. But they usually add that "he" poses as a physician. They comprehend correctly his professional attire and the role he seems to play in the hospital situation. The introduction of the issue of disguise and deception by the patient is evidence that there has been no dissolution of the referential symbol. In such cases one may indeed assume that the referential and the experiential symbols coexist; the former is recognized, but is not acknowledged because of the overwhelming power of the latter.

Misidentification of certain aspects of the environment may at times be the result of a formal thought disorder in schizophrenia. The patient arrives at his false conclusions without, however, being either delusional or disoriented within the terms of our hypothesis. In my experience faulty reasoning on the basis of predicative identification leads to such falsifications of identity. Thus one of my patients, who noted that I was swivelling in my chair, said: "Are you related to Doctor G.? He swivels in his chair just like you do." Another patient said quite congenially to one of my colleagues, who happened to be a Negro: "You must be a brother of Doctor X., because he is also a colored doctor." Although, strictly speaking, neither of these patients had misidentified anybody, they had both drawn a false conclusion in the general area of identity by the process of predicative identification. In neither case was the element of familiarity the determining factor, even though the source of their error was a person familiar to them.

Max Levin reports the case of a schizophrenic patient who, during a superimposed bromide delirium, believed himself to be in China or Japan when in actuality he was in the Harrisburg State Hospital. The patient himself, after recovery from the delirium, explained how he had seen somebody putting shoes on a fellow patient, who made a wry face, as if in pain, "and this made me think of China, where feet are bound tight." Levin comments on this seemingly random conclusion by the patient as follows: "It shows the far-fetched reasoning of the schizophrenic, the identification in terms of the remote and the bizarre."[5] I would like to add to Levin's comment that what is posed here is an example of predicative identification of a rather malignant degree. The connecting link of experiencing pain when putting on a shoe equates this event, as observed by the patient, with the well-known Oriental custom of manipulating or mutilating the feet in order to make them smaller and thus more appealing. The predicative similarities are so remote, irrelevant, and insufficient that only a schizophrenic would find them strong enough to bridge the gap between Harrisburg and China! Levin adds: "A delirious man who was not at the same time schizophrenic might . . . have thought he was in a shoe store watching a fellow customer being fitted."[5] Such a contingency accurately describes the typical mechanism of dissolution of the referential symbol toward the subjectivity of the familiar, as it occurs in and is characteristic of organic disorientation.

DELIRIUM

The cognitive transformation of the personality in delirium differs so significantly from that which is associated with dementia that a separate presentation of this syndrome seems appropriate. It must be admitted that this view is not generally accepted, although clinical and neurophysiological data tend to support the rationale of distinguishing dementia from delirium. I would, therefore, find it difficult to agree with Engel and Romano when they state that "the distinction between dementia and delirium is a somewhat arbitrary one, established by convention."[6] It is, of course, true that both dementia and delirium are the clinical expression of an essentially cognitive failure or insufficiency of the brain, the former being more chronic and the latter more acute. There is even a certain interrelationship between them. An existing dementia, representing an already weakened cognitive faculty, constitutes a potent predisposing element for delirium, although the reverse is much less likely. The cognitive insufficiency of dementia is the result of a loss of nerve cells which can not be replaced; thus dementia is, to this extent, an irreversible process. Delirium, on the other hand, is considered to be the expression of metabolic failure within the brain. These metabolic abnormalities, whatever their nature and origin may be, are usually reversible; consequently delirium is, too. Another feature which supports the view of making a distinction between dementia and delirium derives from the respective electroencephalographic findings reported in these conditions. All authorities, including Engel and Romano, agree that cortical metabolic insufficiency is reflected in the electroencephalogram by diffuse slowing of the frequency to about 7 per second, or less. If we can equate dementia with cortical cell death and delirium with faulty or reduced metabolism of these cells, two conclusions may be drawn. First, we may view the usually insidious course of dementia as being the clinical equivalent of cell death, while the more acute and dramatic (but reversible) phenomena of delirium would reflect equally acute and reversible reductions and/or alterations of cell metabolism. The second inference derives from electroencephalographic readings. It has been noted that there is no convincing evidence of diffuse slowing in the EEG in dementia. Engel and Romano, who noted this fact, state that the abnormally slow potentials arise from damaged, but not from dead neurons; they say also that "the EEG in dementia is less consistently slow as compared to that in delirium."[7] Reduced oxygen or glucose metabolism, both frequent contributory factors in delirium, is characteristically accompanied by diffuse slowing of the EEG. The cognitive insufficiency—which is so typical for both dementia and delirium—may, of course, be produced either by the death of or by deranged metabolism of the affected cortical cells.

Engel and Romano define delirium as "a derangement in the general functional metabolism of the brain [that] is reflected at the clinical level by a characteristic disturbance in cognitive functions and at the physiologic level by a characteristic generalized slowing of the electroencephalogram."[8] The authors continue: "The diagnosis of delirium is unequivocally established when it can be shown that the level of awareness correlates with changes in EEG frequency, reduction being accompanied by further slowing of the EEG and improvement by relative acceleration of the EEG."[9] Thus delirium may be considered to constitute a nosologic entity; its causes are manifold and its clinical expressions, which surround the invariable core of cognitive insufficiency, are to some degree modified by the intensity of the cerebral decompensation, by the particular provocative causes, and by the premorbid personality traits of the patient.

The most frequent cause of delirium is probably endogenous and exogenous poisoning and intoxication; in each instance a particular biochemical abnormality converges on the brain, resulting in the derangement of its metabolism. It is very likely that many cases of mild or moderate delirium could be found on general medical and surgical wards; these patients may suffer from delirium which is secondary to anoxia or other serious biochemical dysfunction resulting from disease in organs other than the brain. Delirium caused by ingestion or withdrawal of exogenous poisons—such as alcohol, bromide, barbiturates, and many other agents—is a well-known phenomenon. Patients with simple dementia are, as already stated, highly susceptible to delirious episodes; the cognitive decompensation may be precipitated by the normal sensory and social "deprivation" during night time, or by metabolic abnormalities the effect of which is compounded by the already existing weakening of the brain resulting from cell death.

The clinical manifestations of delirium include three groups of symptoms: cognitive decompensation, release phenomena, and signs and symptoms reflecting the nature of the precipitating cause. The cognitive insufficiency of delirium is most consistently expressed in various degrees of disorientation; lowering of the general level of consciousness, with difficulty or inability to attend to stimuli or to comprehend the meaning of questions directed to the patient; and, consequently, in the display of confusion. In mild forms of delirium patients may, with great effort, overcome some of these failures or at least hide them behind a veneer of evasiveness or good humor. The cognitive insufficiency is, of course, most marked in severe delirium, but in all instances it will be more pronounced if the patient is exposed to the demands of abstract or unfamiliar situations. There is great difficulty in forming memory traces for immediate recall. It has been stated that the cognitive failure is accurately reflected in a corresponding slowing of the EEG; the latter's frequency will increase as soon as the delirium improves. Engel and Romano make the interesting observation that in severe slowing of the EEG "the characteristic disruption of the pattern by opening the eyes is no longer observed, a physiologic correlate of the reduced impact of externally derived perceptions."[10] Fluctuations in the level of consciousness and (therefore) in cognitive capacity are rather typical.

Release phenomena in delirium may consist in the presence of illusions, hallucinations, and bizarre thoughts as well as in intense dysphoric affects. This group of symptoms lends a certain weird and eery quality to delirium; it may be appropriate to recall, at this point, that the Latin word *delirium* means insanity. Visual hallucinations predominate over auditory ones in delirium, although the latter may also occur. Many visual "hallucinations" are actually illusions. Considering the apperceptive weakness of the patient and the generally obfuscating effect of dusk, dawn, or night, objects are seen by the patient not only considerably altered in shape but also as if in slight motion. These two factors may account for the frequent and proverbial tendency of delirious patients to hallucinate animals. Illusional experiences of familiarity occur also in the auditory sphere; patients readily mistake voices of strangers for those of friends or relatives. Brightly colored visual hallucinations of people who are seen as if they were very small characterize delirium caused by certain toxic substances, such as cocain; they are aptly, and poetically, called "Lilliputian hallucinations." Tactile or haptic hallucinations also occur, particularly in delirium tremens; these abnormal perceptions are often delusionally elaborated by the patients, who then complain that animals (such as insects or roaches) are crawling on their skin. Abnormal sensations resulting from the polyneuropathy of alcoholism may give rise to these tactile phenomena. Generally speaking, the combination of cognitive insufficiency and hallucinatory experiences strongly supports the diagnosis of delirium.

A substantial number of delirious patients show evidence of intense anxiety—even panic—associated with great restlessness. Many of these individuals believe themselves to be threatened or in some kind of danger, and some of them experience hallucinations that confirm their fears. It is sometimes said that the paranoid experiences of delirious patients, in contrast to those of the schizophrenic, lack the element of self-reference. The delirious patient, it is claimed, is under the impression that everybody around him is threatened by the same dangers. In my experience this is not true for all patients suffering from delirium. Bizarre thought content suggestive of schizophrenia may be found in some cases of delirium; we assume that the basic metabolic derangement can, in "predisposed" individuals, release a schizophreniform syndrome. The differential diagnosis rests mainly on a consideration of the cognitive and electroencephalographic status of the patient. There are no disturbances in these areas in dementia praecox.

The signs and symptoms relating to the precipitating causes of delirium can always be noted if one is sufficiently sensitive to the frequency of cerebral cognitive insufficiency. When one considers the etiologic hypothesis concerning delirium, these signs range far and wide. Their detection is at times of the greatest importance because they may be the only clue leading toward effective therapy for the condition.

REFERENCES

1. E. Sapir. *"Selected Writings." In:* D. G. Mandelbaum (ed.). *Language, Culture and Personality.* Berkeley, Univer. of California Press, 1958, p. 564 ff.
2. E. A. Weinstein and R. L. Kahn. "Symbolic Reorganization in Brain Injuries." *In:* S. Arieti (ed.). *American Handbook of Psychiatry.* New York, Basic Books, 1959, vol. 1, p. 964 ff.
3. *Ibid.*
4. J. Taylor (ed.). *Selected Writings of John Hughlings Jackson.* New York, Basic Books, 1958, vol. 1, p. 26, footnote #1.
5. M. Levin. "Delirium: A Gap in Psychiatric Teaching." *The American Journal of Psychiatry,* vol. 107, 1950/51, p. 689.

6. G. L. Engel and J. Romano. "Delirium, a Syndrome of Cerebral Insufficiency." *Journal of Chronic Disease*, vol. 9, #3 (March 1960), p. 274.

7. *Ibid.*, p. 274.

8. *Ibid.*, p. 276.

9. *Ibid.*, p. 268.

10. G. L. Engel and J. Romano. *Op. cit.*, [6] p. 270.

5

The Significance of the
Reticular Activating Systems

Human behavior—despite its ascendancy and complexity—is
at its neurobiological source profoundly, and even crudely,
affected and supported by ancient and centrally located functional systems: the several reticular activating systems of the brainstem. These
structures, extending in man from the medulla up to the midbrain and
into parts of the basal ganglia, are "similar in all vertebrates from the
amphibians to the primates,"[1] and are in the lower forms of vertebrate
life probably the sole mediators between the organism and its environment. In man they interact with the infinitely complex cortical acquisitions in accordance with the principle of encephalization of function.
They are the most elementary neurological source of the most elementary
aspects of human mental life: awareness and reactivity.

In this chapter it is our purpose: (1) to present the essential anatomical and physiological features of the several reticular activating systems
(RAS); (2) to contrast these systems' contributions to mental life with
those of the cortex in terms of *source* and *content*, respectively, of awareness and reactivity; and (3) to describe the pathology of behavior that
results from disease of the several RAS's.

LOCATION AND FUNCTION

In 1945, H. Magoun[2] described the location and presumed
function of an ascending RAS in the brainstem. It is a centrally located reticular formation, distinct from the more laterally placed
ascending or afferent long pathways to respective cortical endstations.
It appears that this reticular formation exerts a nonspecific alerting and
arousing effect on the cerebral cortex, an effect which in animal experi-

ments could be obtained and electroencephalographically verified when this formation was directly stimulated or if an electric stimulus was applied to the afferent long pathways. Thus it was inferred that ordinary sensory stimuli—such as touch, sound, or light—simultaneously "fired" the RAS, carrying a charge of the latter's alerting potential with them. It was further concluded that the states of sleep and wakefulness were closely related to the inactivity or activity, respectively, of the RAS of Magoun; the deafferentiation in sleep was not to be confined to the exclusion, by various means, of ordinary sensory stimuli. It thus seemed plausible that the chances of any afferent event's making itself cortically "heard" or significant were greatly enhanced by the intrinsic and concomitant arousal function of this nonspecific reticular formation. In 1953, Linn[3] suggested a distinction between cortical information and cortical arousal. In his paper he also advanced certain ideas concerning a possible physiological basis for some well-known psychological and psychoanalytical hypotheses. Perceptions, Linn said, arrive at the cortex accompanied by their normal quota of nonspecific alerting impulses from the RAS. At the cortical level an analysis and evaluation of the significance to the individual of sense data (and of ideas?) take place. Three general possibilities may be envisioned. If the afferent mental content is meaningful, it is conceivable that additional and reinforcing motivating impulses are set in motion via (assumed) corticofugal pathways. The resulting intensified awareness could, I think, ultimately serve cognitive, affective, or instinctual needs and purposes. At the other end of the hypothesis, the cortical scanning process may spot the actual or potential, painful and anxiety-provoking character of sense data, in which case corticofugal pathways may deactivate the alerting mechanisms, thus leading to a result akin to suppression or repression. Finally, indifferent material would receive or evoke only marginal attention. Linn's ideas are mentioned not only because they are plausible but also because they present the biological counterpart to our psychodynamic formulations. I may add that clinical data suggest that the function of *sustained* and *circumscribed* awareness is probably more related to the activities of the *specific* alerting systems, as will presently be shown.

Ventral to the RAS of Magoun there exists a nonspecific activating system which facilitates conative (motor) and, possibly, emotionally expressive behavior in animals and in man. Removal of the tectum or quadrigeminal plate in monkeys by Denny-Brown[4] rendered the animals mute and reduced or abolished facial expression or mimetic responses ordinarily evoked in the course of their social behavior. In man lesions of this system cause akinetic mutism (see below). It has been found that without the intact globus pallidus the pyramidal system does not induce movement. The function of this conative system is *nonspecific* in the sense that it seems to control reactivity at its neurobiological core and not at a higher, psychological level of ideation and affectivity.

There exists still another distinct alerting system, the thalamocortical circuits. As they functionally connect certain thalamic nuclei with their corresponding cortical areas, they may be considered "specific." It is assumed that their function is that of maintaining a state of sustained awareness or vigilance, the nature and manifestations of which are, of course, determined by the respective cortical functions to which these circuits address themselves. Thus lesions in the thalamoparietal bundle (or circuit) result in various degrees of loss of awareness of the contralateral half of the body—ranging from episodic forgetting of its existence to its total, permanent sequestration from the body image. While the body half may still be seen and recognized as *a* body part, it is no longer *experienced* as a part of one's *own* body; the contribution of the specific thalamoparietal circuit of elevating body perception to body experience is lost.

Of even greater psychiatric significance are the activating circuits between the dorsomedial nucleus of the thalamus and the prefrontal cortical areas. Their function may be surmised from the nature of the psychological changes following prefrontal psychosurgery. The intensity of affect previously attached to delusions and hallucinations is drastically reduced following severance of these circuits; the patient is no longer motivated to *act* in accordance with his false beliefs, the mere verbal remnants of which he has in no way forgotten. He may continue to hear voices, but they no longer compel him to obey them, or arouse his anger. It has been said that lobotomy does not change the *structure* of the psychosis; it may be added that only its explosive potential is reduced or removed—the psychological bomb has been defused. It is furthermore assumed that these thalamoprefrontal circuits sustain self-awareness in a manner and to a degree that enhance adaptation; the person takes himself and his goals seriously, but not *too* seriously. His motives and capacity for attention are nourished and helped to endure, but not to the point of becoming compulsive or constituting an obsession.

AWARENESS AND REACTIVITY

Basic to any form and aspect of human behavior are the *fact* and the *content* of awareness and reactivity. The state of being conscious, in its constant normal and pathological fluctuations, has—in accordance with the general plan of the nervous system—its sensory and motor (executive) components. This is what is meant by awareness and reactivity. There is enough clinical and experimental evidence now available to permit a conception of an "anatomy of con-sciousness," with cortical and subcortical levels, and with sensory and motor components.

The ascending reticular activating system of Magoun alerts in a non-specific manner the entire afferent cortex. To it we owe the *fact* of being capable of awareness, of being capable of attending to sensory stimuli. If I may use a simile, it illuminates the mental scene just as a screen is illuminated by the bright square field of light from a motion picture projector before the picture itself is run. The less its activity, the dimmer the state of alertness or wakefulness. In severe lesions of the RAS the patient is rendered comatose; but in less severe cases he readily lapses into, and emerges from, a state of somnolence. This condi-tion is also known by the term *coma vigil*. It is instructive to compare the respective contributions to the state of awareness made by the cortex and the brainstem. The cortex, the end station of the long ascending pathways, enables us to perceive, store, recall, conceptualize, and reflect upon the sense data of the outer world and their unbelievably complex elaborations. This is an accomplishment which in man culminates in the deposition of a microcosm of his life experiences ultimately derived from the macrocosm surrounding him. This is what I meant when I spoke of the *content* of awareness. Impairment of memory and orienta-tion and ideation are examples of content pathology, and hence are of cortical origin. A patient with massive cortical loss will not be ren-dered unconscious, but he will be permanently deprived of what he formerly had been conscious of. A patient with a lesion in the RAS is rendered unconscious; but if he recovers, then his microcosm will still be available to him. Such comments, of course, describe phenomena of the state of being conscious as we observe them in human beings, with their highly developed cortex. One could perhaps also include those primates who, in this context, differ from man only in the somewhat inferior quality and complexity of their content of consciousness—both in regard to awareness and to reactivity. It is literally true that the reason that horses do not laugh is that they have nothing to laugh about! In the course of vertebrate evolution, little of consequence has been added to the reticular formations as such, apart from their connec-tions. In the lowest forms these formations are the sole mediators of be-havior patterns that are wholly sufficient for survival and adaptation. Brain-stem existence guarantees returns that, while meager, are utterly reliable. There are neither the opportunities nor the possible pitfalls of ontogenetic development. Neither the capacity for thought nor the sus-ceptibility to error has yet found a place to interpose itself between sensory intake and motor output. Reactions occur in response to *signals*, not *symbols*; the former are unequivocal, but the latter need not be. The turkey hen will not attack or kill her chick because it emits a sound of a definite quality the reception of which reliably inhibits her aggression.[5] But a schizophrenic mother killed her baby girl because she wanted her to die a virgin. Had it not been for this parasymbolic content pathology on the part of the mother, her aim could have been accomplished—with some cooperation on the part of the daughter—in a much less gruesome manner, and at any rate death could have been postponed. There is, after all, a difference between dying and being killed.

A similar duality can be observed with regard to the subcortical and cortical contributions to reactivity: the former supplies the source, the latter the content of motor or conative functions. Midbrain lesions may render a patient motionless and speechless, to various degrees—*not* because he is paralyzed or aphasic (or, for that matter, depressed or catatonic) but because he has lost the potential for reactivity. The *fact* but not the content of the motor component of the conscious state is impaired. This condition, which was first described by Cairns *et al.*[6], has been given the name *akinetic mutism*. The patient suffered from an epidermoid cyst of the third ventricle. During the mute akinetic period emotional responses were almost absent; after the cyst was tapped, normal awareness and reactivity returned. Motility at the cortical (pyramidal) level is voluntary, skilled, environmentally oriented, capable of being symbolic, and in the service of ideation. Disease at the highest level causes loss of voluntary motility (that is to say, paralysis), loss of skilled movement (such as apraxia), and loss of capacity for motor symbolic expression of thought (as in aphasia). Such a derangement constitutes content pathology. None of these defects is found in akinetic mutism, in which condition all these functions are suspended rather than destroyed.

The elementary, although impersonal, effect on awareness and reactivity of these deep-seated reticular formations may have induced Denney-Brown[4] to speak of the midbrain tectum as the site of the "physiological ego," a hypothesis with which I cannot agree. The ego is formed by the interaction of a part of the id with the outer world. To accomplish this transformation the participation of the cortex, with its perceptual and executive content components, is indispensable. The physiological counterpart of the metaphorical concept "ego" is in the cortex.

CLINICAL IMPLICATIONS

It remains now to describe the clinical picture of patients with verified lesions in these nonspecific reticular (and extrapyramidal) systems that control the fact of awareness and reactivity.

I have chosen two case reports from the literature and a case which I recently discussed before a clinicopathological conference.[7] Denney-Brown[4] reported a patient with bilateral necrosis of the globus pallidus caused by asphyxic anoxia. This patient lapsed into a state of unresponsiveness, with his arms and legs moderately rigid in semiflexion. His face was expressionless and he reacted to painful pinpricks only by slowly scratching the spot. Swallowing was possible only if fluids were introduced far back into the mouth. There was also dystonia. Dennis Williams[8] reported a patient whose autopsy revealed postencephalitic lesions in the midbrain and the substantia nigra. This middle-aged man began losing drive and interest. He appeared apathetic, as if depressed. He never spoke spontaneously. All command movements were performed well, but very slowly. He did not move in response to painful stimuli and showed inertia of voluntary pharyngeal movements. The third case was a 69-year-old man in whom his family had noted a gradual deterioration of memory for about a year prior to admission. He was also observed to have changed in that he participated much less in family activities and generated very little spontaneous speech. He seemed slowly to shrink into himself and was reluctant to walk a distance of more than a few feet. He exhibited occasional tremors of the extremities. A neurological examination upon his admission to the hospital disclosed no abnormalities. He was occasionally disoriented, facing away from people and curling up. His posture, because of generalized flexion of all extremities, was described by a psychiatric observer as "a fetuslike position." He would lapse into sleep soon after being aroused. He showed diminished gag reflexes and the suggestion of left central facial paralysis on about the eleventh hospital day. He did not respond to painful stimulation. He did not move any of his extremities. After slipping slowly into stupor, he died on the nineteenth day. I concluded my discussion with the following:

During the year prior to his admission he presented a picture of dementia with conspicuous absence of spontaneity of movement, speech and interest. I would have determined that he was neither paralyzed, nor aphasic, nor depressed. Patients with mere arteriosclerotic dementia are prone to show at least episodic periods of excitement or emotional incontinence. They have difficulty in initiating mental tasks only if such tasks are presented to them propositionally. Akinetic dementia is found in the frontal variety of Pick's disease. Such patients are more inert than demented; the impairment of initiative is at a higher level, so to speak, than in akinetic mutism caused by subcortical disease. I think that the patient's age, even before the development of his terminal symptoms, rules out a diagnosis of Pick's disease. Massive hemispheric neoplasm must be considered. It would have to be massive in order to account for the considerable degree of cognitive decompensation. But there is no evidence in the protocol of increased intracranial pressure; the long pathways were not compromised until questionable lateralizing signs appeared at the very end. Such pyramidal signs as were noted could be found in any old person with dementia. Rapidly progressive neurological signs are even more common in metastatic cerebral neoplasm. I would of course have arranged for air studies, skull plates and an EEG. But I do not think, judging from the protocol in its entirety, that he had a brain tumor. The striking features in the terminal phase of his illness are really an intensification of what he may well have shown to a lesser degree while still at home, about a year before hospitalization: tremors, flexion of his extremities, somnolence and unresponsiveness. He did not move any of his extremities; yet he was not paralyzed. He did not respond to painful stimulation; yet he was not comatose. He was in fact described as being disoriented, which indicates some degree of awareness, albeit the regressive awareness of dementia.

I visualize diffuse and discrete cortical and subcortical pathology, the latter within the deep midline reticular systems and possibly extending into the extrapyramidal gray matter.[7]

Autopsy revealed a rare form of a diffuse degenerative process first described by Okazaki *et al.*,[9] involving ganglionic cells throughout the cerebral cortex, substantia nigra, and the brainstem reticular systems. This condition ("Lewyosis") is identified by the presence of nonviral inclusion bodies, and clinically characterized by a combination of dementia, brainstem abnormalities of the type presented by the patient and elaborated upon by me in this chapter, and, typically, by quadriplegia-in flexion.

What is the relevance of the physiology and pathology of the several RAS's to the study of clinical psychiatry? In addition to what has already been said, a final comment is offered as an answer. I think that for certain reasons we are at times inclined to overlook—and even to look down upon—the ancient structures (neurological as well as endocrinological) that influence behavior at its root. It is true that pathology in these areas lacks the intricacies and intellectual elegance of content pathology. Yet, a clinician should have a balanced view and realize that a patient who is "sick at the core" is entitled to the same professional competence as the one whose psychopathology is conveyed to us in words, dreams, and fantasies. One of the problems in psychiatry, as recently stated by Kalinowsky, is that "Clinical work with the severely sick patient is being neglected by a large section of the profession in favor of over-concern with mild deviations."[10] Let there be balance and broad familiarity. No psychiatrist would permit himself the luxury and sense of immunity to hazard "interpretations" in patients with impersonal organicity, which is subject to biological or postmortem proof.

REFERENCES

1. O. R. Longworthy. "The Neurophysiology of Motivation." *American Journal of Psychiatry*, March 1966, p. 1033.
2. H. Magoun. "Ascending Reticular Activating System in the Brainstem." *Archives of Neurology and Psychiatry*, vol. 67, 1952, pp. 145–154.
3. L. Linn. "Psychological Implications of the Activating System." *American Journal of Psychiatry*, vol. 110, #1, 1953, pp. 61–65.
4. D. Denney-Brown. "The Midbrain and Motor Integration." *Proceedings of the Royal Society of Medicine*, 55: 527–538, 1962. Cited by Longworthy.[1]
5. K. Lorenz. *On Aggression.* New York, Harcourt, Brace & World, 1966, p. 117.
6. H. Cairns, *et al.* "Akinetic Mutism with Epidermoid Cyst of Third Ventricle." *Brain,* 64: 273, 1941.
7. Clinical Neuropathological Conference. *Diseases of the Nervous System,* vol. 28, #6 (June) 1967, pp. 407–412.
8. D. Williams. "Old and New Concepts of the Basis of Consciousness." In *The Brain and Its Functions.* Springfield, Ill., Thomas, 1958.
9. H. Okazaki, *et al.* "Diffuse Intracytoplasmic Ganglionic Inclusions (Lewy type) Associated with Dementia and Quadriparesis in Flexion." *Journal of Neuropathology and Experimental Neurology,* 20: 237, 1961.
10. L. B. Kalinowsky. "Problems in Psychiatry." *Comprehensive Psychiatry,* vol. 7, #3, June 1966, p. 144.

6

Memory and Memories

Paul Schilder once defined memory as "the reawakening of the past in the service of the present."[1] If one observes how lower animals handle similar situations today exactly as they did yesterday, one may conclude that they seem not to have forgotten. This, however, does not mean that they are capable of memory as we understand this phenomenon in man. Not until the evolutionary process had created a brain of sufficient complexity and, presumably, of a corresponding capacity for conscious experience could the ontogenetic past be reawakened in the form of a memory and "in the service of the present." As we ascend the phylogenetic ladder, the ontogenetic past of the individual organism gradually joins the hereditary "memory" of phylogeny; but the lesson of the phylogenetic evolutionary past has been fully given and "learned" at the moment of conception. Phylogeny shapes organisms but not personalities, anlagen but not skills. It supplies memory but not memories. As the capacity for the recording and retaining of perceptions and experiences unfolds somewhere below the summit occupied by man, and to the degree to which the separation of self from nonself becomes possible and meaningful, memory emerges in the form which Schilder chose to call the reawakening of the past in the service of the present. It is a curious fact of the psychopathology of memory that there are some patients who cannot remember and others who cannot forget. Further, Freud discovered that there are even some patients who cannot "forget" because they cannot remember. This statement is neither a contradiction nor meant to be a semantic nicety. It is a perhaps somewhat startling phrasing of Freud's contention that the hysteric suffers from (repressed but dynamically potent) memories which cannot be dissipated ("forgotten") until they have been made conscious in the course of psychoanalytic treatment.

Thus the term "memory" is only a very broad and sweeping generality that refers to the fixation of mental input, the "material record of a past activity,"[2] and the fate of such engrams within the nervous system.

The term hardly suggests the complexities of this faculty, or the momentous consequences to the individual that accrue from memory's operational characteristics. Just as McCulloch said that he did not "like any theory of memory which suffers from what I consider the fallacy of simple location,"[3] so must the clinical psychiatrist avoid the fallacy of assigning a simple equivalence to the many varieties, categories, and destinies of things capable of becoming memories.

INFORMATIVE AND FORMATIVE
MEMORY TRACES

It requires very little self-observation and reflection to become aware of the multitude and variety of recorded mental input. The first striking discovery is the complexity and composite nature of even the simplest and most deliberately isolated memory traces—such as those attending "simple" perception. It is true that symbolic representation in the form of words and language introduces an element of compactness and isolation, but this is illusory and is immediately dissolved if the object or perceptual experience is stripped of its semantic reference.

It appears almost certain that from an early age onward no *isolated* recording of perceptions occurs, that their memory traces become incorporated into pre-existing memory organizations that are pertinent to the perceptions of the moment, and that they are thus brought into the configurational context of relevant past experience. Otherwise neither recognition nor appropriate recall of such simple, self-explanatory, and emotionally indifferent perceptions—such as that of a familiar object—would be possible. When I see two birds in flight the visual image is, of course, recorded as a Gestalt, a configurational whole; but their shape, color, distance, speed, and spatial relatedness are by no means ignored, even if these attributes are not consigned to the center and summit of the mnemonic process. There may be even more deep-seated (preconscious and unconscious) reverberations; these two birds in flight, by an act of symbolic transmutation, may become the fleeting representation of extrapolated primordial fantasies surrounding the mysteries of "whence," "whither," togetherness, and so on. In the psychopathology of confabulation (see below) any of these satellite memories may move into the center of the patient's awareness, thus determining his distorted substitutions. In literate societies a huge segment of the compass of data committed to memory presents itself in the form of verbal or numerical symbols, read rather than heard. Such memories play a very great role in the learning process. The relationship between memory and language is twofold: language may be incorporated into our mental content, either as a transitory or permanent memory; and the memory of events and experiences may in the course of time become, or be reduced to, a mere verbal trace—an "abstract memory" as Penfield called it, a "gut memory" eviscerated. Complex semantic constructions (ideas and inter-related ideas) are remembered, provided they are comprehended; here is a link between memory and intelligence. A special variety of fixation of experience results in our awareness of our body image, parts of which are "forgotten" in the case of lesions in certain parts of the brain (see Chapter 11). Feelings are remembered either as faint (Jacksonian) images or as verbal factual abstractions; they may be recalled and relived in much greater intensity under a number of ordinary and exceptional circumstances—such as a recurrence of an experience or event of the same emotional significance as the original one; a dream; an intense transference reaction during psychoanalytic treatment; and in certain patients by experimental electrical stimulation of distinct cortical areas of the temporal lobe (see below.) Finally, there are memories whose panoramic breadth, continuity, and significance to the individual call for a special designation and consideration. As examples one may cite the continuity of self-awareness or the composite memory which one has of a significant person, such as a parent. The clinical psychiatrist and psychoanalyst is constantly confronted with problems resulting from the psychopathology of memory and of memories, both in the area of diagnosis and therapy.

One may ask whether the two fundamental aspects of psychic life—the pleasure principle and the reality principle—and their interrelation (the latter evolving from the former) may not also be reflected in the area of the psychology and psychopathology of memory; whether, to put it differently, "the intellectual function is . . . distinct from the affective process."[4] The mere fact that the psychopathology of memory encompasses organic as well as functional disorders should call our attention to the likelihood that the formation and fate of conceptual memory traces may be quite different from those of dynamic ones. The phenomena of memory and memory disorders will, therefore, be presented in accordance with an assumed and perhaps relevant existence of two organismic categories. Although "memory-function may be conceived as built on an autonomous inborn apparatus, which in the course of maturation plays a double role,"[5] there are ample reasons for an exposition of contrasting features of this dual role.

Ego Relationships (Informative)

Whenever we observe and test memory impairment in a patient suffering from organic dementia we notice that he is most incapacitated with regard to the immediate recall of verbal material. The patient's failure to form memory traces is proportionate to the amount of cortical cell loss and is compounded by the complexity and not by the emotional significance of the material offered. The term "complexity" in this context connotes some or all of the attributes which tend in the direction of abstraction. *Verbal* tasks closer to conceptual memory schemata are failed when more concrete memories of simple *motor* tasks (such as hiding and retrieving an object) can still be retained, or recovered within a short time. Whatever aid comprehension might have contributed toward success in the area of memory is no longer available to these patients. What is the nature of the faculty of recording and retaining conceptual memory traces, and how does it evolve?

The material whose immediate recall is so conspicuously impaired in organic dementia consists characteristically of verbal representations of conceptual thought. The memory frames of reference involved are therefore quite different from those which "are originally organized around drives and arise in consciousness as representations of these drives . . . ."[6] In *Emotions and Memory* Rapaport suggests that, during the early phases of life, memories are organized around drives, which in the very young child certainly represent the sole or main psychic content.[7] Later both thought and memory organizations revolve around "partial drives," "attitudes," and "interests" until—with the maturation of the psychic apparatus and the introduction of the reality principle— "drive thinking" is supplemented by conceptual thinking; at each developmental stage the corresponding memory schemata or organizations emerge. This idea clearly reflects the broader psychoanalytic view regarding what Freud once called "the two principles in mental functioning;" it is, in fact, a paraphrase of the doctrine of ontogenetic sequences such as underlie the relationships between the primary and the secondary process, the pleasure ego and the reality ego, affectivity and thought. Rapaport concludes, "Thus the drive organization of memories yielded to a conceptual organization . . . [and] this yielding occurred not in the form of replacement."[8] This normal, gradual development "yielding without replacing" of the two memory organizations, in the order suggested by Rapaport, results in their ultimate *coexistence.* Clinical considerations also support such a dual conception of the memory function. Is the inability of the adult brain-damaged person to retain five *neutral* words really comparable to the inability of an adult neurotic to recall (or "forget") five *significant* words said to him in his childhood by a significant person? Rapaport himself notes that "the impressive fact of retention . . . has indeed a certain degree of autonomy."[9] Therefore we may seriously consider whether a significant distinction should not be made between memory traces which pertain to *experiences* and those which are fixations of *conceptual data* (in whatever form) and whether such a distinction does not in fact exist in the psychopathology of the memory function. This discrimination, in simple terms, underlines the essential and contrasting qualities of what in the realm of mental input may be called, respectively, *formative* and *informative*.

The patient suffering from the memory disorder of organic dementia not only has great difficulty in retaining conceptual informative data for immediate recall, but he also shows a progressive loss of such memory traces which in the past had aided him in his adaptation. I refer to those aspects and components of the memory function which are at the disposal of the conflict-free ego—engrams representing information received in the past, tools for the handling of information offered or impinging upon the mind in the present. All this has nothing to do with character formation. (In fact, it is a well-known clinical observation that certain character traits which formerly were contained become disturbingly manifest and prominent in patients with coarse cortical brain disease.) If we may thus assume that the memory impairment of the brain-damaged patient affects (1) fixation and recall of conceptual rather than affective input, (2) data which are closer to learning than to experiencing, and (3) tasks which are beyond his capacity because of their impersonal complexity rather than their personal significance, we must conclude that the "selection" of memory organization affected in patients with coarse brain disease meets all the pathognomonic requirements of organicity. The psychopathology of the conflict-free ego and its component tools is subject neither to motivation nor to repression precisely because of the qualities of this part of the ego, which in a way is closer to the outer world than to the id. The same may be said of the memory traces which it monopolizes.

Id Relationships (Formative)

The other major category of memory traces is in many ways closer to the id. The memory organizations which in the early phases of our life consist largely of instinctual experiences are the precursor of all those subsequent fixations in our mnemonic apparatus which accompany the formation and vicissitudes of drive derivatives. They differ in principle from the memory traces which, as we saw, attend the adaptive processes of the conflict-free ego. They are affective rather than conceptual, even though in the course of time and with the development of the language function they are cast in semantic garb. But we know the techniques by which they can be made to appear in their original nakedness and significance; they can be "relived," not merely recalled. These memory traces are, therefore, always of a substantial and complex character. They are "formative" in the sense that they represent the permanent deposit of those aspects of character formation which are rooted in instinctual and thus affective soil and have been shaped by emotional, interpersonal, or social influences. They are subject to repression and to the miscarriages of repression in the form of psychoneurotic symptoms or parapraxes. A clinical illustration of formative memories would in fact be tantamount to the material which a patient under therapy produces, material derived from various depths of his psyche and recovered after successive removal of repressions. They combine what Kubie called the "I" and "non-I" components of the symbolic process,[10] the former representing the somatic or "visceral" experience, which is always primary, and the latter representing the corresponding reference, at times a mere appendage, that links them to the outer world. In neurophysiological terms they are both archipallial and neopallial. When patients refer to such memories in bland and well-structured sentences—that is, in coded semantic abstractions—we may well wonder how and why formality has replaced intimacy, and verbal memory, "gut memory." This transformation would not be possible if in man the secondary process did not interpose itself between the id and the outer world. Hartmann put it in these words: "The more precise division of labor between the ego and the id in adult man . . . *increases the alienation of the id from reality.* In animals these two institutions, ego and id, would be closer to a middle position in regard to reality."[11]

In summary then, the "dynamic" memory traces belong to the drive organizations and their derivatives; they tend to play a prominent role in personality development, normal and abnormal. In the case of the latter they are the experiential source of special transformations known as psychoneurotic symptoms (hysterical and obessive-compulsive) and thus pathogenic and nonadaptive; their psychopathology is not one of "not remembering" but one of not being able to "forget."

NEUROPHYSIOLOGICAL CONSIDERATIONS AND CORRELATIONS

A great deal of experimental work has been done, both with animals and with humans, by clinical psychologists investigating the effect upon the learning process and upon the closely related recording of memory traces, of any number of facilitating or inhibiting factors. The relevance of most of these studies to the practice of clinical psychiatry and psychoanalysis is marginal. On the other hand, any neurophysiological research which would suggest or establish significant correlations between the functional localization of mechanisms within the various "suborgans" of the brain, and corresponding manifestations in the broad area of "memory" and its disorders would be of utmost clinical importance. Such correlations would, of course, have a mutually corroborating effect.

In his paper "The Fixation of Experience," R. W. Gerard raises a number of formidable questions: "What experience is retained; under what conditions; where does the change occur; is it local or diffuse; what is the nature of the change, chemical, electrical, structural; and how does fixation occur, at the molecular and at the cellular levels?"[12] We have already mentioned the issue concerning the "fallacy of simple location." There is, of course, the actuality of memory engrams having a location, but not necessarily a locality. "It is highly doubtful . . . that each remembered item is located at a particular neuron or synapse."[13] But it is not only a question of innumerable "items" that make up the total mental input during a lifetime; there are also, as was already pointed out in some detail, so many different categories or prototypes of memory traces—which differ from each other in origin, content, function, and ultimate destiny—that a corresponding variety of implementing suborgans within the brain must be taken for granted. Furthermore, it is also a fact that almost any instance or fragment of memory could be and is likely to be represented in several equivalent modes—emotional, perceptual, verbal—flowing in time or static like a marker. There must be an equally extensive and versatile functional location. The rather wide distribution of mental input within the brain, even if such input is experimentally restricted to one isolated passage of entry, strongly supports the conclusion that both hands learn even if only one has been taught. Nevertheless, some broad but constant topographic aspects of memory function must be stated in order to present the balanced picture of this intricate faculty. Most learning, with its indispensable fixations of memory traces, involves the cortex; there is, in fact, "a general parallel between learning and memory capacity on the one hand and general cortical size on the other."[14] As a result of Penfield's experiments (see below), the cortex of the temporal lobe (or certain parts of it), has been found to be a site of recording and storing of structured and compound memories. The memory facets of the language function must be closely associated with the speech areas and the leading hemisphere; yet it may be well here to recall Hughlings Jackson's reluctance to localize speech within too narrow confines: "To locate the damage which destroys speech and to locate speech are two different things."[15] The role of the parietal lobe and its connections in the evolution and dissolution of the memory traces which comprise the body image, in all its experiential qualtities, should be noted. There is still another topographic fact to be mentioned—namely, that the capacity to form durable memory traces seems to depend on the intactness of certain parts of the so-called

"Papez circuit" such as the mammilary bodies, the fornix, and the amygdala; lesions in these areas are seen in Korsakoff's syndrome. Apart from topographic considerations there are also basic functional issues which ought to be considered. Thus Gerard raises this question: "When does a dynamic [reversible] memory become a structural one, much as the spoken word becomes fixed in writing?"[16] A general and tentative answer to this question may point out (1) that the need for permanency may derive from the great adaptive value of those memory traces which in the course of the learning process are destined to become and remain the tools of the conflict-free ego; (2) that others become "fixed" because of their affective significance; and (3) that still others remain operative ("structural") by being decisively implicated in the neurotic process; their unconscious determination is reflected in their "repetitiveness"—be it a psychoneurotic symptom, a perversion, or a neurotic character trait (see Chapter 12.)

Clinical Description

It may be assumed that neurophysiological corroboration of psychological observations will be more promising if the latter are of the simplest possible kind. In the area of memory the temporary fixation of impersonal data, which in man may be perceptual or conceptual, seem to fulfill such a requirement. Experimental studies along these lines have been made with animals and by employing methodical extirpation of relevant cortical areas. The results and inferences drawn have recently been summarized by Konorski. He states that "it is now almost generally accepted that recent memory is based on the activity of reverberating circuits"[17] within such cortical areas as are relevant to the particular nature of the memory trace investigated. In one group of experiments the "delayed response" method was used, in which the animal is restrained for a short time before being permitted to respond to a previously learned signal indicating the location of food. It was found that the animals "remembered" the location of the signal. The author concludes that delayed responses are apparently contingent upon an "orienting reaction" by the animal—one that involves movements and positions of its body, particularly its head and eyes—in response to the original stimulus. But "delayed responses are dramatically impaired or abolished by prefrontal lesions in monkeys and apes."[18] These lesions were, of course, set in the form of cortical (prefrontal) ablation. These prefrontal apes could not, after an enforced period of delay, go to where the food was located (as indicated to them by appropriate clues). It would appear that the prefrontal-induced reduction of function consists of the loss of the memory trace of the orienting reaction, which is essentially a question of motor intent. There seems to be a loss of the mastery of the future at a most concrete level of destination in *space*. This is not surprising if the functional relationship of the entire frontal brain— not only to motility but also to the *future*—is considered (see Chapter 8), although allowance must be made for the natural reduction of this particular function in primates as compared with man. At the human level this (prefrontal) mastery of the future embraces the much more "abstract" dimension of *time;* the future is anticipated, reflected upon, planned; and human "orienting reactions" are not postural, but ideational.

In other experiments the animal's ability to discriminate visual or auditory stimuli after appropriate conditioning was abolished by bilateral lesions within the association area close to the arrival platform of the respective perceptions. Therefore, these adjacent association areas were considered to be the site of the temporary memory traces.

In reporting on these studies, Konorski makes a comment which is of special interest to the clinical psychiatrist: "the respective central representations of the stimuli are excited for a much longer time than the duration of the stimuli themselves."[19] This observation brings to mind a speculative idea which Freud expressed (in "A Note upon the 'Mystic Writing Pad'") to the effect that the functions of perception and of forming memory traces "in mnemic systems" are mutually exclusive, and that these mnemic systems lie "behind" the perceptual systems ("behind" is, of course, meant in a temporal sense).[20] Decades later neurophysiologists have shown in experiments that memory traces require time to develop and that they can in fact be prevented from forming altogether if electric shocks follow the learning process within a very short time.

It is even more gratifying to *infer* psychological conclusions from physiological data than to *imply* physiological probabilities from psychological observations. It appears that this goal has been pursued with notable success through experimental stimulation, in man, of the "memory cortex" of portions of the temporal lobe by Penfield and by the psychological and psychoanalytical inferences drawn by Kubie in his discussion of Penfield's work.[21] Penfield discovered that in patients suffering from temporal lobe epilepsy certain kinds of memories could be evoked if various points along the convexity of the temporal lobe were stimulated with an electrode. While the electrode was applied, the patients, all of whom were fully conscious during these operations and experiments, perceived a very real and vivid reliving of "a specific situation which progresses and evolves just as in the original situation."[22] It was as if a coherent sequence of a past event or happening had been "played back" to the patient, who was, at times, both the participant and the observer. Penfield called these evoked memories "recollective hallucinations" and stressed some of their characteristic elements. They could not be evoked by any known means from any other part of the cerebral cortex, and not even from the "memory cortex" of the temporal lobe, unless the subject suffered from temporal lobe seizures. Obviously, the seizures were not the reason for the recording of these memory traces, although they became accessible upon electric stimulation apparently because of a facilitating effect of the underlying paroxysmal disorder. The evoked memories were a composite of the event and the patient's total interaction with it; they were "a reproduction of what the patient saw and heard and felt and understood."[23] Also, it was "a single recollection that the electrode evoked, not a mixture of memories or a generalization."[24] In this sense the phenomenon differed from the recollective condensations and temporal incongruities of the dream, as well as from the ordinary verbal generalization by which we refer to those past events which are preserved in semantic code. Finally, Penfield thought that "the thread of continuity in evoked recollection seems to be time."[25] Here are some samples of recollective halucinations, reported by Penfield: "There was a piano there and someone playing. I could hear the song, you know." When the point was stimulated again the patient said: "Someone speaking to another, and he mentioned a name, but I could not understand it . . . It was just like a dream." Another patient said: "I just heard one of my children speaking . . . It was Frank, and I could hear the neighborhood noises."[26] It must be realized how these recollective hallucinations differ from "elementary hallucinations" that can be evoked by an electrode from the primary sensory areas of vision, hearing, or touch (Orton's first platform of sensory reception). In this instance there will be only an experience of the inborn character of the corresponding sensory modality (a flash of light, a sound, a tingling sensation), but never a structured organization of objects and events, or of acquisitions by the sensory apparatus derived from scanning and surveying the outer world.

Penfield suggests a hypothesis concerning the neurophysiology of the recording, recalling, and reliving of memories. He suggests the existence of a centrally located integrating and activating system that is akin to or perhaps constitutes the uppermost extension of the reticular activating system of Magoun. This suborgan at the upper end of the brain stem has been given the name "centrencephalic system" (CES) by Penfield. It is in anatomical and functional contact with all sensory projection areas of the cerebral cortex as well as with the memory cortex of both temporal lobes. Thus perceptions and sequences of perceptions (such as happenings and experiences) are relayed from their cortical points of reception to the memory cortex of the temporal lobes via the CES, provided that they received sufficient attention by the individual to lend them the quality of *significance*. The recording of such experiences includes, as the term "experience" clearly implies, more than the mere photographic *imprint* of composite sensory stimuli; it also contains the emotional *impact* and the intellectual *import,* both of which are the contributions of the personality of the receiver and recorder. "Only in this CES can summary and fusion of all types of sensation be achieved."[27] In other words, the memories relayed in this manner contain both extero- and enteroceptive elements. They are, in the words of Kubie, both neopallial and archipallial. Voluntary recall of such memory patterns can never approach the degree of vividness, detail, and temporal progression of the event noted in the Penfield experiment. Further, after a certain time has elapsed, voluntary or associational recall occurs in the form of mere verbal symbolization of past events— shrunken in feeling, contracted in time, and devoid of detail: a mere mark of identification. It is, in fact, quite likely that a separate system of recording is required and used in order to accommodate these verbal or abstract transformations of what at the time of occurrence were the equivalents of recollective hallucinations. Like a barren tree in the winter these verbal remnants hold the promise of bloom and fragrance. It is at this point that the psychotherapist raises an issue. The question is this: If change and insight (in this order!) are contingent upon reliving the *totality* of traumatic and pathogenic experiences, upon total memory, extero- and enteroceptive, I and non-I, neopallial and archipallial, verbal and non-verbal, what is the psychotherapists's tool which would equal Penfield's electrode in efficiency of evocation and surpass it in accuracy of selection? Let us consider the second part of the question first, it is easier to answer. The psychoanalyst has learned to recognize hints and indirect indications of the general nature and content of pathogenic memories through various behavioral expressions by his patient. These "unintentional indiscretions" include symptomatic acts, slips, spontaneous denials or negations, dream elements, fragments of free association, fleeting emotional reactions, screen memories, and responses during the administration of projective psychological tests. While the identification of the area of conflict or pathogenic memory is prerequisite to the therapeutic process, it is not yet therapy; it is diagnostic. The more difficult task is to transform this information as well as verbal recollections supplied by the patient into total relived experiences. While this is not the place to dwell upon therapeutic methods and difficulties, it is nevertheless appropriate to illustrate the very real relevance of the neurophysiology of certain memory mechanisms for psychoanalytic procedure. We have all been aware that the patient's so-called *intellectualizations* must sooner or later be stopped; otherwise analysis will stop. Verbal memories are never therapeutic; nor are verbal constructions by the physician therapeutic interpretations. Words are not only "a way of avoiding action"[28] but also of avoiding memories. Yet words will have to be used throughout this process that aims at enabling the patient to recollect and relive significant and pathogenic memories. Upon the whole, the trend is to have words assigned, in an ever-increasing measure, to the task of expressing feelings rather than to report upon facts or thoughts. The first encouraging step in that direction taken by the analyst may well consist of setting the example for his patient by using—with utmost circumspection—the kind of language to which Macaulay referred when he spoke of "the ruder age of simple words and vivid impressions."[29] But this is no more than a beginning. Even if the patient is encouraged and follows our lead, he will derive only a very limited benefit from a purely verbal abreaction. The supreme therapeutic task that is required is yet to be undertaken: freeing the repressed pathogenic memories, establishing the link between screen memories and their dynamically significant origins and contexts, and correlating fantasies, transference reactions, and acting out with unconscious memories in the form of an experience equal to and as convincing as Penfield's (nonpathogenic) recollective hallucinations. It was Freud's contention that both *verbal memories* (e.g., dissociated and screen memories) as well as *repetitive acting out* of symptoms and "pathological traits of character"[30] (all of them replacing temporarily the reliving of the pathogenic memories) are the staging area from which the battle of the transference neurosis ("working through") is launched. And "the path that starts from the analyst's constructions ought to end in the patient's recollection."[31] If this battle is to be won, verbal memories and repetitiveness (and any other substitution) must give way to reliving of total memories with total intellectual and emotional involvement of the patient.

One may muse whether Dr. Penfield's electrode would be equally effective in evoking recollective hallucinations if it could be guided to touch upon pathogenic or repressed memory traces within the memory cortex, wherever this hypothetical structure may be.

A great deal of neurochemical and electrophysiological research and experimentation during the last decade has been carried out in an attempt to discover the material basis and processes in the formation of permanent and transitory memory traces. In considering the present state of our knowledge and speculation in this area, I have chosen to discuss only those items that might be relevant and applicable to the broader theme of clinical psychiatry.

It is now thought that RNA plays a definite role in the memory function, but it is not yet known what this role really is. Neurochemical studies revealed that the RNA content of cerebral tissue increases and decreases in accordance with clinically observable rise and decline of the memory function. Ewen Cameron[32] and others have reported that administration of RNA to patients with dementia was followed by noticeable improvement in these individuals' ability to retain information. It is, however, not established that "a unique set of RNA molecules functions as specific permanent memory traces."[32] Since it is known that RNA enhances protein synthesis in the neuron, the respective (and reciprocal?) role of the latter, as well as of RNA, in the formation of permanent memory traces would still have to be investigated. Another reciprocal relationship, which is also of great interest to the clinical psychiatrist, is that of the respective role of molecular (such as RNA) and synaptic processes. We have already stated that in the opinion of many neurophysiologists synaptic mechanisms—in the form of reverberating circuits—represent the material counterpart of what we clinicians call "immediate recall." It has also been thought that the recall of memories that had already become "fixed" required their being "transformed" into reverberating circuits. It is easy to see that even the most modern advances in this field have as yet not even come close to supplying the organic concomitants to such urgent clinical issues as repression of memories, psychodynamic effects of unconscious memories on overt behavior, screen memories, and symptom formation, to name just a few.

PSYCHOPATHOLOGY OF KORSAKOFF'S SYNDROME

A special form of memory-function psychopathology is found in Korsakoff's psychosis, which is also known by the term "amnesic syndrome." The condition is physically characterized by polyneuritis; the mental symptoms are complex, and despite detailed investigations are still not yet fully understood. There is, of course, general agreement that patients with Korsakoff's psychosis are usually severely disoriented; bland, indolent, but sometimes euphoric in their affective display; strikingly lacking in the capacity to remember current perceptions and events; and given to substituting confabulation for accurate immediate recall. Clinical observations strongly suggest that despite the obvious inability of the patient to form adequate fixation or notation of mental input, the memory traces are not entirely annihilated. It has, in fact, been suggested that "the organic mental syndrome is the result of a combination of attention and memory disorders,"[33] and that the latter is "one not of registration but rather of recollection."[34] The complexity of this clinical appraisal is matched by the diversity in the distribution of the lesions within the central nervous system. In many instances systematic investigations of the connections between the nature of the confabulations in response to verbal mental input clearly indicate the peculiar transformation of the latter into the former. Various mechanisms are apparently used in this process. In an experimental study,[35] S. Betlheim and Heinz Hartmann explored and defined the means of distortion used in the confabulations of patients with Korsakoff's psychosis. Subjects were asked to repeat, after as many readings as were necessary, simple but emotionally charged stories, none longer than a few sentences. Two of the stories described a rape, one an act of incest, and one was a very brief account of young men being killed by lightening. The following distorting mechanisms were isolated: substitution of associated ideas falling within the compass of the original ones; condensations and displacements; symbolization; and reduplication of the events and persons of the stories. We will quote some examples which illustrate these mechanisms, and comment on them.

This is one of the "rape stories" which was read to the patients: "A young man attacked a young girl, pulled up her skirt and pushed his stiff organ into her sheath." The following confabulatory contaminations were produced by patients:

"He pulled up her stiff skirt [condensation and displacement] . . . my sister-in-law got wounded . . . on the head . . .they shot at her . . . a soldier went after her . . . and wanted to knife me." The mechanisms employed in this confabulation are symbolization of rape (shooting, knifing), reduplication of persons (sister-in-law, patient herself), and some degree of dissolution of the temporal frame of reference.

"He pulled up her skirts and wanted to abuse her. But she struggled and he didn't succeed. My cousin also told me about it." This is another instance of reduplication paramnesia, which is characteristic of Korsakoff's psychosis. Rapaport comments that "a past experience of that affect or impulse is connected with partly or entirely different contexts."[36] His interpretation seems to stress the preservation of the "impulse organization of memory," which is part of the primary process, whereas the secondary process in the form of the "organization in memory frames-of-reference" undergoes dissolution, leading to reduplicative confabulations.

In these experiments it was further noted that there was no clear correlation between registration disturbance and confabulation; that the various parapraxes (symbolizations and introduction of associated ideas) tended to be perseverating; and that the most contradictory statements were stoutly defended. This last observation, so familiar to the clinician, may well result from the fact that "successive impressions extinguish each other"[37] in the amnesic syndrome. It was finally noted that the intensity of confabulation increased with the lowering of the state of consciousness.

As we have already suggested, the mere fact that the patients' confabulations consist in distorted reproductions of the verbal input indicates that the memory function, although grossly defective, has not been entirely destroyed. It has, in fact, been said that in this syndrome "the concept of registration-disturbance describes . . . only a phenomenological characteristic" and that the disorder "originates at a level which is a prerequisite of and preparatory to memory function."[38] Considering that the neuropathological changes in Korsakoff's psychosis are found in such areas as the mammilary bodies and in some of their functionally related structures, far away from the cortical mantle, it is not surprising that a more basic alteration of the entire personality has been hypothesized. The essential nature of this alteration is believed to be affective, thus explaining the peculiar indifference and lack of introspection and even euphoria found in these patients. "The most general background of the disorder seems to be the defect in the personal sphere, the passivity and paralysis of the vital layer,"[39] and "the entire structure of emotionality and drives is altered."[40] It almost appears as if the emotional and associational underpinning necessary for the integration, retention, and internal continuity of the mnemic microcosmos is missing or at any rate severely reduced. Thus it is suggested that "affective resonance exists only while the experience is present,"[41] and it has even been observed that patients who display Korsakoff's syndrome cannot properly hold on to such painful and direct events as being stuck with a pin during a handshake[41]—instead they express in the vaguest form some reservations when the hand is offered a second time, thus adverting to the "forgotten" painful experience in the most indirect and remote manner.

We have already spoken of the means or mechanisms which these patients resort to in their confabulations. It remains now to offer a suggestion as to why they confabulate at all. It is usually said that they do so in order to fill in the gaps of memory; this is certainly the end result of the confabulation, but the material which they use does not seem to come from the depth or continuity of their personality. Instead the fleeting moment of an event or of a question becomes "over-valent,"[42] expanding momentarily at the outermost fringes of the personality, and then recedes leaving only a tenuous and distorted trace.

REFERENCES

1. P. Schilder. "Studies Concerning the Psychology and Symptomatology of General Paresis. *In:* D. Rapaport. *Organization and Pathology of Thought: Selected Sources.* New York, Columbia Univer. Press, 1951, p. 540.

2. R. W. Gerard. "The Fixation of Experience." *In: Brain Mechanisms and Learning.* Oxford, Blackwell Scientific Publications, 1961, p. 21.

3. L. S. Kubie. "Some Implications for Psychoanalysis of Modern Concepts of the Organization of the Brain." *Psychoanalytic Quarterly,* vol. 22, 1953, footnote p. 27.

4. S. Freud. "Negation." *In: Collected Papers.* London, Hogarth, 1950, vol. 5, p. 182.

5. D. Rapaport. "Toward a Theory of Thinking." *Op. cit.,*[1] p. 711.

6. *Ibid.,* footnote #122a, p. 630.

7. D. Rapaport. *Emotions and Memory.* Baltimore, Williams & Wilkins, 1942.

8. D. Rapaport. "Toward a Theory." *Op. cit.,*[1] p. 697.

9. *Ibid.,* p. 710.

10. L. S. Kubie. "The Distortion of the Symbolic Process in Neurosis and Psychosis." *Journal of the American Psychoanalytic Association.,* vol. 1, 1953, pp. 59–86.

11. H. Hartmann. "Ego Psychology and the Problem of Adaptation." *In:* D. Rapaport. *Op. cit.,*[1] p. 383.

12. R. W. Gerard. *Op. cit.,* pp. 25–26.

13. *Ibid.,* p. 26.

14. *Ibid.,* p. 27.

15. J. Taylor (ed.). *Selected Writings of John Hughlings Jackson.* New York, Basic Books, vol. 2, p. 130.

16. R. W. Gerard. *Op. cit.,*[2] p. 24.

17. J. Konorski. "The Physiological Approach to the Problem of Recent Memory." *In:* R. W. Gerard (ed.). *Op. cit.,*[1] p. 120.

18. *Ibid.,* p. 117.

19. *Ibid.,* p. 128.

20. S. Freud. "A Note Upon the 'Mystic Writing-Pad.'" *In: Collected Papers. Op. cit.,*[4] pp. 175–180.

21. W. Penfield. "Memory Mechanisms." *Archives of Neurology and Psychiatry,* vol. 67, no. 2, 1952, p. 178.

22. *Ibid.,* p. 183.

23. *Ibid.,* p. 183.

24. *Ibid.,* p. 180.

25. *Ibid.,* p. 186.

26. *Ibid., passim.*

27. *Ibid.,* p. 187.

28. L. S. Kubie. *Op. cit.,*[3] p. 48.

29. Thomas Babington Macauley. *Critical and Historical Essays.* London, J. M. Dent and Sons Ltd. [1907, 1st printing], 1961, vol. 1, p. 153.

30. S. Freud. "Recollection, Repetition and Working Through." *In: Collected Papers. Op. cit.,* vol. 2, p. 371.

31. S. Freud. "Constructions in Analysis." *In: Collected Papers. Op. cit.,*[4] vol. 5, p. 368.

32. D. E. Cameron. "The Process of Remembering." *British Journal of Psychiatry,* vol. 109, #460, 1963, pp. 325–340; D. E. Cameron *et al.* "Effects of Ribo-

nucleic Acid on Memory Deficit in the Aged." *American Journal of Psychiatry,* vol. 120, 1963, pp. 320–325.

33. D. Rapaport. *Op. cit.,*[1] footnote #2, p. 650.

34. *Ibid.,* footnote #6, p. 651.

35. S. Betlheim and H. Hartmann. "On Parapraxes in the Korsakow Psychosis." *In:* D. Rapaport. *Op. cit.,* pp. 288–307.

36. D. Rapaport. *Op. cit.* Footnote #25, p. 295.

37. H. Buerger-Prinz and M. Kaila. "On the Structure of the Amnesic Syndrome." *In:* D. Rapaport. *Op. cit.,*[1] p. 682.

38. *Ibid.,* p. 652.

39. *Ibid.,* p. 684.

40. *Ibid.,* p. 652.

41. E. Claparede. "Recognition and 'Me-ness.'" *In:* D. Rapaport. *Op. cit.,*[1] p. 69.

42. H. Buerger-Prinz and M. Kaila. *Op. cit.,* p. 685.

7

The Role of the
Temporal Lobe

In a book on clinical psychiatry, there are good reasons for
including special chapters on the known and presumptive
functions of the temporal and frontal lobes. These huge suborgans of the
brain are traditionally and somewhat arbitrarily defined and demarcated
by the familiar but gross landmarks of the major fissures of the cerebral
hemispheres. It would be naïve to derive from this delineation, which
is superficial in every respect, the conclusion that these lobes are as
simple, as uniform, and as unequivocal in their functional contributions
as they appear to be in their anatomical distribution. The psychopathology that accompanies lesions or ablations in these areas is marked by
an immense and bewildering variety of clinical symptoms and behavioral
features—all well known, but many of them ill understood. Evolutionary
considerations (supported by animal experimentation) as well as such
insights into the depths of human psychic life that Freud, first and
foremost, offered compel us to look toward these regions of the brain
for a better understanding of many of those psychic processes which
make man the human animal he is.

It has been known for a long time that the posterior lobes of the
brain are closely related to sensory functions, while the anterior frontal
lobe is "motor." Many years ago Hughlings Jackson said: "I have long
held the hypothesis that the whole of the anterior lobe is (chiefly)
motor . . . [and] that the posterior part of the brain is (chiefly) sensory."[1] One may wonder whether Jackson was fully aware of the pro-
phetic implications of his proposition. If perception and motility are
mapped upon the continuum of temporal experience it will be seen
that the beginning of every perception is in the *past* and the consumma-
tion of every movement in the *future*. It does not really matter, in principle, whether the time interval in either of these contingencies is a

fraction of a second or a number of years. We look at stars which are light-years away; and, if "making a move" may be taken to be a tempered derivative of "making a motion," T. S. Eliot reminds us in his poem "The Hollow Men"

> Between the idea
> And the reality
> Between the motion
> And the act
> Falls the Shadow

The "shadow" in Eliot's poem is, of course, a metaphorical allusion to the theme of "The Hollow Men"; but in our context the "shadow" is *time*. Human consciousness is unique not only in what it can contain at the moment but also in what it can perpetuate from the past and anticipate about the future. In contrast to lower animals human consciousness is not telescoped into the immediate present, with perhaps a slight and slender hold on what has just passed and what will instantly follow. The gorilla and the chimpanzee, the anthropoid apes closest to man, have a rather rudimentary prefrontal lobe as compared with man's, and the remainder of the premotor frontal brain rapidly shrinks in size as we descend the phylogenetic scale. As far as the temporal lobe is concerned, comparative anatomy reveals a striking reduction in size of the true olfactory brain, which in the course of evolution has in ever greater measure been supplanted—almost replaced—by the hippocampal structures. At the same time man's temporal neocortex has reached the size, prominence, and highest-level evolution of an "association area." Thus the old and the new and, as will presently be seen, the individual's past and future meet at this crossroad and juncture that we call the temporal lobe.

OLFACTORY AND NONOLFACTORY PERCEPTION

The qualifying connotations in the above subhead are meant to represent the phylogenetic, anatomical, and functional divisions of the temporal lobe into its two major components: the neocortical and the archipallial. "Archipallial" includes all that is ancient in evolutionary terms, all that is derived from the original olfactory system—which in man has achieved a modified prominence as the so-called limbic system. Also included are all those structures which are apparently involved in the affective and autonomic functions. "Archipallial" is also what MacLean[5] so tellingly described as the "illiterate, visceral brain" and which he contrasted with the neocortical "word brain." These distinctions are also implied in certain metapsychological conceptions and formulations which we owe to Freud, although in his time he did not have the evidence to make significant physiological-anatomical correlations. Freud speaks of the contrasting features of the pleasure principle and the reality principle; of the pleasure ego and the reality ego; of the ego and the id; of the primary and the secondary processes. Olfaction, even in man, is in every sense much closer to all those archipallial and their corresponding metapsychological criteria and qualities of which I have spoken.

Neocortical *perception* turns toward, scans, recognizes, and rediscovers the objects of the outer world. The end result of these processes, which presumably occur in that order, coincides with what one may call the "understanding" of perceptions. We understand an object cognitively if we can answer the question "What is it?"—and we understand it apperceptively if we can answer the question "What is its significance?" In the previous chapter we reported and discussed the recollective hallucinations which Penfield obtained during electrical stimulation of the "memory cortex" of the temporal lobe in patients who suffered from temporal lobe epilepsy. We stressed that the content of these hallucinated memories is not only composite and coherent but also includes the feelings of the patient. By contrast, elementary hallucinations consist of nothing more than a vivid hallucinatory awareness of a representation of action of the sensory modality in which they occur. Elementary hallucinations are the result of an irritative process within the cortical arrival area of a sensory category; if it is visual, the patient will experience flashes of light; if the auditory cortex is involved he may hear sound of a certain quality. It seems that the inherent quality of the respective cortical sensory area is sufficient to produce such hallucinations and to determine their particular sensory quality. It therefore follows that temporal lobe hallucinations, unlike elementary ones, could not occur without the existence and availability of previously recorded perceptual experience.

Illusions, which are so characteristic for temporal lobe disease, are usually defined as pathologically altered perceptions. For a description and discussion of illusional perceptions the reader is referred to the chapter on the epilepsies. It may, however, be stated at this point that illusions differ from agnosias in that, in the case of illusions, the patient recognizes the identity of the object. Considering the almost limitless number of variables or details of all sorts which make up the appearance of a single object—for example, a dog—it is indeed surprising to realize that, although no two dogs are ever alike, any dog will be instantly recognized as such because of the ascendancy during the perceptual process of common and essential similarities of total patterns. This common denominator, it will be recalled, is known as a "universal." The sight or other representation of any dog leads ultimately to a three-letter word: *dog*, or at least to the idea of *dog*. It has been asked: How does the brain perceive universals? As far as neocortical or cognitive universals are concerned, including those in the area of hearing, thalamocortical scanning and clocking devices seem to offer plausible explanations.[2] These neocortical universals, operating perhaps on the Gestaltist principle that the whole determines the significance of the parts and is, in any case, more than their sum, are quite reliable, particularly since their ultimate representation is verbal. "Affective universals" (see below) are far less unequivocal; nor can they be represented by a single word. It may be of interest to note that in certain schizophrenics perceptual scanning of an object, or of a Rorschach ink blot, may result in an overdetermination of an irrelevant detail; such patients, in a reversal of Gestalt principle, fail to arrive at the appropriate universal, either by inversion of figure and ground or by permitting a part to determine the qualities of the whole. These reversals of Gestalt laws will be noted mainly in such patients' Rorschach performances because the ink blot is by its very nature more equivocal than an ordinary object would be.

Despite Penfield's startling discovery of the existence of composite memory traces within the temporal-lobe cortex of certain patients, it does not appear likely that the temporal lobe is the place where all of the individual's previous experiences are stored; it could certainly not be the only place if one considers the fact that past experience and its microcosmic repository, the "ego supplement" of Ostow, is represented in so many different forms and modalities. Citing Critchley, Ostow states: "Because the parietal lobe seems to be concerned with speech formulation, with calculation and with space and form comprehension, I am inclined to attribute to it the functions of the ego supplement, namely, the formation of images of objects, preconscious memory, thought, and the capacity to predict."[3]

Thus if we keep the tenuous correlation between (1) psychological functions and (2) their localization, in mind, we may—in connection with the theme of the temporal lobe—present a special form of perceptual abnormality: namely, depersonalization. This term includes a variety of abnormal experiences which, however, share a subjective feeling of estrangement or unreality with regard to objects, one's own body, and one's self. As paroxysmal phenomena they are part of the temporal-lobe epilepsy symptomatology and as such are usually equated with other forms of illusory perceptions found in this condition. But it must be admitted that depersonalization is characteristic neither of a certain localization nor of any single nosological disease process. In addition to temporal-lobe epilepsy—in which depersonalization is the reverse of the illusion of *déjà vu*—the phenomenon may occur in the neuroses, in schizophrenia, in depressive states, and in normal persons in states of fatigue. Generally speaking the specific manifestations of feelings of estrangement or unreality are as follows. The patient complains of a certain lack of feeling or emotional participation of the kind he knows he ought to experience and remembers having experienced in the past in the given situation. There is, in fact, not only such an awareness but usually an almost compulsive comparison of his present with his past emotional response. Self-observation is heightened in the sense that the difference between the "then" and the "now" is keenly and painfully noted. Sometimes the patient feels as if he were split into an observer and a doer; a feeling of automatism or lack of will may attend this state. However, except in the case of schizophrenic depersonalization, the condition is not attributed by the patient to outside influences; nor is it described in bizarre terms. It is not uncommon that patients in the early stage of schizophrenia complain of depersonalization both with respect to objects and their body or its parts. In that case they are likely to feel a sense of panic or at least puzzlement, and they readily seek and find causes to which they attribute these alterations in con- sciousness. In other words, they elaborate the depersonalization experi- ence into a delusion. The "as if" quality—which is so characteristic during temporal-lobe seizures or in states of fatigue in normal people—is then lacking.

If we consider the wide range of the phenomena of feelings of estrangement and unreality, both with regard to their duration and par- ticularly to their point of reference, we may draw certain conclusions as to the localization and nature of the underlying cerebral mechanisms. It is true that in every instance of depersonalization a "matching process" fails to take place, which deprives the patient of the normal experience of familiarity. The more circumscribed and isolated and indeed *simple* the point of reference is, the more likely it is that a localization is known or may be presumed. Thus in the area of body-image disorders caused by organic lesions, a patient will feel that his arm or leg does not belong to him, or he will at least have lost the feeling of bodily familiarity with respect to the involved extremity; then we know that the matching process is interfered with as a result of interrupted function in the contralateral thalamoparietal bundle. Even in the instances of paroxysmal unfamiliarity of perceptual experience in temporal-lobe dis- ease, we can hypothesize about a matching mechanism within that struc- ture—one that deals with relatively simple and objective perceptual experiences. But beyond this point—as, for instance, in the feeling of the schizophrenic that the world has changed and everything, himself included, is unreal and strange—the issue of localization becomes an impossible and therefore irrelevant undertaking.

AFFECTIVITY

There are compelling reasons for including the issue of affectivity in discussing the role of the temporal lobe in clinical psychiatry. The primeval quality of emotion in the interactions between the organism and its environment can not be denied and must never be ignored. From whatever direction the student of human or animal behavior may approach this phenomenon—from evolution, neuroanatomy, neurophysiology, clinical psychiatry, or psychoanalytic metapsychology—he will be somewhat discomforted by our still incomplete knowledge of this fundamental and immensely complex function. I may also mention "the obviously primitive, phenomenological and conspicuously prescientific descriptions and definitions of emotional behavior"[4] with which, as clinicians, we tend at times to conclude our observations in the area of affective psychopathology. This is perhaps the place to recall what Sir Charles Sherrington said in his Rede Lecture at Cambridge, in 1933: "I reflect with apprehension that a great subject can revenge itself shrewdly for being too hastily touched." Emotional manifestations, in contrast to cognitive or conative performances, are, of course, largely subjective, somewhat intangible, and consequently very difficult to describe, grade, and differentiate both as to intensity and finer nuances. It is indeed rare that a clinical psychiatrist, when appraising the emotional display or endowment of a patient, will feel impelled or even prepared to attempt to make a judgment with respect to, say, the state or level of maturity or refinement of the patient's affectivity. When one ponders this broad question it would seem that the refinement of emotional expression and experience ought to parallel the refinement of the conscious experience of the object or issue toward which affectivity is cathected. The concept of evolving levels of basic psychological functions is generally accepted. As to affectivity, MacLean quotes Papez as follows:

The central emotive process of cortical origin may . . . be conceived as being built up in the hippocampal formation and as being transferred to the mammillary body and thence through the anterior thalamic nuclei to the cortex of the gyrus cinguli. The cortex of the cingular gyrus may be looked on as the receptive region for the experiencing of emotion. . . . Radiation of the emotive process from the gyrus cinguli to other regions in the cerebral cortex would add emotional coloring to psychic processes.[5]

In a comprehensive review of experimental studies of emotional behavior in animals that had been subjected to various and deliberately placed lesions within the central nervous system, Brady[6] demonstrated the existence of a succession of "emotional sub-organs" that apparently mediate emotional responses of increasing complexity as one progresses from the lowest level of the reticular formations to the highest level of the neocortex. Such hierarchical integrative progression is, of course, entirely in accord with the principles of evolution of mental-apparatus functions, regardless of the particular nature of such functions. In the area of affectivity, Brady distinguishes four ascending levels of emotional integration and expression as outlined in the following paragraphs.

Midbrain Reticular Influences. Animal preparations reduced to this lowermost level react to nociceptive stimuli with emotional responses that have aptly been described as "pseudoaffective behavior." The responses are extremely brief and do not even outlast the duration of the stimulus. At the efferent end they seem only to go through the motions of an emotional reaction.

Diencephalic Participation. Animal preparations whose brains were severed above the level of the hypothalamus are capable of accelerated defense reactions for fight and flight; they also exhibit the phenomenon of sham rage. "But the functional limitations of such gross reaction patterns contrast sharply with the more delicately balanced and restrained discriminative emotional behavior of which the normal organism is seen to be capable."[7]

Limbic System. It is not within the scope of this presentation to describe the anatomical and presumptive physiological details of this large and intricate array of cerebral structures. These complex arrangements of gray and white matter, linking rather circuitously the archipallial portions of the temporal lobe with the cingular gyrus of the frontal lobe, are considered to be the mediators and modulators between perception and affectivity. The momentous significance of such a function was first and tentatively proposed by Papez in 1937,[8] and the corresponding structures have since been referred to as the "Papez circuit." Phylogenetically they are part of the ancient forebrain structures, comprising hippocampal gyrus, hippocampus, and the latter's efferent tract, the fornix, which leads into the mammilary bodies. From these bodies fibers reach anterior thalamic nuclei and ultimately the cingular gyrus of the frontal lobe. The amygdaloid nuclei are likewise parts of the limbic system. Papez thought that these circuits "constitute a harmonious mechanism which may elaborate the functions of central emotion, as well as participate in emotional expression."[9]

In order for the clinical psychiatrist to appreciate the far-reaching significance of this system, it is necessary to trace the origins of primordial "affectivity" to those species in which it is solely in the service of ecological adaptation and, indeed, survival. We must return to the times and organisms in which the sense of smell was, and is, supreme. In lower mammals and even more so in lower vertebrates the hippocampal area—which in man is only one, although a significant component of the limbic system—comprises the bulk of the telencephalon. What is, however, more significant, is that its function is entirely olfactory; it is truly a rhinencephalon. Such animals test their environment by means of olfactory information, which in turn guides their reactions of pursuit or avoidance of such basics as food, sexual partners, and enemies. Thus olfaction is a prime phylogenetic modality of reality testing; and nature has, at that juncture, entrusted the preservation of the life of the individual and the species to the sense of smell. Ostow, speaking of man, says that "it has long been observed that almost all odors are immediately classified as pleasant or unpleasant."[10] We may thus infer that in the "rhinencephalic creatures" all odors are immediately classified as either life-preserving or life-threatening. It is a reasonable assumption that the olfactory mechanism is the prototype for all later affective evaluations and discriminations. In the course of evolution, as soon as other sensory modalities emerge, particularly the distance receptors of vision and hearing, these elements begin to "exert a greater influence in directing the movements of the animal"[11] and, it may be added, its motivations. In man, ancient, primordial, and archipallial olfaction—having been relegated to a subordinate "visceral" role—has been superseded and almost replaced by the neopallial and nonolfactory array of perceptual capabilities. Nevertheless, this perceptual apparatus continues to maintain most intimate contact with the emotional centers of the limbic system, particularly the hippocampus, and to receive from them informative guidance. The hippocampus in man has largely ceased to be an olfactory center, but it now receives impulses from all sensory cortical areas through the intermediary function of the hippocampal gyrus. The linkage between perception and affectivity remains unbroken; indeed, it increases in complexity, compass, and continuity: "But the hippocampus never loses its close connection with the paleocortex and ultimately its afferent [affective] supply from the paleocortex is far larger than its direct olfactory supply. . . ."[12] Erect man's nose, it is true, is no longer sniffing and searching the ground in order to find a safe way through life. But man is now also in danger of being misled by wrong or obsolete road signs on his journey. We will return to this issue later in this chapter.

Among the many experimental animal studies on the subject of affectivity and its role in behavior, the classical observations by Klüver and Bucy[13] are perhaps of special relevance to clinical psychiatry. The authors removed both temporal lobes of a large series of rhesus monkeys; both the neopallial and the archipallial components of the temporal lobes were extirpated. The resulting behavioral abnormalities of these "bitemporal monkeys" are frequently referred to as the "Klüver-Bucy syndrome."

One of the most outstanding behavioral changes in these animals was their apparently irresistible impulse to react to all visual stimuli and to contact every object in sight. This phenomenon is known as hypermetamorphosis. If only the temporal neocortex was removed, the monkeys did *not* show any evidence of hypermetamorphosis. This fact is significant; the inability of the animals to recognize the *meaning* of objects through vision must have "deeper" reasons. Any conceivable object—whatever its physical attributes, animate or inanimate, edible or inedible, familiar or unfamiliar, still or moving—is rapidly and indiscriminately contacted; "the fact of an object being an object . . . is in itself sufficient for eliciting this impulse."[14] This frantic and uncritical contacting and subsequent smelling or mouthing of objects within sight of the animals has been referred to by the term "psychic blindness." However, careful analysis of the behavior of the bitemporal animals does not suggest that we are dealing with a purely cognitive defect within the visual sphere, or not even with a visual agnosia. Klüver and Bucy concluded that the "tests gave no evidence that the ability to 'generalize' in responding to visual stimuli was impaired."[15] While the animals were able to recognize that a stick was "longer than" or "nearer than," they were unable to use it as a tool—that is, "to recognize the 'tool' character of a stick."[16] This is indeed a significant fact, perhaps an indicator of an affective defect. There is, of course, a difference between the properties and the utility of an object. The utility of the object (its tool character) and thus its potential promise of gratification of an instinctual need can no longer be determined merely by visual scrutiny, as would normally be the case in most situations. These animals can make such determinations only by either smelling the object or by establishing its value or danger by introducing it into their mouth; "certain properties of the objects, their being 'dangerous,' 'inedible' or 'indifferent' have suddenly become ineffective in determining visually guided reactions."[17] The animals may contact a nail and put it into their mouth for as often as a hundred times within a single hour, and "it is evident that the animal has no capacity for expressing aversion [or indifference] to any stimulus unless it has had oral or olfactory contact with it."[18]

The outstanding feature of the changes in affective behavior seems to be loss of the so-called negative affects, of "the motor and vocal reactions generally associated with anger and fear. . . ."[19] Deprived of their temporal lobes, the monkeys have been rendered tame and docile, and they no longer seem to be afraid. However, they are fearless without being courageous. It is easy to see that the loss of the capacity to mobilize negative affects such as fear, aversion, and anger may seriously disable the animal to deal with environmental dangers effectively and in good time, either by fight or flight. It has been suggested by Ostow that "the psychic function of the temporal lobe is the formation of apperceptive judgments, especially negative ones."[20] There is considerable clinical evidence to support such a view, and we will present the clinical material later in this chapter. We believe that it would not be an unreasonable extrapolation from these animal experiments to draw attention to the possible relationship, at the human level, between the temporal lobe and various mental mechanisms, including repression, which support and sustain adaptation and instinctual containment in the form of "negative apperceptive judgments," not necessarily at the conscious level. In this connection the striking abnormalities in the sexual behavior of the bitemporal monkeys are of interest. They not only appeared to be "oversexed" but they also engaged in sexual practices—either alone or with a partner of either sex—of such a deviant character as to resemble what at the human level would be designated as polymorphously perverse.

Neocortical Functions.   At this level affectivity reaches its highest measure of integration. The corresponding structural representation are the thalamoprefrontal circuits. Much of the frontal-lobe syndrome must be attributed to interruption of these pathways, a matter that will be discussed in Chapter 8.

APPERCEPTION

The processes by which the mental apparatus makes a determination as to the *significance* of a perception constitute a distinct function known as apperception. The faculty of apperception thus leads to an introspective continuation and elaboration of the original perceptual process. It enables us to understand a perception or experience in terms of a previous perception or experience. On the other hand it may disable us by limiting our understanding if it is based only on such terms. Without apperception the continuity of psychic life would not be possible. There is sufficient experimental and clinical evidence to support the assertion that temporal-lobe structures play an indispensable role in the various apperceptive judgments.

There are two principal types of apperceptive judgments: *cognitive* and *affective*. In his paper "Negation" Freud stated with regard to cognitive judgments:

The other sort of decision made by the function of judgment . . . is a concern of the final reality-ego, . . . that is, of the faculty that tests the reality of things. It is now no longer a question of whether something perceived (a thing) shall be taken into the ego or not, but of whether something which is present in the ego as an image can also be re-discovered in perception . . . .[21]

As to affective apperceptive judgments he said:

Originally, the property to be decided about might be either "good" or "bad," "useful" or "harmful." Expressed in the language of the oldest, that is, of the oral, instinctual impulses, the alternative runs thus: "I should like to eat that, or I should like to spit it out."[21]

Cognitive Apperception. In this area of the apperceptive process the determination of the significance of a perception lies in the recognition of the identity of the object through what Freud called its rediscovery. Cognitive apperception takes place as our distance receptors scan the outer world of sounds and objects. Once cognitive universals have been perceived and the question "What is it?" has been answered, the apperceptive process, with the aid of the temporal lobe, will address itself to the task of matching the present percept with the cognitive memory traces of the ego-supplement. It seems that the temporal lobe is necessary to answer the question "What is it *like?*" Cognitive universals, being much closer to the secondary process than "affective universals," are much more reliable tools of adaptation. Furthermore, cognitive universals are ultimately verbal; thus, to use MacLean's example, the neocortex will "conceive of the color red in terms of a three-letter word or as a specific wave length of light"[22] and of nothing else. Cognitive apperception will not condense, for affective or parasymbolic reasons, "such diverse things as blood, fainting, fighting, flowers, etc . . . ."[22] into the color red. *Affective* apperception, however, will do just that.

Affective Apperception. The structures within the temporal lobe that presumably participate in affective apperception are part of the limbic system and include especially the hippocampus and hippocampal gyrus. The archipallial character of these structures reflects to some degree their functional contribution to the making of affective judgments and of equally primal, and even primordial, affective symbolizations. The latter may perhaps be designated as "affective universals." This latter term is proposed to designate the highly individualistic common affective denominator and unifier that connects, equates, and thus recategorizes diverse and objectively unrelated parts of our psychic experience. Thus the "affective universal" embodying the sadness, horror, or loneliness of "death" may assemble under its affective pall such diverse items as snow, silence, the color black, falling autumn leaves, or a musical theme.

Because the hippocampus has access to all neocortical perceptions, which are carried to it via the hippocampal gyrus, and as it is also in close functional contact with the emotional and autonomic centers of the hypothalamus, it is generally accepted that this is the place where perception and affect meet. It is the emotional participation in perception which gives the latter the qualities and significance of an *experience*. "It is possible . . . that the hippocampus is the site of the comparison of stimuli with acquired memories, and therefore the structure in which, or from which, affects are elaborated."[23] It is the purpose of affective apperception to recognize, through this comparison, whether a given and present situation is *likely* to result in psychic pleasure or pain. "According to psychoanalytic theory, apperception proceeds by the superimposition of the perception of the external data upon some idea or memory which has independently no access to consciousness. This unconscious idea contributes an affect to the apperceptive experience."[24] We used the word "likely" with respect to the goal of affective apperceptive judgments. This is a significant characterization of this function. While it is true that "when the match is especially good, a feeling of recognition appears . . . ,"[25] we must nevertheless keep in mind that after a situation has been affectively recognized, the psychic apparatus would still have to "decide" whether to pursue or avoid involvement— that is, "whether to eat it or to spit it out." It seems that affective apperception takes place with one foot in the past and with an eye toward the future. Ostow has made the observation that "Phylogenetic and experimental evidence suggests that somatic pleasure and pain do not require the hippocampus . . . . In other words, the temporal lobe mechanism is needed not to answer the question 'How do I like this experience?' but 'How would I like such an experience?' "[26] Since we know that the temporal lobe elaborates especially negative apperceptive judgments, it is easy to see that lobe's probable role in the initiation of avoidance reactions. MacLean summed it up by using a most felicitous simile when he said that "the hippocampus suggests a keyboard on which the various elements of the sensorium can play."[27] Nor did he overlook the possible mistakes that may occur on, and the dissonances that are built into, this ancient instrument.

The term "affective universals" was suggested both as an analogy and as a contrast to the more familiar idea of cognitive universals. MacLean agrees that "it has been implicitly assumed that the hippocampal formation provides the kind of analyzer that can derive universals from the particulars of experience and relate them symbolically in the experience of emotion."[28] He adduces neurophysiological data which are rather convincing. The question that must be raised here is this: Suppose it is true that in the course of individual maturation affective and symbolic equivalences are subject and responsive to the corrective influence of experience and the secondary process. Does it then follow that failure of such corrections to take place, will, in the form of symptoms, reflect the essentially primitive and unreliable nature of "affective or symbolic universals?" A simple clinical illustration may be used to help us clarify the point. Let us assume that a certain situation has been frightening to a child. Not only will the particular event remain a frightening memory but any innocuous events coinciding with it may become involved if at that point an affective identity is established. If this connection is subsequently permitted to continue uncorrected, the basis for the development of a phobia is laid. MacLean puts it this way:

If the visceral brain [hippocampal structures] were the kind of brain that could tie up symbolically a number of unrelated phenomena, and at the same time lack the analyzing ability of the word brain [neocortex] to make a nice discrimination of their differences, it is possible to conceive how it might become foolishly involved in a variety of ridiculous correlations leading to phobias, obsessive-compulsive behavior, etc.[29]

We will return to these issues later when we present clinical illustrations. But here I should like to make one more observation on the psychology of apperceptive judgments. When I first read *The Old Man and the Sea* I was struck by the emotional impact of the sentence "It was an hour before the first shark hit him." It then occurred to me that only the artist, with the aid of the aesthetic illusion, can achieve such an awesome anticipatory emotion in his listener by informing him of the certainty of a dreaded event, while its victim has not yet had even the slightest clue upon which to base an apperceptive judgment.

CLINICAL ILLUSTRATIONS

The complexities of the functions of the various structures within the temporal lobe are reflected in the diverse and baffling features which attend disease and dysfunction of this part of the brain. This fact is underlined by the variety and disparity of the clinical syndromes involved. They include temporal-lobe epilepsy, which regardless of the nature of the epileptogenic lesion produces *irritation* of and discharge within temporal-lobe structures; the Klüver-Bucy syndrome, a result of surgical *elimination* of the temporal lobes; irregular *destruction* of the temporal lobe, as will result from brain tumor; schizophreniform psychoses which have been observed in the wake of long-standing temporal-lobe epilepsy; and, finally (and surprisingly), cases of fetishism, a condition rooted in psychodynamic psychopathology.

The nature and interpretation of the symptomatology of the temporal-lobe epilepsy will be presented in the chapter on "the epilepsies." At this point we wish also to direct attention to studies which have revealed a correlation between behavioral abnormalities in both epileptic and nonepileptic patients, and temporal-lobe electroencephalographic deviations in the form of the so-called "temporal spikes."[30]

In 1955 Terzian and Ore reported what must be considered a rare case of the Klüver and Bucy syndrome in man.[31] The patient had undergone surgical removal of both temporal lobes, including most of the uncus and hippocampus. The resulting abnormalities in his behavior are of the greatest interest, not only because they confirmed the essence of this syndrome (which was first described in the bitemporal monkey), but also because of the modifications of the features of the syndrome in man. We will follow closely Terzian's classification of the postoperative findings and comment on the significance of their modifications.

Psychic Blindness. The first postoperative behavioral abnormality was that the patient did not "recognize anyone, including his closest relatives." He treated his mother exactly the way he did the nurse, calling her "Madam." It is natural to associate this abnormality with the "psychic blindness" noted in the bitemporal monkeys. What might be the nature of this cognitive failure, and is it in fact "cognitive?" In a way this kind of "disorientation" is the reverse of what one sees in a delirious patient. The latter will mistake the nurse for his mother, or for his wife; the substitution of the more familiar and therefore more concrete person for the less familiar one (the nurse) represents the positive symptom of the uniform dissolution in delirium. It would also appear that the quality of familiarity includes affective components. By contrast, the bitemporal patient perceives mother and nurse alike; neither familiarity nor affectivity are of any help to him. It is, in fact, stated that Terzian's patient had been unusually affectionate toward his mother and that after the operation he manifested no particular affection for her. He first addressed her as "Madam" and somewhat later as "Mother," but without any warmth. Terzian and Ore report that the patient "no longer recognized persons in their emotive value." Might not this failure to recognize people be the result of an affective deficit, an emotional estrangement rather than the manifestation of a purely cognitive failure? The patient was no longer able visually to make an affective apperceptive judgment. "Mother" had been reduced from an experience to a designation.

Hypermetamorphosis. About two weeks after the operation the patient showed hypermetamorphosis just as the bitemporal monkeys had— except that his compulsive and indiscriminate urge to make contact included humans as well as objects. "The patient would stop anyone he met . . . . He picked up objects, limiting his interest to a superficial inspection of them, passing from one to another, picking up the same object again and again . . . ." One may ask whether such behavior could be the result of the patient's postoperative inability to make either negative affective apperceptive judgments, or at least judgments of emotional indifference; if so, an assumed innate conative drive to contact objects perceived by the distance receptor of vision could have been "set free" by the amputation. One is reminded that children, perhaps before they have learned to develop the necessary mechanisms for negative apperceptive judgments, also tend to contact all objects in sight. In contrast to the bitemporal monkeys, the patient did not show any evidence of "oral tendencies" such as smelling and mouthing; he did, however, reveal bulemia, which the authors ascribe to his now simple vegetative state.

Sexual Deviance. Abnormalities in the sexual area became obvious 15 days after the operation. He became boisterous about his sexual potency, exhibited himself before the doctors, masturbating and expressing verbal invitations to them along homosexual lines. However, no (homosexual) aggressiveness was noted.

Memory Impairment. The patient showed marked impairment of memory, and it is said that "he did not remember anything of his past . . . the patient felt completely isolated, without a past to remember and consequently without any future whatever." The authors state that it was not possible "to analyze his memory functions," and it may be assumed that they referred to the question of immediate recall. It seems that the patient's memory disorder consisted in an amputation of his past, of his "ego-supplement," of the repository of affective as well as cognitive records of past experience; neocortical *and* archipallial temporal-lobe structures had been removed bilaterally, and it appears certain that *both* partake in the formation of those memory traces that

Penfield elicited electrically and called recollective hallucinations. The effect of bitemporal amputation on the continuity of psychic experience is rather impressive.

Disordered Affects. Profound alterations were noted in the area of affective display. The patient appeared to have become totally indifferent to his surroundings; he displayed neither affection nor resentment toward persons whom he had previously either loved or hated. Nor did he give any indication of experiencing emotions in his contacts with personnel in the hospital. His face was vacant and there was noticeable absence of gesturing. His voice had become monotonous. The avoidance reactions of fear and anger had disappeared, just as they had in the bitemporal monkeys.

Other Findings

In 1963 Slater and his co-workers reported on the relationship between temporal-lobe epilepsy and schizophrenialike psychoses.[32] Their work is a contribution to the broader issue of the occurrence of schizophreniform psychoses in the presence and course of organic brain disease such as general paresis. We may also recall that schizophrenialike psychoses have been observed in alcoholic hallucinosis, various chronic intoxications, and in epilepsies other than the temporal-lobe variety. Slater et al. carefully studied and followed 69 patients, and their observations and conclusions may be summarized as follows. Although both temporal-lobe epilepsy and schizophrenia are rather common diseases, it was believed that their coexistence was not randomly determined. The patients did now show evidence of a schizoid premorbid personality, and the possibility that the epilepsy "released" a "latent" schizophrenia was dismissed. It was further noted that the duration of the epilepsy and not the frequency of the seizures correlated with the appearance of the schizophreniform symptomatology; the mean age of onset of the latter was about 30 years, and 14 years after the start of the epilepsy. The schizophrenic symptomatology consisted of delusions and hallucinations of a kind considered pathognomonic for schizophrenia; evidence of a formal thought disorder and auditorization of thought; affective disturbances of various types, including blunting of affect, although this feature was not so pronounced as one would expect; and religious and ecstatic ideas and feelings—a feature which is perhaps as much a part of the epileptic as of the schizophrenic personality.

In 1954, Mitchell et al.[33] reported a case of epilepsy associated with fetishism; the patient was relieved of both of these conditions by temporal lobectomy. Since then several papers—notably the one by

Epstein[34]—have been published with the view of stressing, at least phenomenologically, the relationship between temporal-lobe dysfunction and certain psychiatric features noted in a large and well-documented series of patients suffering from fetishism. This most unusual sexual perversion—like all perversions and their "negative" counterparts, the neuroses—lies clearly within the domain of psychoanalytic theory and treatment, but perhaps not exclusively. There is, so it seems, an opportunity to hypothesize about the possibility of a correlation between known and assumed temporal-lobe functions and psychoanalytic concepts and, indeed, doctrine.

Before returning to the subject of fetishism and temporal-lobe function and dysfunction, some general observations may serve to prepare the ground.

At birth and for some time thereafter all feelings and perceptions, such as they are, arise from and concern themselves with the body. Existence at that period of life is purely instinctual and "visceral." Gradually the child learns to distinguish self from nonself. Ego boundaries emerge and are recognized and respected. A similar progression takes place in the area of affectivity and drives. To the originally enteroceptive visceral feelings there are added feelings about objects which are perceived by the distance receptors. Apperceptive judgments are made as to whether such objects may be *desirable* or not (even *suitable* or not) for instinctual gratification from whatever visceral point of view that may be appropriate. If one adheres to the theory that all pleasurable affective cathexes are derivatives, equivalents, sublimations, displacements, aim-inhibited expressions, and so on, of instinctual, libidinal, and "visceral" appetites, then the question about the possible existence of nonlibidinal affects, emotions, and motivations would never arise. But let us raise this question. One loves to look at an object because it is beautiful. If the object is a beautiful woman (or even a picture of one) and the viewer a man, no particular difficulty or dispute in psychological theory is likely to arise. But suppose the object is a flower or the starlit sky. Is aesthetic visual pleasure to be equated with "sublimated" voyeurism? On the subject of sublimation, Fenichel, after having disposed of the less controversial instances, says: "It is even possible that an activity opposite in direction to the original instinct may really have replaced the original instinct."[35] And Freud, in one of his rare comments on the psychology of beauty, says in a footnote, "I have no doubt that the concept of 'beauty' is rooted in the soil of sexual stimulation and signified originally that which is sexually exciting. The more remarkable, therefore, is the fact that the genitals, the sight of which provokes the greatest sexual excitement, can really never be considered 'beautiful.'"[36] It is true that Freud made this statement in the context of the beauty of the human body, and it is significant that it did not occur to him to enlarge at this point upon the nature of the aesthetic experience in general. Nobody will deny that in many instances of seemingly nonlibidinous or nonaggressive emotions or motives very intricate, subterranean, and disguised pathways will lead us to a libidinous or aggressive source from which they came. But must all interest or curiosity in, or enjoyment of, objects in the outer world first undergo a process of "desexualization" before it can be regarded as merely contemplative or aesthetic?

A similar question may be asked about the assumed and essential identity, in principle, of incorporation and identification. Incorporation, also called "primary identification," refers to what Freud called "oral mastery of the object;" in the early phases of infancy this means quite literally to take the object into the mouth and devour it. Secondary identification (or identification proper) "is the consequence of incorporating the object within the psyche of oneself. . . . It is as if the instinctual impulses were asked to take a substitute . . . for the real object."[37] Implicit in all these considerations is the question whether a clearly nonlibidinous (nonvisceral) emotion or motivation in regard to an object is merely a disguised or attenuated derivative of its essentially libidinous (visceral) source, or whether it is entirely different and separate from a libidinous (visceral) source. It is the question whether, in certain forms of psychopathology, we should speak of dynamic fluctuations within one system of instinctual organization, or of a *trespassing* from one psychic system into another. I must admit that I feel quite comfortable with an idea expressed by MacLean in the following words:

It is to be noted that many of the seemingly paradoxical and ridiculous implications of the term "oral" result from a situation, most clearly manifest in children or primitive peoples, where there is a failure or inability to discriminate between internal and external perceptions that make up the affective qualities of experience. Visceral feelings are blended or fused with what the individual sees, hears, or otherwise senses, in such a way that the outside world is often experienced and dealt with as though it were incorporated.[38]

As an illustration of this hypothesis MacLean quotes from H. Werner that a child looking at a leaf may say, "It tastes green."[39] In such an instance—in which a primitive, visceral, and enteroceptive (oral-incorporative) drive, almost appetite or "taste," finds a totally unsuitable, exteroceptive neocortical perception (green) an appropriate object for its satisfaction—one may perhaps see the prototype for the kind of "trespassing" of which I have just spoken.

All this is, of course, even more dramatically suggested by the phenomenon of fetishism. Although the fetish may be any conceivable object, ranging from a piece of velvet to the exhaust pipe of a car, the object is almost invariably inanimate. There exists a significant incongruity between the affective sexual (visceral) intensity which it provokes and the grotesquely nonsexual character of its appearance. Freud stated categorically that every fetish represents a penis, specifically the penis which the boy found missing when he discovered his mother's genitals, so that intense castration anxiety was aroused in him.[40] But even Freud had to admit: "One would expect that the organs or objects selected as substitutes for the penis . . . would be such as act as symbols for the penis in other respects. This . . . is certainly not the determining factor. It seems rather that when the fetish comes to life . . . some process has been suddenly interrupted. . . ."[41] Let us remember that the only reason why the issue of fetishism is being discussed in this context is the fact that in some—perhaps in many—instances of this perversion, certain temporal-lobe symptoms were noted. Epstein[42] refers to a large group of episodic behavior patterns in a rather extensive number of reported cases of fetishism; these patterns are quite characteristic of temporal-lobe epilepsy: paroxysmal visual hallucinations resembling "dreamy states," visual illusions, olfactory hallucinations (such as are experienced in uncinate fits), episodes of "forced thinking," and bursts of emotions unrelated to any present situation or mental content, as well as automatisms and short-lasting psychotic states. Of particular interest is the history of the patient reported by Mitchell *et al.* in 1954.[33] It appears that since his early childhood this patient was fascinated by the sight and possession of shiny safety pins, of which he had quite a collection. He recalled having once seen a safety pin on his mother's underwear. These pins, even at the early age of around 4 years, gave him what he later described as a "thought satisfaction . . . better than sexual intercourse . . . the greatest experience of his life."[33] After several years of marriage (and one child) he became impotent; his reaction to this calamity was that the safety pin had replaced his need for a sexual outlet. There was clinical and electroencephalographic evidence that the sight as well as the thought of safety pins could provoke temporal-lobe-type seizures, and focal evidence was found in the EEG over the left frontotemporal region. It was assumed that the safety pins, a sexually charged object for him and thus his fetish, constituted the epileptogenic stimulus. A left partial temporal lobectomy, including excision of parts of the uncus and the hippocampus, was performed. Following this procedure both the seizures and the fetish disappeared completely. In this case the relationship between fetishism and temporal-lobe dysfunction has been proved in both directions, so to speak; the fetish could bring on temporal-lobe seizures, and removal of the involved temporal lobe abolished the psychopathology of the fetish.

Some Conclusions

What might be the nature of this relationship? One can only speculate in such an attempt to reconcile psychoanalytic and neurophysiological data, hoping that either point of view in its own way illuminates identical processes. A truly visceral affect and activity (namely, orgasm) occurs here in response to a truly nonvisceral and nonsexual object. It looks as if we were dealing with a conditioned reflex. Who or what "conditioned" the patient? Psychoanalytic investigations have shown that the ultimate purpose of the fetish is to remain "a token of triumph over the threat of castration and a safeguard against it."[43] But since "probably no male human is spared the terrifying shock of threatened castration at the sight of the female genitals,"[44] one may reasonably ask the question why (and how) only a handful of fetishists safeguard against this threat in this particular manner; one may also wonder whether a psychopathology as incapacitating and monstrous as fetishism could in any sense be regarded as a "triumph" over a universal human psychological hazard, even if only to the extent of a "token triumph." The real triumph over the "castration threat" is the resolution of the Oedipal conflict. Nevertheless, for the fetishist the fetish does apparently accomplish that aim. All authors agree that the fetish is to its beholder an object which he also admires, even worships, in addition to finding it sexually arousing. We can note quasiaesthetic value judgments in the instance of Mitchell's patient. I myself have studied a patient who, while not a fetishist, maintained well into adulthood an excessively overdetermined sexual preference and "admiration" of women's buttocks—and, I might add, paraphrasing Freud's choice of words, of only *special* buttocks. He had a decided bias against heavy women; they were to him not only sexually unattractive but "in a strange way" (affective-symbolic "universal") "stupid," "dirty,"—unaesthetic. Women with slender buttocks were, of course, endowed by him with the opposite qualities. He would jokingly and "ignorantly" say: "What an intelligent rear end." He remembered that as a child of about 4 or 5 years he would sleep at times in his parents' bed in a position which they called "tooshy-sleeping" and which consisted actually in a back-to-back position with the buttocks being the only point of contact. The patient does not remember ever having touched buttocks with his mother, but only with his father. A few years later—and, in fact, for a considerable time during his teens—he would "rate" his classmates' intelligence or social standing in such terms as "good tooshy" or "bad tooshy," and it did not in the least matter whether they were boys or girls; in fact they were mostly boys. Those who were "bad tooshy" he would in fantasy subject to severe physical punishment. He never confided these facts or the words he used to anybody prior to his analysis. It may be added that his mother was of unusual intelligence and that he had always adored her, "although from a distance."

It has long been known to poets and psychiatrists alike that lovers cherish an object which belongs to the beloved. Such objects are not fetishes; they are substitutions and do not by themselves arouse sexual feelings. Sometimes they are used as charms. The fame of a great man is reflected in the value society attaches to any object he used, or an insignificant letter he wrote; his greatness is also reflected in the price which such objects will command. In these *pars pro toto* transactions the connections are transparent, and the objects in question do not incite the viscera.

From our present and admittedly incomplete knowledge of the functions of the temporal lobe we may now attempt to interpret some of the phenomena of fetishism in terms of these functions. There are two reasons for making such an attempt. Clinical experience clearly points to the likelihood of such a correlation; and further research in this area may lead to the discovery of neurophysiological mechanisms which correspond to our present psychoanalytical formulations. Thus I may repeat in part MacLean's statement which was quoted previously, and complete it as it might be completed in this context. "Visceral feelings are blended or fused with what the individual sees, hears, or otherwise senses in such a way that the outside world is . . . experienced and dealt with as though" it were, by its nature, equipped to satisfy a visceral need. The existence of the fetish seems to indicate that in this form of psychopathology a strong, positive affective apperceptive judgment coexists with a normal cognitive apperceptive judgment without a sense of contradiction. From this point of view fetishism is the reverse of a phobia. Finally, the infantile fusion, or trespassing during the formation of the fetish (the original affective-symbolic equivalence or "universal") had never been corrected. The archipallial functions within the temporal lobe, for some reason, prevailed over the neocortical apperceptive process in a major psychological realm. Only in such a way will "the leaf taste green."

REFERENCES

1. J. Taylor (ed.). *Selected Writings of John Hughlings Jackson.* New York, Basic Books, 1958, vol. 2, p. 79.
2. W. Pitts and W. S. McCulloch. "How We Know Universals: The Perception

of Auditory and Visual Forms." *Bulletin of Mathematics and Biophysics,* vol. 9, 1947, pp. 127–147.

3. M. Ostow. "The Biological Basis of Human Behavior." *In:* S. Arieti (ed.). *American Handbook of Psychiatry.* New York, Basic Books, 1959, vol. 1, p. 78.

4. J. V. Brady. "Emotional Behavior." *In: Handbook of Physiology, Sect. I., Neurophysiology,* vol. 3, Washington, D.C., American Physiology Society, 1960, p. 1543.

5. P. D. MacLean. "Psychosomatic Disease and the Visceral Brain." *Psychosomatic Medicine,* vol. 11, 1949, p. 339.

6. J. V. Brady. *Op. cit.*[4]

7. *Ibid.,* p. 1535.

8. J. W. Papez. "A Proposed Mechanism of Emotion." *Archives of Neurology and Psychiatry,* vol. 38, Oct. 1937, pp. 725–743.

9. J. V. Brady. *Op. cit.,*[4] p. 1536.

10. M. Ostow. "A Psychoanalytic Contribution to the Study of Brain Function." *Psychoanalytic Quarterly,* vol. 24, 1955, p. 397.

11. P. D. MacLean. *Op. cit.,*[5] p. 343.

12. M. Ostow. *Op. cit.,*[10] p. 395.

13. H. Klüver and P. C. Bucy. "Preliminary Analysis of Functions of the Temporal Lobe in Monkeys." *Archives of Neurology and Psychiatry,* vol. 42, #6, Dec. 1939, p. 979 ff.

14. *Ibid.,* p. 988.

15. *Ibid.,* p. 995.

16. *Ibid.*

17. *Ibid.,* p. 988.

18. M. Ostow. *Op. cit.,*[10] p. 412.

19. H. Klüver and P. C. Bucy. *Op. cit.,*[13] p. 991.

20. M. Ostow. "Psychic Function of Temporal Lobe as Inferred from Seizure Phenomena." *Archives of Neurology and Psychiatry,* vol. 77, #1, 1957, p. 85.

21. S. Freud. "Negation." *In: Collected Papers.* London, Hogarth, 1950, vol. 5, p. 183.

22. P. D. MacLean. *Op. cit.,*[5] p. 348.

23. M. Ostow. *Op. cit.,*[10] p. 400.

24. M. Ostow. *Op. cit.,*[20] p. 83.

25. M. Ostow. *Op. cit.,*[10] p. 403.

26. *Ibid.,* p. 411.

27. P. D. MacLean. *Op. cit.,*[5] p. 346.

28. *Ibid.,* p. 347.

29. *Ibid.,* p. 348.

30. F. Ervin, *et al.* "Behavior of Epileptic and Non-epileptic Patients with 'Temporal Spikes'." *Archives of Neurology and Psychiatry,* vol. 74, 1955, pp. 488–497.

31. H. Terzian and G. D. Ore. "Syndrome of Klüver and Bucy." *Neurology,* vol. 5, #6, 1955, pp. 373–380.

32. E. Slater, *et al.* "Schizophrenia-like Psychoses of Epilepsy." *International Journal of Psychiatry,* vol. 1, #1, 1965, p. 6 ff.

33. W. Mitchell, *et al.* "Epilepsy with Fetishism Relieved by Temporal Lobectomy." *Lancet,* vol. 2, 1954, pp. 626–630.

34. A. W. Epstein. "Fetishism: A Study of its Psychopathology with Particular Reference to a Proposed Disorder in Brain Mechanism as an Etiological Factor." *Journal of Nervous and Mental Diseases,* vol. 130, #2, Feb. 1960, pp. 107–119.

35. O. Fenichel. *The Psychoanalytic Theory of Neurosis.* New York, Norton, 1945, p. 143.

36. S. Freud. "Three Contributions to the Theory of Sex." *In: The Basic Writings of Sigmund Freud.* New York, Modern Library, 1936, p. 568.

37. L. E. Hinsie and J. Shatzky, *Psychiatric Dictionary.* London, Oxford Univer. Press, 1940, p. 277.

38. P. D. MacLean. *Op. cit.,*[5] p. 344.

39. *Ibid.*

40. S. Freud. "Fetishism." *In: Collected Papers,*[21] vol. 5, p. 198.

41. *Ibid.,* p. 201.

42. A. W. Epstein. *Op cit.*[34]

43. S. Freud. "Fetishism." *Op. cit.,*[40] p. 200.

44. *Ibid.,* p. 201.

8

The Role of the
Frontal Lobe

In the opening passages of the chapter on the temporal lobes
we said that evolutionary considerations compelled us to
look at the forebrain for a better understanding of all those psychic
processes which make man the human animal he is. Embracing the
fact of evolution of organismic life, as all scientists will, and comparing
human behavior, capacities, and experience with what we can see or
infer during our observations and studies of the social apes (our closest
evolutionary kin), we might understandably try to account for whatever
differences exist or are suspected by pointing to the additional mass
of brain in man. The idea that "more of the same can really lead to
a qualitative difference" has been put forth by an authority such as
Gerard.[1] The most striking increase of brain tissue in man occurred
in that area of the frontal lobes which extends from the premotor (area
6) and adversive fields (area 8) forward toward the frontal poles. This
prefrontal portion of the forebrain (which is also known as the anterior
association area), its functions, and its psychopathology are the subject
of this presentation. It is, of course, understood that the subcortical
circuits of the prefrontal lobes are included as integral parts of this
uniquely human suborgan of the brain.

Whenever we attempt to define and tabulate the essential differences
between man and social ape we are not really at a loss to single out
human characteristics. We speak of language—but there is also communication amongst animals. It is true that the latter communicate
through signals, not through symbols; there is an enormous difference
between "sign language" and human speech. We can point, as Sir Julian
Huxley did, to the human capacity of conceptual thought, of tool-making, or of using the forelimbs as hands instead of as means of locomotion.
We recognize that only man can transmit a record of his thoughts.

knowledge, and activities to a future generation of man. Man is driven to learn from such records by curiosity and psychosocial necessity alike. Only man creates culture. In addition to all these accomplishments there are the symbolic representations of art. There is the knowledge of his death and the need for spiritual-ideational organizations in whatever forms, all of which may be called religion.[2] But despite the unquestioned uniqueness and predominance of man in his position of evolutionary ascendancy, we can recognize in subhuman species, particularly in primates, at least the beginnings of similarities to many of the human characteristics. The reader will find many instances of astonishing confirmation of this fact in the observations by zoologists such as Tinbergen and Konrad Lorenz. Thus, with an eye on the human prefrontal brain, we may well ask ourselves whether we are different merely because we have "more of the same" or whether we are more than social apes because of something that is indeed different. We quote Huxley:

After man's emergence as truly man, the same sort of thing [as at the infra-human level] continued to happen, but with an important difference. Man's evolution is not biological but psychosocial. . . . Accordingly, major steps in the human phase of evolution are achieved by breakthroughs to new dominant patterns of mental organization . . . ideological instead of physiological or biological organizations.[3]

These breakthroughs required and created not just sharper tools and greater complexities of organismic faculties. As soon as man knowingly began shaping his environment instead of being shaped by it, he took his future into his own hands. This was not a providential act, although it gave birth to the idea of Providence; rather, it was the result of man's conquest of consciousness of the future. At the same time, he acquired the capacity for taking himself seriously—an individual world in a world of individuals. Without the prefrontal brain of man this doubly fateful extension of consciousness in *depth* and in *time* would have been impossible. Safe ignorance had finally given way to the uncertainties of knowledge.

THE FRONTAL-LOBE SYNDROME
IN PRIMATES

In an exhaustive study entitled "The Frontal Lobes and their Function," Denny-Brown has given us a complete review of the literature and his own authoritative conclusions on the subject.[4] We have, therefore, used his monograph as our main source of reference in the preparation of this chapter. As far as ablation experiments on the prefrontal lobes in primates are concerned, the clinical psychiatrist is, of course, much more interested in behavioral than in neurological changes following such procedures. But there is one area of function which seems to occupy a crucial spot along the transitional progression of integration within the frontal lobe: the gaze to the side, with corresponding turning of the head. The adversive fields of the frontal lobes (area 8 of Brodmann), which mediate this function, are the "last" specific and circumscribed centers which the electrode can detect and define on its searching course forward from the precentral gyrus toward the frontal pole. Is this where we ought to look for the evolutionary hinge in the frontal lobe of man? Having already committed ourselves to the view that the frontal lobe represents in some way man's conquest of the consciousness of the future, we are tempted to dwell for a moment on the prescience of language—which has wrought such a natural link between a sensory and temporal modality, particularly as exact science has found no reason to gainsay this display of semantic wisdom. We speak of "a man of vision" because he can foresee the course of future events; we "listen" to the echoes of the past, but we try to "peer" into the mysteries of the future. We speak of "foresight," and we sense the ripple of derision with which the almost paradoxical word and idea of "hindsight" is scorned.

The results of experimental removal of the adversive fields in primates may be summarized as follows:[5] The animals do not seem to recognize objects in the affected fields; but it would be more accurate to say that rather than suffering from "frontal-lobe blindness," their "behavior fails to be appropriately activated by a purely visual stimulus"[6] and that "some more subtle feature of the visual stimulus, which gives it specific meaning, fails to excite reaction after frontal lobe lesion."[6] Bianchi noted that "the animal looks at everything, but without fixing herself to anything. Her senses are excited but not attracted."[6] Blinking at a threat within the corresponding field required a larger stimulus than ordinarily; the animal would also fail to pay attention to food left on the side which corresponded to the visual field opposite the lesion. They did not seem to know what to do with the food; they exhibited a wooden expression and in general reflected a loss of frontal-lobe function which in Denny-Brown's words "is concerned with the direction of behaviour as a whole by events that are primarily visual."[7] Once visual interest and understanding had been impaired or abolished by the ablations, either contralaterally or bilaterally, the animals showed a compensatory (?) hypersensitivity to auditory and tactile stimulation. All observers agree, Denny-Brown concludes, "that ablation of the whole frontal area produces the syndrome . . . with much greater certainty and persistence."[8] To this we may add that the loss of attentiveness to objects within the adversive fields is merely the prototype for a more elaborate loss if the ablations are carried forward toward the frontal pole—namely, an incapacity not of just *seeing*, but of *visualizing*, and not only of visualizing *objects*, but *objectives* and consequences. This assumption seems to be borne out by the results of ablations of the entire frontal lobes in monkeys and by prefrontal lobotomy, lobectomy, or disease in man.

The bifrontal ablation experiments on monkeys by Bianchi rank in importance with the classical findings obtained by Klüver and Bucy with their bitemporal monkeys. With regard to the visual-perceptual alterations, Bianchi concludes that the bifrontal monkey seems to be left with "a defect in perception which seems to be reduced to a more elementary level and lack some of the factors necessary to the formation of a more complete judgment."[9] Sociality has been compromised, even for a monkey. "She no longer plays with the other two monkeys who are her companions. . . . If she wishes to empty her bladder or bowels, she does not move off to some spot as she used to do . . . [she shows] no curiosity or interest in what is happening around her."[10] Affective reactions seem not only to be telescoped in immediate responses but also to have lost whatever refinement had been at the animal's command prior to the ablation. "The primitive emotions . . . persist. The higher sentiments, such as friendships, gratitude, jealousy . . . self-esteem . . . and above all, that of sociality . . . are lost."[11] Bianchi also observes that the animals "never again acquired that vivacity, that malicious, crafty and suspicious mobility which is so characteristic of the monkey."[11] No longer crafty, indeed; craft, as was once remarked by Winston Churchill, is common both to skill and deceit. Finally, it was noted that movements performed lacked any definite objective and that a certain incoherence of conduct prevailed "due to incapacity to represent and to sustain an objective in the focal point of consciousness."[12]

Lashley's frontal-ablation experiments on rats indicated that intelligence was impaired diffusely rather than selectively after removal of frontal-lobe tissue. "Deterioration of a trained habit did not occur in relation to one or another component, but in relation to ability as a whole."[13] Jacobsen and his co-workers stressed the greater susceptibility of the prefrontal animal to the disrupting effects of newly impinging and distracting internal or external stimuli.[14]

THE FRONTAL-LOBE SYNDROME IN MAN

Although the clinical manifestations of the frontal-lobe syndrome are to a certain degree influenced by the nature, location, and extent of the respective lesions, there is general agreement as to the specificity of the symptomatology of disease affecting the most anterior portion of the forebrain. Beginning with the famous "cross-bar case" of Harlow,[15] one hundred years ago, and carried to current times by investigators such as Thompson,[16] who linked sociopathic behavior to abnormalities within the thalamoprefrontal circuits, all authors express agreement that an alteration of personality—cognitive, affective, and social—follows disease or ablation within the prefrontal region of the brain. Each writer, while recognizing more or less the same defects noted by his fellow workers, would understandably emphasize a certain aspect of the symptomatology and try to accommodate it within the broader framework of his own theories and conceptualizations. A few authors have attempted to formulate a uniform hypothesis aimed at defining a unitary function of this latest evolutionary acquisition of the brain. In this chapter we will present the most notable observations on the psychopathology of the frontal-lobe syndrome, as well as prominent contributions to our understanding of the disorder. Although we will describe deficits in the broad areas of intellectual, emotional, and social performances in such patients, we must not forget how little enumerative separateness reflects clinical unity; it would, in fact, be contrary to modern conceptions of integration of brain function to allow for any kind of parcelling in this respect.

If the frontal-lobe syndrome is produced in man by therapeutic cutting of fibers within the thalamoprefrontal circuits, verbal intelligence shows little or no impairment.[17] Performance on the "impersonal" intelligence tests may, in fact, be better after the operation because of the resulting lessening of anxiety and tension that might otherwise accompany an ambitious desire to do well. As such procedures do not destroy cortical tissue, there is no loss of memory engrams—although there will very likely be a change in the significance which the patient will attribute to whatever memories he may summon into use. Of all these cognitive traces and instrumentalities of the past it may be said, with Walter Freeman, that it is "not a question of intelligence . . . it is a question of the employment of intelligence and the satisfaction gained therefrom. . . ."[18] If, on the other hand, the frontal-lobe syndrome results from a lesion which destroys large parts of the frontal cortex—such as a tumor or general paresis—there will, of course, be a very definite intellectual deficit, a dementia. But such a dementia, per se, does not seem to be different from one that eventuates from equally extensive destruction of more posterior parts of the isocortex. There will be the same impairment of abstract capacity (Kurt Goldstein), of synthesis of engrams (Brickner), of registering more than one stimulus at a time (Ackerly), and of maintaining a set toward a goal (Malmo). The hypothesis of mass action suggests that as far as these highest-level adaptive functions and complex mechanisms are concerned the clinical deficit will be in proportion to the amount of isocortical tissue lost, regardless of the site of the lesion.[19] "Many attempts to reduce this phenomenon [of the prefrontal personality] to terms of a single basic intellectual deficit have been made, but none is satisfactory."[20] On the other hand, the attitude of patients with frontal-lobe dementia toward their intellectual failures is quite different from the "catastrophic reactions" found in the so-called simple dementias. The prefrontal patient is quite indifferent toward his cognitive failures and equally nonchalant toward what normal people would consider social fatuity. There will be some reduction of the more complex intellectual capacities after bilateral prefrontal ablation, but the most severe and most characteristic deficit will be found in that sphere of intelligence which is required when one deals with other *people*. Thus it has often been said that in order to appreciate prefrontal "stupidity" one has to observe the patient's behavior within the circle of his family, in his dealings with the man on the street, or in the presence of a person of the opposite sex. Brickner speaks of the puerility of these patients; Freeman remarks that they seem to display all the Boy Scout's virtues in reverse. These are very pretty and also accurate descriptions, but what is the explanation? Denny-Brown notes "the preservation of the immediate aspects of the personality after lobectomy."[21] The patient's behavior may be quite inconspicuous and even adequate as long as he has to deal only with simple and habitual stimuli or situations of the moment—but only of the moment. Then his "immediate" reactions will be appropriate and sufficient. Because his cognitive and affective appreciation of the future has been amputated together with his prefrontal lobes, he will fail whenever called upon to consider *consequences*. Consequences, particularly social consequences, must be anticipated so that they may serve their purpose as feedback in the complicated patterns and continuous modifications of social intercourse. Psychosocial survival depends on this capacity. The prefrontal patient will overreact to the present, but underreact to the future in his state of telescoped awareness. A good illustration of this phenomenon is his reaction to pain. "The immediate effect is natural, or more often exaggerated, and can certainly be remembered as a colorless event, but all other effects cease within a few seconds."[22] Lobotomy does not abolish pain, but it does abolish "suffering" and is for this very reason at times carried out as a last resort in the presence of intractable pain. The general tendency of the prefrontal patient to emotional overreaction to momentary stimuli has been aptly described by Rylander as "emotional incontinence." It is a prefrontal symptom only because it is accompanied by an inability to experience sustained emotional reactions or remote affects—such as remorse, hope, faith, bitterness, dread, or desire for retaliation. The well-known euphoria of the frontal-lobe syndrome is not to be confused with joy; rather, it is the bland and barren expression of a stunted affectivity. This does not mean that the prefrontal patient has lost his capacity, and even gusto, for immediate gratification of basic instinctual needs. Like Bianchi's prefrontal monkeys he pursues his primitive drives, wolfing his food (bulemia) and giving free and offensive expression to his sexual desires. Another manifestation of the affective amputation of the future is the lack of initiative and enthusiasm. Implicit in the meaning of both of these terms—in their clinical as well as general usage—is the idea of a sustained, strong, and highly personalized emotional investment in the future, aided (as the case may be) by the cognitive effort of visualizing the merely possible. Thus the meaning of the Chinese proverb, "A journey of a thousand miles must begin with a single step," can never be truly appreciated by the prefrontal patient, let alone be applied in his behavior. This issue of prefrontal initiative, which was stressed by Kleist and even given a tentative location in his diagrammatic chart of frontal-lobe functions, has received the same thoughtful but speculative attention by the psychoanalysts, who refer to it as "motivation." Ostow[23] hypothesizes that the frontal lobe is the site for the elaboration of instinctual derivatives, beginning with the formation of infantile fantasies, some or all of which in the course of mental-apparatus maturation are replaced by suitable equivalents. It is assumed that all of the individual's life experiences, all of his emotional and cognitive power of pursuit (as well as of restraint), and his capacity for symbolization and indirect representation participate in the complicated task of attaining gratification of primarily biological needs in a setting of psychosocial realities and restrictions. Ostow contends that "the greater the amount and energy and ingenuity brought to bear in the creation of derivatives the more opportunities the individual will find to gratify instinctual desires despite repression and external obstacles. . . ."[24] He considers successful derivative creation a task of "respectable intellectual magnitude."[24] Thus, in disease of the frontal lobe motivation is "attenuated in intensity and diminished in complexity."[23] This assumption is certainly suggested by clinical observation of these patients. Stanley Cobb's idea of a "long-circuiting" function of the frontal lobes and its reduction to "short-circuiting" in case of disease is a simple but valid parallel to Ostow's hypothesis.

Walter Freeman was particularly impressed by the loss of fantasy life and "depth" in the wake of prefrontal lobotomy. It is not at all a matter of these patients having lost, after the operation, the power of creating great works of art or imagination; most of them never could have done this with their frontal lobes intact. What they did lose was the capacity for imagining the "merely possible" (as Kurt Goldstein called it)—for including the "make believe" attitude in their psychosocial considerations and behavior. It is their failure of "visualizing motor and affective resultants"[25] in the clear presence of a given situation and even more so in the "make believe" situation that is of the essence. It is one of man's unique endowments to be able to impose upon an object a meaning which the object does not inherently possess; that is to say, the symbolic "perception" of such subjective meanings can not be accounted for by the natural capacities of our perceptual apparatus. This is how man may objectify some of his beliefs. This is how a pair of sticks crossed at a right angle becomes a *cross*, with all that implies. The prefrontal patient will still be able to recognize the *pattern* of the cross but not its symbolic significance. Nothing is known about any localization or neurophysiological mechanism of the human capacity for symbolic apperception of objects. But it is known that the prefrontal lobe is necessary for the "make believe" attitude, and thus for foresight and for thinking the "merely possible" and wishing it, or, at times, for striving to avoid it.

We have already mentioned the primarily visual mechanisms of the frontal lobe. This may be the proper place to quote Denny-Brown's significant summing-up statement.

We conclude that . . . the [pre]frontal lobes are the chief executive organs of visually directed behavior, sharing some of this function with . . . the temporal pole. Within the large zone of the frontal and prefrontal cortex . . . behaviour is oriented in terms of vision, with a dominant factor of expectancy. . . . In all zones there is some evidence of sub-specialization, but this has the aspects of elaboration of the effect of special qualities of stimulus, rather than special parcellation of function.[26]

Clinical Observations

It may be useful to match these highly academic formulations with some clinical illustrations. I will first quote a typical remark that a patient of Freeman and Watts made after lobotomy: "Now that I have done it, I can see that it was not the thing to do, but beforehand I couldn't say whether or not it would be right."[17] Brickner made exhaustive studies over a period of several years following bilateral prefrontal lobectomy in a 41-year-old man with a large meningioma. Apart from irritability, boastfulness, puerility, and some impairment of social sense in the patient, Brickner noted intellectual changes which he considered to be quantitative rather than qualitative; he speaks of "a kind of quantitative frontal localization of a part which increases the degree to which a

PROPERTY OF WASHINGTON
SCHOOL OF PSYCHIATRY
LIBRARY

given process may be elaborated."[27] In his opinion the frontal lobes
are necessary for the elaboration of relatively simple mental engrams
into more complex ones; if confronted with the latter the patient would
either fail altogether or perform at a much slower rate than a control
subject. Brickner's patient showed, of course, the characteristic lack of
appreciation of the gravity of a situation and a total absence of concern
and anxiety about his future.

I remember a patient with general paresis (in which case there is,
of course, considerable cortical prefrontal destruction as well as cortico-
thalamic loss) who accidently dropped his cigar while leaning out of
a window; without hesitation he jumped through the window to get
his cigar back, breaking a leg as a result of the fall. He told me later
that at the moment of jumping it did not occur to him that he might
get hurt; all he wanted was to get his cigar back. He certainly had
taken the short circuit! It should be noted that the patient had been
quite well oriented and that there was no indication of cognitive confusion. As an example of how this particular prefrontal "factor of expectancy" operates in every-day social situations let us assume that I
am sitting alone at a table in a sidewalk cafe when I notice a "meter
maid" ticketing cars parked at meters that have run out of time. I remember that my own car is parked at a meter in the next block; it will
probably be ticketed too. Rather than risking a fine I walk to my car
and put a dime into the meter. But if, in the identical situation, I were
having lunch with an executive to whom I had applied for a very promising position and who wanted on this occasion "to look me over," I
would not run off to avoid a ticket—I would not wish to give the impression that I am fearful of a small fine, or of authority. This "prefrontal
judgment" entails, in Brickner's words, the fact that "the individual must
be able to conceive of emotional compensations for the emotional sacri-
fices which are required."[28]

Behavior guided by such considerations presupposes the intactness
and even the attainment of a prefrontal faculty which is at times described as "social intelligence." All authors are agreed on the marked
impairment of "sociality" in patients (and animals) with prefrontal lesions. Social intelligence is a complex function comprising quite an imposing array of techniques of dealing with the most significant, most
unpredictable, most needed, most desirable, most dangerous, and most
elusive of all objects—another person. As soon as in the course of evolution the impersonal "anonymity of the flock" had given way to the
"group," "the attachment reactions [became] . . . inseparably linked
with the individualities of group members."[29] The impersonal interactions within the anonymous flock are the result of built-in adaptive
mechanisms over which a nonexisting individuality could, naturally, not

exercise any control. Sociality—notwithstanding its strong pressures toward cultural uniformity—is nevertheless based on complete individual separateness with the result that in social relations no individual can really be exchanged for another. The physiological correlate for this separateness, as a subjective experience, must be sought in those still-unknown processes of maturation within the brain which culminate in adult, human self-awareness. And one of the cardinal consequences of this awareness of self is the capacity of becoming aware, objectively and reciprocally, of another person as an independent and yet interacting social entity. The reduced social intelligence of the prefrontal patient bears some resemblance to the as-yet-undeveloped social intelligence of the child. The patient's notorious inability of "role-taking," of sensing, recognizing, or anticipating the thoughts, feelings, and reactions of the other person is comparable to the ego-centered world-picture of the young child; the patient's reduction of visualization of the more distant events and consequences is not unlike the child's world of "nearness at hand."[30] However, we must be careful in all such comparisons of the normal mentality of the child with psychopathology in the adult; the similarities are there, but the differences are by far greater. Thus similarities have been recognized to exist between the thought processes of small children on one hand and primitive peoples as well as schizophrenics on the other. Still, as far as any possible relation between child psychology and ethnopsychology is concerned, Werner warns us that "any hypothesis of recapitulation has to be rejected."[30] The *puerility* of the prefrontal patient contains none of the redeeming qualities of the *little boy*.

A "FOURTH DIMENSION?"

We have proposed the hypothesis that the essentially "motor" function of the anterior brain and particularly the phenomenon of lateral gaze, represented in the adversive fields, could be correlated with man's conquest of the consciousness of the future. Many of the features of the frontal-lobe syndrome seem to suggest that the prefrontal patient looks at his future with less interest and concern and also with reduced cognitive capacity for prediction and planning. Before attempting a generalization concerning the presumptive essential function of the frontal lobes we must again emphasize that personality changes, both in kind and in degree, depend on the nature and location of the pathology. One would not expect the clinical picture of general paresis to be the same as that of a patient who underwent a judiciously placed lobotomy for relief of a severe obsessive-compulsive neurosis. It is also necessary to point to those studies which suggest that there might be functional differences among the various cortical regions of the prefrontal lobe, such as the areas of its convexity, the cingular portion, and the orbital gyri. Despite all these qualifying facts and considerations, there can be little doubt that an authentic frontal-lobe syndrome exists. For our present purpose we will permit ourselves a somewhat simplified view of the frontal lobe, with one of its "suborgans" comprising the entire prefrontal cortex, while the other unit is represented by the thalamoprefrontal system, possibly augmented by its further hypothalamic connections. The former is closer to the cognitive aspects of the personality, the latter to the affective.

Developmental psychology has convincingly demonstrated that the evolving relationship between the organism and its environment, between subject and object, proceeds from syncretic primitivism toward an ever-sharper delineation and polarization between self and nonself. This progression—with all its attending characteristics and increasing complexities—affects all components of mental life: cognitive, conative, and affective. It can be traced by observing the transformations of behavior of organisms in the course of their phylogenetic, ontogenetic, and cultural-anthropological evolution: from lower to higher animal; from child to adult; from primitive to sophisticated man. In disease of the prefrontal lobes we can expect the resulting dissolution to reverse the evolutionary direction—toward primitivity.

Some of Werner's comments on the nature of syncretic *action* (conation) are relevant to our theme: "the primitively acting organism is intimately bound up with the concrete situation. . . . The growth and differentiation of the personal factor in action are demonstrated in the emergence of a specifically personal *motivation*. . . . In brief, the striking characteristics of primitive concrete action are *immediacy, limited motivation,* and *lack of planning*."[31] He also speaks of "the extension of the action beyond the visibly given field"[32] as one of many signs of release of the organism from primitivity. He uses the term "visibly" in the literal sense. We are familiar with the "immediacy" of action and reaction by the prefrontal patient, regardless in what form or guise it may manifest itself clinically—"concreteness," "short-circuiting," "tactlessness," or "emotional incontinence." We recall how disease or removal of the prefrontal lobe results in an "amputation of the future," both cognitively and affectively, with a resulting (or rather remaining) conative affinity to the *immediate* situation only—that is, to the present. "Limited motivation" appears in the prefrontal syndrome as apathy, inertia, indifference, and lack of sustained interest; but it also includes the impoverishment and coarseness of mental life that results from loss of fantasy, and the inability to create "instinctual derivatives" of "respectable" complexity and versatility. Lack of planning may be the result of either cognitive or affective prefrontal deficits, or of both. If the lesion has destroyed a significant portion of the cortical mantle, all those aspects of abstract behavior which are required for the choice, pursuit, and ultimate attainment of goals are compromised. The affective deficit in the area of planning consists in the emotional irrelevance, to the patient, of the future—as well as in his inability to view certain future eventualities with appropriate concern and to meet them by appropriate planning.

At the infrahuman level the great constructors of biological evolution—namely, gene shuffling, mutation, and the survival of the fittest—determine the future of the species. As far as the individual organism is concerned there is at these lower levels a striking intraspecific uniformity, little diversity of behavior or habit (even across the span of countless generations), and little more than "instinctual understanding" of the environment by a creature as yet incapable of contemplation or of shaking off "the shackles of time-present."[33] The individual's past can do little, if anything, to assist in shaping the individual's future. Parental care for the young is biological, not cultural. Life consists of a mere sum and series of discontinuous and repetitive adaptive performances—solid enough, but not yet soaring. No "time-binding" faculty that would meaningfully elevate sequences to continuity has yet arrived on the evolutionary scene. Fossils, but not cultural imprints, are the sole reminders of a past existence.

It has been said that human ontogeny repeats and retraces phylogeny, at a rapid pace and with some modifications. Accordingly, we recognize the fact that even a very small child with his prefrontal lobes still inoperative is already in the process of becoming more human than a grown social ape. Thus any attempt to define the essential function of the frontal lobes of man must include a search for the appearance in man of mental qualities not found even in his closest phylogenetic predecessor, which happens to be the gorilla. We must address ourselves to the question of whether this specifically human area of the brain which we call the prefrontal lobes is responsible not merely for the obvious difference between animal and man but also for a difference in *kind* rather than only in *degree*—whether, in other words, it is true that a "new dimension" has been created with man. Critchley puts it this way: "Has a new factor been abruptly introduced into the evolutionary stream at some point. . . . Can it be that Darwin was in error when he regarded the differences between man and animals as differences merely in degree?"[34] He does not come forth with an unequivocal answer, but he admits that "it is tempting to doubt whether anything like a smooth gradation has occurred."[35] I am tempted to add that changes in degree may well appear as changes in kind—even as a change in color is caused by a purely quantitative increase in the wavelength of light. The clinical picture resulting from bilateral removal of the prefrontal lobes or from substantial bilateral lobotomy may be compressed into a formulation that considers the cognitive and affective alterations, if any, of the personality in regard to temporal continuity: past, present, and future.

Clinical Signs of Prefrontal Impairment

1. There is no significant loss of knowledge, memories, or skills acquired in the past; they are all available, even if the patient does not (for other reasons) avail himself of these assets in the pursuit of goals.

2. There is some blunting of whatever affective charge had been attached to thoughts and actions of the past. Feelings such as regret or remorse are not likely to be experienced by the patient, even if he should, like the psychopath, give lip service to them.

3. There is marked impairment of cognitive anticipation of the future. It is doubtful whether the prefrontal patient could be relied upon to drive his car "defensively" or to figure out whether the recipient of antimissile missiles was the aggressor or the attacked. It is certain that he could not play a good game of chess.

4. The most significant defect seems to be the inability of the patient to project himself affectively into the future. The pursuit of ideals as well as the threat of dire consequences have become meaningless to the patient.

5. As to the present, there is little incapacity for dealing with its demands and opportunities. However, it must be realized that in human social living an isolated performance within the present, except for very concrete or habitual acts, does not exist. Even animals will use objects as tools to solve a problem of the moment; *but never will they afterwards put the tool aside for future use. If they did they would be human.*

It therefore appears to this writer that the human frontal lobes add a "fourth dimension" to the world of self and objects *in presentia;* namely, *the world of self and objects in the future (in absentia).* Critchley makes a similar observation in the area of human language. "Man's utterances . . . possess the superlative advantage of applying to events in time past, present and future and to objects *in absentia*. This endowment has been called the 'time-binding' property of human language."[36] The conquest of the consciousness of the future, which we attribute to the frontal lobes, is, of course, not confined to the area of language. It must apply to all mental and behavioral processes which we consider to be characteristically human. Thus only *homo sapiens* uses symbols; and "symbols can refer to things out of sight and outside present experience."[37] Tool-making with an eye to the future—rather than tool-using strictly within a "present" orientation—is uniquely human; and there is not a single conscious creative thought or act, from the simplest to the most sublime, which could conceivably occur without the awareness of, and hope for, and belief in a future, however remote, however transcendental. Huxley asserts that "one of man's unique qualities is that in his evolution he is able to preadapt to the future."[38] And we may perhaps add that, in so doing, man has divided his attention and foresight equally between his future in this world and in another one to come.

We have already posed the question of whether the conquest of the "consciousness of the future" and its related instrumentalities and consequences represent a qualitative or quantitative evolutional progression. This point is mentioned here not so much for its own sake but for reasons closer to the issues of clinical psychiatry. While precursors or equivalents of human characteristics have been described not only among the social apes but also considerably lower down along the phylogenetic scale, the balance of authoritative opinion does not favor a quantitative gradualism in the emergence of *homo sapiens, loquens,* and *faber.* But with the decisive qualitative change having been accomplished (so we think) at some point between the anthropoids and man, a quantitative element may be required in order to account for individual differences in the display of prefrontal capacity among otherwise "normal" persons. These differences are found in such areas as social intelligence, sense of responsibility, capacity for certain forms of abstract thought and behavior, and "judgment and wisdom which the diencephalon normally derives from the frontal lobes."[39] This formulation, from which we must infer that the emotional hypothalamic centers rely on the frontal lobes for reasonable and wise guidance, proposes a hierarchical order in which neopallial ascendancy is depicted as our last best hope. When we survey the vast panorama of neopallial and particularly prefrontal accomplishment, we cannot possibly fail to see its greatness; but we also dare not overlook its dangers. Our frontal lobes have tampered with the atom before our hypothalamus has learned to temper its potential for aggression. Our cultural evolution has even targeted in on the innermost source and secret of biological evolution, the gene, pondering how to make man in man's image. All the distortions and incomprehensions of reality caused by disease of the mental apparatus may already have become a far less dangerous event for mankind than the precision and comprehension of some of those new realities which in our unwisdom and vanity we idolize as achievements of that very same mind.

CLINICAL ILLUSTRATIONS

Psychopathy

George N. Thompson has recently advanced an entirely novel hypothesis concerning the nature and causes of psychopathy—namely, that it is "an organic control disorder of frontal lobe-hypothalamic connections,"[40] either in the form of a neuronal deficit or of intermittent paroxysmal irritation within these circuits. The history of the concept "psychopathy" reflects the lack of precise knowledge concerning the etiology and, therefore, the treatment of this condition. This confusion was unavoidable as long as one thought that the essence of psychopathy lay in the habitual inability of the "sociopath" to conform with social requirements, to emulate current social mores, and to obey the law. It is quite obvious that failure to do so may be the result of a great variety of psychopathological deviations. Patients suffering from character disorders with prominent tendencies toward rebelliousness or with an unconscious need for punishment may "act out" their conflicts in a manner resembling psychopathy. Schizoid or paranoid personalities often commit crimes or else behave in an extremely offensive manner; they are, I submit, as little psychopaths as are the so-called professional criminals. Patients with epileptic automatisms and mild schizophrenics, whatever their antisocial behavior may be, should offer less difficulties in being diagnosed for what they are. It has, of course, been known for some time that there exists a group of patients who can not be diagnosed as neurotic, schizophrenic, or organic, but who show in their conduct—although not usually in their deportment during a psychiatric examination!—that kind and persistence of unbelievable social irresponsibility and stupidity which has been described in such terms as "moral insanity" (Prichard), "anethopathy" (Karpman), and "semantic dementia" (Cleckley). The designation of "constitutional psychopathic inferiority" is equally vague and, according to Thompson's thesis, even misleading. Thompson maintains that psychopathy exists in all societies, including the most primitive aborigines of Australia, and that a hypothetical person who spends his entire lifetime alone on an uninhabited island would still be a psychopath or "sociopath" provided that he had suffered the kind of brain damage that can produce this condition. It is the nature of psychopathy that society is merely the arena for its vagaries, and its members at times the victims of this abnormality. After all that was said in this chapter concerning the presumptive function of the prefrontal lobes it will not surprise us that in Thompson's view the first and fundamental symptom of psychopathy, almost its essence, is the patient's inability "to formulate a concept of time concerning himself. Thus he has no concern with the past or future, only with the present."[41] Thompson lists twelve important signs and symptoms— such as lack of concern for the consequences of one's actions; inconsiderateness; inability to profit from experience; irreversibility of behavior which is totally refractory to the usual methods of psychotherapy; his tory of brain injury or brain disease (e.g., encephalitis); high incidence of neurological and electroencephalographic abnormalities. If psychopathy according to this theory is representative of organic disease of the frontal lobe–hypothalamic connections, it follows that there is no evidence of ordinary (cortical) dementia. It has, in fact, been said that the psychopath is usually of better than average intelligence, as far as purely verbal or impersonal tasks are concerned. Some observers, Thompson included, have stressed the ingratiating tendencies of these patients and their verbal adroitness, which they enlist in presenting a front of reasonableness, almost of empathy, and which can be so deceptive that Cleckley aptly called it a "mask of sanity." Thompson further supports his hypothesis by reminding us that alcohol "will make, temporarily, almost any person a psychopath;"[42] and we know, of course, that alcohol, as well as drugs, can impair frontal-lobe function for the duration of the intoxication. It appears not unlikely that the exaggerated reaction of brain-damaged persons to relatively small amounts of alcohol, referred to as "pathological intoxication," represents such a temporary psychopathic state.

Pick's Disease

This particular variety of presenile psychosis (the other being Alzheimer's disease) is the result of a slowly progressive degenerative process which affects the phylogenetically most recent portions of the neopallium, i.e., the frontal and temporal poles. As the disease progresses, additional regions within the frontal and temporal lobes become involved. If, as is often the case, the atrophy is most extensive in the prefrontal region a typical frontal-lobe syndrome—manifested by inertia, lack of interest and concern, and deterioration of the higher intellectual and symbolic functions—presents itself. There are certain special features noted in Pick's disease which deserve some description. In the early stages of the disease the patients seem to be more demented than they actually are; it is their reluctance and loss of initiative to perform intellectual tasks rather than their inability to do so. This situation reflects cortical loss that underlines the "prefrontal" quality of the condition at its inception. Memory traces are also preserved for a long time. In the later stages the loss of abstract capacity is, of course, pronounced. The general transformation of personality is either in the direction of

akinesia, inertia, and affective blunting, or, less frequently, of hyper-
kinesia, euphoria, and excitement. Both syndromes, as was pointed out
by Brickner, are consistent with frontal-lobe involvement. Another feature
of Pick's disease is the occurrence of repetitive utterances and stereotyped movements. Instinctive grasping may be interpreted as a (compensatory?) extraordinary sensitivity to tactile and proprioceptive impressions in the wake of prefrontal loss of reactivity to the visual aspects
of the environment. Although aphasic disturbances will occur with a
more posterior distribution or extension of the lesion, the prefrontal
variety is characterized by an aversion toward speech rather than an
inability to talk.

General Paresis

As the pathology in general paresis invariably involves the frontal lobes
without, however, sparing the more posterior portions of the cerebral
cortex, the disease usually presents the picture of a "contented dementia."
In a very large proportion of patients the prefrontal contentment reaches
the stage of euphoria and even of grandiosity. It is a fact that there is
hardly a mental disease easier to diagnose then general paresis; in almost
all instances the spinal-fluid findings are positive in untreated cases. On
the other hand, the early manifestations may be quite subtle and misleading. Not unlike the postlobotomy or postlobectomy patient, the pa-
retic may be able to carry out routine work satisfactorily for a considerable time after the onset of the disease process; but the family who live
in close social contact with him will notice personality changes which are
at total variance with his previous attitudes and social and emotional
attainments. They may become aware that he has grown indifferent to
the feelings of others, to the consequences of his actions, and to social
disapproval. They may, on the other hand, observe minor odd or incomprehensible acts—such as Breutsch's patient,[43] who went into a five-and-
dime store in order to buy a Buick automobile. In other paretics the very
first symptom may be a convulsive seizure. It is well to remember that a
first convulsion in a person in his 40s or 50s requires careful investigation
as to the possibility of either general paresis or hemispheric neoplasm,
the latter most likely being located near the sensory-motor strip. It is
particularly in those forms of general paresis which involve the posterior
as well as the frontal cortical areas (so-called Lissauer type of paresis)
that the disease may be ushered in by a *grand mal* attack or an apoplec-
tiform seizure. In still other cases the first instance of abnormal behavior
may be a purely cognitive deficit, severe enough to attract the attention
of those who live with the patient. As such an example we can report a
patient whose first unmistakable sign of "contented dementia" was re-

vealed when he could not remember where he had parked his car when he was going to the office that morning; he then took a train home, telling his family nonchalantly that he had lost his car somewhere in town. As the disease progresses the dementia becomes more pronounced and unmistakable while at the same time the affective blunting and transformation of the personality become evident. The majority of paretics tend to become indifferent and euphoric to various degrees; a certain percentage shows the classical expansive and grandiose picture with the corresponding delusions. Occasionally a clinical syndrome indistinguishable from schizophrenia presents itself—intermingled, of course, with evidence of simple dementia, typical neurological signs, and the characteristic spinal-fluid findings. Although they occur rarely, such combinations raise significant issues, such as the concept of "symptomatic schizophrenia" and its relation to coarse brain disease or temporal-lobe epilepsy (see also Chapters 10 and 13). In the case of the schizophrenialike symptomatology in rare instances of general paresis, it appears quite obvious that "these psychoses are schizophrenic in form but not in etiology. They are not endogenous but symptomatic."[44] Such combinations also offer the interesting opportunity to observe the coexistence of schizophrenic and simple dementia in the same patient.

CONCLUDING COMMENTS

Neurophysiologists ascribe to the latest phylogenetic acquisitions of the brain (such as the prefrontal association area), a potential for functional capabilities and growth unhampered by predetermined and fixed evolutional commitment to a specific function. Hughlings Jackson assigned to these "uncommitted" regions the faculty of what he called *internal evolution.* He said: "There is what I will call Internal Evolution, a process which goes on most actively in the highest centres. On account of its great preponderance in the highest centres of man, he differs so greatly from animals."[45] But there are also significant and undeniable differences amongst individuals in the human species. As far as the central nervous system is concerned, we venture the hypothesis that the possibility for differences in individual growth—of whatever kind and content—is somehow tied to the highest organizations, whose functional character has not been preempted by lower- or intermediate-level functional assignments. This idea of an evolutionary *"carte blanche"* appears as a provocative concept in its possible relationship to the concept of equipotentiality and the presumptive function and extent of the "neuropil." Every man has, so it seems, the same frontal lobes, but not the same degree of foresight, imagination, creativ-

ity, richness of instinctual derivatives, emotional refinement, persever-
ance, or appreciation for the significance of experience. It would, of
course, be naïve to suggest anything like an "anatomy of creative talent."
On the contrary, we realize the fact and the extent of the contribution
that nonfrontal territories make toward creative accomplishment, be it
modest or exceptional. But might not the prefrontal lobes be the organ
of ultimate implementation? The musician must draw on his especially
gifted temporal lobes; the sculptor on his parietal lobes, which endow
him with such astonishing artistic mastery of spatial relations; the painter
could not produce the artistic blending of perspective and color without
the help from the parietal and occipital lobes—how, we do not know.
But none of these artists could create without his especially endowed
prefrontal lobes. This has been proved in the case of creative patients
who had undergone prefrontal lobotomy. It also seems that this elusive
faculty is operative to various degrees in people other than those with
exceptional talent. Nor must we for a moment overlook the importance
of many extraneous factors to the ultimate outcome of the issue. But
any attempt toward devising a typology of man must include the prefrontal differential. Clinical investigation has revealed that patients after
lobotomy or prefrontal lobectomy no longer dream. But some men with
intact frontal lobes, of a certain quality as yet undefined, will while
so deeply awake, "dream things that never were and say why not?"

REFERENCES

1. S. Tax (ed.). "Issues in Evolution." *In: Evolution After Darwin.* Chicago, Univer.
   of Chicago Press, 1960, vol. 3, p. 201.
2. A. Koestler. *The Ghost in the Machine.* New York, Macmillan, 1967, p. 297.
3. S. Tax (ed.). *Op. cit.,*[1] p. 251.
4. D. Denny-Brown. "The Frontal Lobes and Their Function." *In:* A. Feiling
   (ed.). *Modern Trends in Neurology.* London, Butterworth, 1951, pp. 13–89.
5. *Ibid.,* pp. 51–57.
6. *Ibid.,* p. 56.
7. *Ibid.,* p. 57.
8. *Ibid.,* p. 56.
9. *Ibid.,* p. 59.
10. *Ibid.*
11. *Ibid.,* p. 60.
12. *Ibid.*
13. *Ibid.,* p. 62.
14. *Ibid.,* p. 63.
15. J. M. Harlow. *In: Publications of the Massachusetts Medical Society,* 1868 2:329.
16. G. N. Thompson. "Sociopathic Personality: Its Neurophysiology and Treatment."

In: M. Rinkel (ed.). *Biological Treatment of Mental Illness.* New York, L. C. Page, 1966, p. 131.

17. W. Freeman and J. W. Watts. *Psychosurgery.* Springfield, Ill., Thomas, 1950.

18. *Ibid.,* p. 21.

19. L. F. Chapman and H. G. Wolff. "The Human Brain, One Organ or Many?" *Archives of Neurology,* vol. 5, 1961, pp. 463–471.

20. D. Denny-Brown. *Op. cit.,*[4] p. 78.

21. *Ibid.,* p. 79.

22. *Ibid.*

23. M. Ostow. "A Psychoanalytic Contribution to the Study of Brain Function: 1. The Frontal Lobes." *Psychoanalytic Quarterly,* vol. 23, 1954, pp. 317–338.

24. *Ibid.,* p. 332.

25. D. Denny-Brown. *Op. cit.,*[4] p. 83.

26. *Ibid.,* p. 84.

27. *Ibid.,* p. 72.

28. *Ibid.,* p. 71.

29. K. Lorenz. *On Aggression.* New York, Harcourt, Brace & World, 1966, p. 166.

30. H. Werner. *Comparative Psychology of Mental Development.* New York, International Univer. Press, 1957, p. 26.

31. *Ibid.,* p. 191.

32. *Ibid.,* p. 194.

33. S. Tax (ed.). *Op. cit.,*[1] p. 297.

34. *Ibid.,* p. 307.

35. *Ibid.,* p. 308.

36. *Ibid.,* p. 294.

37. *Ibid.,* p. 300.

38. *Ibid.,* p. 254.

39. G. N. Thompson. *Op. cit.,*[16] p. 134.

40. *Ibid.*

41. *Ibid.,* p. 133.

42. *Ibid.,* p. 135.

43. W. L. Bruetsch. "Neurosyphilitic Conditions." *In:* S. Arieti (ed.). *American Handbook of Psychiatry.* New York, Basic Books, 1959, vol. 2, p. 1006.

44. E. Slater, *et al.* "Schizophrenia-like Psychoses of Epilepsy." *International Journal of Psychiatry,* vol. 1, #1, 1965, p. 27.

45. J. Taylor (ed.). *Selected Writings of John Hughlings Jackson.* New York, Basic Books, 1958, vol. 2, p. 71.

9

Delusions and Other
False Beliefs

As may be inferred from the title of this chapter, delusions
are a special type of false beliefs. It is generally accepted
that a patient who entertains delusions suffers from a malignant mental
illness—a psychosis. Thus delusions are malignant false beliefs. Actually,
matters are not quite so simple as that. Terms such as "psychosis," "false
beliefs," and "malignant'" are far from unequivocal. Although we will
attempt to clarify some of these uncertainties and ambiguities we can
not hope to remove the controversy with which they are still sur-
rounded. Nevertheless, such an attempt may be of value in guiding
the judgment of the clinical psychiatrist when he is confronted with
a patient who believes in something which is not, or could not be,
true.

Criteria of the concept "psychosis" have been advanced both on theoretical and clinical-pragmatic grounds. As psychoanalysis is the most
sophisticated and detailed theory of psychodynamic psychopathology
one should not dismiss whatever Freud has had to say on the nature
of the psychotic process. In "The Interpretation of Dreams" he made
the following statement:

Sleep guarantees the security of the fortress which has to be guarded. The
state of affairs is less harmless when a displacement of energies is produced,
not by the decline at night in the energy put forth by the critical censorship,
but by the pathological enfeeblement of the latter, or the pathological reinforcement of the unconscious excitations. . . . The guardian is then over-
powered; the unconscious excitations subdue the Pcs., and from the Pcs.
they dominate our speech and action, or they enforce hallucinatory regres-
sions. . . . We call this condition phychosis.[1]

This purely psychodynamic formulation rests on the premise that the
unconscious excitation by virtue of its *content* and *intensity* seriously

conflicts with the facts and demands of reality; the result is that the patient's capacity to comprehend and deal with the world of objects is lost. It is clear that no psychodynamic theory can be applied to a formulation concerning the essential nature of the cognitive transformation of personality that we note in patients who are suffering from coarse brain disease. Freud's statement refers to the *breakthrough* of the primary process whereas the essence of organic dementia lies in a *breakdown* of the secondary process. Thus psychosis may come about either way. Land can be rendered useless by a flood as well as by a drought. We should also remember that the limited, circumscribed, and contained breakthrough of the primary process in the form of either a hysterical or obsessive-compulsive symptom is not in itself sufficient, precisely because of its isolated compactness, to cause any impairment in the testing and comprehension of everyday reality; therefore it will not necessarily lead to a psychosis. At this point we must be aware of a notable lack of correspondence between theoretical and clinical considerations.

Clinical psychiatry has traditionally associated certain symptoms, such as delusions and hallucinations, with the concept of "psychosis." In these particular instances no allowance was to be made for qualifying considerations. While such an approach is clinically and pragmatically quite sound and workable it does not shed much light on the problem what the essence of psychosis is. But there exist qualifying factors, both clinical and theoretical, the consideration of which is relevant to our theme. Let us take the example of hallucinations. Suppose that a patient experiences elementary visual hallucinations because of an irritating lesion in the calcarine area. It would never occur to any psychiatrist to make a diagnosis of psychosis on that basis; the same applies if the patient complains of olfactory hallucinations because of uncinate fits. It is not sufficient to say that neither of these patients is likely to present any symptoms commonly associated with a psychotic disorder. The reasons why such hallucinations can not be designated as psychotic manifestations are more complicated. In a paper entitled "The Distortion of the Symbolic Process in Neurosis and Psychosis," Kubie[2] proposes the hypothesis that each symbol is bipolar, having both an internal (visceral, archipallial) and an external (nonvisceral, neopallial) component. He designates the former as the "I" component and the latter as the "non-I" component. "As a consequence of this characteristic of the evolving learning process . . . all percepts of the outer world must establish points of reference to inner, bodily percepts and concepts."[3] The "non-I" component is necessarily in closest contact with an object of the outer world; distortion of that point of contact, says Kubie, represents the essence of the psychotic process, within the sphere of symbolizations. By contrast, the neurotic process is characterized by a distortion of the "I" component of the symbolic process, a component which is deeply rooted within the body experience. As an illustration Kubie compares a cat phobia with a delusion about cats. He states that in the former (neurotic) distortion there is no abnormality

of the patient's understanding of the meaning of CAT whether as percept, concept, or language symbol. In the psychotic process, however, one or more of these components of the symbolic process will have been dislocated from its relationship to the presenting object: so that a CAT and its symbolic derivatives actually mean to the patient something other than itself.[4]

Let us return to the question of elementary hallucinations. They may very likely occur within the modality of our most accurate and reality-oriented distance receptor, vision. But because they are "elementary," their content will never concern itself with objects but only with the inherent qualities of the corresponding sensory modality. For this reason there is also nothing about such hallucinations which could conceivably represent the symbolic process. The situation is, of course, entirely different if a schizophrenic attributes a hallucinated hissing sound to evil outside sources. In that case the hallucination, while not a "voice," has all the connotations of bearing a message. Kubie suggests that we may be inclined to overlook the truly hallucinatory character of those myriad bodily sensations that occur in neurotic and non-neurotic persons; he cites as examples "the commonplace sensations of pain, itching, sleepiness, heat and cold . . . ;"[5] he also emphasizes the lack of precision which attends proprioceptive percepts as compared with exteroceptive ones. We may again add that such bodily hallucinations would be, and in fact are, of a psychotic nature only if the patient—in elaborating about their origin and consequences—implicates objects or their equivalents within the outer world, and in so doing distorts the "non-I" component of the symbolic process. As far as delusions are concerned we will in this presentation attempt a distinction between false beliefs which are not indicative of a psychotic process, and those which are and which we therefore refer to as "delusions."

Another clinical criterion of psychosis rests on a consideration of the quantitative factor and the intensity of a given symptom. How severe, we will ask, is the impairment of immediate recall in a particular elderly man with cerebral arteriosclerosis? How many words will he be able to produce upon request? Is he certain about the date and the day of the week? At what point of failure in these cognitive tasks will we conclude that he is "psychotic?" How much about the outer world of objects must a patient be able to comprehend, recognize, remember, and deal with effectively in order to be judged (psychiatrically and by his society) sound and responsible, even though his cognitive and adaptive tools may have been somewhat dulled and enfeebled by age or disease? Clearly such a judgment would have to reflect the degree of loss of function and the demands of adaptive requirements; it would have to be rendered in every given case in accordance with the special circumstances prevailing; it would never be a judgment of principle. The criterion of incapacity must be applied with circumspection in any attempt to define the concept "psychosis." A patient with a severe traveling phobia will be decisively incapacitated if his livelihood depends upon traveling; similarly, a patient who suffers from a neurotic sexual impotence or from homosexuality will be greatly incapacitated in an area of living that is of decisive importance for his mental health and happiness. Yet, in none of these instances is there any falsification of everyday reality or an incapacity in comprehending it. A neurosis may be totally disabling, by itself and because of the circumstances under which the patient has to live; but it will not be considered "malignant" if it is judged by theoretical and academic standards of psychopathology. A patient who suffers from a mild and stationary form of simple schizophrenia may well be much less incapacitated while he is performing routine work, under benevolent supervision, and has little opportunity to become involved in conspicuous conflict or controversy with the world of objects. This situation, of course, arises from the blunting and passivity of his emotional potential.

There is one more consideration with regard to the meaning of the concept "psychosis." We must be careful not to confuse the *enormity* of an aspect of behavior with its *malignancy*. Here the psychiatrist might be treading (or should we say trespassing?) into delicate and controversial ground. Let us take the example of murder in the first degree—the unbridled and carefully premeditated and deliberately unleashed aggression of homicide. Already we have made a social judgment, we have defined a crime. In most of us murderous impulses are either repressed (and thus remain "unconscious excitations" without access to "motility") or are rendered ineffective by the various possibilities of symptom formation or aim-inhibited discharge. The "nonpsychotic murderer" distorts neither the facts nor the demands of reality; the former he weighs carefully and accurately, the latter he ignores or considers merely as a calculated risk. If our conception of psychosis rests upon the presence of a distortion of the symbolic process in the broad area of the object, the "non-I" component of the symbol, then such an act of murder in the first degree—while "enormous"—is, psychiatrically speaking, not "malignant."

Even in the case of far less dramatic forms of behavior than murder great difficulties arise when we attempt to sort such aspects as "enormity" and "'malignancy." As psychiatrists we often ask ourselves whether a certain patient is dangerous to himself or to others, and at times society asks us this same question and takes action in accordance with our answer. We all know that certain character neuroses, theoretically "benign" conditions, can be highly destructive both to the patient and to his family. History itself offers a melancholy catalogue of victims who either could not tell false gods from true devils, or, if they could, were helpless to escape their influence. It is indeed rare that a person or a group of persons will be destroyed by a schizophrenic, apart from an occasional and isolated victim.

SOME DIFFERENTIATIONS

Against this background of so many ambiguous and qualifying statements it may indeed place one in a precarious position to offer a definition of "psychosis," despite the fact that the experienced clinician is not likely to come to grief in his judgment and treatment of the patient on such grounds. I suggest that we make a distinction between the qualitative and the quantitative aspect of this issue. Qualitatively we recognize the existence of a distinct form of psychopathology which we designate the *psychotic process*. We hypothesize that it differs in principle from other forms of psychopathology. Its criteria tend to be theoretical rather than clinical-pragmatic. Quantitatively we recognize the existence of a loss of the reality-testing capacity of the ego of such a degree as to render the patient incapable of autonomy. If—owing to the lack of a better term—a semantic ambiguity will be pardoned, we may say (in accordance with a clinical colloquialism) that such a patient has regressed into the *"psychotic" stage* of his illness. In this contingency the criteria tend to be clinical-pragmatic rather than theoretical.

Qualitatively, the psychotic process consists in the pathological transformation and replacement of one or several aspects of the outer world of objects and their verbal, ideational, and affective equivalents. This transformation and replacement is the result of an ascendancy of normally contained and archaic cognitive and affective psychic forces and potentials. It occurs in accordance with the inherent qualities of these forces and potentials. In the psychotic process it is not so much a question of what the patient has lost, but of what has been set free.

Quantitatively, the stage of "psychotic" decompensation may result either from an intensification of the psychotic process as defined, or else a patient may enter the "psychotic" stage of a mental illness that is primarily the result of dissolution within the conflict-free ego sphere—

such as dementia or delirium. In that case it is much more a question of what the patient has lost rather than what, in addition, may be set free. In either case the patient will no longer be able to deal with the outer world of objects, of tangible, noncontroversial everyday reality, but in each of these two contingencies for a different reason. If one may use a simile one could say that the patient with dementia sees *too little* of the outer world or has to look at it at close range—*concretely*, as we call it, like a myopic. But the schizophrenic sees *too much* of it, and what he sees is distorted, like the images of the astigmatic.

A delusion is usually defined as a false belief which can not be attributed either to results of the patient's upbringing or to cultural influences; its morbidity from this point of view lies in the fact that it is not an aspect of the character structure of the patient. In the following we will attempt to present the issue of delusions from the formal rather than the dynamic angle. We will examine the nature and validity of the various criteria of delusions as well as the degrees of intensity and malignancy. These steps will enable us to make correlations with various nosological entities in which delusions and other false beliefs are found, and to discuss the clinical problems of differential diagnosis. We will stress much less those factors which determine the particular content of delusions and other false beliefs (such as the patient's early and subsequent life experiences and their interaction with his biological make-up).

As delusions are false beliefs we should at the outset present a definition of what a belief is. A belief is defined as a *feeling* of truth or as a conviction of truth based on *faith*. But there is also *clinical* evidence that a delusion is at its core a form of psychopathology born of a morbid affect. This fact will become clearer if we recognize the difference between what Bleuler called the "basic" or primary delusion in contrast to secondary or accidental ones. The latter are resorted to by the patient in order to rationalize, prove, and reinforce his basic delusion. Bleuler states quite clearly: "The basic delusion . . . develops only under affective influences. . . ."[6] The question is often asked whether a delusion is a thought disorder. The basic delusion is not anything of that kind. It is the verbal expression of a morbid feeling, an affect masquerading as a thought. A patient who believes that he is being persecuted by the F.B.I. or that he is God may state his conviction without any disorganization of the formal aspects of thought and language, even if he should be a schizophrenic; if he should suffer from (nonschizophrenic) paranoia, he will certainly be free of a formal thought disorder. The inability to organize thought is not the same as the inability to judge its validity and truth. The situation is quite different in the case of the secondary or accidental delusions that are almost always present.

Here the affective pressure inherent in the primary delusion forces the patient to interpret his environment either by the application of paleologic reasoning, such as predicative identification, or by delusional perceptions in which formal thought disorder may well play a significant role. Thus it is only in regard to these secondary delusions in and through which the patient vainly attempts to square reality with his primary delusion that he will, and must, resort to pathological reasoning or thought processes. These ancillary pathological processes deserve to be presented in some detail, and in conjunction with clinical illustrations.

Whenever we attempt to explain to ourselves an observation or event which attracts our attention we do so by trying to determine its cause as well as its purpose. Deterministic causality is cognitive, objective, and impersonal; a passing car on a rainy day will splash me with water if I stand too close to it. Most people will reason along such lines in this situation without assigning evil intent to the driver; they may curse the effect but they will not suspect intent. Whatever degree of anger or helplessness may be felt is reactive and has been fully determined by an appropriately provocative event rather than by a pathological and pre-existing affective or characterological sensitivity. Deterministic causalty is, of course, maximally objective, cognitive, and impersonal during, let us say, a scientific investigation of natural phenomena or in mathematics. But there exists another form of causality which is much closer to affectivity and subjectivity. It has been referred to by Arieti as teleological causality because the observer "looks for a cause in a personal motivation or an intention."[7] If pathological and pre-existing delusional or characterological beliefs determine the interpretation of an event, a purpose will be suspected when none was intended, and a personal reference inferred when none existed. This imposition of affective subjectivity upon an indifferent object or event is known as *projected psychological causality.* A patient with a primary paranoid delusion will readily and with the aid of projected psychological causality form secondary delusions of persecution. In such an instance we are dealing with an inferiority of reasoning, a paleologic regression that, as a phenomenon, is quite common. It is important to recognize that it may manifest itself in various degrees of malignancy; we see the effects of this form of paleologic "thoughtless" reasoning in the countertransference, in which case the causes are usually unconscious; we also see it in the behavior and the false beliefs of patients with character neurosis, and with an increasing display of incongruity in psychosis.

A patient may find confirmation of a primary delusion's validity by still another method of paleological reasoning which is known as *predicative identification.* Whereas the normal logical mind establishes an identity on the basis of identical "subjects," a delusional patient may accept as valid an identity which is based merely on one or more common predicates. Predicates are either certain physical qualities of an object or any conceivable fact or event in the person's life; predicates of contiguity refer to simultaneity of occurrence or contiguity of space. The principle of "subjective identification" is known as the Von Domarus principle, after the man who first proclaimed it. It should be noted that normal people adhere to this principle automatically, but that violation of it in the form of predicative identification is not by any means restricted to delusional patients in their attempts and need to justify their primary delusions. An example will illustrate the application of the Von Domarus principle and its paleologic regression in the form of predicative identification. To quote Arieti: "if a normal man is told, 'All men are mortal; Socrates is a man,' this normal person will be able to conclude, 'Socrates is mortal.' "[8] On the other hand, if given the major premise "Every President of the United States is a person who was born in the United States," and also the minor premise "John Doe was born in the United States" (a fact which is only *one* of many of John Doe's predicates), it will normally be noted that the minor premise is not contained in the major one; nevertheless, a person resorting to predicative identification would illogically conclude that John Doe *is* the President of the United States. A person with mediocre intelligence who is incapable of and unaccustomed to the application of logical thought may also draw such an erroneous conclusion. In a delusional patient, predicative identification comes about in a different way. His primary delusion is by necessity at variance with reality. But the strong affective psychopathology of the primary delusion demands verification derived from his observation of that very same reality. In addition, there may be, as Arieti has suggested, a decrease in the efficiency of the highest levels of mentation. Predicative identification would seem to be the "ideal" way to prove identity of causes, motivations, and meaning—even in situations in which none exists; all that needs to be done is to find flimsy similarities (predicates) to support weighty conclusions and connections. The wider the gap between the irrelevance of the predicative link and the significance of the conclusion of identity, the more malignant is the process of predicative identification. Thus a paranoid schizophrenic who has been dismissed from his job will kill *any* person who is still employed by that firm, and in fact he may kill a person merely because he saw him enter the building which houses the business. Here the coincidence of spatial contiguity (predicate) replaces the essential identity of the boss who had dismissed the patient. Predicative identification need not always spring from an intense morbid affect and lead to such disastrous results. It may in some instances be closer to a formal thought disorder than to thoughtless affective reasoning. Bleuler[9] reported a schizophrenic who, when a table was removed from his bedside, remarked, "Farewell, I am Christ!" Bleuler comments: "The leave-taking, obviously in reference to the table, arouses in him the image of Jesus. For this patient, the enormous differences between Jesus' farewell and his bidding farewell to a table, do not come into play . . . but the minimal similarity of the patient's situation with that of Christ suffices . . . to make him identify with Christ."[9] There is probably a gradual transition in a patient's resorting to predicative identification from an affective need to verify a primary delusion to the mere drawing of a false conclusion which may well be fleeting and of little or no affective significance. One of my patients once smilingly remarked to me when he noticed that I was swivelling in my chair: "You must have spoken to Dr. G., he also swivels in his chair."

In most instances delusional patients enlist the paleological reasoning of predicative identification because of the affective pressures inherent in the primary delusion. Bleuler states:

If such false conclusions are to generate delusions the concurrence of affective factors is of course necessary. . . . The patient refers a perception, on the basis of inadequate logical reasons, to a complex which happens to be in the foreground of his interest at the time. The *delusion of reference* ("pathological self-reference") can be seen in their crassest form in schizophrenia.[10]

What Bleuler here calls "crass" is what we meant by the term "malignant," or by the significance of the width of the gap between the irrelevance of the predicative link and the significance of the conclusion. Bleuler reports on this point one of his own observations. "A child passes in front of the patient; he protests, 'I am not the father of this child.' "[10] This is indeed a crass instance of predicative identification; "*a child*' is being equated with "*my* child" merely on the basis of the predicative link of simultaneity and contiguity. It does not appear to be unreasonable to assume that the patient may have felt that he was, or would be, accused of having fathered a child.

In a more subtle manner, but also for affective reasons, predicative identification underlies the deplorable tendency toward what is referred to as "guilt by association." The intrinsic inferiority of predicative identification as a means of testing reality is also underlined by Freud's discovery of the primary process and its manifestations in the dream work. Displacement, substitution by allusion, and symbolization are examples. In the first two instances a dream element is modified by the addition of a feature or attribute ("predicate") which belongs to an element not directly represented in the dream. In accordance with the demands of the censorship, the dreamer is not supposed to "get the hint"—but in the subsequent process of interpretation of the dream the intended *pars pro toto* identification will become evident. As to symbolization, it will suffice to mention, as one of many similar examples, that in the view of Freud any object capable of containing something, such as a room or a ship, may stand for the female sexual apparatus; the quality of "capable of containing" constitutes the predicative link.

In the preceding presentation we have attempted to show how secondary delusions must, under affective pressure from the primary delusion, resort to paleological reasoning, either in the form of projected psychological causality, or of predicative identification. A different psychological problem presents itself in the case of so-called delusional perceptions. "In delusional perception an abnormal significance, usually in the sense of self-reference, despite the absence of any emotional or logical reason, is attributed to a normal perception."[11] Thus K. Schneider[12] had a patient who saw a dog lift its front paw and who "knew" immediately that this signified that he (the patient) was being persecuted. Because we have no information as to how and why the patient drew this particular conclusion from that particular observation, we are confronted with the problem of how to account for a quite incomprehensible connection. There must, of course, be what Schneider called a "link from the normal perception to the unusual significance." Two possibilities are offered as follows.

Distortion by Semantic Disorder. The formal thought and language disorder seen in schizophrenic dementia may distort the verbal representation of a perception in such a way as to become the link to the pre-existing primary delusion. Desymbolization of the word, semantic shift, and system shifting may become the catalytic event which will cause or facilitate the emergence of affectively determined delusional content in connection with such a perception. The "linoleum incident" described by Fish and quoted in Chapter 14 is such an example. Another illustration of such a possibility is reported by Bleuler: "During a meal, a catatonic is asked by his sister whether he wants some more bread; in a wild rage he wants to stab her because she thus referred to his unemployed status. (In German his 'breadlessness')."[13] The operative thought disorder which served as the catalytic event for the delusional interpretation seems to be in the area of system shifting, from the literal "being without bread during a meal" to the figurative "being unable to keep body and soul together." On the other hand, Bleuler thought that "the releasing factor" was the reference to the emotionally charged complex of the patient. However, in another passage he does state that often words will satisfy the need for causal explanations. Another patient of Bleuler "saw an epileptic girl fall down in one of her convulsive attacks. He accused himself of trying to rape her; she fell during the struggle."[14] Unfortunately, the patient's own explanation for his conclusion is not given. Most specifically in the German language "a fallen girl" is one who has sinned in the sexual sphere. Thus if the double meaning of the word "fallen" provided the catalytic event for emergence of the delusional self-accusation in connection with perceiving the seizure, we would then have an example of a semantic shift's constituting the link in delusional perception. Further research is required to substantiate this hypothesis and the patients' own explanatory comments would seem all that is necessary. The latitude of ideational possibilities afforded by desymbolization of the word, semantic shift, and system shifting, all of which are found in the schizophrenic thought and language pathology is, of course, in sharp contrast with the semantic stringencies of logical thought and language, and this very latitude becomes the trap in this particular possibility for delusional perceptions.

Sudden Delusional Perceptions.   It is much more difficult to account for those sudden (or "apophanous," as Conrad called them) delusional perceptions that remain incomprehensible, so it seems, regardless of our efforts to find an explanation from various quarters. There is no pre-existing morbid affect to which one can ascribe what Fish[15] called the abnormal consciousness of significance that occurs in connection with a given experience. No link based on the verbal representation of the perception—however transmogrified owing to the presence of a thought and language disorder—either exists or can be elicited. The suddenness with which the "establishment of a reference without cause" (Gruhle) comes about has in addition the quality of an apparition; Conrad therefore suggested the term "apophany" for this phenomenon. The previously mentioned patient who knew that he was being persecuted when he saw a dog lift its paw is such an example (at least as long as the patient has not supplied a link of the kind we are looking for). Bleuler has observed similar instances in which "the delusions seem to emerge 'primordially' from the unconscious in their complete and finished form."[16] Thus one of his patients heard a rumbling noise; she thereupon concluded that the Prince of France (who otherwise played no particular role in her ideas) had been murdered.[17] The incomprehensibility in delusional perception resembles that of the manifest dream. Furthermore, in both situations we are dealing with visual perceptions, images, pictures—at least predominantly so. We also know the abstract ideas of the latent dream content have been transformed into concrete images, both pictures and visible events. In this process (known as the dream work), condensation, plastic representation, symbolization, and displacement of psychological accent create an array of nonverbal representations the extent and potential ramifications of which are almost without limitation. When we said before that the latitude of ideational possibility afforded by the schizophrenic dementia at the *verbal* level is considerable, the latitude of meanings inherent in the *pictorial* dream images is incomparably greater. We propose that in delusional perception the schizophrenic *reverses* the direction of the psychological processes of dreaming by transforming rational pictures into irrational ideas, and that he does so by resorting to mental mechanisms similar to those employed in the dream work. It is important that we should not confuse the schizophrenic *language of pictures* with metaphoric or poetic *figures of speech*. We may say metaphorically: "The jowls of the Russian winter devoured Napoleon's Grand Army." This expression is a metaphoric abstraction, not to be taken literally; it is intended to be a comparison, not an identity. The Russian winter has no jaws and no French soldier was devoured, although many froze to death. Most important, the metaphor and any other form of normal symbolic representation through language takes place independent of the presence of the perceptual image to which the symbolization addresses itself. By contrast, delusional perception can occur only in response to a present perception or event. The following is an example which may be considered a suitable counterpart. Alfred Storch reports how "a schizophrenic suffering from persecutory delusions cast anxious glances at a moving door and exclaimed: 'The animals are eating me.' The anxious affective attitude of the patient to all movements in the environment caused her to include the harmless act of opening the door under her guiding idea of 'devouring.' "[18] Storch also points out that "upon occasion a doorway may be called the jaws of a monster."[18] Apophanous delusional perceptions of schizophrenics may be, but need not be accompanied by a formal (verbal) thought and language disorder. The patient's belief in the validity of his parasymbolically expressed interpretation does not seem to be different from the belief of the ordinary dreamer in the reality of his dream. In either case it would appear that an affective need sustains the deception.

Factors in Delusion

Let us at this point recall that we had raised the question whether a delusion is a thought disorder. I think that we are now in a position to improve the formulation of this issue. The relevant question is: What role may be assigned to formal (verbal) thought and language disorder, to paleologic reasoning, and to autistic parasymbolic distortion in the origin, expansion, and expression of the secondary ("explanatory") delusion? The wider the gap between the content of the delusional beliefs and the facts—and, indeed, possibilities of reality—the more regressive or "malignant" must be the psychopathological mechanisms required to bridge it. We have seen how projected psychological causality—a mild form of emotional, subjective reasoning—exists both in psychopathology and in human frailty. We have tried to demonstrate that predicative identification as a paleologic phenomenon may be resorted to in different degrees of malignancy, ranging from its socially accepted and shared ritualistic application to its use as an autistic and socially incomprehensible method of attempting to prove a nonexisting identity. We have shown how verbal thought and language pathology may act as a catalytic agent in the mobilization of a morbid affect, and how in apophanous delusional perception the most primordial and regressive parasymbolic distortions (in the form of a "language of pictures") have attained more than parity with their affective confederates.

We must therefore conclude that the source and core of every delusion is an affective abnormality—regardless of the presence or prominence of pathological language, or the reasoning or symbolizations in and through which the delusions are verbalized. Any of these cognitive abnormalities may noticeably recede into the background whenever a schizophrenic, as of the moment, may not be under the affective influence of his complexes. But "for the construction of the 'phantasy reality' . . . the archaic primitive thought forms are very useful foundations, because they alone possess the necessary elasticity to permit the erection of his tottering thought world. . . ."[19] To this we would only add that although the thought world may be tottering, its affective underpinnings and foundations are solid. The prevailing intensity of affect may influence the phenomenology of delusions in various ways. Delusions may be transient or abortive if the affective pressure is only temporary; conversely, if the morbid affect is prolonged and sufficiently intense, paranoid ideation that otherwise may have consisted merely in fugitive ideas of reference may expand into irreversible delusions of persecution and spread by an increasing elaboration of secondary explanatory delusions to encompass a very considerable portion of the patient's mental content. This process is known as "systematization of delusions of persecution." Similar features are found in the phenomenology of delusions based on feelings of unworthiness or grandiosity. It is also well to remember that after electric shock treatment or prefrontal lobotomy—both of which tend to reduce, or may even extinguish, the morbid affect—the patient no longer believes in the truth of his former delusions and also ceases to act in accordance with them, although he will remember the now-ineffective verbal shell in which they had previously been encased.

THE RELATIVITY OF REALITY

We intend, of course, to restrict the meaning of this sub-heading to the question of what we mean when we say that the belief which a patient entertains is "false." The issue has already been rendered somewhat contentious by our use of the designation "patient." If he is a "patient," he is automatically a member of a minority and, in a manner of speaking, its only representative. No one else shares his beliefs; thus he must be wrong. *Realities* may be decided by the will or the vote of a majority, but not *reality*. Impartial observation does not support the conclusion that beliefs are true merely because a majority, even an overwhelming majority, entertains them. As will be presently shown, difficulties arise as soon as the concept "reality" is applied in connection with phenomena which are (to whatever degrees) in their essence, intangible, impossible of proof, or difficult to prove, and hence controversial and in any event outside the sphere of "everyday reality." Equally important to our theme of the psychiatric judgment with respect to the existence and malignancy of false beliefs is our recognition of the fact that both *cognitive* and *affective* limitations may interfere with the appraisal of *any* aspect of reality; if this is so, the psychopathologist will have to make a significant distinction between these two contingencies. A few illustrations may be given for clarification.

Let us consider the steady advancement of our interpretation and understanding of reality in the sciences. Science is, of course, a mental activity rooted in cognition, objectivity, and (ultimately) in perceptual evidence. A solid discovery, while often merely adding evidence to previously established truths, may on occasion prove yesterday's "truths" to have been false. Further, discoverers—particularly great ones—are always a minority. But this is not the main issue. Scientists do not have, or ought not to have, an emotional investment in their appraisal of reality or truth with regard to scientific data and their possible meaning. One would expect that scientists would welcome any correction of an error. But if there should be an emotional investment, the discovery of a contradictory truth may be ignored. The history of science contains many poignant examples of the humiliation and even the martyrdom of the discoverer. It may be just as difficult to correct errors as it is to remedy false beliefs; but the latter may be more dangerous to him who will make the attempt. In a psychiatric sense cognitive limitations do not result in false beliefs or delusions, but in errors or false conclusions. In children—owing to the normal cognitive limitations of their ego and, at times, because of ignorant encouragement by their elders—

false beliefs and conclusions are frequent and are in no way comparable to the delusions or false beliefs of adults. It is normal for a child of a certain age to believe in the various myths about birth; but if an adult woman believes herself to be pregnant because a man accidentally touched her arm, she is suffering from a malignant delusion. A four-year-old child once asked where milk came from and was told it came from the cow. She then added spontaneously: "And coffee comes from the horse because the horse is brown." This is not a thought disorder; in a child of that age, as in primitive man, this is merely an example of the predominantly sensory or perceptual character of the thought processes, which in these instances are much more under the domination of images than of ideas. The cognitive limitations inherent in the formal thought and language disorder of schizophrenia may likewise lead at times to false conclusions that are only minimally related to affectivity. One of my patients, when asked how much $1 + 1$ was, replied "three." There is a reason why I have just used both numerals and a "verbal" form of "three." When I asked him to explain his answer, he said: "When two people get together they have a baby, so there are three now." The patient had slipped from the abstract numerical frame of reference into a more concrete one, the particular choice of which was very likely codetermined by a sexual image. I would not call his false conclusion a false belief.

Delusions and false beliefs are the result of those *affective* limitations the psychopathology of which we have discussed in the previous sections of this chapter. We also suggested that, while every delusion is a false belief, not all false beliefs are to be equated with delusions. In general and practical clinical terms we may say that (1) delusions are contradicted by what we have called tangible, noncontroversial, everyday reality; (2) that their content is not shared by contemporary society and is not part of the culture in which the patient lives or grew up; and (3) that the patient himself did not, prior to the onset of his mental illness, entertain such beliefs. The very opposite features characterize most nondelusional false beliefs. In the latter, so frequently seen in neurotic illnesses and neurotic character deformations, the distortion of reality affects not so much tangible or objective reality as it does the formation of judgments and feelings of truth with respect to matters that are less tangible, more subjective, socially determined, and often arbitrary. It may not be an overstatement to say, within this context, that cosmic reality is quite different from man-made realities.

There are different aspects of reality which a patient who entertains delusions or other false beliefs may falsify; there are also degrees of malignancy in such distortions of reality. We will present four categories of criteria which can guide the clinical psychiatrist in evaluating the nature and significance of "false beliefs." We recognize that the ultimate judgment is the result of both aggravating and attenuating factors within these proposed categories of criteria.

Possible and Impossible Delusions

In the case of a "possible" delusion, the content is "false" as a result of psychopathology—but it *could* be true, both from the point of view of logic and general experience. Many elderly patients with senile or arteriosclerotic psychosis accuse their relatives of conspiring to steal their money or other possessions, of "railroading" them into mental institutions, or of poisoning their food. Singly or in concert, fear of the future in the presence of increasing and obvious helplessness to cope with the demands of the present, resentment concerning loss or curtailment of autonomy, and the partial release of previously contained tendencies toward suspiciousness may lead to the emergence and expression of such paranoid delusions. They are characterized by a certain simplicity of substance and lack of eccentricity, and have at times been described as being "pedestrian." Their unimaginative character may derive partly from the general dearth of ideation, but may also reflect the fact that there is no "breakthrough" of the primary process in simple organic dementia. The content of a delusion may be an event that would be rather unlikely to occur, but it still could be "possible." Let us consider delusions of jealousy. An elderly man believes that his wife, in her early 60s, has sexual relations with another man. We would call such a believe a "possible" delusion for a number of reasons. First, while it is unlikely to happen at her age, it is certainly possible. But let us also assume, as is often the case in such situations, that the husband is either impotent because of his advanced age, or has noted evidence of declining sexual power. He may then feel inferior as a male and suspicious of other men who are still sexually vigorous. His delusion of jealousy would then be "possible" because it is also *understandable*. In referring to Jaspers' hypothesis of *verstehende* (comprehensible) psychology, Fish would call the husband's false belief a "delusion-like idea" that "can be understood as secondary to some other psychological change, such as an endogenous or reactive emotional state, unpleasant experiences. . . ."[20] We can project ourselves into the psychological state of a patient with such "possible" delusions and, while we do not share the false beliefs, they do not strike us as being outside the bounds of comprehensibility. Nevertheless, even a "possible" delusion is a delusional false belief because it contradicts that aspect of reality which is based on exteroceptive data; it is less malignant to distort a reality that is more subjective because it is based on enteroceptive data. (We will return to this issue later in this chapter.) "Possible" delusions are found both in schizophrenic and in nonschizophrenic psychoses; their presence, therefore, does not in itself rule out a diagnosis of dementia praecox. It must, however, be noted that a "possible" delusion may change into an "impossible" one if the patient's psychosis worsens in certain ways. Such a deterioration may be the result either of an intensification of the affective morbidity or the emergence of more malignant paleologic or formal thought pathology.

We have already said that an impossible and/or incomprehensible delusion is characteristic of schizophrenia. Admittedly, there may at times be some disagreement among clinical observers as to whether a certain delusional belief meets these somewhat subjective criteria, particularly with respect to the issue of comprehensibility. We tend to circumvent the problem by referring to the delusions of schizophrenics as "bizarre," "esoteric," and "recondite." However, such expressions of violent rejection of the illogical are insufficient because they do not define the special nature of the schizophrenic's unique incomprehensibility which we call *autism*. It is certainly illogical in the extreme to believe in astrology; yet such beliefs are quite common and in no way suggestive of schizophrenia. We propose that the decisive issue in schizophrenic incomprehensibility is not merely that of establishing a "reference without a cause," but to do so in a *manner* and in a *matter* that contemporary society is not prepared to accept.

Schizophrenic incomprehensibility results from the application of obsolete paleologic and parasymbolic distortions to tangible, everyday reality. Let us return for a moment to the example of astrology, the belief that the course or station of, say, the planets at a certain time, determines our fate. Anyone, even if he rejects the alleged significance of the horoscope, can follow and comprehend a line of thoughts which may perhaps run something like the following: "God, in whose hands our Fate rests, is in Heaven—Heaven and sky are in a way related, one to the other—I recall a line from Kipling, who referred to childhood as that beautiful time when sky was still Heaven—I will think now of the immutable courses and orbits of the celestial bodies, and by way of a metaphor of the immutable divine predetermination of Fate." None of these considerations and beliefs, however, will prevent a person from exercising common prudence in his daily activities, from trying to anticipate the possible consequences of his behavior, or from recognizing tangible reality for what it is. But if a schizophrenic has the delusion that an "influencing machine" causes him to say certain words or think certain thoughts, or that it produces certain alterations or transformations of his organs, then we are no longer dealing with such broad and somewhat intangible generalizations as divine guidance or wrath. The essential difference between the schizophrenic delusion of the "influencing machine" and the belief in astrology is that in the first instance one man's autism distorts and replaces tangible reality whereas in the second contingency mankind's emotional needs and conflicts (which as such are not different from those of the schizophrenic) are met and served by shared beliefs that neither distort nor replace tangible reality, but rather coexist side by side with it. If an ultimately organic alteration of brain function is accepted as the decisive factor in the causation and unfolding of the schizophrenic process we would have to conclude that even amongst the most primitive peoples whose everyday beliefs strike us as totally "impossible and incomprehensible," one of their own schizophrenics would find ways to express his autistic delusions; and that his fellow men would notice and react to his schizophrenic "impossible and incomprehensible" beliefs.

The Relative Reality of the Future

Much of the psychopathology of the neuroses consists in a psychodynamically predetermined distortion of future events. Certain aspects of the future are thus experienced by the patient as if they had already happened. The neurotic patient is usually aware of the fact that his affective apperceptive judgments about the future are, or might be, contradicted by alternative predictions which may be based on logic or an objective appraisal of the evidence. The awareness of contradiction is most pronounced in the case of patients who suffer from obsessive thoughts, which are one of several features of the obsessive-compulsive psychoneurosis. In his classical description of this type of neurosis Freud said: "it is . . . striking that in this condition the *'opposite values'* (polarities) pervading mental life appear to be exceptionally sharply differentiated."[21] The patients tell us that they "know" that their thoughts about dreadful future events are "silly," but that such "knowledge" does not remove the reality of the feeling. A patient can not rid herself of the belief that she will become blind; she does not bother to ask herself when, why, and how this dreaded event will occur. She does not even bother to have her eyes examined. She does not adduce evidence to support her obsessive thought. The psychological mechanisms of isolation and displacement are even more pronounced in those patients whose obsessive thoughts are, in their words, "silly," and they repudiate them without, however, being able to rid themselves of their grip. All obsessive thoughts, whether they pertain to the future or not, are ego-alien and in many instances we may consider them to be "affects without belief."

We will speak at this point of phobias within the limited context of the heading "The Relative Reality of the Future." We will also limit ourselves to those phobias which Freud called "specific phobias, the fear of special circumstances that inspire no fear in the normal man."[22] Such fears must therefore be rooted in falsifications and can not be considered to be mere exaggerations of "normal" fears. In a phobia an object or a situation is avoided because it is *felt* rather than *thought* to be dangerous to the patient. The patient feels that if he avoids the phobic situation he will thereby avoid its feared consequences. He has no specific idea, beyond the awareness of dread, as to what these consequences may be; at times he may come up with simple and transparent rationalizations. After a successful psychoanalysis he would, of course, realize that the phobic object or situation had represented, by various mechanisms of disguise, a very real danger during his childhood or early life.

Let us compare a food phobia that is a nondelusional false belief with a delusion that the food is poisoned. The delusional patient will elaborate on the identity, methods, and motivations of certain persons who have poisoned his food. His psychopathology expresses itself in a paranoid distortion of the past, which is, together with the present, the only unequivocal reality; it is, so to speak, "on the record." The future, on the other hand, while predictable to a certain degree, has still to become reality and will in fact become reality only when and after it has happened. The patient with the delusion that his food is poisoned will avoid eating it just as the patient with a food phobia does. However, in the latter case the psychological emphasis is not on the past, but on the future consequences of exposing himself to the phobic object or situation. There is also another reason why the phobia is not a malignant false belief. The phobic patient has, of course, no explanation for his fear of the food; he abstains both from the food and from rendering a judgment. Thus he can not arrive at false conclusions or beliefs at the expense of tangible reality. To paraphrase the old saying that the good people content themselves with dreaming about what the wicked do, we may add that the phobic patients content themselves with remaining blinded to what the delusional patient falsely sees.

In the character neuroses the patients' affective apperceptive judgments and anticipations of consequences—particularly in the sphere of interpersonal relations—are so strongly woven into the pattern of their personality structure that we must consider them to be ego-syntonic. Thus a young man will, as a result of powerful unconscious negative affects concerning heterosexual activity, falsely believe that any woman would receive and reject his sexual advances with disdain. If his sexual inhibition is the result of a feeling of sexual inadequacy he will anticipate the woman's rejection accompanied and compounded by derision. Other patients anticipate that an expression of any of their most reasonable requests or requirements would invariably arouse the annoyance or anger of the other person. In these instances, as in innumerable similar ones, the patients have little or nothing to offer in evidence that their respective anticipations of a future event are based on identical experiences in the past—as far, or rather as little, as they know it. We consider these false beliefs benign because they represent themselves as a distorted appraisal of a future event. We shall presently suggest even more compelling reasons why the false beliefs of neurotics are not malignant and therefore not delusional, as we use this term.

Exaggeration and Falsification

It seems to be a reasonable assumption that the mere exaggeration of the significance of an awareness would be a less malignant psychological event than an outright falsification of identity or meaning of reality. Clinical experience and psychiatric consensus support this assumption, with some qualifications. The inaccurate beliefs of neurotic patients do not entail falsifications of the sort we encounter in the delusional beliefs of psychotic patients. But, as is true so often, matters are not quite so simple under the scrutiny of theoretical and even clinical investigation as the respective entries in the dictionary would make us believe. We recall that Freud distinguished between common and special phobias. The former he described as "an exaggerated fear of all those things that everyone detests or fears to some extent: such as night, solitude, death . . . etc."[23] In the case of special phobias such as agoraphobia or food phobia, it appears that some transformation has taken place which *amounts* to a falsification, but which in a significant sense is not a falsification at all. We have already spoken of the difference between a "cat phobia" and a delusion about cats (see page 132). In the case of a special phobia, which is not a malignant process, a "falsification" has occurred at the level and within the domain of the unconscious—for instance, by the mechanism of displacement, desexualization, etc.—but the all-important "non-I" component of the symbolic process has not been falsified. Thus the term falsification, as used in this context, applies only to the object.

Let us consider another example. An apprehensive neurotic will take a more serious view of the possible consequences of even the slightest violation of his ego-ideal, or of the "letter of the law" of the land, than a normal person would. As therapists we know that the intensity of his reaction, while exaggerated as far as the occasion is concerned, is quite commensurate with the aggrandizement of his idealized image, or the rigor of his conscience. At this point we are merely dealing with an exaggerated feeling of either shame or guilt; the patient will, in effect, say that he feels *very* ashamed or *very* guilty. Again, the "falsification" remains unconscious. It consists of his unknowingly equating an innocuous present-day violation with a more virulent one of the past. But a more malignant falsification would have to be diagnosed if the preconditions, as described, would lead either to a paranoid distortion of any aspect of the outer world of objects in reference to the present violation, or to an equally malignant internalization of the same psychodynamic process. In the event of the latter course, we hypothesize that the superego "persecutes" the ego in retaliation for the offense, and an act of suicide, should it take place, could be considered as having replaced the delusion of being killed by others. We know, of course, that in many clinical instances the situation is not quite so unequivocal and that considerable fluidity and interaction of several criteria have to be considered. But it may, nevertheless, be useful to have drawn a distinction between exaggeration and falsification, provided that didactic attempts at clarity do not lead to clinical inflexibility.

Transcendent Beliefs

Despite the somewhat philosophical flavor of this subheading, beliefs of this kind are those that are most commonly encountered by the practicing psychiatrist, and particularly by the psychoanalyst. We propose to consider two possible meanings of the term "transcendent." The dictionary defines it as being something which is beyond the limits of all knowledge. In this restricted sense we may briefly refer to what Masserman[24] called man's "Ur-defenses" and "Ur-delusions" of his invulnerability, his immortality and of man's kindness to man. Masserman even suggested that man, or at least most men, may be better equipped to deal with their primordial anxieties with the aid of these transcendent beliefs.[24] But more relevant to our immediate purpose of finding criteria for an evaluation of the clinical character and malignancy of false beliefs are those somewhat transcendent feelings of truth which neurotic patients entertain about what is right or wrong, good or bad, adequate or inadequate, worthwhile or worthless, superior or inferior. Before giving a few illustrations of these commonplace phenomena we wish to state that from an academic and theoretical point of view, false beliefs of this kind are benign. The reality under dispute is intangible and many of these false (or at least "unwholesome") beliefs are shared by others; furthermore, the "reality" of value judgments is entirely man-made—men can, and have, reversed them. The distortion is in the "image," which is closer to the "I" component of the symbolic process;

it is not in the "object," which alone represents the "non-I" component. Also, in contrast to delusions, value judgments—even if acquired later in life—are not episodic but, rather, are permanent components of the character structure.

The following is a brief and abridged account of a patient's character structure and his distorted value judgments, in this instance in the sexual sphere. It is from our point of view representative of a vast number of neurotic problems. The patient is a 26-year-old single man whose presenting symptom consisted of an inability to urinate in the presence of other men, as for instance in a public toilet. At such moments he felt embarrassed because he realized that any man present could notice his difficulty from the absence of the splashing noise which signifies urination. There was not the slightest evidence at any time of delusional thinking or of ideas of reference. In the course of treatment it became increasingly obvious that the patient entertained certain beliefs on such issues as "masculinity," "sinfulness of sexual activity," being a "good" son, having a "good" mother. Specifically, he believed that women do not desire sexual intercourse, but merely "endure" it, although he "knew" that this was not always true. He further believed that every act of intercourse was "mental rape" against the woman and therefore "bad," but that on the other hand sexual intercourse with as many girls as possible (with "no questions asked") was a desirable evidence of "masculinity" and virility—both of which he greatly coveted. He described his father as a physically powerful man, capable of intimidating everyone by a prodigious display of aggressiveness; he felt that his father would have little regard and respect for gentle and shy men, and would be outright contemptuous of men who could not impose their will upon a woman (particularly in the sexual area). By a most unfortunate contrast, his mother considers all sexual advances as "bestial" and an insult to the woman or wife. She has often told her son that it would be better never to be married, not to "make" children, and to be very "modest"—meaning that one should not expose one's body. She always praises him for being "mother's little helper" and the patient has in turn always been very much "devoted" to her and feels sorry and even horrified at the thought that she may be "exposed" to the "pain and disgrace" of conjugal sexual relations. Every psychiatrist is, of course, thoroughly familiar with the manner in which parental value judgments, in the sexual or any other area, are transmitted to (at times *visited upon*) the child, overtly and covertly. We recognize the importance of the mental mechanism of identification in the formation and deformation of the ego-ideal and of the character structure of the individual in general. It is tempting to extend the scope of the hazardous process of uncritical identification to the field of so-called mass psychology. A great deal of ink and blood has been spilled to bear witness to the tragic consequences of the peculiar type of surrender of personal autonomy to another person's authority and (at times) wicked will. This disastrous variety of surrendering one's individuality in exchange for an anonymous identity with evil, in whatever disguise, is the result of a miscarriage of what Koestler calls "self-transcendence."[25] This is what occurs in a way, on a much smaller scale, in the development of many neurotic traits. The power of parental values is too strong for the child, who is as yet incapable of independent judgment, unaware of alternatives, and at the same time susceptible to the highest degree. Later in life the self-transcending tendency may be equally indiscriminating in some people. Perhaps only very few can retain their *responsible* individuality in the face of social pressures or temptations. When we spoke earlier of a second possible meaning of the term "transcendent," we had this form of surrender in mind. In the field of psychopathology it is indeed paradoxical that a theoretically and potentially "benign" mental mechanism such as identification may nevertheless ruin a man's life merely because some such beliefs are significantly false. But who or what will ultimately determine whether a transcendent belief is "false?" As therapists we must be careful not to play God. It was Mephistopheles who mockingly wrote out a prophesy for the naïve student who had already surrendered himself to what he thought was Faust's presence: "You shall be like God knowing the difference between Good and Evil."

This is not a book on the goals and techniques of psychotherapy. But it may be said at this point that the psychotherapist may direct his efforts toward pointing out the disadvantageous consequences and the alien origins of such transcendent beliefs. As a physician he is much less interested in whether they are true than whether they work. In some patients some "false" beliefs do work.

REFERENCES

1. S. Freud. "The Interpretation of Dreams." *In: The Basic Writings of Sigmund Freud.* New York, Modern Library, 1936, p. 510 f.
2. L. S. Kubie. "The Distortion of the Symbolic Process in Neurosis and Psychosis." *Journal of the American Psychoanalytic Association, 1:* 1953, p. 59.
3. *Ibid.,* p. 72.
4. *Ibid.,* p. 79.
5. *Ibid.,* p. 81.
6. E. Bleuler. *Dementia Praecox or the Group of Schizophrenias.* New York, International Univer. Press, 1950, p. 382.
7. S. Arieti. "Schizophrenia: The Manifest Symptomatology, the Psychodynamic

and Formal Mechanisms." *In:* S. Arieti (ed.). *American Handbook of Psychiatry.* New York, Basic Books, 1959, vol. 1, 1959, p. 482.

8. *Ibid.,* p. 478.

9. E. Bleuler. *Op. cit.,*[6] 19.

10. *Ibid.,* p. 133.

11. F. J. Fish. *Schizophrenia.* Baltimore, Williams & Wilkins, 1962, p. 30.

12. K. Schneider. *Clinical Psychopathology.* New York, Grune & Stratton, 1959.

13. E. Bleuler. *Op. cit.,*[6] p. 134.

14. *Ibid.,* p. 123.

15. F. J. Fish. *Op. cit.,*[11] p. 30.

16. E. Bleuler. *Op. cit.,*[6] p. 135.

17. *Ibid.,* p. 133.

18. A. Storch. *The Primitive Archaic Forms of Inner Experiences and Thought in Schizophrenia.* Nervous and Mental Disease Monograph Series #36. New York and Washington, Nervous and Mental Disease Publishing Company, 1924, p. 10.

19. *Ibid.,* p. 36.

20. F. J. Fish. *Op. cit.,*[11] p. 29.

21. S. Freud. *A General Introduction to Psychoanalysis.* New York, Liveright, 1935, p. 230.

22. S. Freud. "Obsessions and Phobias: Their Psychic Mechanisms and Their Aetiology." *In: Collected Papers,* vol. 1. New York, Basic Books, 1959, pp. 128–137.

23. *Ibid.,* p. 136.

24. J. Masserman. "Faith and Delusion in Psychotherapy: The Ur-defenses of Man." *American Journal of Psychiatry, 110:* 324, 1953.

25. A. Koestler. *The Ghost in the Machine.* New York: Macmillan, 1967, p. 229.

10

The Epilepsies

A student of the history of psychiatry may fairly conclude
that the subject of epilepsy played a similar role in the
evolution and maturation of the thinking of Hughlings Jackson as did
the study of hysteria in the case of Freud. Being nature's experiment
in paroxysmal, "fast-motion" dissolution and evolution of function, epilepsy is quite naturally of immense interest to the clinical and neurophysiological psychiatric researcher and observer. Some epileptic phenomena, such as temporal-lobe seizures and epileptic automatisms,
present symptomatology that calls for special efforts and skills in differential diagnosis. The very fact that epileptic discharges will, depending
on their point of origin and subsequent spread, produce a great variety
of symptoms seems to make any attempt at defining the condition in
clinical terms difficult and even undesirable. However, the task of denoting the essence of the condition became quite feasible with the advent
of the science of electroencephalography. We can conclude that epilepsies are short lasting, paroxysmal, repetitive, and patterned alterations
of functions in the broad areas of awareness and reactivity; that the
particular features of these alterations are largely determined by the
location and spread within the central nervous system of the pathological
electrical discharges; and that epileptic paroxysms are accompanied by
distinct alterations in the electroencephalogram.

It is easier to state with clarity the general characteristics of all epileptic paroxysms than to find a relevant basis for their classification.
The traditional division into idiopathic and symptomatic forms appears
to rest on etiological considerations, but it actually merely reflects a
gap in our knowledge. We do not yet know what abnormality underlies
those "idiopathic" epileptic discharges which occur in the absence of
demonstrable, structural brain disease. But whatever their nature may
be we may be sure that they are, if viewed from the broad perspective
of etiological principle, the manifestations of defective and impersonal

mechanisms or alterations. They are thus just as "symptomatic" of organicity as all other forms of epilepsy with which they are still being contrasted.

Epileptic discharges have been classified in accordance with a significant distinction as to their origin within the central nervous system. If the epileptogenic focus is anywhere within the hemispheric gray matter the resulting seizure would be "focal," and its clinical manifestations would be determined by the particular cortical site involved. If, on the other hand, the epileptic discharge originates within the centrencephalic system—the hypothesized central integrating system of the higher brain stem—the ensuing seizure would be "centrencephalic" and, in Jackson's term, a "highest-level" seizure. The limitation of this classification lies in the clinical fact that seizures which begin as "focal" phenomena, such as temporal-lobe discharges, may spread subcortically into the centrencephalic system, thus terminating with automatism (a "highest-level" paroxysm). Nevertheless, it seems that despite the possibility of transitional spread, a classification based on the involvement, at least initially, of either cortical or centrencephalic structures is physiologically sound and clinically practicable. Accordingly we intend to discuss the epilepsies in the following order, after the arrangement of Penfield and Jasper,[1] with only slight modifications:

I. Seizures in which cortical (focal) phenomena are the initial or most important ictal event
   1. Motor and sensory seizures
   2. Temporal-lobe seizures
II. Centrencephalic seizures
   1. Petit mal
   2. Grand mal
   3. Psychomotor automatism or epileptic twilight state.

CORTICAL PHENOMENA

Motor Focal Seizures

If an epileptic discharge originates within the precentral gyrus and, in the course of its progression, remains confined to this pre-Rolandic area of motor representation, it will result in movements of the corresponding body parts on the contralateral side. The sequence of these movements reflects the order of progression of the cortical excitation. There will be no loss of consciousness. This is known as a Jacksonian seizure and its patterned progression as Jacksonian march. The precentral gyrus is the site of those motor representations which Jackson assigned to the middle level. He once remarked that the cortex knows nothing of muscles and that it knows only of movements. Yet, the movements produced during Jacksonian seizures are incoordinate and "there is no evidence of any difference in response between skilled and unskilled individuals, old and young."[2] This is the first occasion in this presentation to point out that epileptic phenomena are neither in the service of ideational expression nor of symbolic representation. It is, of course, a well-known clinical fact that in Jacksonian (motor) seizures those body territories which are capable of the most delicate and potentially most skilled motor performances are the ones most likely to be affected: the thumb–index finger combination, the mouth area, and the great toe. They are the "leading parts" because they have the widest anatomical representation at the middle level and, also, "because the movements concerned have the widest fields of low threshold excitability."[3] We assign to these areas and functions in the context of epilepsy merely an anatomical and physiological ascendancy. In front of the precentral gyrus are the so-called adversive fields, the cortical centers for lateral gaze. The discharge during Jacksonian fits often spreads into these areas, which causes the eyes and head to turn in the opposite direction—away from the site of the cerebral irritation (adversive seizures). Jacksonian fits are almost in all instances indicative of a structural epileptogenic lesion and, therefore, are of great localizing value. Quite often they are followed by a generalized grand mal seizure with the discharge spreading subcortically into the centrencephalic system. In that case the Jacksonian fit is preictal; it constitutes an "aura."

Sensory Focal Seizures

Epileptic discharges that originate within, and remain confined to, the postcentral gyrus produce tingling or numbness and occasionally a sense of movement in the contralateral corresponding body territories. Almost every point of principle which was made in connection with Jacksonian (motor) seizures can be applied to their sensory counterpart. There will be a Jacksonian march, and if the excitation remains focal there will be no loss of consciousness. The middle-level nature of all sensory seizures, including those affecting the modalities of vision and hearing, is reflected in the fact that the ensuing sensations are "elementary;" the patient experiences the sensory qualities of the modality, but not the complex and compounded sensations which attend the perception of objects by touch, vision, or hearing. Thus it is debatable whether these epileptic sensations, which are sometimes referred to as "elementary hallucinations," should be designated as hallucinations at all. More important than this semantic ambiguity, however, is the unequivocal clinical significance in locating the lesion that causes these phenomena. Thus sensory focal seizures involving vision and causing the patient to experience flashes of light, colored lights, and at times even darkness going on to the point of blindness, are indicative of a focus at the arrival platform of visual impulses in the occipital lobe (area 17 of Brodmann). Many, but not all, patients experience these visual disturbances in the contralateral field.

Temporal-lobe Seizures*

Although the clinical expressions of epileptic discharges within the temporal lobe are, as subjective experiences of the patient, rather diverse, we can in each instance recognize the unitary features which characterize pathology that affects that part of the brain. Penfield and Jasper, who call temporal-lobe epilepsy a "psychical seizure,"[4] attribute to it a localizing value equal to that of sensory seizures or Jacksonian (motor) seizures. They also pair and compare temporal-lobe epilepsy with epileptic automatisms. In both disorders, significant alterations of function at the highest integrative level of the personality are noted; both, therefore, present themselves as psychic states and must be differentiated from similar, nonepileptic psychic states. In the patient with temporal-lobe epilepsy, the psychopathology is mainly within the realm of perceptual awareness and experience; the patient knows of his altered state, and for this reason the condition has been referred to as a "positive psychical state."[5] In the various epileptic automatisms, on the other hand, the psychopathology is in the sphere of conation, of reactivity and behavior; it is accompanied by irretrievable amnesia, and the patient knows nothing of what he did while under the attack. This, Penfield and Jasper contend, is a "negative psychical state." Temporal-lobe seizures are usually ictal; however, they may be followed by short-lasting automatism, or represent merely an aura to a grand mal seizure.

A temporal-lobe seizure will manifest itself by the paroxysmal and short-lasting appearance of any or all of the following phenomena: illusional perceptions; bursts of emotions, all of which are of an unpleasant quality; and hallucinatory states of a dreamlike nature but with consciousness preserved, and which if accompanied by olfactory hallucinations are known as "uncinate fits." In addition, we find in many instances of temporal-lobe epilepsy bouts of masticatory movements and occasionally attacks of so-called "forced thinking."

Illusional perceptions occur both with respect to objects and to the

* See also Chapter 7, "The Role of the Temporal Lobe."

patient's own self. Objects may appear larger than they are known to be (macropsia), and the patient has the feeling that they are close or are moving close to him. Or, objects are seen as being unusually small and as if far away (micropsia). Sounds may be heard louder and nearer, or from far away. There may be changes in the vividness of objects. One of my patients told me that during his attacks objects seemed to lose their tridimensional quality and appeared "flattened out." These altered perceptions of the physical attributes of objects never interfere with the *recognition* of the object; even in the case of illusions of unfamiliarity or estrangement the patient, in his state of ictal "double consciousness," recognizes the incongruity of his perceptual experience. The epileptic discharge apparently distorts that aspect in the perceptual process which is concerned with the scanning and recognition of what Ostow has called "the accidental parameters" of the object, without presenting interference in the area of pattern perception. Ostow says: "In the temporal lobe there is a mechanism that divides any perception into essential pattern and accidental parameters, so that the two sets of data may be used independently. For this reason focal temporal lobe seizures may evoke illusions limited to those sensory qualities that have to do with these accidental parameters."[6] Penfield and Jasper make this comment concerning the possible nature of the illusory perceptual alterations during these seizures:

It would seem that there is a ganglionic mechanism within the temporal cortex that is utilized in making such judgments [of accidental parameters] and that this mechanism has an organization that is somehow separate from the mechanisms utilized in the recording of contemporary experience. . . . when the interpretation mechanism becomes the site of epileptic discharge, a . . . change takes place in the subject's interpretation of sensations and experience. . . ."[7]

The illusions which we have so far described concerned themselves with rather tangible, indeed *physical* attributes of percepts. Less tangible and perhaps closer to an emotional experience are the alterations in the sphere of familiarity which occur during some seizures. As with all these phenomena, the reverse—a feeling of estrangement—may be noted. In these instances the doubly conscious patient becomes aware of an incongruity when he attempts to match a present perception or experience against its appropriate counterpart within his memory or, as Ostow calls it, against the "microcosmic representation" within the "ego supplement."[8] The *déjà vu* phenomenon as well as its opposite, the feeling of strangeness, are, of course, always experienced by the patient as puzzling events and at variance with his "better judgment;"

he knows whether the perception or situation ought or ought not to be familiar to him. This is the case even in those nonepileptic instances of *déjà vu* which are observed in patients suffering from hysterical illness. In the latter condition, however, the illusion of familiarity (or estrangement) is motivated and triggered by the psychodynamic suitability of the experience; in temporal-lobe epilepsy it is triggered by the fact of the seizure, and the sole importance of the situation lies in the coincidence of its occurrence.

Bursts of emotion are often the first sign of a temporal-lobe seizure. The patients may complain of a sudden feeling of fear, sadness, remoteness, or of a feeling too ineffable to be described by words. There is no obvious or existing relationship between these emotions and a cause other than the attack itself. It is significant that these emotions are never of a pleasurable character. All observers agree on that: "our experience [indicates that] neither localized epileptic discharge nor electrical stimulation is capable of awakening any such [pleasurable] emotion."[9] It may be recalled in this connection that "the psychic function of the temporal lobe is the formation of apperceptive judgments, especially negative ones,"[10] and that the arousal of unpleasurable affects is a very potent and reliable tool in making such negative judgments. It seems wholly likely that for this same reason the olfactory hallucinations during uncinate fits invariably are described as bad or disagreeable odors.

The elaborate hallucinatory states which occur in the course of temporal-lobe discharges correspond to what Hughlings Jackson called "dreamy states." He observed them with meticulous care and consummate clinical judgment and, like Penfield, compared them with epileptic automatisms—but from a different point of view. Jackson considered both phenomena to be "positive symptoms" that were *set free* during a state of partial dissolution of consciousness (negative symptom) brought about by the epileptic attack. He also noted that the patient during a "dreamy state" is doubly conscious but does not act, whereas the patient with automatism acts without having any consciousness of his actions. He described how a "dreamy state" may terminate in automatic behavior, and how it may merely be the aura for a grand mal. We now know that the electrically evoked recollective hallucinations of Penfield closely resemble in character and even in content the spontaneous seizures of these patients. (The reader is referred to the chapter on memory and memories for a detailed description of these recollective hallucinations.) As to the particular content of these psychical hallucinations the question may be asked whether—and if so, to what degree— that content represents a psychodynamically significant pattern and is determined by a psychodynamic priority. Are all these epileptic evocations the haphazard echoes of random electrical discharges, criss-crossing like the proverbial cat's paws the ganglionic keyboard of the memory cortex of the temporal lobe? Or is there significant meaning, or at least a preference, hidden in and behind these desultory apparitions? Research along these and related lines was suggested in the course of a discussion by Kubie of Penfield's work.[11] At this point we may attempt to make some comments on this broad question. We shall use two case reports of Penfield and Jasper[12] in connection with which they themselves raised the question of a psychological precipitation of an epileptic attack.

Case Studies.   The first patient was a girl of 14 when first seen because of seizures. History revealed that at the age of seven years she experienced fright when a man came up behind her. She ran across a meadow to seek refuge with her brother. Subsequently this scene was re-enacted in the form of nightmares. At the age of 11 she began to have "epileptic seizures in which she showed fright, screamed, and clung to people."[12] During the paroxysm of fright she "saw . . . a little girl identified as herself in the same meadow where the event occurred, and she was filled with terror lest she be struck . . . from behind."[12] Some of the seizures were followed by major convulsions, with temporary left-sided weakness and a transitory Babinski sign. Craniotomy revealed meningeal adhesions of the type that follows a subdural hemorrhage. It was assumed that this hemorrhage had occurred during infancy when she had had a single convulsion during a coma, after administration of a general anesthesia. At that time there had also been a short-lasting left hemiparesis. Cortical stimulation during craniotomy "initiated the visual hallucination of her ordinary attack."[12] Penfield and Jasper conclude:

It would seem reasonable to surmise that the same set of neuronal communications which was established that day in the meadow had served for memory, for "nightmare," and for seizure. The pathological condition established in infancy eventually gave rise to epileptic discharge in that region and the discharge took place along the neurone pattern established by a vivid experience.[12]

What is the relationship between the "epileptic discharge in that region" and "the neurone pattern established by a vivid experience?" How do electrodynamic and psychodynamic forces interact in such a situation? *Despite the fact that both of these forces asserted themselves jointly, it does not appear that they were conjoined.* The traumatic memory did not need an epileptic discharge to awake it; sleep and a dream had sufficed. And the local pathology found during craniotomy obviously did not *require* a ganglionic record of a vivid experience in order to cause a seizure to take place, whatever content the latter may reveal. Why in fact *did* the discharge galvanize this particular neuronal pattern? One may consider a topographic explanation. On this point Penfield and Jasper expressed themselves as follows: "One might argue . . . that experiences are classified and that those of a similar character are recorded in patterns that are adjacent to each other or are somehow closely related."[13] Results of electrical stimulation of the memory cortex as reported by these workers seem to indicate that repeated stimulation of the same point may or may not evoke the same memory trace. Furthermore, memory traces are more likely to be recorded in overlapping patterns than in adjacent partitions, and thus be evoked by facilitation of arousal and transmission in accordance with principles other than mere contiguity. We have good reason to surmise that, under the circumstances under discussion, the availability of memory traces is very likely related to the threshold of excitability; the lower the threshold the greater the possibility of evocation. It would indeed be tempting to correlate psychological priority or significance of a memory with a lowered threshold, provided that allowance is made for the fact that these same psychological attributes may for defensive psychodynamic reasons lead to the opposite result: unavailability of the memory trace because of repression.

In the second patient an epileptic seizure was triggered by certain perceptions and memory traces related to them. This patient was a 20-year-old man with a slow-growing benign cholesteatoma "just anterior to the left temporal lobe." His first attack occurred at the age of 17 years when, during a military-school exercise, he saw a cadet grab a rifle out of the hands of another young man. This episode immediately led to a recollection of his having grabbed a stick out of a dog's mouth when he was 13 years old. In his mind he associated these two incidents. At this point he became confused, lost speech and consciousness, and had a convulsion. Six months later, while in a night club, he heard a man say "Give me my hat" and then saw him grab the hat from the hat-check girl. He again immediately experienced the memory of grabbing the stick from the dog's mouth, became confused, and had an attack of automatism. The attacks then occurred with increasing frequency and the content of the preictal phenomena changed. During craniotomy the memory cortex of the temporal lobe was stimulated at a certain spot on at least two occasions and a recollective hallucination of "somebody grabbing something" was evoked each time.

In this case the relationship between an epileptic discharge at a certain point within the memory cortex and the neuron pattern established by a vivid experience is somewhat different from that in the previous patient. In the second patient an actual experience had on two occasions become immediately associated with a memory trace with which these two experiences, in Penfield and Jasper's words, shared "an abstract resemblance." The resemblance they had in mind is the idea of "grabbing something from someone." It is uncertain whether cognitive or affective elements are the basis for the identification in the form of "adjacent patterns" of the several instances of "grabbing." If the determining element was cognitive, the process would be comparable to the creation of "universals;" if the link was affective or psychodynamic, the phenomenon would be comparable to the mechanism of displacement. In any case, there can be no doubt that an identity exists and that it had played a role in the precipitation of the attacks. Again it may be asked what the relationship between the electrodynamic discharge from the region of the cholesteatoma and the psychodynamic discharge from the cumulative patterns of "experience → memory" is and entails. We wish to draw attention to the following comment, which is addressed to this very question concerning the latter patient:

In the case of a man whose minor seizure begins with sensation in the hand, tactile stimulus of the hand may precipitate a seizure. . . . By analogy, we may argue that the arrival of the impulses which establish the memory record of each new example of "grabbing" are guided to a special portion . . . of the temporal cortex. Thus the arriving impulses activate the recollection and precipitate the seizure.[14]

Thus a seizure—even if precipitated by a psychological or psychodynamic event—still remains an epileptic phenomenon, just as a burst of emotion in temporal-lobe epilepsy is of no psychodynamic significance. It is suggested that there is a difference between a memory that precipitates an epileptic seizure by physiological augmentation, and a memory that repeats itself in a hysterical seizure by psychological concealment.

CENTRENCEPHALIC PHENOMENA

It should be noted that in all of the seizure phenomena discussed above, consciousness is preserved—although its content and quality may be pathologically altered. In the centrencephalic seizures there is always, and by necessity, a *loss* of consciousness. This fact is not a coincidence. The forms of epilepsy in which the centrencephalic system (CES) is the site of the epileptic discharge were designated by Hughlings Jackson as highest-level fits, and he thought the ultimate integration of sensory and motor *re*representations formed the material neural correlative of consciousness. He fully endorsed Herbert

Spencer's contention that "the seat of consciousness is that nervous centre to which mediately or immediately the most heterogeneous impressions are brought.[15] Jackson's only error was that he assumed that the anterior frontal cortex fulfilled Spencer's requirements. We know now that "if we are to use Jackson's term 'highest level' it must be applied to the centrencephalic system."[16] In addition the term, "highest level"—if applied to the CES—must be more precisely defined. It will be recalled that Jackson made a distinction between higher, middle, and lower levels of performance to illustrate the evolution of functions. This hierarchical progression has, of course, its neuronal correlative in the cortex, as far as the highest- and middle-level functions are concerned. The CES has not only a different anatomical location, but its physiological preeminence is also of an especial character—namely, the integration of all cortical processes regardless of their functional level.

It seems likely that the various cortical areas are projections of the diencephalon and that their separate functions can only be carried out when diencephalic center and cortical area are acting together as a unit . . . the centrencephalic system functions normally only by means of employment of the various cortical areas.[17]

In other words, a distinction must be made between the highest-level qualities attained in the *evolution of functions*, and the highest level of *integration*—without which function at *any* level would not be possible. A simple simile may illustrate this reciprocal contrasting relationship. While banknotes exist in different denominations of "lower," "middle," and "highest" amounts, their validity is guaranteed only by the authority and solvency of the government which issues them; but the government will make this guarantee with complete impartiality as far as different denominations are concerned.

Centrencephalic seizures result from epileptic discharges (preictal, ictal, and postictal) within or spreading into that area of highest-level integration that mediates voluntary activity as well as understanding and introspective judgment; paralysis of this area as a result of seizure discharges abolishes activity or reduces it to automatic acts, as well as abolishing consciousness and the capacity to record memory traces for the duration of the attack.

Petit Mal

The effect of the discharge upon the ganglionic area of the centrencephalic system (CES) is "negative" or inactivating; thus consciousness ceases at the moment of and during the duration of the attack, and so does activity. In some instances, however, the patient may perform automatic acts of which no memory traces are recorded. As soon as a petit mal attack starts there is an immediate effect upon the entire cortex in both hemispheres; simultaneously all awareness and activity of a voluntary and understanding nature ceases. A pathognomonic electroencephalographic pattern emerges, which consists of the familiar "dome-and-spike" tracings obtained from both cerebral hemispheres, with one side being the mirror image of the other. When this electrophysiological signal appears all mental processes, regardless of their intrinsic complexity, are suspended: "the cortical mantle lies dormant."[18] This is true even if at times some sensorimotor integrations, in the form of automatisms, may "survive" during the seizure, like dislodged and aimlessly roving stragglers and remnants of a former cohesive organization. For "without an integrated system for control . . . upon local cortical functions of the two hemispheres, coordination of cortical function as a whole would be impossible."[19]

Clinically, not all petit mal seizures are of the same intensity; therefore, variations in the symptomatology occur. Minimal seizures that last several seconds may pass unnoticed by others, although the patient realizes he has experienced a lapse of consciousness. Such attacks are fairly frequent in children, and since as many as a hundred may take place during a day, their cumulative effect is sufficiently substantial to interfere with the child's learning capacity and thus with his scholastic accomplishments. Occasionally such children are erroneously considered to be defective, while electroencephalographic examination would easily reveal the true nature of the condition. In a petit mal attack of average intensity the patient will suddenly stop in his tracks—in speaking, writing, or engaging in any other activity—turn somewhat pale, and stare ahead with uncomprehending eyes. When the seizure has passed he will resume the activity at the exact point at which it had been interrupted. Occasionally a petit mal forms the aura for an ensuing generalized convulsion.

Grand Mal

In the case of centrencephalic grand mal, whatever the nature of the abnormality within the centrencephalic system may be, its effect must be a massive activation of the ganglionic maze at the highest level. The convulsion is the clinical expression of this positive state. It is followed by a negative state of ganglionic exhaustion, which is reflected in the EEG. In contrast to those types of grand mal which are secondary to focal epileptogenic cortical lesions—such as scars, tumors, or inflammatory cerebral disease—the pathogenesis of centrencephalic generalized convulsions is still obscure. Hereditary predisposition—as suggested by a high incidence of cerebral dysrhythmia amongst blood relatives—should be noted. The clinical manifestations and their sequences are well known. The patient, either instantaneously or after a brief aura of dimming of consciousness or peculiar epigastric sensations, loses consciousness completely and will (unless he happened to be supine) fall to the ground as he emits a cry. Generalized tonic contractions of all extremities occur next, with head and eyes often turned to the side. Respiration ceases and there will be cyanosis. The tonic phase soon gives way to clonic rhythmic movements of the entire body and their gradual fading out signals the approaching end of the attack. Fixed pupils and a positive Babinski sign may accompany the seizures. The violent contraction of the muscles of the jaws accounts for the patient's typically biting his tongue and lips. Penfield and Jasper state:

The sudden rapid generalization of the attack is in marked contrast to the slowly progressive march of the Jacksonian motor seizure. It seems reasonable to assume, therefore, that generalization of the motor seizure does not take place by spread of excitation through cortical circuits. It must spread through the more closely interrelated neuronal network of the . . . centrencephalic system with symmetrical functional relationships to both sides of the body.[20]

At the moment of cessation of the convulsion, the patient enters the postictal state. Clinically this phase manifests itself either by sleep followed by gradual return of consciousness and of the faculty of understanding and discrimination, or else the patient may for a while be in a state of partial dissolution (particularly with respect to his cognitive powers) but show automatic movement and behavior; the latter may consist of aimless actions that are harmless, or he may become violent and dangerous, especially if he meets with interference by others. There is also total amnesia for these automatic twilight states. During the postictal phase, EEG tracings indicate paralysis or "exhaustion" of the ganglionic apparatus. Further evidence of this "negative state" is found in the occasional occurrence of circumscribed postictal paralyses, known as Todd's paralysis. If a patient has suffered many grand mal seizures within a short time (status epilepticus), he may remain in a state of cognitive dissolution for a considerable time, even for several days, so that in the absence of a history of recent seizures or of clinical evidence such as marks of injury or tongue bite a problem of diagnosis may arise. Generally speaking, epileptic phenomena are not difficult to diagnose, provided one has considered the possibility of their existence.

It is sometimes necessary and difficult to differentiate epileptic grand mal seizures from hysterical attacks or "fits." At the risk of overstating the case, we submit that the distinction is of extreme importance. In accordance with our view about the impersonal etiology and character of organicity, the epileptic seizure is intelligible only in terms of neuro-anatomy and neurophysiology; the alterations in these spheres are projected and transformed into motor activity. On the other hand, hysterical attacks are "phantasies projected and translated into motor activity and represented in pantomime."[21] Thus hysterical fits, in accordance with their psychological character and purpose, avail themselves of the same means and mechanisms as dreams do and can therefore be made intelligible by the same methods which we employ in our attempts to undo the dream work. In his paper "General Remarks on Hysterical Attacks,"[22] Freud lists some of these psychological mechanisms: condensation, multiple identification, reversal of the sequence of events, and antagonistic inversion of the innervation. The latter denotes the presence of postures or movements which would be the reverse of those actually (unconsciously) intended. None of the clinical manifestations, regular sequences, and neurological signs noted in all epileptic grand mal seizures are found in hysterical fits. There is, of course, nothing symbolic or pantomime in epilepsy. It may be recalled in this context that Freud made his sharp delineation on the basis of clinical as well as theoretical considerations, and without the benefit of objective evidence supplied by electroencephalography. Even without such objective diagnostic tools Freud was quite prepared to make the delineation stick, and it appears doubtful that he would have agreed with Fenichel's statement that "there is a gradual transition between genuine epilepsy and conversion hysteria (hystero-epilepsy)."[23] It is perhaps significant that not a single reference cited by Fenichel lists a work by Freud with respect to hysteroepilepsy. It is difficult to see how one could allow for such transitions without inferring radical changes in psychoanalytic doctrine concerning the evolution and meaning of the hysterical conversion symptom: As late as 1928 Freud said:

It is therefore quite right to distinguish between an organic and an "affective" epilepsy. The practical significance of this is that a person who suffers from the first kind has a disease of the brain, while a person who suffers from the second kind is a neurotic. . . . In the second case the disturbance is an expression of his mental life itself."[24]

Psychomotor Automatism

As an ictal phenomenon, epileptic automatisms may be defined as paroxysmal states of dimming or suspension of consciousness, but with preservation of motor and behavioral capability, and accompanied by irretrievable amnesia. These "epileptic twilight states" are believed to be the result of epileptic discharges within the centrencephalic system. Penfield and Jasper state:

there must be some form of division between the mechanism within the centrencephalic system that is devoted to physical co-ordination and that devoted to memory and mental processes. Automatism is produced by functional interference with the latter portion of the centrencephalic system.[25]

As these psychomotor automatisms are *ictal*, they are the sole expression of the epileptic attack and are not preceded by any other epileptic manifestations, such as grand mal or temporal-lobe phenomena.

It is indeed a strange fact that these patients—while in a state of suspended consciousness and at that moment totally lacking in the capacity for introspection and understanding—are nevertheless able to carry on certain motor or behavioral activities; the latter range from "seemingly normal" to "odd" and even "absurd," and they may at times be of a violent character. Whatever the nature of such behaviors—either in terms of their social or antisocial character and consequences or as viewed in the light of their obvious unintelligibility—they share the quality of being *automatic*. Jackson considered them for this reason "external signs of crude mental states."[26] The clinical psychiatrist will be particularly interested in the singular phenomenology of these automatic acts; he will compare and contrast them with other "unintelligible" acts, such as obsessive-compulsive rituals and symptomatic acts of known psychodynamic significance; and he will have to face the issue of criminal responsibility of some of these patients, if their automatisms should be socially offensive or harmful to others.

It may be best first to give a random sampling of verified epileptic automatisms so that the reader may be able to grasp the general flavor of these odd performances and derive a general impression of the clinical manifestations and their range. These examples are taken from Jackson's paper "On Temporary Mental Disorders after Epileptic Paroxysms,"[27] and from the case reports of Penfield and Jasper.[28] A patient blew his nose on a piece of paper while in an omnibus; when he got off he gave the conductor 2 £ instead of the usual small change for the fare. Another patient was seized with a fit while taking a man's pulse; when he "came round, in another room," he began to feel his sister's pulse, *she being near him*. Some patients show what has been called "an invariable type of pseudovoluntary activity"[29] that repeats itself during each fit and may therefore be called "stereotyped." Such individuals may clutch their throat, tear their clothes, or wander about aimlessly. But other patients seem to have limited understanding of their actions and manage while in an automatic state, to walk through traffic with a good "sense of direction and in perfect control of vision and hearing."[30] One of Jackson's patients would invariably look at his pocket watch after a seizure; one day he found the candle extinguisher in his coat pocket and it appeared that he had mistaken the extinguisher for the watch during the loss of consciousness. Another patient, during a fit which occurred in church, took his coat off; subsequently he suffered a seizure in a different church and took his shoes off—and on many other occasions he would unbutton his coat and his trousers, once in the presence of four women. During still another automatism he took a knife out of his pocket and grasped it, not by the handle, but by the blade. Finally, we will report and compare the automatisms of two patients whose actions were obviously "determined" by the accidental circumstances existing at the moment of the attack. The first patient, just prior to the onset of the attack, was about to make some cocoa. He was informed by relatives who found him shortly thereafter that he was mixing cocoa in a dirty gallipot that was half filled with bread and milk intended for the cat, and was stirring the mixture with a mustard spoon. The second patient, who was about to cut bread for her children at the moment of the seizure, thereupon inflicted severe cut wounds on her arm with the knife she happened to hold in her hand.

Jackson, like Freud, combined astuteness of observation of detail with perspicacity in recognizing broad principle. It is, therefore, not surprising to discover how much Jackson was able to infer from the clinical manifestations of epileptic automatisms. He stated for instance "that the alteration is sometimes not in the 'form' of the action, but in the 'contents' of that form."[31] Thus the patient who blew his nose on a piece of paper (long before the use of facial tissue paper replaced the handkerchief) performed an act which *resembled* very closely the normal, customary activity, and the general *form* and conformation of the various motor sequences are sufficiently preserved to reveal the meaning of the act. On the other hand, its implementation *contains* an incongruous element—namely, the substitution of a scrap of paper for a handkerchief. The same may be said about the patient's giving the conductor of the omnibus a banknote instead of the coin. (It is, of course, to be taken for granted that he did not expect to receive change from the conductor). Both automatic acts *differed* from a normal performance in the faulty introduction of a detail. The situation is also very similar in the instance of the patient who mixed cocoa in such an absurd fashion. In all these examples just mentioned crude resemblances are preserved, but finer discriminations have apparently undergone dissolution. We may recall a comment which Jackson made, although in a different context: "There are two halves of thought, tracing resemblances and noticing differences. The former is the more automatic."[32]

Jackson also observed that the degree of conative dissolution occurred in proportion to the degree of dimming or loss of consciousness. He said: "It is not enough borne in mind that the more imperfect and shorter the paroxysm, the more likely is it that *elaborate . . .* automatic actions will follow."[33] Thus the epileptic nature of such acts may not be recognized, and should they happen to be socially offensive, let alone harmful, the patient's accountability may not even be questioned. Jackson also thought that in these mild fits with only partial loss of consciousness or of introspection automatic acts are developed by the external circumstances, as they existed at the moment. But even in more profound seizures of the centrencephalic type, external circumstances become significant by coincidence rather than by any design or motivation on the part of the patient. This fact is of great practical and, also, of some academic interest. Patients during epileptic twilight states will, or may, attack another person not because they are motivated but merely because that other person happened to be there, and particularly, because he may unwisely and (if it should be a psychiatrist) ignorantly try to interfere with the patients' automatisms. Thus the patient who was about to cut bread when the attack started cut herself severely with the knife; Jackson would contend that, had she held a spoon in her hand at that moment, instead of a knife, no harm would have come to her, or to anyone else. Jackson emphasized that the absurdity and not the enormity of the automatic acts was the significant fact and perhaps the key to the understanding of their nature. This leads us to the last point in our discussion of psychomotor automatisms. How do these behaviors differ from other simple but "absurd" acts?

Both Jackson and modern clinicians consider that centrencephalic seizures are "highest-level fits." It must be kept in mind that the effect or nature of the epileptic discharge in such cases is to "paralyze" or "deactivate" these highest centers—that is, to create what Penfield called "a negative state." In Jacksonian terms this negative state is indicative of dissolution, and the ensuing automatisms represent the positive symptom. They are *set free.* This fact, of course, accounts for their inappropriateness, functional inferiority, and, at times, absurdity. Unintelligibility and absurdity also attend the manifest features of such psychoneurotic conative phenomena as obsessive-compulsive rituals and symptomatic acts, at least until psychoanalytic investigation has revealed their latent meaning. It is, therefore, necessary to distinguish between the *setting free of the primitive* and the *return of the repressed.* Generally speaking, the performances in the first contingency are reduced in their efficiency and mutilated in their execution; it is for these reasons that they are, *and remain,* unintelligible. The situation is quite different in the case of the psychoneurotic ritualistic or symptomatic acts. While they are inefficient except insofar as their inherent primary gain relieves anxiety or permits a substitutive cathexis, their unintelligibility owes to a disguise which is the result of well-known mental mechanisms, and which is reversible by a process akin to decoding. Furthermore, it may be of interest to note that an unintelligible act may result either from dimmed consciousness or from unconscious motivation. In the automatisms, impaired consciousness accounts for the dissolution and incoherence of the motor performance whereas in the case of the psychoneurotic symptom the substitutive nature of the derivatives of the unconscious defies understanding only when viewed as a surface phenomenon. There is also the difference between (1) the irreversible amnesia for automatic acts of which no memory traces have been recorded and (2) the reversible ignorance of the patient concerning the nature and origin of his psychoneurotic symptom. Paying for one's dinner with a scrap of paper while in a twilight state and not being able to remember having done so is quite different from remembering later that one had "forgotten" to pay for one's dinner, an omission which may well have been motivated. And if it was indeed motivated and if, therefore, we would have to call it a symptomatic act and thus an alloplastic equivalent of a hysterical conversion mechanism, rooted in ontogeny, we could only conclude that the parapraxis of forgetting in the present was the dynamic effect of a repressed memory from the past. There is no "statute of limitation" for pathogenic memories.

Competent investigators who are noted for their understanding of neurodynamic and psychodynamic processes in psychiatric symptom formation do not seem to endorse an issue of principle in the delineation of the "setting free of the primitive" in organicity and the "return of the repressed" in the neuroses. Ostow says in his paper "Psychodynamic Disturbances in Patients with Temporal Lobe Disorders": "It is suggested that [the identity of neurodynamic and psychodynamic factors in temporal-lobe seizures] . . . can be explained by the psychoanalytic thesis that neurosis arises from unsuccessful repression . . . [and that] presumably some forms of organic disease of the temporal lobe can act . . . to weaken repression . . . in fairly specific, narrow areas."[34]

The primitive element that is set free in organicity represents a lower but transitory level of functioning in ontogenetic maturation. Its destiny in the child is, in the normal process of growth of the mental apparatus, to evolve into, and become supplanted by, the gradually emerging higher levels, thereby remaining subordinate to the latter. Thus automatic response gives way to voluntary action, concreteness to abstract capacity, restricted awareness to expanded consciousness, crude affectivity to modulated and discriminating emotional orchestration of thought and behavior; the undistorted dreams of children gradually avail themselves of the sophisticated mechanisms of the dream work. If all this is true, how could one then reconcile the predominance of the "primitive" in childhood, let alone equate it with the "return of the repressed"? The forces of repression are, in psychoanalytic doctrine, strongest during that very period of childhood; they are said to cause childhood amnesia, the lifting of which is prerequisite to psychoanalytic therapy. And ought there not be a substantial difference between that which is meant to evolve into a form and manner that will enrich the psychic potential and that which is normally denied emergence into the psychic life of man so as not to endanger it and him? As a manifestation of psychopathology each contingency is, of course, a disadvantage, a step backwards. But in organicity it is the antiquated that has taken over; in neurosis it is the disowned and disavowed.

REFERENCES

1. W. Penfield and H. Jasper. *Epilepsy and the Functional Anatomy of the Human Brain.* Boston, Little, Brown, 1954, p. 20 ff.
2. *Ibid.,* p. 76.
3. F. M. R. Walshe. "Contributions of John Hughlings Jackson to Neurology." *Archives of Neurology,* vol. 5, #2, 1961, p. 124.
4. W. Penfield and H. Jasper. *Op. cit.,*[1] p. 438.
5. *Ibid.,* p. 438 (footnote #2).
6. M. Ostow. "Psychic Function of Temporal Lobe as Inferred from Seizure Phenomena." *Archives of Neurology and Psychiatry,* vol. 77, #1, 1957, p. 80.
7. W. Penfield and H. Jasper. *Op. cit.,*[1] p. 446.
8. M. Ostow. "The Biological Basis of Human Behavior." *In:* S. Arieti (ed.). *American Handbook of Psychiatry.* New York, Basic Books, 1959, vol. 1, p. 75.
9. W. Penfield and H. Jasper, *Op. cit.,*[1] p. 451.
10. M. Ostow. *Op. cit.,*[6] p. 85.
11. W. Penfield. "Memory Mechanisms." *Archives of Neurology and Psychiatry,* vol. 67, #2, 1952, pp. 178–198.
12. W. Penfield and H. Jasper. *Op. cit.,*[1] p. 464 and p. 138.
13. *Ibid.,* p. 140.
14. *Ibid.*
15. *Ibid.,* p. 470.
16. *Ibid.,* p. 473.
17. *Ibid.,* p. 474.
18. *Ibid.,* p. 482.
19. *Ibid.*
20. *Ibid.,* p. 494.
21. S. Freud. "General Remarks on Hysterical Attacks." *In: Collected Papers.* London, Hogarth, 1950, vol. 2, p. 100.
22. *Ibid.,* p. 19.

23. O. Fenichel. *The Psychoanalytical Theory of Neurosis.* New York, Norton, 1945, p. 267.

24. S. Freud. "Dostoevsky and Parricide." *In: Collected Papers. Op. cit.,*[21] vol. 5, p. 227.

25. W. Penfield and H. Jasper. *Op. cit.,*[1] p. 538.

26. J. Taylor (ed.). *Selected Writings of John Hughlings Jackson.* New York, Basic Books, vol. 1, p. 122.

27. *Ibid.,* p. 119.

28. W. Penfield and H. Jasper. *Op. cit.,*[1] p. 497 (footnote).

29. *Ibid.,* p. 517.

30. *Ibid.,* p. 520.

31. J. Taylor (ed.). *Op. cit.,*[26] p. 124.

32. *Ibid.,* footnote #1, p. 124.

33. *Ibid.,* p. 123.

34. M. Ostow. "Psychodynamic Disturbances in Patients with Temporal Lobe Disorder." *Journal of the Mount Sinai Hospital* (New York), vol. 20. #5, 1954, p. 307.

11

The Body Image
and Its Disorders

To each of us our own body is a most unique, almost enigmatic object. On one hand "it constitutes the idea of I,"[1] and
yet we know that the I is something beyond the body experience because
the latter can become the object of the former. Thus the body seems
to occupy an intermediate position along the perceptual spectrum, somewhere between the world of objects which are clearly outside and
"non-I" and the purely subjective awareness of one's self, of the world
within. This singular fact is fundamental to the evolution of the concept
and experience of the body image. Fenichel states that the body "is
distinguished from all other parts of the universe by the remarkable
fact that it is perceived through two types of sensation simultaneously:
through external tactile sensations and through internal sensations of
depth sensibility."[2] To this observation may be added the fact that we
become aware of our body through the simultaneous participation of
all extero- and enteroceptive sensory modalities. The resulting "body
image" is, therefore, a synesthesia—a concomitant sensation.

At birth and for some time thereafter all experience is restricted to
the body, and body experience to sensations. Ideas and affects concerning the body and its various parts, functions, and destiny appear later.
But in the beginning stages of the emergence of the ego, body awareness
is its sole content, and even later in life the body remains its nucleus.
"The sum of the mental representations of the body and its organs,
the so-called body image, constitutes the idea of I and is of basic importance for the further formation of the ego."[3] However, to the clinical
psychiatrist the concept of the body image and its disorders is restricted
to essentially perceptual, not libidinal issues. Neither the pleasures nor
the pains of the body are included, although this does not gainsay the
secondary role of affective forces in the ultimate clinical manifestations
of certain forms of body image disorders.

It is worth noting that the classical erogenous zones lack a representation in the body image as well as in the outline of cortical representation (Penfield's homunculus) that is commensurate with their role in the development of infantile sexuality. The fact that the mouth (as well as the tongue) does have an enormous sensory-motor cortical representation must be attributed to the highly complex and skilled sensory-motor functions of this area—particularly in connection with the faculty of articulation—and *not* to any signal libidinal cathexis. This observation clearly underlines the essentially cognitive character of the body image proper, or at least of that component of the total body experience which is mediated by the peripheral and central nervous systems along localizable pathways, and which, precisely because of its cognitive rather than instinctual-affective qualities, is closer to the outer world than to the id.

THE CONCEPT AND COMPONENTS
OF THE BODY IMAGE

Clinical and neurological data suggest that our perceptual awareness of our body is a composite of a number of component functional parts or units. The resulting total body experience is traditionally referred to as the "body image." However, the term as used here does not apply to any mental representation of any aspect of the body which results primarily from psychopathology. The following subdivisions of the body image are suggested:

1. The system of postural awareness of body parts (Head's postural model).

2. The system of general body orientation.

3. The system of organization and awareness of extrapersonal space, an extension of the corporeal body image.

4. The system mediating the awareness of "me-ness" with respect to body parts and territories.

5. The system mediating awareness of basic ego functions, such as motility, vision, and hearing.

Postural Awareness

In 1911, Head and Holmes[4] suggested that the awareness of position or of change in position of body parts was accomplished by a process of matching new postures against a pre-existing standard of postural

impressions, a "postural model." This postural model or frame of reference, located in both interparietal regions, may be viewed as a gradually
evolving repository of proprioceptive input that is capable of constant
modification but is permanent as a functional unit. It may be considered
as a cortical center for kinesthetic recognition. Each movement is relayed
to it, and the awareness of the new position occurs as soon as the matching process has been completed. Visual impulses seem to play only a
subordinate role in the creation and activities of the postural model.
This is not surprising if it is realized that less than half of the mass
and surface of the body is accessible to visual perception and scrutiny.
Thus, in the case of a phantom limb, the "proprioceptive conviction"
of the presence of the amputated extremity is in no way influenced
by the visual evidence of its absence.

The Phantom Limb.   This may be the appropriate place to make some
comments about the phenomenon of the phantom. It may be a matter
of dispute whether a phantom could be rightly considered to be a false
perception. As the kinesthetic representation of the extremity within
the body schema or postural model is not affected (at least not immediately) by the amputation, the postural awareness continues in the
patient's consciousness like a central "prosthesis." There is ample clinical
evidence to support such a neurophysiological explanation. It is, for
instance, well known that congenital agenesis or "amputation" of a limb
does not in later years ever lead to the awareness of a phantom; there
has simply not been an opportunity for a sensory-motor representation
of the absent extremity to come into being within the cortical regions
of the postural model. But in an adult in whom such a representation
has been established and firmly entrenched, sudden peripheral amputation as little extinguishes central postural and proprioceptive memories
as blindness in later life will destroy visual memory. However, in the
course of several years certain modifications of the phantom are known
to take place. These changes, too, seem to confirm the neurophysiological
nature and explanation of the phenomenon. The patient notices that
with time some parts of the phantom appear to him less vivid than
others. Those portions of the limb, such as fingers (and also the great
toe) that, for obvious reasons, have the most extensive representation
in the neurological homunculus of the sensory-motor cortex resist the
process of fading or gradual extinction of the phantom for the longest
period of time and also the most successfully. Thigh, upper, or lower
arm and calf—for which we may assume a much less extensive cortical
representation—fade out very early. These orderly reorganizations within
the phantom ultimately lead to what is sometimes referred to as the
"telescoping phenomenon,"[5] the hand (or the foot) phantom appears

to move more and more in the direction of the proximal stump; for a time the emptiness of the intermediate gaps may be felt by the patient, but ultimately such awareness drops out. Head reported a patient in whom a phantom disappeared after the individual had suffered a thrombosis in the "corresponding" cortical region within the postural model.

General Body Orientation

General body disorientation with inability to recognize the various parts of the body and to comprehend their normal topographic relationships has been observed to accompany isolated lesions of the supramarginal and angular gyrus, on the dominant side of the brain. This condition was first described by A. Pick, who proposed the term "autotopagnosia." In some instances patients were also unable to recognize and comprehend the body parts of others. There was never an aphasic disturbance to account for this disability. Nor was there an agnosia for any other objects, animate or inanimate. Autotopagnosia is a rare condition, but one of its varieties or subdivisions confined to disorientation in the area of one's fingers is not so uncommon. It is known as "Gerstmann's syndrome," after the worker who first described the condition (in 1924). The usual combination of symptoms—finger agnosia, inability to name fingers, acalculia, agraphia, and left-right disorientation may at first sight strike us as being a rather irregular assortment of defects. The disability extends to the fingers of both hands, at times to the fingers of other persons. That the fingers should be particularly vulnerable to any process of dissolution within this system of body-image integration could be viewed and explained as an illustration of "Jackson's law." It must, however, be noted that in cases of a Gerstmann syndrome, lesions of the angular gyrus and its immediate surroundings on the dominant side have been described. The directional disorientation never affects the dimension "up-down" or "front-back." The reasons for the much greater susceptibility to dissolution of the dimension "left-right" are rather obvious. Awareness of "up-down" is part of our adaptation to gravity, a fundamental aspect of our environment and thus presumably mediated by well-organized, least-complex, and "lower-level" neuronal arrangements. The same implication may be advanced with regard to the dimension "front-back." Our most important distance receptor, vision, aims forward—perhaps it *determines* the direction "forward;" we normally walk in that direction and our mouth, as an instrument of verbal communication, cooperates and coincides with this general scheme. But the ability to discriminate left from right must be learned; it takes a child some time to form these concepts, the basis for which must at first appear to be rather arbitrary. This aspect of our body orientation is usually taught us first in connection with our hands. Here cerebral dominance may serve as a reinforcement, and semantic symbolization as an aid. The right hand, so the (right-handed) child is told, is the "nice" or "good" hand; the multivalent meaning of "right" in adult language is, of course, well known. I have observed a patient in whom a pathological symbolic reorganization was superimposed upon coarse brain disease in the area of confusion of laterality. He was a 62-year-old man, right-handed, who after a cerebral thrombosis showed signs of left-sided paralysis with anosognosia, amnesia of the left half of the body, and in addition presented some of the features of a Gerstmann syndrome consisting in finger agnosia and left-right disorientation. For several weeks he thought that he was taken to the hospital in order to be "tested," to "justify" himself and to prove that he could tell "right from wrong." It was also noted that his failure to designate directions was most pronounced if the problem was presented to him propositionally or abstractly; thus he was either unsure or wrong in his replies to questions such as, "Where is 'up'?" or "left" or "right", etc., at a time when he had already sufficiently recovered so that he could, upon command, point to his left arm, his right eye, or to the wall on his right. The agraphia in the Gerstmann syndrome is, of course, not the result of a loss of symbolic function; rather it must be attributed to right-left confusion and motor awkwardness resulting from the finger agnosia. A similar pattern of disturbances is thought to play a role in some cases of reading and spelling disabilities in children and adolescents.[6] It would be interesting to investigate the possibility that the acalculia—the inability to perform *simple* calculations—is the result of dissolution of a digital decimal scheme that, during an early stage in childhood, acts as a bodily abacus.

Extrapersonal Space Organization

Several components of the body image exert and extend their functional qualities into the space immediately surrounding our body. This space, which may be called "extrapersonal space" (EPS), is not the space of physics. It is the space which is accessible to the grasp of our hands and to the stride of our legs. Its directional identity in terms of "left," "right," "up," and "down" is contingent upon the position of our body at the moment and also upon our directional body image itself. "Left" in the EPS is on the side of what I know to be the left side of my body; an object located in my left EPS will when I turn around a half circle be in my right EPS. Furthermore, clinical experience shows that the body-image system which mediates the awareness of "me-ness" in regard to our body parts (see below) incorporates the adjacent EPS into its sphere of vigilant attentiveness, thus bringing it into the orbit of a quasicorporeal extension of the body. Objects within this EPS that are normally dealt with if they are significant, or avoided if they may cause harm, are in case of lesions in the corresponding areas of the brain ignored or overlooked. We will not discuss here disturbances in the recognition of distances of objects in space because this form of pathology does not directly pertain to the present subject matter of body-image disorders. It should, however, be mentioned in this connection that the judgment of distances of objects in space is largely based on a correlation of several mechanisms: seeing the object, recognizing it and thus knowing its usual size, and concomitant feedback from oculomotor proprioceptors on one hand, as well as proprioceptive postural "memories" within the territories of the upper and lower extremities on the other.

Disorders in the perception of EPS occur in combination with certain body-image disturbances. In many cases of neglect or amnesia of the left half of the body resulting from lesions within the right thalamoparietal circuits (see below), the left EPS is concomitantly (and to various degrees of completeness), eliminated from awareness. This syndrome may manifest itself in a number of ways. Russell Brain[7] described an agnosia of the left homonymous EPS associated with contralateral lesions. The spatial abnormality may consist of a general avoidance of the left EPS so that the patient will invariably move toward the right, even if he wants to move toward the left; he will look for an object, which he recognizes and "knows" to be on his left, in his right EPS. Or he may not pay attention to objects in the left EPS and collide with them. Acoustic stimuli coming from the left are reacted to and perceived as if they had come from the right, which represents a variety of alloesthesia. There have been reports of patients with left-body amnesia and agnosia of the left EPS who were unable to recognize the left half of objects, persons, and pictures. In those patients who show a combination of body and EPS amnesia the lesions are in the contralateral parietooccipital body image areas of the brain. My own patient with the incomplete Gerstmann syndrome (whom I briefly mentioned above) showed an extension of his directional body disorientation into the entire EPS, including all dimensions.

Mediating the Awareness of "Me-ness"

The system within the total body-image experience that mediates the awareness of "me-ness" with respect to body territories seems to belong within the general scope of the specific thalamocortical circuits of the reticular activating suborgans of the brain. As far as body awareness is concerned the thalamoparietal bundle is the operative functional unit. Lesions which disrupt the thalamoparietal circuit may produce alterations in the awareness of the contralateral (usually the left) half of the body, ranging from episodic forgetting to permanent sequestration from consciousness and thus from attention. The patients behave as if that part of their body did not exist; their general orientation, both in the perceptual and in the conative sphere, is toward the opposite (right) side. Tactile, visual, and auditory perceptions entering from the left may be perceived on the right, or as if they originated from the right. This transposition of sensory stimuli is known as alloesthesia. On simultaneous bilateral stimulation either extinction or alloesthesia may be observed. There is no evidence of perceptual impairment in any other sphere and, in Gerstmann's words, "the activity of the mind as a whole is uninterrupted."[8] Cases of this kind were reported as early as in 1913 by Zingerle.* and subsequently by Nielsen and Ives (1937),† Nielsen (1938),‡ and Frantz (1950).§ One of Nielsen's cases may be cited for being particularly representative of this syndrome. The patient was a 48-year-old dentist who after a period of slight euphoria and irritability showed episodic neglect of his left body half and of the left EPS. His wife noted that he would not try to avoid people or objects on his left when driving his car; when this was brought to his attention he became somewhat angry but tried to pay more attention thereafter. Shortly afterwards he suffered left-sided Jacksonian seizures. Signs of unmistakable unawareness or forgetting of the left side of his body became quite evident. When undressing he would remove only the right parts of his clothes; he would try to go to sleep with his left shoe and sock on; he would dry only the right side of his body after a bath. He could not find his left hand unless he actually *looked*. Craniotomy revealed a spongioblastoma in the right upper parietal region. The patient died soon after the operation and no autopsy was performed.

In other instances of left body amnesia an associated left homonymous hemianopia and/or left hemiplegia, with or without anosognosia, was also present. The alienation which such patients feel toward the dissociated body parts expresses itself in various forms or degrees. Some patients refer to the involved arm without the personal pronoun; this pattern is reminiscent of an observation by Weinstein and Kahn[9] that patients with a denial syndrome tend to use the third or second person

* *Monatschr. Psychol. Neurol., 34:* 13, 1913.
† *Bull. Los Angeles Neurol. Soc., 2:* 155, 1937.
‡ *Bull. Los Angeles Neurol. Soc., 3:* 127, 1938.
§ *J. Nerv. Ment. Dis. 112:* 240, 1950.

when talking about their illness. The general attitude displayed by patients with amnesia for the left half of their body is quite often of a kind that Weinstein and Kahn called "forms of implicit denial." But they refer to patients who deny their disability (e.g., hemiplegia or blindness) and indeed anything connected with the disability. But is there not a significant difference between denial of a defect such as a paralysis and the implicit or explicit denial or disregard of a perfectly normal part of the body? Patients with an amnesia for the (left) side of their body may or may not have an associated left hemiplegia; if they are also paralyzed they may or may not deny the existence of their paralysis. Such cases were reported by Nielsen and Ives (1937), Frantz (1950), and in Nielsen's series of five patients with left-body amnesia without anosognosia (1938). We must therefore conclude that the mechanisms which lead to neglect, amnesia, and even denial of "me-ness" of a body territory differ in principle from the denial of a paralysis which in itself could be viewed as a motivation for such a denial. But what could be the possible motivation for the symptoms and behavior of patients with body amnesia, but without anosognosia? What could be the possible motivation for the frequent alienation with which they literally look at the involved body territory and for the even more far-reaching psychopathological elaborations they entertain about it? If a body territory has to be dissociated from awareness or from functional activity for psychological reasons—that is to say, in response to a compelling psychological motivation rooted in conflict— then the only known way in which this is accomplished in man is by the various mechanisms of conversion hysteria. Body amnesia is the result of a lesion and not the expression of a motivation to undo or mitigate a psychological dilemma. The psychopathological elaborations concerning the involved body parts may perhaps be viewed as a positive Jacksonian symptom—that is, as an inferior form of perception; in extreme degrees this alienation transforms the body part into one belonging to another person. One of Olsen's patients, as cited by Nielsen, insisted that her arm and leg belonged to the physician. In such cases, as a result of the dissolution within the body-image area concerned, the corresponding "ego boundaries" no longer exist and a part of one's own body is experienced as if it were an object of the outer world. Weinstein and Kahn published samples of Human Figure Drawings by some of these patients.[10] The drawings clearly indicate the absence of the mirror-image half of the body of the figure, who was always drawn facing the patient. As the omission appears in the form of a mirror image of the patient's body amnesia, we conclude that it is not a true representation of the idea of "loss of the left side." The drawings must be considered as an extension of the patient's body-image defect into EPS.

Mediating the Awareness of Ego Functions

It is still a matter of considerable doubt and even controversy whether the various syndromes of denial or imperception of defects such as hemiplegia or (central) blindness are to be viewed and explained as disorders of the body image caused by lesions within a corresponding system. We have referred to a system that mediates awareness of basic ego functions such as motility, vision, and hearing. The contention of such authors as Redlich and Dorsey (1945), Dusser de Barenne and McCulloch (1938), and Stanley Cobb[11] has been that specific thalamo-cortical circuits play the same role in the sustained awareness of basic body *functions* as they do with respect to the feeling of "me-ness" of body *territories*. Nielsen likewise suggested adding to the anatomical or corporeal body-image concept a functional counterpart.[12] However, in view of the multiplicity and uncertainty of the etiological and contributing factors in cases of denial or imperception of defects and illness, it may be best to begin with the clinical presentation of these body-image disorders and to address ourselves to the theoretical problems later.

It is necessary to define the term anosognosia. Originally it was used by Babinski to denote imperception or denial of left hemiplegia. It is now also applied to imperception or denial of blindness and deafness. We will *not* use this term in any other sense.

THE CLINICAL SYNDROMES
OF ANOSOGNOSIA

Patients with anosognosia of hemiplegia usually show a sudden onset of paralysis, almost invariably on the left side (in right-handed patients). Disturbances of sensibility on the affected side are almost invariably present; they are most severe in the modality of deep-sensibility. Also, there is in most instances an associated left homonymous hemianopia, with or without neglect of left EPS. There is furthermore a *general body orientation to the right:* head and eyes are turned to the right not because of a paralysis of lateral gaze to the left, and not even because patients do not want to look to the left, but because there is nothing on the left for them to look at. This posture is invariably present in those patients who also show loss of awareness of their left body half. In accordance with the general orientation toward the right there is often alloesthesia, the "transference" of left-sided stimuli to the right side of body and EPS; in milder forms this phenomenon appears as extinction of left-sided stimuli upon simultaneous left-right stimulation, as the left side can not successfully compete in this perceptual rivalry with the intact right. The general mental attitude of the patient toward his incapacity may vary. The terms "denial" and "imperception" are quite representative of the two basic attitudes which have been noted by all observers of anosognosia. "Denial" connotes an active, verbal disavowal of the paralysis; the patient acts and talks as if he could or did use his paralyzed extremities; Poetzl referred to this reaction as an unwillingness to acknowledge the defect (*Nichtbemerkenwollen*); it corresponds to Weinstein and Kahn's "explicit verbal denial." This group of patients is usually euphoric and resorts to rationalization or minimization to come to terms with whatever incongruity they may dimly feel when fact and fancy collide. Quite a different attitude is displayed by those patients who are totally unaware of the existence both of the paralysis and the paralyzed half of the body. They show many of the features of apathetic and indolent indifference that Weinstein and Kahn describe as "forms of implicit denial;" Poetzl called it imperception (*Nichtbemerken*). It should be noted that in either group the respective abnormal attitude is restricted to the involved body territory and function. In some instances of anosognosia of hemiplegia, reduplication phenomena may be noted; the patients say that there are "several arms," and some of these arms having been eliminated from the total body experience, are attributed to other persons or projected into space—as if the "amputation" had been peripheral instead of central. It is even possible that such an extremity is experienced as if it was a lifeless object, such as a stick, a sheet, or a board. A few patients complained that a stranger was lying next to them, occupying the affected side of the body—as indeed was true in a fashion. It appears that the vacuum created by the body-image disruption had to be filled and that psychological factors determined the nature of these symbolic substitutions. Gerstmann called these phenomena bizarre illusory transformations or "somatoparaphrenia." In the majority of cases of anosognosia of hemiplegia normal awareness of the defect returns within weeks, depending on whether the patient survives the cerebral lesion which caused the hemiplegia.

Anosognosia of (central and peripheral) blindness is also known as *Anton's symptom*, despite the fact that Monakow and not Anton was the first worker to report the condition. Since then quite a few cases of denial and imperception of blindness have appeared in the literature. The clinical features are, of course, largely determined by the causes of blindness in a given case; but the general mental attitude of the patients is remarkably uniform regardless of whether *central* or *peripheral* blindness is denied or ignored. Anosognosia of central blindness occurs usually in patients who had in the past suffered a hemiplegia, say, on the left, with left homonymous hemianopia, and who subsequently developed a thrombosis of the right posterior cerebral artery, thus being rendered blind because of bilateral interruption of the posterior optic radiations. In some of these patients there was also loss of visual memory, as if the fact of vision itself had been "amputated" from their awareness. Thus, if the awareness of the faculty of vision is lost, the concomitant fact of blindness can not be noticed. However, in other patients no such loss of visual memory was found. Some patients will deny outright that they are blind; others will use rationalizations, such as "I can not see so well without my glasses" or "I can not see because it is too dark here." These externalizations seem to indicate that the patients realize the existence of *a* defect, but not *their* defect. Confabulation reminiscent of the Korsakoff syndrome may be present in some patients, while others show apathy and still others demonstrate euphoria. Peripheral blindness may be denied if it is accompanied by increased intracranial pressure, as in brain tumors or, occasionally, in subarachnoid bleeding. It appears that in such cases a general lowering of the level of awareness is a major and perhaps a decisive factor in the development of the Anton symptom. Weinstein and Kahn, who described a large number of such cases, said that "a milieu of function sufficient for the development of anosognosia could be produced by a lesion anywhere in the brain if it were associated with increased intracranial pressure or subarachnoid bleeding."[8] They noted that in all such cases a bilaterally abnormal electroencephalogram (slow wave activity of 1 to 7 cps) was obtained while the patients were in the state of denial; when, however, the knowledge of the defect (hemiplegia or blindness) returned, the EEG reverted to a focal pattern, such as would be consistent with the brain tumor. If peripheral blindness is associated with frontal-lobe disease (such as general paresis) the latter condition— by creating a state of euphoria, of diminished concern with the self, and of "organic repression of the future"—may well be a powerful factor in the facilitation of the anosognosic attitude. Lunn's patient,[13] who suffered from general paresis with progressive diminution of visual acuity, was for 6 years intensely aware and despairing of his failing eyesight. Following a relatively minor head injury he developed a fulminating luetic meningoencephalitis during which period he was markedly euphoric, insisting that he could see. The diagnosis was confirmed at autopsy. Most cases of denial of peripheral blindness described in the literature were associated with intracranial hypertension or frontal-lobe disease or both.

Theoretical Considerations

In view of the tendency to extend the concept of denial of illness beyond the limits suggested in this presentation, it appears appropriate to state the reasons for our more restricted use of the term. As a body-image disorder anosognosia is ultimately the result of a perceptual defect; it is an *exceptional* failure in corporeal or functional body awareness resulting from certain focal and/or diffuse cerebral lesions, and it must be realized that the *majority* of patients with hemiplegia or blindness, but *without* those cerebral lesions, are aware of their paralysis or loss of vision. The concept of anosognosia is thus largely influenced by what one would include in the concept of the body image. Schilder[14] expanded the body-image concept far beyond its perceptual-cognitive pith; he added two dimensions when he introduced the idea of the libidinous and of the sociological structure of the body image. There can, of course, be no doubt about the close, intricate, and exceedingly frequent interrelations between the body and "libidinous" as well as other psychodynamic forces, both normal and abnormal. There is in fact hardly a possibility that psychopathology resulting from disorders of our instinctual and affective organizations will not, directly or indirectly, include our body; it may alter or abolish some of its functions, create abnormal sensations, distort our image of our body through false beliefs and delusions, make us fearful of sicknesses which we do not have, and cause us to ignore and even to deny those that we have. Yet, how we feel our body is not the same as how we feel *about* it. If the body-image concept remains restricted—as I believe it ought to be—to the perceptual-cognitive schema, both corporeal and functional, then body-image disorders will be recognized by these criteria: the etiology will be "impersonal"—that is, organic; the psychopathology is essentially cognitive, not affective; the distortion is perceptual, not symbolic; psychodynamic forces, while participating in the totality of the clinical picture, are not its source; and the involved body parts and body functions are not the target of abnormal cathexes but of specific dissolutions. The advantage of restricting the concept of the body image in this sense and in accordance with clearly defined clinical syndromes lies in the demarcation of organic from functional psychopathology; it would, perhaps, be more capricious not to stress this demarcation.

These reflections lead us to a consideration of the causes and the suggested motivations (or at least advantages to the individual) of denial of illness in the form of anosognosia. It will already have become transparent to the reader that the etiology of anosognosia is a complex and unsettled problem, even if one were to consider only structural and functional alterations within the brain. Nevertheless, there is considerable clinical evidence and broad general agreement that two types of mechanisms are capable of bringing it about: relatively circumscribed or focal lesions within the corresponding thalamocortical circuits and/or more diffuse pathology that results in specific and distinct perceptual dissolutions of the entire cognitive apparatus.

Focal Lesions. In many instances of amnesia of the left half of the body an associated hemiplegia has been ignored or verbally denied by the patient. It was, therefore, quite reasonably deduced that, as the patient was not even aware of the existence of his extremities, he could not be aware of their paralysis either. There appeared to be primarily a disorder of the system mediating awareness of "me-ness" in regard to body territories, of the "anatomical" component of the body schema (Nielsen) leading by necessity to anosognosia if a paralysis happened to coexist. However, this explanation could not be applied to those anosognosia-hemiplegia patients in whom no loss of awareness of the involved body half could be demonstrated. Thus a "physiological" or functional counterpart to the "anatomical" component of the body schema was stipulated. Both systems are presumably within the thalamo-cortical activating circuits; lesions within either produce curiously contrasting effects, as was pointed out be Nielsen[15] and others: in body amnesia an existing body territory is felt to be absent while in anosognosia a lost function is felt to be intact. Nielsen believed that a lesion in the right thalamus or in its immediate surroundings was the cause for the imperception of a contralateral hemiplegia, while lesions in the right posterior parietal cortex (particularly in the supramarginal gyrus) accounted for neglect or amnesia of the contralateral body half. Similar focal possibilities that might account for the imperception of central blindness have been entertained by some investigators, and have been mentioned in the course of this presentation. Central blindness is necessarily caused by a bilateral defect. Therefore, lesions within the corresponding physiological or functional body schema system—namely, the thalamooccipital circuits—will cause Anton's symptom in this focal fashion and in a manner that since Anton's time has in fact been spoken of as the "amputation theory."

Clinical experience suggests that in imperception or denial of central (and even more so of peripheral) blindness, certain *diffuse abnormalities* of cerebral function create perceptual impairments which are particularly conducive to the establishment of what may be called the organic anosognosic milieu. There are three distinct varieties which must be noted.

The Level of Consciousness. It has been noted by many clinical observers that a transient initial clouding of consciousness seems to favor a later development of anosognosia (Barkman, 1925). Even more convincing are the observations by Weinstein and Kahn[16] on patients with denial of gross defects accompanying brain tumor associated with increased intracranial pressure. These authors invariably found bilateral and diffuse slow-wave activity in the electroencephalogram accompanying the period of anosognosia; whenever the EEG reverted to its focal pattern of abnormality consistent with the nature and location of the tumor, the denial syndromes disappeared and the defects were acknowledged by the patients. Then, if lowering of the level of consciousness was induced by administration of amytal, the denial syndrome could be reproduced—almost at will. Weinstein and Kahn conclude:

In summary, the conditions of brain pathology were those which by virtue of rapidity of development, diffuseness, bilaterality or midline situation or through the effects of increased intracranial pressure or subarachnoid bleeding produced diffuse delta wave activity in the EEG record.[17]

Impairment Resembling Korsakoff's Syndrome. The tendency of many patients with denial of central blindness to resort to extensive rationalizations—usually accompanied by a bland and even euphoric emotional attitude—has been noted by many observers, including Anton himself. There are also usually indications of partial disorientation. For these reasons the possible role of this Korsakoff-like state in the production of the denial syndrome has been considered and investigated by a number of workers. It appears, however, that this "amnesic-confabulatory" attitude of the patients is rather restricted to the issue of blindness and its denial or minimization. Kleist even thought that the patients had a vague notion of their defect, but suffered from an inability to become or remain sufficiently attentive to their loss of function. Although the precise nature of this particular perceptual impairment and its contribution toward the ultimate formation of an Anton syndrome are far from well understood, any number of observations by students of the Korsakoff psychosis could conceivably play a contributory role.

"Repression" of the Future. Because peripheral blindness is at times closely associated with disease of the frontal lobes—either in the case of general paresis with optic atrophy or in the case of large frontal-lobe neoplasm leading to a Foster Kennedy type of peripheral blindness—it may be asked whether the well-known lack or loss of concern that is associated with frontal-lobe pathology may be a factor in bringing about imperception or denial in such cases. A mental attitude such as this may be judged as being an equivalent of a perceptual impairment in the sense that the loss of the capacity to appreciate the meaningfulness and significance of an event, such as the loss of vision, may well encourage a degree of indifference tantamount to oblivion. In that case the patient would be less motivated by a desire to protect himself against psychic pain with the aid of psychological defense mechanisms, but rather would have been rendered incapable of appreciating psychic pain because of a structural loss of tissue. The subjective result in either case would be quite similar, but the ways in which it was accomplished would be quite different. It is for this reason that the phrase "repression of the future" was suggested. It may be added in this connection that Stengel considered the affective transformation of the personality following prefrontal lobotomy to be very similar to that seen in many patients with Anton's symptom. On the other hand it must be admitted that not all patients with peripheral blindness and associated frontal-lobe disease show the denial syndrome. Obviously there are still some factors at work which have so far eluded us.

To summarize, we may say that the final clinical picture in any given case of anosognosia is, as far as structural pathology within the body-image systems is concerned, the result of focal and/or diffuse lesions; the latter create various specific perceptual impairments, each of which could conceivably foster the imperception or denial of the defect. It appears, however, fitting and indeed necessary to make some final comments concerning the possible participation of psychological processes in the etiology and expression of anosognosia.

Psychological Processes. Since the preservation of anatomical and functional integrity of the body is without doubt a universal need and goal, it would appear reasonable to investigate the role of motivation in anosognosia. Motivation is "the general name for the fact that an organism's acts are partly determined . . . by its own nature."[18] We have learned to recognize the significance and power of that aspect of our "own nature" which we call *instinct*. The psychoanalytic theory of normal and abnormal behavior rests on this fact. Motivation, broadly speaking, may be *instinctual* if its goal is to satisfy an instinctual need; it may be *anti-instinctual* if its goal is to ward off the dangers to the ego that may arise from pursuit of an instinctual goal or the giving-in to an instinctual need. We also know that compromise patterns between instinctual and anti-instinctual forces occur in the form of certain psychoneurotic symptoms, such as conversion. There does not appear to be any conceivable or even comprehensible sexual or aggressive motivation to account for the phenomenon of anosognosia. On the other hand, both the needs and the goals of the ego instincts—the self-preservative forces within us, primordial and enduring—are powerfully and painfully challenged, thwarted, and endangered by the fact and awareness of paralysis, blindness, or deafness. We could not possibly dispute the fact that a motivation for the preservation of motility, vision, and hearing exists. If this motivation is in conflict—e.g., with a sexual instinctual need—the representations of the self-preservative instinct are more often than not compromised and sacrificed, as they are in hysteria. One may also make a good case for the intelligibility of a motivation to spare a patient the awareness of his paralysis, blindness, or deafness. However, the question that must be raised is this: Are those mental mechanisms that we know as being capable of preventing painful awareness to enter consciousness operative in anosognosia? What could be the clinical and theoretical evidence that this is, in fact, the case? What is the evidence that it is not?

There are four defense mechanisms which in one way or another exclude painful awareness from consciousness: repression, negation, rationalization, and projection. The first two are of a rather radical and therefore effective nature. Freud once said that "negation is, at a higher level, a substitute for repression."[19] Both are essentially anti-instinctual and in the service of warding off sexual and/or aggressive impulses. One could theorize that these two mechanisms might be equally useful if they could protect us against the awareness of a threat to, or loss of, our bodily integrity. They may indeed accomplish this end, but only, so it seems, with regard to ideas and affects pertaining to illness and *not* at the level of elementary perceptions of light, sound, and movement. Schilder's concept of "organic repression," which he offered in explanation of anosognosia, is a purely semantic attempt to apply psychodynamic principles. As to the defensive value and fitness of the mechanisms of repression and negation in anosognosia it must also be recalled that the body image, as we understand this term and its limited application, is very much a part of the objective world, even to its owner. Repression and negation, however, are mechanisms of defense which are not at all primarily directed toward a threat or a painful awareness emanating from without; on the contrary, their prime target is the id, the innermost core of the psyche. Along similar lines, it would appear most unlikely to see the phenomenon of alloesthesia as a mechanism akin to displacement (as we all understand this term), which would be an integral component of the primary process.

The second group of defense mechanisms which aim at the avoidance of painful awareness, rationalization and projection, is quite evident in certain patients with anosognosia. Some reference has already been made to such observations in the clinical description of the syndrome. The tendency to minimize or to rationalize the dimly perceived loss of function is seen in those patients who, while denying their paralysis, will nevertheless (or rather instead) complain that their arm feels heavy or clumsy; rationalizations are even more common in patients with Anton's symptom. My patient[20] would never admit to blindness, but he frequently made such remarks as "I am not blind, but I have to change my glasses . . . my eyes are kind of weak now, but they are picking up" and so on; he also confabulated a great deal, giving a detailed but totally wrong description of the examiner, without a trace of hesitation. His general mental attitude was quite compatible with that of the Korsakoff syndrome. Many patients with denial of blindness attribute their visual difficulty to external but untrue causes, as was already stated. In effect they complain of *darkness*, but not of *blindness*. Some psychiatrists may consider such expressions as "externalizations" of causality, but we feel that the term and idea of projection is quite accurate as a designation. In anosognosia of hemiplegia the paralyzed extremity, usually the arm, is at times projected into space or on to another person. Speaking about the mechanism of projection, Fenichel makes certain observations which are pertinent to our hypothesis:

Projection is a derivative of the first negation; it has the content "I want to spit it out" or, at least, of "I want to put distance between it and myself" . . . . while everything painful is experienced as being non-ego. . . . this primitive mechanism of defense can be used extensively only if the ego's function of reality testing is severely damaged . . .[21]

Two conclusions are offered concerning the role of projection in anosognosia: the projection indicates *some* awareness of a defect and seems to deal with those remnants of insight which have not been completely obliterated; the required reduction of the capacity to test reality is to be found in an organically rooted perceptual deficit.

REFERENCES

1. O. Fenichel. *The Psychoanalytical Theory of Neurosis.* New York, Norton, 1945, p. 36.
2. *Ibid.,* p. 418.
3. *Ibid.,* p. 36.
4. H. Head and G. Holmes. "Sensory Disturbances from Cerebral Lesions." *Brain, 34:* 1911, p. 102.
5. L. C. Kolb. "Disturbances of the Body Image." *In:* S. Arieti (ed.). *American Handbook of Psychiatry.* New York, Basic Books, 1959, vol. 1, p. 761.
6. R. D. Rabinovitch. "Reading and Learning Disabilities.." *In:* S. Arieti (ed.). *Op. cit.,*[5] p. 867.
7. R. Brain. "Visual Disorientation with Special Reference to Lesions of the Right Cerebral Hemisphere." *Brain, 64:* 1941, p. 244.
8. E. A. Weinstein and R. L. Kahn. *Denial of Illness,* Springfield, Ill., Thomas, p. 6.
9. *Ibid.,* p. 63.

10. *Ibid.*, pp. 106–107.

11. S. Cobb. "Amnesia of Left Limbs Developing into Anosognosia." *Bulletin of the Los Angeles Neurological Society, 12:* 1947, p. 48.

12. J. M. Nielsen. *Agnosia, Apraxia, Aphasia: Their Value in Cerebral Localization* New York, Hoeber, 1936.

13. V. Lunn, "Ueber mangelnde Wahrnehmung der eigenen Blindheit (Anton's Symptom)." *Acta Psych. Neur., 161:* 1941, p. 191.

14. P. Schilder. "The Image and Appearance of the Human Body." *Psychological Monographs* #4. London, Kegan Paul, 1935.

15. J. M. Nielsen. *Op. cit.*[12]

16. E. A. Weinstein and R. L. Kahn. *Op. cit.,*[8] pp. 337–342.

17. *Ibid.*, p. 87.

18. H. B. English and A. C. English. *A Comprehensive Dictionary of Psychological and Psychoanalytical Terms.* New York, Longmans, Green, 1958, p. 330.

19. S. Freud. "The Unconscious." *In: Collected Papers.* London, Hogarth, 1950, vol. 4, p. 119.

20. H. Oppenheimer and M. Weissman. "On Anosognosia." *American Journal of Psychology, 108:* 1951, pp. 337–342.

21. O. Fenichel. *Op. cit.,*[1] pp. 146–147.

12

The Essential Nature and Unity of the Neurotic Process

This chapter, as its title suggests, aims to identify the psychopathology which is essential and common to all psychiatric illnesses referred to as neuroses. We proceed from the premise that a nosological entity called neurosis does exist, and that despite its protean manifestations and clinical ambiguities it differs in principle from any other psychological state, including mental health. In pursuing this common denominator we will not be particularly concerned with etiology, symptom formation, content pathology, or treatment. We hope to recognize in the myriad individual clinical manifestations of neurosis representations of a single basic psychopathological process, even while we may not yet know, or fully know, why this process should ultimately appear in so many different forms or cloaks. Most certainly more questions will be raised than can be answered. In tracing the evolution of the concept of the neurotic process we will, quite naturally, begin with a consideration of Freud's ideas, as far as they are relevant to our theme; we will take issue with his topographic conception of the nature of neurosis. Next, we will consider the question of the reliability and validity of phenomenology in the search for the principle we are seeking to isolate. We hope to find this principle, following Kubie's suggestion, in a general dynamic formulation according to which the essence of the neurotic process can be seen in the distorted repetitiveness of isolated or comprehensive aspects of behavior that arise from a predominantly unconscious determination of such behavior. Finally, a number of variations of neurotic repetitiveness will emerge that, although resembling a "classification," are, in our opinion, more in the nature of alternative forms of the same "psychological stuff."

NEUROSIS AS A PROCESS

The concept of neurosis has been considerably expanded, diluted, and even polluted since Freud's epochal discoveries and clarifications. Freud dealt principally with the hysterias and the various obsessive-compulsive syndromes, in all of which the symptomatology is both conspicuous *and* enigmatic. His aim, as was once said, was to make the seemingly irrational rational and the seemingly rational irrational. Thus he confined himself largely to these most structured, condensed, coded, symbolic, and indirect expressions of the psychopathology of the psychoneuroses. His views, after they had matured, had all the advantages and limitations of a look through the high-power lens of a microscope; all phenomena were seen in their isolation *and* minuteness: the conversion of conflict into abnormal cerebrospinal innervations or the allusions to significant past events in the form of present-day semantic or conative-ritualistic pointers (all fragments of the primary process). This viewpoint may account for Freud's conclusion that the difference between neurosis and health prevails only by day. This statement is, of course, invalid if one includes—as we must—character deformations among the clinical possibilities of the neurotic process; but, as we said, Freud did not particularly concern himself with the latter. On the other hand, except for his conviction concerning the universally sexual origin and etiology of all neuroses, Freud made only few and brief statements about the possible nature of what one might call the constant, uniform, and unifying factor in which the essence of the neurotic process lies. Those statements were, despite his professed "dislike of simplification at the expense of truth,"[1] eminently true and of disarming simplicity. Thus he says in *A General Introduction to Psychoanalysis* that "an extraordinary and unprofitable attitude towards life . . . is a universal trait common to every neurosis."[2] and a few pages later, referring to the impossibility of control by the patient over his obsessive ritual, "it will be followed. It must be followed."[3] Here, although restricted to *one*, but a particularly suitable neurotic manifestation, is an allusion to the idea and character of inevitability of neurotic processes in whatever form they may present themselves; but Freud did not see in this quality the essence of the neurotic process.

In a paper, "Neurosis and Psychosis," Freud defines the essence of neurosis as a *"conflict between the ego and its id."*[4] This formulation is based on what is known as the topographic or structural frame of reference, according to which the mental apparatus is made up of three major structural components after it has matured and completed its ontogenetic evolution. As is well known, its oldest component, the id, is given at birth; the ego, by virtue of its capacity to interact with the outer world of reality, is considered to emerge as a specially differentiated portion of the id, a kind of mediator between biological needs and external possibilities as well as a hindrance to the endless striving for instinctual satisfaction. The third component, the superego, may be considered as a repository of parental and social influences, permitting, encouraging, postponing, or interdicting human strivings as well as creating incentives of the kind known as values or ideals. When Freud defined the essential nature of neurosis in the aforementioned topographic terms he made, so it seems, a generalization intended to carry within it the force and principle of a psychological law without room for doubt or obscurity. Still, he warns us in the next paragraph "to be suspicious of such simple solutions of problems."[4] I do not construe this topographic definition to mean that neurosis is the *only* or inevitable outcome of a dynamic interaction between the ego and its id. While a contest may be decided in an arena, it is not the arena which decides the contest; nor does it necessarily determine the events which could take place in it. I therefore submit that the normal and painful growth from psychological childhood to adult mental and social maturity requires within this same topographic framework a transformation and taming of the id, or rather of a part of it, into what will then emerge as a healthy ego. The participation of the outer world and its various introjects in this process is well known. It is relevant to distinguish in principle as well as in detail between ordinary "growing pains" and neurotic deformity and distortion. The dynamic forces operative in the successful "passing of the Oedipus complex"—Freud's central theme—as well as in the accomplishment and resolution of other required adaptations may occupy the same topography and engage the same dynamic forces and conformations as do their less fortunate counterparts, such as hysteria or a perversion. Again, it is not the metapsychological allocation, not even the content of the conflict, that is responsible for the development and essence of the neurotic process. A neurotic conflict, unless successfully treated, remains in most instances unsettled and self-perpetuating; and yet, a conflict may be settled and thus terminated without leading to a neurosis.

The Role of Phenomenology

We will, for the moment, postpone questions concerning the general validity of phenomenology and consider the value of specific phenomenological clinical facts as possible indicators of the neurotic illness and process, albeit with some qualifications. It is, for instance, quite possible to define the neurotic symptomatology by pointing out those major areas of psychological functions which are *preserved*. Such an approach, although pragmatically sound, is nevertheless a way of identification by stressing a negative issue, and we will later advance more positive evidence. Nevertheless, the following few comments, which are all applicable to the phenomenology of neurosis, have the additional distinctive but incidental advantage of serving as some lines of demarcation between "neurosis" and "psychosis."

There is no abnormality in the area of formal use of language and thought in the neuroses, such as would be found in organic or schizophrenic dementia. While reasoning in neurotic character disorders is bound to be mildly illogical owing to an ascendancy of critical emotional needs or attitudes at the expense of objectivity, even such reasoning will not confound the observer because it lacks the quality of incomprehensibility. There is no *breakdown* of the secondary process in neurosis, and whatever *breakthrough* of the primary process may occur in the symptomatology of the psychoneuroses is limited in degree and delimited in extent. Nor does the neurotic symptomatology contain hallucinatory disorders of perception within the modalities of the distance receptors of vision and hearing. This fact is related to a subtle but significant aspect of reality testing and is relevant to the present context. Freud, in a paper entitled, "Negation," examined the function of reality testing by "the final reality-ego" and "the previous pleasure-ego." He said, "once more . . . the question is one of *external* and *internal*. What is not real, what is merely imagined or subjective is only *internal;* while . . . what is real is also present *externally*."[5] Various abnormal sensations within the several fields of the enteroceptors, which mediate internal stimuli, are very common in certain types of neuroses. Some authors think that they may even be of a hallucinatory nature. But unless they are delusionally elaborated as to their origin, meaning, and consequences (and this does *not* happen in neuroses in a manner comparable to that seen in psychotics) they are as benign as neurosis is itself. It is, of course, the function of the distance receptors, as instrumentalities of the reality-ego, to test outer reality by perceiving, rediscovering, and thus recognizing it. There is also no fragmentation of the personality in neurosis. Hysterical paralysis, for instance, while, in Freud's words of *"excessive intensity,"* also *"shows an exact delimitation."*[6] All psychoneurotic symptoms are, in fact, safely and distinctly insulated from the remainder of the soma and psyche. It is a well-known fact that even severely conflicted and distressed patients suffering from a character neurosis remain clinically and socially coherent, and, despite crippling limitations, so to speak, in one piece. There is one more significant negative feature in the psychopathology of neuroses—namely, the absence of delusions or malignant false beliefs. Nevertheless, the neurotic entertains many "false beliefs" of a certain kind, as was pointed out in the chapter called "Delusions and Other False Beliefs." In other words, the relationship of the neurotic to reality is not entirely undisturbed. It seems to me that in his paper, "The Loss of Reality in Neurosis and Psychosis," Freud addresses himself more to the psychoneuroses than to the character neuroses. Thus his statements "Neurosis does not deny the existence of reality, it merely tries to ignore it," and "in neurosis a part of reality is avoided,"[7] would explain, from this point of view, the difference between a cat phobia and a delusion about cats. But I wonder whether it throws sufficient light on other well-known features of neurotic false beliefs, such as their anticipatory rather than retrospective nature or their tendency at times to exaggerate rather than to "ignore" reality without in any sense denying its existence. There is another subtle, but potent distortion of reality in many neurotics, and perhaps amongst most of mankind: while people do not experience true visions, they maintain false images as to what constitutes right and wrong, good and evil, superior and inferior, even normal and sick. This distortion of reality, essentially the result of introjects, is "relative" in the sense that it has no reliable standards or basis in the world of objects and not even in the history and social structure of man. Beliefs of this kind have thus lead us into the largely man-made realm of values and evaluations, and their influence on human behavior is enormous. While at times masquerading as health, such beliefs actually constitute significant albeit elusive components of neurotic behavior, which Kubie aptly called "masked neuroses."[8]

We are now in a position to consider the validity as well as the fallacy of phenomenology in our search for the essence of the neurotic process. In the symptomatic neuroses, and particularly in the psychoneuroses, the validity of phenomenology is considerable. Thus in the hysterias and the obsessive-compulsive syndromes the symptomatology is most conspicuous and least comprehensible to the uninformed observer; it is most condensed and least ego-syntonic; it is most clinical and least social. It is also least "contagious" in a social sense as compared with the various character neuroses. In the latter, the possibility of error arising from the unreliability of surface phenomena is much greater. Let me present some clinical illustrations. Certain character traits— because of their inflexibility more than their prominence—are likely to be neurotic. "Civility is not a sign of weakness," President Kennedy said in his Inaugural Address; but to display amiability toward each and everybody, and under circumstances which would seem to call for dissent if not for outright resentment, seems to indicate fear of the wishes of others rather than courage of one's own. Let us consider the issue of aggressiveness. A distinction must be made between healthy aggression, which in its manifold forms is a normal and desirable survival function,[9] and neurotic aggression. The former is much closer to initiative, enthusiasm, and the capacity to make real efforts—within secular and moral law. Neurotic aggression, put briefly, aims toward vindictiveness and destruction, not vindication and accomplishment. The neurotically aggressive person would, of course, fail to see any difference between these two sets of aims. Perhaps one more of many possible examples may be mentioned—namely, the compulsive need for certainty. At first consideration such a trait appears to be eminently healthy. But the real question is whether its motivation is, or is not, rooted in a fear of uncertainty, for whatever reasons inherent in the past experiences or conditioning of the patient. If one is afraid of darkness one does not merely *enjoy* sunshine, one *needs* light.

A few words may be added to indicate and indict the ambiguity and unwholesomeness of certain social criteria as applied to such areas as conformity, success and failure, utility and sacrifice. The question whether conformity in a given instance is healthy or neurotic is considered here strictly from the clinical psychiatric point of view. We are, therefore, not debating compliance with the law; there is nothing to debate in this context. Conformity motivated by fear is different from conformity based on reason and social responsibility. The former is not likely to make allowances for exceptions under any circumstances; it is compulsive and automatic. The latter, because it is healthy, will be discriminating; and if circumstances call for nonconformity, the healthy person will not experience embarrassment or fear of consequences—even though often enough there are bound to be grievous consequences. On the other hand, noncomformity may represent a compulsive and automatic need to rebel, to appear to be different or superior. It is not the act itself, but the motivation, or rather its psychological source, which determines in this as in many other situations the healthy or neurotic quality. There are rare but eminently sturdy acts of behavior which are judged as foolish and even offensive by less vigorous members of one's society, and there are many neurotic traits which an unsuspecting majority admires. This dramatic paradox of being incapable of telling the giant from the pygmy brings to my mind a comment once made (and hopefully with justification) by the late Winston Churchill about a contemporary politician: "He has all the virtues I despise and none of the vices I admire."[10]

TOWARD A UNIFYING CONCEPT

In our search for the essential nature of the neurotic process we have traversed metapsychology, clinical phenomenology, social and adaptive criteria, and have, in fact, reached a point of apparent reversal of the respective meanings of neurosis and normality. Nevertheless, if the premise of a common denominator is prerequisite to forming a hypothesis of the essential unity of neurotic psychopathology—and it is—then such a unifying feature must be found. In 1954 Kubie proposed that the essential difference between normality and neurosis lay solely in the respective preponderance of dynamic forces among the systems Cs, Pcs, and Ucs in their determination of a single (and preferably simple) act of human behavior or element of mental content.[11] To the degree to which the Cs-Pcs "alliance" determines a psychological event, such an event will not only be normal but will also be characterized by certain features and functional qualities inherent in the system Cs-Pcs. On the other hand, if unconscious dynamic forces are the decisive determinants the resulting psychological event will reflect certain qualities of the system Ucs; and it was in the presence, or dominance, of these qualities in which Kubie saw the universal and thus essential nature of the neurotic process. It must be understood and appreciated, however, that the issue does *not* depend on the level (Cs, Pcs, or Ucs) at which the event *occurs*, but on the level, or levels, which on balance are dynamically responsible for its occurrence. Nor does it matter what the nature of the particular event may be; it may be ideational, affective, conative, autoplastic or alloplastic, or comprise larger psychological units of behavior (such as character traits). Kubie expresses, in fact, the ultimate hope that increasingly comprehensive and complex individual and even cultural phenomena may be included in, and comprehensible within, this scheme. What concerns us here, then, is not the subjective experience of fluctuations in the state of consciousness, but rather the functional or dynamic characteristics of these three distinct levels or modes of psychic life. A simple clinical example will serve to illustrate this distinction. A patient will be intensely conscious of his compulsive rituals or phobic anticipations; but this intense awareness does not represent the qualities of the system Ucs that cause, shape, and sustain the ritual or the phobia. Nor does it negate them. To various degrees every act and aspect of human behavior is the result either of participation or exclusion of the systems Cs, Pcs, and Ucs, and in this sense expresses their respective qualities and dynamic contributions. Generally speaking, an act or aspect of behavior will tend to be disadvantageously automatic and repetitive, the more its occurrence is determined by unconscious forces. Conversely, voluntary and discriminating behavior requires a preponderance of capacities most apposite to the system Cs. Thus a surgeon will wash his hands thoroughly and conscientiously before an operation because his is aware of the need for aseptic cleanliness. But a patient suffering from a hand-washing ritual will wash his hands just as thoroughly and conscientiously because he is *not* aware of his need for cleansing himself of, let us say, a sense of guilt. Despite certain similarities in the performance of the same simple act it is easy to see the decisive differences between health and neurosis, within the general terms I have just used.

As a final illustration, let us compare in depth the psychopathological issues involved in, let us say, a patient's opening the wrong door either because the act took place at a lowered level of consciousness or because it was determined by forces operating at the level of the unconscious. Dissolution owing to fatigue, mild intoxication, or postictal lowering of the level of alertness reduces precise discrimination to approximate or peripheral similarity of the nature of an act. Such a performance may be considered erroneous as a result of inflicted reduction in efficiency, as appreciation of differences is of a higher order than the recognition of similarities. "The doctrine of evolution implies the passage . . . from the most general to the most special."[13] But an identical act, also seemingly "committed in error"—if it occurs because of unconscious determination—represents a neurotic process, in this case perhaps a symptomatic act. Here, the quality of apparent error does not indicate loss of discrimination and subsequent reduction to loose and overinclusive similarity. On the contrary, in such instances precise unconscious determination only feigns loss of capacity for discrimination. These differences are crucial.

Psychodynamic Determinants. Let us now be more specific. Unconscious determination of neurotic symptoms or traits may be the result of a repression that has miscarried. This is particularly the case in the psychoneuroses. The original infantile impulse has neither been silenced nor modified in such a way as to voice its claim with discrimination, reasonableness, or in deference to the reality principle. It seems as if a persistent and predominantly unconscious motivation would indicate that some aspect of our mental life had somehow been left behind, become isolated, pursued its own devious ways, and had thus never been given the opportunity to grow and mature toward a normal integration. Freud, speaking of conversion hysteria, said that "the [hysterical] lesion, then, would consist in the abolition of the accessibility of the concept 'arm' in association. The arm acts as if it did not exist in the interplay of associations."[14] The arm ceases to be an important instrument of utility to the ego; after having been both ideationally and affectively endowed with the special and significant attributes of the conflict, it is relegated—through the mysterious leap of somatic compliance—to the encased, symbolic, and useless existence of such objects as are relics of the past. Also, because substitutive or obsolete gratifications or attempts at solution neither gratify nor solve anything, the unaware patient will, naturally, ceaselessly repeat the neurotic attempt. In so doing he will disregard utility, flexibility, reality testing in its more subtle forms, as well as the lessons of reward and punishment. He has no choice. Instead, his responses as well as his more circumscribed symptom are automatic and repetitive. The present situation is powerless to modify behavior because "the processes that have set it in motion predetermine its automatic repetition."[15] One may indeed apply to neurotics the wording of a judgment (attributed to Talleyrand): "They have learned nothing, and forgotten nothing."[16] It is in this sense that automatic and repetitive behavior is pathognomonic of the neurotic process. The definition is psychodynamic.

By contrast, the dynamic qualities of the system Cs-Pcs are such as to enable men to be reflective, flexible, realistic, imaginative, and creative, that is to say, healthy. The system Pcs contains that part of our mental life which is more or less readily accessible to full consciousness. Some preconscious elements are merely tangential or irrelevant to whatever may be at the focus of our awareness; they are normally excluded, with or without screening, from consciousness or expression by the ego. Other preconscious regions contain material of unique relevance that is capable of augmenting and even enriching mental life. I will mention but a few examples: fantasy, ideational expansion of thought, and "inspirational and elaborative creativeness"[17]—such as allusions, metaphors, and the felicitous choice of multivalent, multidimensional words. While this is not the place to elaborate upon the nature of the preconscious process, a few things may be said to reinforce our theme. Preconscious determination is not representative of the neurotic process because of the nature of its psychodynamic qualities. While pursuit of elaborative thought may be painfully slow and elusive, it nevertheless draws from the potential of the conflict-free ego sphere; and no counter-cathexis stands in the way of its ultimate emergence into consciousness in whatever form. While intuitive thought is not planned, it is nevertheless willed. While it may come at times without effort, it is not automatic. While its arrival will not come as a surprise, its timing is quite unpredictable.

Conscious determination of behavior, minimally and therefore insignificantly modified by unconscious promptings, has the quality and indeed the advantage of being guided by reflection and aided by the capacity for discrimination. Outer reality, representing either stimulus or target for an act of will, is viewed objectively for what it is, not subjectively for what it appears to be or symbolizes to a mind disqualified by previous conditioning that is unknown to itself. This being the case, conscious determination is freed from unwholesome past predeterminations and free to consider future purposes and consequences as well as to present alternatives. In this sense conscious motivation is most voluntary and least automatic. There is a choice; there is also the risk and the toil of a choice.

This emphasis on the superiority of voluntary option over automatic and compelling repetitiveness in the psychic life of man (and thus within the highest Jacksonian levels) invites a digression which will qualify and clarify what might otherwise be regarded as a dogmatic oversimplification. Repetitiveness of thoughts, feelings, actions, and even larger units of behavior is by no means necessarily pathological; quite the contrary. Consistency of purpose, habits, social or religious rituals, and the innumerable minor but essential activities to be carried on day in and day out—all these are really closer to stability than to crippling, neurotic immobility. As an illustration one may consider some significantly different examples of "repetition" in the field of music. When the artist is practicing a difficult musical phrase, he will have to repeat it time and again until the problems of mechanical and expressive execution have been mastered. This is repetition in the service of learning and attaining skill. Similarly, the composer will repeat a phrase in his score if musical aestheticism calls for it, or he may repeat a musical idea (then called a theme) by writing a long set of variations—the musical equivalent of a metaphor. This is repetition in the service of enjoyment and enrichment. And then there is the proverbial "broken phonograph record." Obviously, something went wrong and will remain wrong, unless one does something about it. In a paper, "The Repetitive Core of Neurosis," Kubie traces the normal function of repetitiveness in the development of the child, from the primitive repetition of somatic and instinctual activities to the "repetition of effort . . . inherent in living,"[18] so that the child may learn and acquire adaptive skills; the author concludes with the idea of repetition of activity for the sake of and as a source of sheer enjoyment of accomplishment. It may be added that exceptional people command an exceptional capacity for repeated, endless toil.

The pathological distortion of repetitiveness, representing the essential feature of the neurotic process, corresponds to the "broken phonograph record" and its dismal reiteration in the life history and symptomatology of the patient. How does it come about and what are its principal manifestations?

If we accept the premises that predominantly unconscious determinations add up to "predominantly unconscious goals, and unconscious symbolic goals are never attainable;"[19] that, however, attempts at attaining them are endlessly repeated; and that "when a repetition thus becomes irresistible, it becomes a neurosis,"[20] questions about the origin, maintenance, and choices of expression of such enormous and intractable psychodynamic forces must be asked and attempts made to answer them. It may be assumed that the stakes in a neurosis are never trivial; but what does that mean in psychological, let alone neurophysiological, terms? Classical psychoanalytic theory maintains the sexual—or at any rate, *instinctual*—source of neurosis. Neither the power nor the recurrent need for satisfaction of an instinct can be denied. Instincts represent one of several principal activating biological factors which affect mental life. Furthermore, if it is realized that the pathogenic "miscarriage of repression" of instincts and their derivatives neither sates nor silences the need for gratification, the resulting stalemate may, in every instance of neurotic repetitiveness, be tantamount to a draw resulting from perpetual check. Other factors pertaining to the questions raised may be added. Human beings, from a certain age onward, have the capacity of many forms of indirect representation: the capacity of the symbolic process. Symbolic representation may be comprehensible or incomprehensible, depending on a variety of very complex circumstances in which it appears or is resorted to; but it will always retain its character of indirectness. Thus, the "aesthetic illusion" in artistic symbolic representation is eminently pleasing and satisfying. But neurotic illusions of gratification through indirect symbolic representation are neither. It seems that the psyche, as well as the soma, requires natural and not substitutive satisfactions; but with the former lacking, the latter, while insufficient, remain nevertheless indispensable. These symbolic pursuits of nonexisting or unattainable goals by indirect and token means is, of course, the hallmark of the psychoneuroses. In addition to recognizing the forces of the instincts, we must also consider the power and ultimately the authority of the counter-instinctual counter-cathexes and their eventual introjects and projections.

Other Criteria.   Neurophysiological research has perhaps not yet advanced far enough towards fulfilling Freud's hope and prediction of finding a biological correlate to psychological phenomena and thus evidence to support psychoanalytic theory. The investigations of Lorente de No, McCulloch and Pitts, and of many other neurophysiologists have produced highly suggestive evidence for the existence within the central nervous system of reverberating and self-sustaining circuits. Even the "exact" sciences of mathematics and cybernetics have testified in support of a demonstrable neurophysiological basis for repetitive phenomena, both normal and pathological, and are even in a position to promise precise measurements of data most relevant and useful to psychoanalysis and psychoanalytic therapy. If it could, for instance, be proved that the refractory state of such self-sustaining circuits as may be the physiological counterparts of "compulsive" drives, ruminations, or traits was either so prolonged or so intense as to withstand any known attempts to "break up" those circuits, then "an organic limitation on the efficacy of . . . psychotherapy"[21] would absolve the patient from the onus of accounting for (and paying for) his putting up resistances; and even the theory of fixation may be improved or perhaps revised. The presenting problems in this whole matter are complex and their solution is probably distant. But the directions in which to think and to proceed have been clearly outlined: "What remains to be worked out are . . . the conditions which determine the degree and kind of awareness with which such circuits may be invested (Cs, Pcs, and Ucs) and . . . the methods and conditions by means of which such circuits can be interrupted."[22] It is, of course, assumed that self-sustaining circuits occur at all levels of consciousness *and therefore* of accessibility. They may encompass the whole range of psychic life, from archipallial, highly emotional "gut memories" to neopallial, highly frigid conceptual references. Significant emotional events may set them into motion; repression caused by either interrupting their "linkage"[23] to the various activating and/or centrencephalic systems or by a process of deactivation within these systems via corticofugal pathways[24] may keep them in a state of self-sustaining potency (unconscious determination!); and, finally, sophisticated mental mechanisms using either direct or indirect representation may account for the repetitive surface phenomena—all this along a path strewn with many unknown landmarks, one of which is time, a path which therapy has to tread from beginning to end, although it would be more accurate to say from end to beginning.

Webster defines classification as a "systematic arrangement in groups or categories according to established criteria." Accordingly, as physicians, we must distinguish between identification of disease entities, and the search for, and choice of, "established criteria" that will justify a subdivision of such disease entities into subgroups. In attempts at classification the emphasis may be put on theory, etiology, phenomenology, or prognosis. The validity and indeed the degree of excellence of the criteria upon which a classification is based determines its value toward better comprehension, better diagnosis, and better treatment of the disease. I can, in fact, see no other significant purpose in our attempting medical and psychiatric classifications. The relationship between phenomenology, understanding, and therapy is rather intricate, and at our present state of knowledge (or ignorance) somewhat incongruous—despite the obvious logic which is implied in the sequence of the component parts. The knowledge of one may not help us much in dealing with the other, and incomplete or controversial understanding may not hinder us much in helping the patient. From the beginning of psychoanalytic thinking the classification of the neuroses has been, and has largely remained, the child of theory. In his final formulations Freud classified the psychoneuroses (and even the psychoses) according to fixation at, or regression to, certain stages of evolving infantile sexuality. Hysteria (conversion reactions and phobias) resulted from psychopathology at the Oedipal level; obsessive-compulsive neuroses were traced to the anal stage, again within the framework of the libido theory. Melancholia and schizophrenia corresponded to an even more profound return to early and earliest (oral and narcissistic) phases of psychosexual immaturity. Perversions were classified depending on whether there was a deviation in aim or object. Freud considered them to be a kind of "reversal" of the psychoneuroses. Whatever was indirectly represented in the psychoneuroses erupted directly in the perversions; whatever was "white" in the former, showed "black" in the latter, and vice versa. Freud meant this quite literally; he used the positive and the negative of a photograph as a simile, and referred to perversions as the positive of the neuroses, the true face of the situation. "I have . . . described the neuroses as the 'negative' of the perversions, because in the neuroses the perverse tendencies come to expression from the unconscious part of the mind, after the repression, and because they contain the same tendencies in a state of repression that manifest perverts exhibit."[25] The lines of demarcation were indeed sharply drawn as the clinical exponents of theoretical formulations were assigned to their respective stations, although the method of treatment remained the same for all.

Because this presentation has stressed the essentially unitary nature of the neurotic process, attempts at classification constitute, as I said at the outset, consideration of alternative forms of expression of the same "psychological stuff." There will be preponderances, but no singular and mutually exclusive modes of expression. Whatever differences in phenomenology exist are not of the essence. Kubie thought that the basic neurotic psychopathology of distorted repetitiveness in behavior would *under certain circumstances* be most prominently displayed in one of three ways (italics mine).[26] The instinctual drive itself, undisguised and unmitigated, is compulsively and, so to speak, nakedly (but by no means always impudently!) gratified through perversion. This category includes "partial" and pregenital instincts within the compass of sexuality. The qualification "nakedly but not impudently" is significant. Perversion, lacking the indirectness of expression which repression usually provides, is indeed a resounding neurotic affront—not only to a Victorian society, but to any society and civilization that repudiates any deviation in aim or object of the sexual instinct. There is, of course, no question of intentional affront by the patient. On the contrary, his emotional reaction toward his perverse impulses and acts is almost always one of shame and depression. Some degree of neurotic character deformation, while playing a subordinate role, coexists. The second possibility is the relative ascendancy of the "negative" of a perversion, a psychoneurosis. Owing to partially successful repression and perhaps for other largely unknown reasons, the symptomatology is coded, condensed, and inoffensive. The respective mental mechanisms operative in the various categories of psychoneuroses see to that. Reiterating Plato's statement that good men content themselves with dreaming of what the wicked do, one may say that psychoneurosis contents itself with discreet concealment of what perversion reveals in the raw. Finally, unconscious determination leading to neurotic rigidity and repetitiveness may attain its end by a more evenly distributed, attenuated, but permanent psychopathology; the neurotic character deformation. Here, too, we are likely to find traces of some of the "alternative forms of expression of the neurotic process," despite the preponderance of a broad neurotic behavioral and emotional disorder. There may be minor phobias and reaction formations against, and sublimations of, perverse tendencies. The relative preponderance of *one* alternative is never unaccompanied by smaller or larger admixtures with components of the remaining ones. Thus diversity of expression need not violate unity of principle. We do not really know the nature of those "certain circumstances" which determine the ultimate "choice" of the clinical manifestations. The availability and effectiveness of repression has probably a great deal to do with it. It is also uncertain in what proportion constitution and life experiences participate in the outcome. Freud once remarked on the possibility that education was not the only factor influencing the effectiveness of repression. There are many traps and pitfalls on the road from unconscious instinctual determination to neurotic illness.

> Between the emotion
> And the response
> Falls the Shadow[27]

It has been the purpose of this presentation to throw some light on this shadow.

REFERENCES

1. S. Freud. A *General Introduction to Psychoanalysis.* New York, Liveright, 1935, p. 249.

2. *Ibid.*, p. 242.
3. *Ibid.*, p. 246.
4. S. Freud. "Neurosis and Psychosis." *In: Collected Papers.* London, Hogarth, 1948, vol. 2, p. 250.
5. S. Freud "Negation." *Op. cit.*,[4] vol. 5, p. 183.
6. S. Freud. "Some Points in a Comparative Study of Organic and Hysterical Paralysis." *Op .cit.*,[4] vol. 1, p. 48.
7. S. Freud. "The Loss of Reality in Neurosis and Psychosis." *Op. cit.*,[4] vol. 2, p. 279.
8. L. S. Kubie. "The Fundamental Nature of the Distinction between Normality and Neurosis." *Psychoanalytic Quarterly, 23:* 167–204, 1954, *passim.*
9. K. Lorenz. *On Aggression.* New York, Harcourt Brace & World, 1966.
10. B. Adler (ed.). *The Churchill Wit.* New York, Coward McCann, 1965, p. 29.
11. L. S. Kubie "The Fundamental Nature." *Op. cit.*[8]
12. L. S. Kubie. "Some Implications for Psychoanalysis of Modern Concepts of the Organization of the Brain." *Psychoanalytic Quarterly, 22:* 29, 1953.
13. J. Taylor (ed.). "Evolution and Dissolution." *In: Selected Writings of John Hughlings Jackson.* New York, Basic Books, vol. 2, p. 58.
14. S. Freud. "Some Points in a Comparative Study." *Op. cit.*,[4] p. 56.
15. L. S. Kubie. "The Fundamental Nature." *Op. cit.*,[8] 182.
16. J. Bartlett. *Familiar Quotations,* 13th (Centennial) ed. Boston, Little, Brown, 1955, p. 384a.
17. E. Kris. *Psychoanalytic Explorations in Art.* New York, International Univer. Press, 1952, p. 59.
18. L. S. Kubie. "The Repetitive Core of Neurosis." *Psychoanalytic Quarterly, 10:* 26, 1941, p. 26.
19. L. S. Kubie. "The Repetitive Core." *Op. cit.*[18]
20. *Ibid.*
21. L. S. Kubie. "Some Implications for Psychoanalysis." *Op. cit.*,[12] p. 23.
22. *Ibid.*, p. 32.
23. *Ibid.*, p. 33.
24. L. Linn. "Psychological Implications of the Activating System." *American Journal of Psychiatry, 110:* 1953, pp. 61–65.
25. S. Freud. "Civilized Sexual Morality and Modern Nervousness." *Op cit.*,[4] vol. 2, p. 86.
26. L. S. Kubie. "The Repetitive Core." *Op. cit.*,[18] p. 39.
27. T. S. Eliot. *Collected Poems 1909–1962.* New York, Harcourt Brace Jovanovich, Inc., p. 82.

13

The Concept of Schizophrenia

Our conceptions about schizophrenia and all its essential
aspects are still evolving; it appears that the vast mass of
clinical and experimental data, the profound reflections of thoughtful
theoreticians, and the great variety of individual patients all constitute
a grotesquely disproportionate weight to be carried by a single diagnostic term, even if qualifying adjectives are employed. Everyone who
reflects upon the essential nature of schizophrenic mental states and
transformations agrees that they are quite different, in many respects,
from the psychopathology that characterizes coarse brain disease,
affective psychoses, neuroses, deliria, mental defect, or psychopathy.
However, it does not seem to be sufficient or scientifically sound to
define schizophrenias in terms of what they are not and thus to reduce
their unquestioned identity to a mere negative reference. By assigning
an identity to "schizophrenia" we do not mean to imply that etiological
factors, phenomenology, types of the disorder, and course and prognosis
are the same or even similar in all instances. The purpose, and the
challenge, of this presentation is rather to consider the many and meaningful diversities of facts and opinions, without, however, having to
abandon a decisive element of uniqueness which sets these mental
disorders apart from all others. In trying to pursue such a course we
will also have to free ourselves from the common but fallacious and
illusory notion that a phenomenon can be extricated from doubt and
ambiguity in which it may be cast by the simple device of giving it
a name. In an article dealing with the historical evolution of the concept
of schizophrenia Wender,[1] quoting the American author Alexander
Bryant Johnson, reminds us how often men are led astray by mistaking
words for things; psychiatrists are not exempt from this hazard.

206

HISTORY OF THE CONCEPT

Morel is generally credited with having been first to apply the term *démence précoce* to the mental illness which Kraepelin some 30 years later called by its Latin equivalent, "dementia praecox." However, clinical descriptions of signal accuracy preceded the appearance of the modern terminology by almost a hundred years. Thus John Haslam, as early as 1809, gave an account of "a form of insanity, which occurs in young persons . . . [and] which in a short time has transformed the most promising and vigorous intellect into a slavering and bloated idiot."[2] From Haslam's astute and detailed description it would appear that this patient had suffered from a schizophrenic process, most likely a hebephrenia. In 1828 G. M. Burrows, commenting on the intellectual alterations in what we now call dementia praecox, said: "It is a defect or a hebetude of the understanding, general or partial, confined to individual faculties of the mind, particularly those concerned in associating and comparing ideas."[3] He referred to this form of insanity as "demency." It is therefore clear that both Kraepelinian and Bleulerian criteria had been observed and singled out since the beginning of the nineteenth century—namely, endogenous causes, early onset, progressive deterioration, dissociation of thought, and even withdrawal (autism). As is well known, Kahlbaum, in 1874, isolated and described a disease entity which was characterized by certain motor and conative abnormalities and to which he gave the name "catatonia," indicating a lowering of "tension" or "will." He must have been impressed by such typical catatonic symptoms as waxy flexibility, automatic obedience, and general abulia. Three years earlier, in 1871, Kahlbaum's pupil Hecker had described a puberty psychosis ending in rather rapid and profound intellectual deterioration and to which he assigned the name "hebephrenia," a term which, incidentally, was first used by Kahlbaum himself. Kraepelin's search for an identity and thus for a concept of schizophrenia turned in the direction of the most obvious and even pragmatic observations of the mentally ill. Some of them seemed to recover, Kraepelin noted, no matter what one did or failed to do with them. Their illnesses were cyclic; affective abnormalities either in the form of mania or of melancholia dominated the clinical picture; and there was no subsequent or even concurrent intellectual deterioration. These patients had a good prognosis, and their illness, Kraepelin concluded, was "manic-depressive psychosis." But the "other group" of patients with endogenous mental illnesses never recovered, no matter what one did with them. While they might also show affective abnormalities, the crucial and characteristic distinguishing feature lay in the presence and progression of an intellectual deterioration that was unusual not only because of its occurrence in the early decades of life but mainly because of its novel and even arcane manifestations. The designation "dementia praecox," which Kraepelin revived and applied to this group of patients, was thus a most accurate if abridged appelation. Kraepelin furthermore concluded that this malignant entity included Kahlbaum's catatonia, Hecker's hebephrenia, a paranoid variety, and (in the 8th edition of his textbook) a "dementia simplex," whose main features, apart from those qualifying it for inclusion into the dementia praecox group, were negative. After having thus accomplished this massive separation of forms of mental illness Kraepelin set out to define and refine a very large number of subtypes. His patience, power of observation, and faith in the value of minute phenomenological dissection must have been enormous, but his major contribution does not rest on these qualities. It will be of interest at this point to quote the appraisal of Kraepelin by such an authority in the field of the history of medical psychology as Zilboorg. He writes: "To Kraepelin a mentally sick person seems to have been a collection of symptoms. He was a true son of the great, energetic and creative age that was interested greatly in humanity but comparatively little in man."[4] Things, or rather patients, were, however, not quite so clear-cut and in conformity with Kraepelin's formulations. There was, for instance, a small group of patients suffering from "dementia praecox," who recovered without residual deterioration. Could there be "dementia praecox without dementia"? This issue is still with us, and we will take it up when we present modern views on classification. There were also in Kraepelin's time patients whose illness closely resembled the paranoid variety of dementia praecox but whose personality and intellectual faculties were far better preserved than those who suffered, let us say, from hebephrenia. Reluctantly and rather belatedly, in 1912, Kraepelin accepted the diagnostic label "paraphrenia" for this group of patients. This term has since given rise to a great deal of confusion. Freud clearly used "paraphrenia" as synonymous with Kraepelin's "dementia praecox" and Bleuler's "schizophrenia." In modern times K. Leonhard has designated one of his three major subgroups of "systematic schizophrenias" as paraphrenias, with several qualifying subdivisions.

When Bleuler in 1911 introduced the term "schizophrenia" he accomplished a great deal more than a mere replacement of the Kraepelinian designation "dementia praecox." It is not always realized how far-reaching the significance of Bleuler's use of the plural was when he gave his classical book the title, *Dementia Praecox or the Group of Schizophrenias*. In 1965 Bleuler's son, Manfred, published a paper entitled, "Conception of Schizophrenia Within the Last Fifty Years and Today."

In his discussion of this paper Leonhard said: "My difference of opinion arises at the outset from the fact that in his paper he [Dr. Manfred Bleuler] almost everywhere uses the singular form 'schizophrenia' and speaks of the 'schizophrenic.' "[5] Eugen Bleuler's conceptual extension achieved through use of the plural took into account the observable fact that mental deterioration is not the inevitable outcome of these illnesses. Accordingly, some present-day psychiatrists are inclined to distinguish between "Kraepelinian" malignant dementia praecox and "Bleulerian" (not necessarily malignant) schizophrenias. The former is characterized by insidious onset and a course leading to the total deterioration of the core of the personality—hence the term "nuclear" or "process type" of the disease. Bleuler further recognized that a schizophrenia might be "released" by physical disease of the brain or other organs and that it might even be provoked by psychological stresses in certain predisposed individuals. There is hardly a point along the compass of modern multidimensional etiology that was excluded by Bleuler in his search for the causes of schizophrenias. The conception of "a group of psychotic reactions rather than one formal disease"[6] is thus in many ways implied in Bleuler's descriptions and interpretation of the schizophrenias. It should also be added that he attempted to integrate some of Freud's discoveries in his formulations of schizophrenic symptomatology. He clearly recognized the significance of ideational-affective "complexes" in the determination of schizophrenic thought and language; he demonstrated the manifestations of condensation, displacement, and symbolisms in the mental processes of the patient; and he created the concept of autism, which he defined (in effect) as the pathological preponderance of wishful thinking and infantile fantasy at the expense and as a replacement of objective external reality.

THE SEARCH FOR DECISIVE SIGNS AND SYMPTOMS

This issue presents itself as a convenient link between the preceding historical account and the contemporary scene of controversy about the existence and nature of phenomenological evidence of schizophrenia. Although intellectual deterioration, strange in its manifestations and occurring so early in the patient's life had always been noted, it was Bleuler who first conceived the idea of "fundamental" or "primary" symptoms that were few in number but pathognomonic of the disease. He said: "The fundamental symptoms consist of disturbances of association and affectivity, the predilection for fantasy as against reality, and the inclination to divorce oneself from reality (autism).''[7] Of these primary symptoms the disturbances of associations rank first in importance as well as in accuracy and comprehensiveness of exposition; and they correspond to the manifestations of what is usually referred to as the formal thought and language pathology in schizophrenia, an issue which is discussed in detail in the following chapter. Since Bleuler's original documentation of the thought and language performances of schizophrenic patients, some of his observations and formulations have been described by students in this field by different names and in the light of subsequent theoretical hypotheses. For example, Kleist also believed that speech and thought disorder occurred to some degree in all schizophrenics, and in some forms of the disease so prominently that it became the basis for his designation of one of his four main types. Being somewhat neurologically oriented, Kleist held that disorders of speech ought to be separated from disorders of thought, with the former resembling a form of pathology not unlike ordinary aphasia. At any rate, it is quite possible and advantageous to describe the schizophrenic pathology of the *word* separately from that of the *sentence* or the associations, although both are the expression of the same pathognomonic primary symptom of *dementia* praecox. Both Bleuler and Kleist stated that "dementia," while always present, may range from hardly noticeable traces to total incoherence of the patient's productions. If the thought and language pathology is minimal and thus not evident during ordinary conversation, special forms of interrogation will bring it to the surface. One may, for instance, ask the patient to define objects, explain differences and similarities, complete sentences (particularly those which require a cause-and-effect judgment), construct sentences from suitable given words, and classify a collective concept into its component parts. We may ask the patient to explain the meaning of a simple proverb. Finally, the Rorschach test is a very sensitive tool for detection of the presence and extent of a schizophrenic thought disorder. It should be added that the purely verbal schizophrenic psychopathology—such as desymbolization, metonymic approximation, and neologisms—will, if at all present, almost always appear in the patient's spontaneous speech.

Disturbances of *affectivity*, Bleuler's second category of primary symptoms, are of decisive importance for the diagnosis of schizophrenia either in the advanced stages of the disease or at any time in the course of the illness if they appear in the form of blunting or stiffness of emotional expression. Schizophrenic affective abnormalities present a more complex problem to the clinician than the various thought and language disorders. There are several reasons why this is so. The inherent subjectivity of emotional experience as well as a subjective element on the part of the observer make an appraisal of affectivity more difficult and less reliable. At any rate, a great deal of clinical experience is required in this area in order to avoid false inferences. An additional complicating factor is the possibility that a schizophrenic illness may exist without the presence of characteristic affective changes at the time of observation. It is therefore not surprising that the psychopathology of affectivity has not been given the same prominence in the diagnosis of schizophrenia by clinicians after Bleuler. But there can be little doubt that in many cases of schizophrenia affective abnormalities of a pathognomonic character exist. They are more likely to be found in the sphere of emotional expression than in the form of a specifically "schizophrenic mood." In fact, any conceivable quality or shade of mood disorder may occur, such as anxiety, depression, perplexity, elation, and irritability. It is true that many schizophrenics show rapid and seemingly unaccountable mood swings; but this lability did not, in Bleuler's view, represent an essential feature of the disease. On the other hand, disorders of *expression* of affectivity are of diagnostic significance. The total lack of any kind of emotional expression associated with the patient's verbal and behavioral confirmation of complete indifference to even the most provocative potential releasers of affect is indicative of schizophrenia; it is usually found in the more advanced stages of the illness and is most pronounced in the end stages of dementia praecox. No other mental illness can produce such a profound depletion of feeling. There is, of course, no longer any diagnostic problem present after the disease has progressed to the point of affective deterioration. But an entirely different situation prevails during the early phases. Some schizophrenics display a characteristic viscosity of affective expression, known as "stiffening" of affect; they maintain, for instance, a faint smile or any other mien far beyond the moment when it had been appropriate; their affective expressions, as Fish put it, change more slowly than in normals. This phenomenon accounts in part for the proverbial incongruity of affective expression in dementia praecox. Another pathognomonic feature in the area of emotional expression is the almost ineffable quality of coldness and stilted artificiality that accompanies verbal and other attempts of contact. We can at this point sympathize with Bleuler when he said that "it is easier to sense these phenomena than to describe them."[8] But an experienced clinician can sense this affective "robot" quality in these patients; disease, not design, has brought about this display of dehumanization. Such a situation was very well portrayed by Bleuler in these words: "If we hear a schizophrenic speaking in a language foreign to us he offers us no indication of what he is talking about."[9] In conclusion it may be said that while a specific psychopathology of affectivity in schizophrenia exists in the area of expressiveness, considerable experience is required for its detection and evaluation if no other confirmatory evidence of dementia praecox is present. The latter contingency, while possible, is, however, not likely to present itself often to the skilled and thorough examiner.

Ambivalence, another of Bleuler's fundamental symptoms, is defined by him as "the tendency of the schizophrenic psyche to endow the most diverse psychisms with both a positive and negative indicator at one and the same time. . . ."[10] Bleuler also stated that this phenomenon is not always quite explicit, but that "its complete absence appears highly improbable."[11] He described *affective* ambivalence as a condition in which pleasant and unpleasant feelings—or at any rate *opposite* feelings—are simultaneously experienced toward the same person or idea. In *ambitendency,* or ambivalence of will, the patient wishes and does not wish to act, and he expresses this alternation of opposite tendencies accordingly and in immediate sequence, e.g., by reaching for and immediately withdrawing from an object. *Intellectual* ambivalence connotes the instantaneous sequence of thought and counterthought or of a word and its opposite. Bleuler clearly recognized that schizophrenic ambivalence resembled and possibly represented a much broader fundamental quality of the psyche—namely, the intrinsic polarity of affective, conative, and cognitive functions. Opposites, if projected against their appropriate supraordinate unity, are closer to each other than are heterogenous words, ideas, and feeling, which lack such a unitary point of reference. Freud gave a detailed account of this principle in his paper, "The Antithetical Sense of Primal Words," in which he quotes the philologist K. Abel as having said that "every conception is thus the twin of its opposite. . . ."[12] The same may be said in regard to affects and acts. Love and hate, to use Bleuler's own example, are infinitely closer to each other than to indifference or guilt. Representation by the opposite is a well-known mechanism of the dream work and may therefore be considered an inherent quality of the primary process. This very same mechanism if put in the service of the secondary process is made use of so effectively in the psychology of wit. Freud has given us many illustrations of this principle in his book, *Wit and its Relation to the Unconscious.* President Kennedy, so it was reported, once referred to the city of Washington as being renowned for its Northern hospitality and its Southern efficiency. In view of the ubiquitous distribution within the psyche of the principle of the "affinity of opposites," of which we have given only a few illustrations, it is necessary that its special expression in the form of schizophrenic ambivalence must be defined in more precise terms. Unless the clinician has this understanding he may suspect "Bleulerian ambivalence" when none exists, as in neurotic conflict and even in normal psychological phenomena. One can, for instance, not equate compulsive doubting, "mixed feelings" toward a person or situation, or the evasive or impotent production of antithetical words in a word association test with schizophrenic ambivalence.

Bleuler thought that ambivalence was "an immediate consequence of the schizophrenic association disturbance."[13] It is not quite obvious how this observation would explain affective or conative ambivalence; but it seems reasonable to hypothesize that intellectual ambivalence may be one of the manifestations of the psychopathology of schizophrenic dementia. Clinical observation shows that intellectual ambivalence occurs most frequently as a spontaneous phenomenon rather than in response to a question. It may be that the association of opposites is, at the moment, the only available associational capacity in a patient; it is certainly a very inferior and meaningless associative performance, and like the similarly pathognomonic enumerative associations, it is of no ideational and communicative value. It seems that catatonic verbigerations are often reduced to the endless repetition of pairs of opposites, such as, "I am, I am not," or "an angel, a devil." At the level of the unconscious these contrary ideas exist side by side and without interacting; at the preconscious level, in the nonschizophrenic person, their word representations are in a state of comparative readiness—but only if it would be useful for the person to make his point by the device of the antithetical word and thought. In his random expansion of a concept, the schizophrenic has no point to make. Bleuler remarks that Schreber's special language included a tendency to replace a word by one with opposite meaning; thus "reward" means "punishment" and "poison" means "food."[14] This phenomenon, if viewed as a purely formal pathology of thought and language, might be explained as an example of "system shifting" (see p. 233); but it also appears possible, and indeed probable, that affective factors may have determined the substitutions in the examples cited, owing to their obviously emotional loading. Inasmuch as ambitendency is really a catatonic symptom, diagnosis should not be difficult because other catatonic motor phenomena are certain to accompany the ambivalence of will. The movements of ambitendency may appear to an observer to reflect doubt or indecision; it is, however, not likely that in a catatonic the corresponding neuronal mechanisms are of such a high order or representative of a psychological conflict. Affective ambivalence as a fundamental symptom of schizophrenia is the one among the antithetical phenomena most likely to cause diagnostic difficulties because the existence of opposite feelings is a very common occurrence. In nonschizophrenic situations a feeling toward a person may be wholehearted because its opposite counterpart has been successfully repressed. In reaction formation the repression of the counter-affect is considered to be less reliable, more "brittle," and there may be clinical evidence of "ambivalence." In that case, however, there would be a situational explanation to account for the unexpected breakthrough of the "ambivalent attitude," accompanied by considerable anxiety or guilt. Even in those instances in which opposite affective tendencies toward the same object alternate—as, for example, in the course of an analysis or during its equivalent in the form of a corrective experience—the patient is fully and painfully aware of the contradiction. He may accept and weigh "ambivalent" feelings and decide in favor of the stronger of the two. None of this is found in schizophrenic affective ambivalence. The emotional antithesis is always patently obvious in the patient, no effort toward integration or resolution is made or attempted, and neither emotional suffering nor cognitive bewilderment is experienced. Thus the characteristic feature of affective ambivalence in schizophrenia seems to lie in the simultaneity and parallelism of the antithetical feelings. The analogy to a parallelism is intended to illustrate not the idea of a correspondence but, on the contrary, a total unrelatedness such as characterizes schizophrenic dissociation in general. Parallels never cross. In schizophrenic ambivalence the defusion is absolute.

Current Attempts

The search for decisive signs and symptoms of schizophrenia has not abated, either in intensity or in ingenuity, since Bleuler's original formulations. In Europe, where the influence of Karl Jaspers has been considerable, psychiatrists have applied his principle of "understandability" as a collective criterion of all schizophrenic phenomena. Jaspers' *verstehende Psychologie* maintains that "the understandability of a symptom is assessed by the observer feeling himself into the situation of the patient, and assessing whether the symptom can be understood rationally or emotionally as arising from the situation and the changes in the patient due to the situation and his emotions."[15] In this sense Jaspers' "understandability" differs, of course, from professional-psychiatric intelligibility. It is, for instance, understandable that a woman with a characterologically determined life-long fear of desertion may, during middle age, develop paranoid delusions to the effect that her husband's young and attractive secretary is plotting to kill her so that she can marry her husband. Such a delusion would be "understandable" in Jaspers' terms, not only because it is "possible" but also because it is *comprehensible* against the backdrop of the patient's emotional makeup and the life situation as represented by a potential rival for her husband's affection. Jaspers called such false beliefs "delusion-like ideas" in contrast to "true delusions," which evolve from incomprehensible circumstances. Both varieties may occur in schizophrenia, but only the latter form would be considered to be pathognomonic by the standard of *verstehende* psychology. These principles can be applied to delusions centering on perceptions as well as to delusional ideas. Thus in delusional misinterpretation of perception the qualities of the percept fit the affective or situational precondition within the patient; his delusional misinterpretation of what he sees or hears is comprehensible against this background and is very likely codetermined by it. A patient with intense, morbid guilt feelings, upon seeing a hearse, may "now" be convinced of the certainty of his imminent death. These mechanisms are, of course, much more characteristic of affective psychoses than of schizophrenia. But if, on the other hand, the qualities of the percept lack any conceivable connection, either with the content of the delusion or the usual predeterminations, then such delusional perceptions are indicative of schizophrenia. The ambiguity of all such formulations is acknowledged, even by their proponents. Fish concedes that regardless of these fine theoretical points of distinction any delusional idea which is very bizarre "is highly likely to be schizophrenic in origin."[16]

The element of bizarreness has, of course, always been associated with the phenomenology of the schizophrenias. "Bizarreness" is not a precise or even clinical term. Nevertheless, its presence in psychopathology has been equated with autism (itself a very controversial term). Consequently a special chapter will be devoted to the concept of "autism" and its place in psychopathology in general. Another well-considered but figurative definition of "bizarreness," particularly as it may apply to schizophrenia, rests on the assumption of a massive breakthrough of the primary process. Jung and others have likened the phenomenology of dementia praecox to that of the dream. But there are some authorities who maintain, with Fish, that "the essential feature of a true schizophrenic symptom . . . cannot be explained by means of the theory of the abolition of defence mechanisms."[17] We will give one more illustration of Jaspers' principle, this time in the area of hallucinations. It would be "understandable" if the voices echo the quality or ideational expression of the prevailing affect; thus guilt feelings may be projected as accusatory or derogatory phonemes and a paranoid affect would be properly represented by hearing threatening voices. On the other hand, it is not "comprehensible" why a schizophrenic should hallucinate a running commentary on his current, innocuous activities, or hear his own thoughts aloud (*Gedankenlautwerden*). Despite its obvious pertinence to our conception of the nature of schizophrenic symptoms, the application of the Jaspersian principle of "understandability" does not solve all the problems that surround this baffling disease. It is, for instance, difficult to find a "comprehensible" counterpart to the phenomena of the thought and language pathology in dementia praecox. Obviously, normal language is not the alternative. Slips of the tongue *resembling* either neologisms or metonymic derailments, and the "coded" incoherence of deliberate free association may perhaps be considered to be "comprehensible" counterparts of their respective schizophrenic representations. (This issue will be considered in the course of the next chapter.) One may perhaps acknowledge that the incoherence of manic flight of ideas is more understandable than schizophrenic asyndetic language because in the former the nature of the associational links is usually quite transparent and often derived from external objects and events. But one must admit that this is not a very impressive example. Another limitation lies in the impossibility of drawing a sharp line between what is, or ought to be, comprehensible and incomprehensible. Nevertheless, Jaspers' discrimination between understandable psychopathological "development" and incomprehensible pathological "psychic process" remains in our view a most useful and significant criterion in the field of psychopathology. The idea of a pathological new "development" has a certain retrospective quality and linkage; on the other hand, the concept of schizophrenia as a new "psychic process" assumes the sinister character of a mysterious visitation, which it is.

In 1957, K. Schneider[18] proposed a listing of certain symptoms, each of which he considered to be pathognomonic of schizophrenia and which he accordingly designated as primary or first-rank symptoms. His search for decisive schizophrenic signs, in contrast to Jaspers', focused on individual rather than collective clinical phenomenology. Yet, Schneider's first-rank symptoms are by and large representative of what Jaspers referred to as the principle of incomprehensibility. They are discussed in the following paragraphs.

1. *Gedankenlautwerden* may be translated as auditorization of thought, thought echoing, or "thought words" being heard out loud by the patient. It is important to determine, before *Gedankenlautwerden* can be assessed, whether the patient really has the vivid sensation of *hearing*, and also that the experience is not projected by him to any place outside his head or attributed to another person; otherwise it would, of course, be an auditory hallucination. Very often such patients realize that they have two kinds of thoughts, the ordinary "silent" ones, and the strong and loud ones. The latter may be localized by the schizophrenic in a certain part of his head because of the symbolic meaning, to the patient, of such a location. Thus one of my patients placed the site of his audible thoughts near the back of his head, saying that they represented his "subconscious mind," which to him meant "that which is in the back of my mind." One may consider the phenomenon of *Gedankenlautwerden* as a precursor of auditory hallucinations; but whereas the latter are found in many psychiatric disorders, the former

is noted only in schizophrenia. Such patients may have the impression that others can "listen in" on their loud thoughts; but the symptom of thought broadcasting, in which the patient has the certain knowledge that others participate in his thoughts, need not be accompanied by auditorization of thought.

2. Schneider considers auditory hallucinations as being diagnostic of schizophrenia if they occur either in the form of a running commentary on the patient's current thoughts and activities, or if they are experienced in the form of a conversation between "two or more people" who refer to the patient in the third person. In Schneider's view schizophrenic phonemes, as far as their formal structure is concerned, are characteristically heard as complete and well-articulated sentences. It should be noted that his criteria with regard to auditory hallucinations ignore content but stress the formal aspects of the phonemes.

3. Somatic hallucinations that the patient attributes to the will, influence, or malice of outside agencies, of whatever kind, are decisive signs of schizophrenia. Bleuler had already pointed out the significance of bodily hallucinations in schizophrenia, but Schneider considers the delusional interpretation of such abnormal sensations by the patient as the decisive element. In nonschizophrenic hypochondriasis or depressions delusions of influence are not resorted to in an attempt to account for the origin of the sensations; their consequences rather than their sources are stressed. The many and ill-defined body sensations which beset the neurotic patient and which are considered to be at times hallucinatory in origin are, of course, never accompanied by delusions of influence; in neurosis, as was described in the chapter on delusions and other false beliefs, the "non-I" component of the symbolic process is never violated.

4. Thought withdrawal, thought insertion, thought broadcasting, and other influences on thought comprise the pathognomonic psychopathology of thought control in schizophrenia. In thought withdrawal the patient suddenly and for no apparent reason ("incomprehensibly"?) ceases to have any thought; this experience is usually referred to as schizophrenic "blocking," or as thought deprivation. Although Bleuler was inclined to attribute its occurrence, at least in many instances, to the emergence of the patients' "complexes," he also admits that this symptom "has something capricious about it objectively for the observer, and subjectively for the patient."[19] Again, patients tend to attribute the experience of thought withdrawal to outside influences. "Blocking" is quite different from the common experience of suddenly losing one's trend of thought because of negative affects or other disturbing interferences; in such instances the reason for the cessation of thought is

entirely comprehensible. Thought insertion connotes the opposite of thought withdrawal; the patient feels that thoughts are put into his mind from "without" and against his will or power to prevent it. In thought broadcasting the loss of control seems to consist in the surrender of the privacy of thought. These patients often and understandably (but "incomprehensibly") entertain the delusion that others can read their mind.

5. Delusional perception, another of Schneider's first-rank symptoms, has already been described.

6. Finally, Schneider lists as symptoms "all events in the sphere of feeling, drive, and volition which are experienced as made or influenced by others."

THE SEARCH FOR A CLASSIFICATION

The late Gregory Zilboorg would at times counsel his students that it is better to understand things which one can not classify than to try to classify things which one does not understand. In view of our incomplete knowledge and understanding of the schizophrenias our search for meaningful classifications has continued without having so far achieved completely satisfactory results or general acceptance. The original and traditional phenomenological classification (hebephrenic, catatonic, paranoid, and simple types), while relatively easy, addresses itself only to syndromes and by no means to all syndromes with which the clinician is confronted. As such it throws little or no light on the uncertainties of etiology and identity of the process. There is as yet no direct neuroanatomical or neurophysiological evidence which would permit a classification of the diverse clinical types of schizophrenia in terms of a disease process that affects corresponding suborgans of the brain, although such an assumption is the basis of the classification of schizophrenias by Kleist and the Frankfurt school. Another difficulty arises from the fact that schizophrenias which progress to the point of permanent deterioration of the personality—whatever the initial and final clinical features may be—are in significant respects different from those phenomenologically similar forms from which patients recover. Several authorities maintain that recovery without residual defect precludes a diagnosis of "true" schizophrenia, regardless of the nature of the symptoms. Schizophrenialike syndromes may accompany various structural (organic) diseases of the brain such as general paresis, Huntington's chorea, and chronic temporal-lobe epilepsy. Finally, there is the difficult problem of how to interpret and classify those psychotic states which are neither clearly schizophrenic nor purely affective and whose lack of identity may be gathered from the variety and ambiguity of terms which have been assigned them—such as "mixed psychoses," "schizophreniform psychoses," and "pseudoschizophrenias." Therefore, it seems best to acknowledge the existence of these issues and uncertainties and to offer several tentative classifications and clarifications, not as alternatives but as a natural consequence of significant but independent areas of relevance concerning the schizophrenias.

One such area of relevance is the conception of dementia praecox as a chronic and progressive disease that invariably leads to clearly recognizable end states and personality "defect." Thus no mental illness from which the patient makes a full recovery, however "schizophrenic" the clinical picture may appear, can be classified as a "true" schizophrenia. The sole criterion of such a classification is the issue of reversibility of the psychopathology. In the United States these "true" forms of schizophrenias are sometimes referred to as *process type* or *nuclear* schizophrenias. In such cases there must be no evidence of coarse structural brain disease, although almost all authorities incline toward a biological rather than psychological etiology of nuclear schizophrenia. This group must now be delineated from so-called *symptomatic schizophrenias.* These are schizophrenic illnesses that are indistinguishable from "true" schizophrenia in their clinical features but are associated with coarse or chronic-epileptic brain disease. The nature of this "association" is still unclear. It may be that a symptomatic schizophrenia can be provoked by coarse brain disease in patients who are already predisposed to schizophrenia; but it may also be that brain damage may be accompanied by a schizophrenialike symptomatology which subsides completely. Alcoholic and other organic hallucinoses are examples of such transitory symptomatic "schizophrenias." Even greater difficulties arise in the case of a third variety of mental illnesses with a schizophrenialike symptomatology but without associated coarse brain disease. This latter group—in which "lack of identity" has already been mentioned and underlined by referring to the various purely descriptive designations given to them—are perhaps best defined in negative terms. They are not chronic, they do not lead to deterioration, they are not classifiable as purely affective or neurotic disorders, and "their independent nature . . . cannot be determined by clinical investigation."[21] The terminology by which they have been described varies among the several authors and even in different countries. This writer prefers the term. *schizophreniform psychoses,* which was introduced by Langfeldt in 1939.[22] They are characterized by psychotic episodic states, usually in response to stressful situations; they resemble schizophrenia phenomenologically, but they differ from process schizophrenia by the all-important fact of being reversible. Schizophreniform psychoses are likely to present the fluidity of symptomatology and relative preservation of the personality which characterize the early stages of the process-type schizophrenias. Some types of Rümke's "pseudoschizophrenias,"[23] particularly the endogenous, characterogenic, and developmental varieties, seem to correspond to the schizophreniform psychoses. Leonhard's "cycloid" psychoses and the "schizoaffective" types of schizophrenia (a designation which is popular in the United States) are closely related to those marginal psychoses the existence of which embarrasses the proponents of sharp demarcation lines between schizophrenias and manic-depressive disorders. Fish, in his monograph *Schizophrenia*,[24] has given us a comprehensive account of these special varieties and of the very great diagnostic and classification difficulties attending them.

The classification which we will now consider aims at a delineation of well-established clinical syndromes among the chronic, progressively deteriorating, malignant (or "nuclear") forms of dementia praecox. We recall that Kraepelin, the first of a long line of classifiers, divided his patients with dementia praecox into the well-known categories of catatonia, hebephrenia, paranoid varieties, and (later) dementia simplex; except for the last one, these terms and identities have been retained by modern authorities on schizophrenia. But changes have occurred since Kraepelin's time in our concepts of these subtypes. Particularly the representatives of the Frankfurt school have attempted to go beyond a merely descriptive approach. They consider that these subtypes are found with unequivocal clinical purity only in the end states of malignant or process schizophrenia; as such, each subtype is indicative of disease of a corresponding functional unit within the brain. This ultimate gravitation of the disease process toward hypothesized functional systems of the psyche explains, it is thought, the phenomenological differences in catatonic, hebephrenic, paranoid, and other syndromes. Kleist believed that such a course was followed by what he called the "typical schizophrenias" and to whose subtypes he added a "confused" variety, in which thought and language pathology was the prominent feature. His pupil Leonhard retained Kleist's principles but substituted the term "systematic schizophrenias" for Kleist's "typical schizophrenias." He also uses the term "systematic paraphrenias" as synonymous with Kleist's "typical paranoid schizophrenias." The reader will find a comprehensive review of the views of Kleist and Leonhard on the classification of the schizophrenias in some of Fish's publications. Our presentation of this subject is less concerned, at this point, with a detailed description of the various forms and manifestations of the subtypes than with the principles upon which these classifications are based, as well as with their possible implications toward a better understanding and future research. If one reflects on the prominence of psychomotor or conative disorders in schizophrenic (and experimental) catatonia, of affective and cognitive deterioration in the hebephrenias, of ideational-psychosocial abnormalities in the form of delusions and auditory hallucinations in the paranoid schizophrenias, and of formal thought and language pathology in the confused types of Kleist, then a hypothesis which aims at correlating such specific symptomatologies with specific functional "suborgans" of the brain and psyche seems provocative and not entirely unpromising. In the atypical (Kleist) or nonsystematic (Leonhard) varieties several functional systems are believed to be involved so that the symptomatology becomes more variable. One cannot escape the impression, when reading and reflecting upon these elaborate classifications, that the image of schizophrenia as a nosological identity seems to recede more and more into the background and that this occurs despite the fact that schizophrenic symptomatology is recognized to be of a kind which, in Bleuler's words, "appears nowhere else in this particular fashion."[25]

In addition to the traditional classifications of schizophrenia several authors have put forth the hypothesis that there are possibly two distinct schizophrenic illnesses: one with a favorable, the other with an unfavorable outcome. The implications of such a radical approach affect not only the issue of prognosis (which is obvious) but also suggest different causes, modes of onset and course, syptomatologies, and precipitating factors. One of the proponents of this classification, Vaillant, lists the following criteria as favoring the existence of the "non-malignant" variety: As to hereditary predisposition, the occurrence of psychotic *depressions* among the family of the patient—not a history of schizophrenia—is significant. Perhaps for the same reason(s) the prepsychotic personality makeup of the patients is never schizoid. The onset of the illness can be traced to precipitating factors or stresses, presumably largely psychological or environmental in nature; this factor may make some of the clinical manifestations more understandable, and thus, by inference, less malignant. The illness develops to its climax rather rapidly, considering the nature of psychological illness in general (namely, within six months). Depressive symptoms dominate the clinical picture; but confusion and disorientation are also found.[26]

We believe that students of schizophrenia will be able to profit from all the described attempts at classification, although it is not possible at this time to predict the outcome of the issue. It is to be assumed that experienced and thoughtful investigators and clinicians would have come forth with some good points. But it may be well to remember that particularly in the field of schizophrenia, an exhaustive "description in depth" comes closest to an identification and, ultimately, to an explanation.

THE SEARCH FOR AN ETIOLOGY

The obvious state of disparity among the various schizophrenias—which makes the search for a classification so difficult
and somewhat less than satisfactory—constitutes only one of several
reasons why one should not assume a single and simple etiology of
the schizophrenias. With very few exceptions the search for an etiology
in mental illness must always include the entire range of biological
and psychosocial (interpersonal and cultural) pathogenic factors. Some
of these exceptions with a single and simple etiology are, for instance,
phenylpyruvic acid oligophrenia at one pole and fainting at the sight
of a grisly event (such as a fatal accident) at the other. Within the
intermediate majority the issue of etiology must include such considerations as predisposing, provocative, aggravating, and protective factors,
both in the biological and psychosocial spheres. The occurrence, intensity, and prognosis of the mental illness are the resultants of the interactions of all these factors, each of which by itself contains a formidable
array of highly complex and intricate parts, some known and many
either unknown or not easily ascertainable.

If we agree with Brosin that "[mental] disease is not an entity but
the name given to adaptive failures of already existing and operating
processes . . ."[27] the concept of etiology will be more adequately defined
in terms of multidimensional evolutions than of linear cause and effect
relationships. As a simple illustration let us take the example of general
paresis. Nobody doubts that the *Spirochaeta pallida* is the *conditio sine
qua non* for the development of general paresis. But this fact does not
fully explain why a certain person has general paresis. To begin with,
not all patients who have acquired syphilis develop general paresis;
this may depend on whether the particular strain of *spirochaetes* with
which they were infected is "neurotropic;" this introduces a secondary
biological or immunological element. Syphilis is in most instances acquired through illicit and/or promiscuous sexual intercourse—for instance, with a prostitute. Thus whether a person does or does not acquire
syphilis, and ultimately perhaps general paresis, may depend on his
having or not having a psychosexual problem in the form of, say, a
perversion or a character neurosis. He may seek out a prostitute because
he desires to experience certain sexual pleasures and activities which
he would be neurotically inhibited to ask of his wife or neurotically
horrified to accept from her. He may, as a result of a previous head
injury, be intolerant of alcohol and have sexual intercourse with a
stranger or prostitute while in a state of pathological intoxication. Multi-

dimensionality of etiology does not imply that the various participating factors are of the same significance in causing the ultimate "adaptive failures;" in fact, they are usually not. But this does not mean that the less significant ones can be ignored; they may be the only ones, in a given illness, toward which therapeutic efforts can be exerted. The example of general paresis is perhaps a somewhat coarse and simplified illustration of the subtle and intricate interplay of etiological contributory factors that lead to ultimate failure in adaptation. Some general observations and illustrations of this interplay of forces, facts, and fate may be in order; but the totality of "multidimensional etiology" is beyond the scope certainly of this book and possibly even of a computer.

Genetic potential for mental illness, psychological hazards of personality development during the first six years of life, and physical and mental constitution at birth may serve as a foundation or point of departure in the search for an etiology of mental illness and failure in adaptation. Genetic predispositions are relevant, both with a view toward a taxonomic orientation and in terms of their particular severity or dominance. Thus in the area of dementia praecox, a malignant mental illness, a strong genetic loading for the development of this illness would relegate all other etiological considerations into a subordinate position. Except for a judicious application of eugenic practices we have as yet not found a way of undoing genetic liability. Let us now assume that a child is born with a "slight" genetic loading or predisposition toward schizophrenia, but that his mother suffers from an active schizophrenic illness. What etiological or pathogenic possibilities are now open? It is not likely that the mother will be able—in view of her overt schizophrenic symptomatology—to give the child even a minimum of a basic feeling of security, reality, and freedom from undue guilt and anxiety, to mention just a few essential requirements for the formation of a viable ego. Such a situation must not be confused with the concept of the "schizophrenogenic mother;" this controversial term purports to define certain character traits in a mother that are likely to "cause" schizophrenia in the child. The traits mentioned in the literature range from overprotectiveness to overt hostility, although most authors single out extreme rejection of, and aloofness from, the child as the most damaging influence. Such a mother will adversely affect the mental health of the child, but the child's innate or constitutional strength may to some degree offset such an adversity. We can not entirely write off constitutional factors—for instance, as far as native intelligence or good looks are concerned. Freud, the outstanding proponent of the psychosexual (psychosocial) origin of the neuroses, said time and again that constitutional "dispositions" may determine the occurrence, type, and severity of a neurosis. We just do not know enough about these things; but even the knowledge of the possibilities within the unknown can be helpful in guiding our judgment.

Before we will report on the current opinions which are determining the directions of our search for etiological factors in the schizophrenias, we wish to conclude the preceding sketch of the issue by once more quoting Brosin:

At all stages of the evolving process, some disorders or deviations may occur. . . . If we accept the hypothesis that all these corrupted processes are resultants of the natural forces made familiar to us by the physical, biological, and social sciences, we can more easily understand that most, if not all diseases, are the disorders of being a member of a species in a physical-psychosocial matrix.[28]

CONCLUDING REMARKS

Certain conclusions suggest themselves from the data contained in this chapter. There is sufficient phenomenological similarity to justify a "concept of schizophrenia" despite the great variety of clinical expression. Attempts at classification of the schizophrenias would lead one to believe that "schizophrenia" may be the final common path or destination of diverse biological and/or psychosocial pathogenic factors. Etiology of almost all forms of behavioral pathology must be viewed as an intricate and interacting evolutionary process among all given and acquired levels of functioning of the most complex organism in a most complex environment. Against such a background one can appreciate the degree of uncertainty and the possibility of error which confront one's search for an etiological understanding, and thus ultimately a therapeutic conquest of this terrible illness. It is not likely that a chemical compound, or a theory of personality development, or a figurative neurophysiological rephrasing of the problem will supply the complete answer.

Kety[29] gives us an authoritative and comprehensive review of the present state of the problem—its promises, its sources of error, its limitations. Kety's paper also gives us 184 references, few of which are much more than a decade old. His main points cover the biochemical hypotheses that implicate oxygen, carbohydrate energetics, amino acids and amines, epinephrine, ceruloplasmin, taraxein, and serotonin. He stresses the extremely high concordance rate for schizophrenia in monozygotic twins. He underlines the direct relationship between emotional stress and resulting biochemical alterations of many kinds—adding, in effect, that the schizophrenic creates more than enough of stressful situations by his behavior and incapacities. He suggests that genetic factors, involving one or more genes, may *effect* abnormal biological reactions or adversely *affect* the correlation of existing normal ones. Such reactions may take place throughout the body or only within the brain, "or even within extremely localized areas of the brain."[30] Although he deals only with the biochemical and genetic aspects of the etiology of schizophrenia his expressed views can hardly be considered onesided, let alone biased. Thus he says: "Even the most uncritical acceptance of all the genetic data, however, cannot lead to the conclusion that the schizophrenic illnesses are the result of genetic factors alone."[31] He considers environmental factors to be "quite as suggestive as the genetic evidence but by no means more conclusive."[32] This writer associates himself with a view succinctly expressed by Fish in these words: "To sum up, schizophrenia is due to genetic predisposition which may or may not be expressed, depending on the overall genetic constitution, the modifications of the constitution during childhood, and the severity of the stress to which the patient is subjected in adolescence and adult life."[33]

REFERENCES

1. P. H. Wender. "Dementia Praecox: The Development of the Concept." *The American Journal of Psychiatry*, vol. 119, #2, 1963, pp. 1143–1151.
2. *Ibid.*, p. 1144.
3. *Ibid.*, pp. 1144–1145.
4. G. Zilboorg. A *History of Medical Psychology*. New York, Norton, p. 452.
5. M. Bleuler. "Conception of Schizophrenia Within the Last Fifty Years and Today." *International Journal of Psychiatry*, vol. 1, #4, p. 516.
6. G. Zilboorg. *Op. cit.*,[4] p. 501.
7. E. Bleuler. *Dementia Praecox or the Group of Schizophrenias*. New York, International Univer. Press, 1950, p. 14.
8. *Ibid.*, p. 42.
9. *Ibid.*, p. 42 (footnote).
10. *Ibid.*, p. 53.
11. *Ibid.*
12. S. Freud. "The Antithetical Sense of Primal Words." *In: Collected Papers*. London, Hogarth, 1948, vol. 4, p. 187.
13. E. Bleuler. *Op. cit.*,[7] p. 53.
14. *Ibid.*, p. 54.
15. F. J. Fish. *Schizophrenia*. Baltimore, Williams & Wilkins, 1962, p. 80.
16. *Ibid.*, p. 31.
17. *Ibid.*, p. 97.
18. *Ibid.*, p. 81.
19. E. Bleuler. *Op. cit.*,[7] p. 35.
20. F. J. Fish. *Op. cit.*,[15] p. 81.

21. *Ibid.*, p. 97.

22. G. Langfeldt. *The Schizophreniform States.* Copenhagen, Munksgaard, 1939.

23. H. C. Rümke. "The Clinical Differentiation within the Group of Schizophrenias." *Second International Congress for Psychiatry*, Zurich, 1957, Report 1, p. 302, Orel Fussli.

24. F. J. Fish. *Op. cit.*[15]

25. E. Bleuler. *Op. cit.*,[7] p. 9.

26. G. E. Vaillant. "The Prediction of Recovery in Schizophrenia." *Journal of Nervous and Mental Diseases,* vol. 135, 1962, pp. 534–543.

27. H. W. Brosin. "Evolution and Understanding Diseases of the Mind." *In:* S. Tax (ed.). *Evolution After Darwin.* Univer. of Chicago Press, 1960, vol. 2: "The Evolution of Man," p. 387.

28. *Ibid.*, p. 388.

29. S. S. Kety. "Biochemical Theories of Schizophrenia." *International Journal of Psychiatry*, vol. 1, #3, pp. 409–446.

30. *Ibid.*, p. 430.

31. *Ibid.*, p. 429.

32. *Ibid.*

33. F. J. Fish. *Op. cit.*,[15] p. 17.

14

Schizophrenic Dementia: An Expression of the Psychopathology of the Conflict-free Ego

This presentation limits itself to those aspects of the language and thought pathology of dementia praecox which are usually called "formal." I will present the clinical material and attempt an analysis of this formal pathology. I hope to be able to propose plausible conclusions as to its nature. A very similar pathology of formal thought will be noted in the nonverbal performances of schizophrenics, while an entirely different pathology of formal thought characterizes organic dementia. Finally, the relative independence of pathology of form from pathology of content in schizophrenic thought and language will be discussed.

I do not believe that the meaning of the term "formal" is to be taken for granted. Implicit in the clinical use of this term is the assumption that psychopathology combines "form," which is impersonal and static, with "content," which is personal and dynamic. There are relatively few forms, in which a limitless variety of content finds expression. As formal phenomena, all phobias, depressions, or delusions are alike; but the psychodynamics which lead up to and lend content to these formal entities are as varied and many as the individual patients. But are all utterances by our patients "content" and, as such, personal and psychodynamic—indicative of conflict and thus traceable to unconscious

This chapter is based upon an article written by the author and published in *Journal of the Hillside Hospital* (*16:* 267–284, 1967), to the publishers of which the author extends grateful acknowledgement of their courteous cooperation.

sources, i.e., to the primary process? It seems to me that no such assumption is warranted with respect to much of the so-called organic symptomatology. Hughlings Jackson's concept of dissolution of function as a reversal of evolution and Kurt Goldstein's "loss of abstract capacities" in organic dementia represent a neurodynamic, phylogenetic viewpoint rather than a psychodynamic ontogenetic one. We may consider organicity essentially as a *breakdown* of the secondary process. By contrast, in the transference neuroses we are observing a *breakthrough* of the primary process, modified and limited though it is, while the secondary process (above all, language) remains intact. In dementia praecox, I submit, there is both a breakthrough of the primary process unmodified and unlimited, and a breakdown—in a unique and characteristic manner—of the secondary process. Their relationship to each other, if any, is a very challenging question. As I see it, the formal thought and language pathology in schizophrenia reflects this singular breakdown of the secondary process. In this respect it resembles, almost suggests, impersonal organicity. It is a manifestation of psychopathology of the conflict-free ego.

CLINICAL MATERIAL

The potential meaning of a single uttered word is subject to immediate or delayed modification. When a single word is flung into the mind of the listener its precise meaning may become obvious only in the context of the nonverbal situation in which it is spoken. The word "fire" has quite different meanings depending on whether the situational configuration is, say, a military setting or a theater. The verbal context of the sentence used has (or should have) the same effect on the word—to lift it from the bottom of potential ambiguity to the summit of precise and unequivocal meaning. This process constitutes an achievement in which the schizophrenic fails: namely, the capacity to form precise and appropriate concepts from the potential, antecedent, amorphous possibilities. Concept formation, as Cameron points out, is accomplished by a process of fusion, which in turn implies an antecedent extension.[1] In the case of a single word this potential extension with its concomitant ambiguity may be "horizontal." I refer to the clusters of more or less equivalent and associated meanings which a single word activates and which, if tangential or irrelevant, are eliminated by the normal mind. In this way only can the semantic configuration emerge as it should. But there is also a "perpendicular" antecedent extension in the potential meaning of a word. A word evolves from the lowest level of its meaningless sound quality to the highest level of its metaphorical meaning. Between these levels are, in descending order, connotation, denotation, and verbalization.

Word Use

Desymbolization of the Word. In its most extreme form the meaning of the word is *reduced* to its sound quality, which gives rise to clang associations. To the question, "Who discovered the North Pole?" a patient answered, "Napoleon." The phonetic similarity "Pole-Napoleon" determined the association of a name famous for quite different reasons. Arieti mentions a statement by a patient in connection with the Japanese attack on Pearl Harbor, "The next time they may attack at Diamond Harbor or Emerald Harbor."[2] Here the geographic concept "Pearl Harbor" has disintegrated to a level of literalness or verbalization that is totally alien to the normal mind.

Semantic Shift. The meaning of a word may also be pathologically *expanded* by the patient in a manner which violates the situational or semantic organization. I refer here to words which potentially have two or more meanings, e.g., the word "admit." Whereas normally the semantic context determines the precise or intended meaning of ambiguous words, such inherent ambiguities give rise, in the schizophrenic, to a pathological ideational derailment; I call this a "semantic shift," a conceptual slippage. One of my patients said, "They asked me all the questions in the admitting office, but I didn't tell them anything." Another example of associational derailment owing to semantic shift appears in a paper on proverb interpretation by schizophrenics. To the proverb, "Where there's a will, there's a way," the patient responded with "Where there's a will, there's relatives to divide what's left."[3] The authors, however, considered the patient's response as indicative of an overinclusion of meaning, similar to placing "carrot" into the category of "fruit" together with "apple." The present writer would not consider these two examples as representative of the same formal thought and language pathology.

Metonymic Distortion. This term, introduced by Norman Cameron, describes the pathognomonic tendency of schizophrenics to use words that only approximately— and at times not at all—convey the required meaning.[4] A metonym neither reduces nor expands the conceptual organization; it *blurs* it. A false equivalence is attributed to the metonymic word by the patient, for various reasons, and this results in various degrees of conceptual contamination. Phonetic resemblance may determine the substitution. In extreme cases of this type the metonym is a mere clang equivalence of the proper word. In less severe cases the acoustic equivalence is partial, as in the metonymic substitution of "currency" for "current." The false equivalence may derive from the inability of the patient to find the precise word; he may then use a word within the cluster of approximate meanings, at various distances from "bull's-eye." A patient may say "menu" when he means "meal." One of my patients declined my suggestion of hospitalization with these words, "A hospital is no exit for me;" he meant: "no way out." In still other instances a metonymic word is resorted to on the basis of a thought disorder itself. One of my patients regularly substitutes the word "half" for the word "part;" to him "half" and "part" are both fractions of a whole. Such false equivalence is based on attributing identity to mere similarity. Some of the most striking examples of metonymic blurring occur in those schizophrenics who tend to use the same word to denote different things. Kleist referred to this phenomenon as the use of "stock words." He considered it to be a disturbance of word storage and akin to verbal paraphasia. F. J. Fish reports on a patient who used the word "vessel" for nearly all objects; a watch was a "time vessel." An even more grotesque form of inappropriate word usage, also quoted from Fish, was resorted to by a patient who called a candle "a night illumination object." This example is somewhat similar to that of Bleuler's patient who spoke of "hay" as "a means of maintenance of the cow."[5] One cannot really say that either of these definitions is untrue; what is wrong, or rather schizophrenic, about such designations is the shifting by the patient into a semantic system of expression or reference that is wholly unsuitable for the context or situation in which the word was used at the moment. Such schizophrenic pseudoprofundities differ sharply from those rare and superior *intentional* circumlocutions which are meant to express by innuendo what would be offensive in the raw. An illustration of the latter is a remark made by Winston Churchill during a speech in the House of Commons. The operative phrase used was "terminological inexactitude," intended as a whimsical circumlocution for "lie."

Neologisms.   The well-known tendency of many schizophrenics to create nonexisting words occupies a special place in the "pathology of the word." As a purely formal phenomenon certain neologistic condensations or combinations of normal words are also found in wit and in the artistic representation of language; in either form they are intelligible in a highly intelligent way and are used in the service of a significant expression of thought. In the schizophrenic, however, they will neither evoke laughter nor enrich meaning. Bleuler considered them one of the manifestations of the intellectual aspects of autism.[6] One of my patients said that her face looked to her "comatic." She felt that she was being "doped" (coma) and driven insane (lunatic); hence, "comatic." The condensation is meaningless, no significant supraordinate idea is alluded to and no tendency is expressed. In other instances schizophrenic neologisms are combinations of normal words based not on social sanction but on individual pathology of thought. A patient says "blueward" when she means "skyward" and explains her neologism by stating that the sky is blue. The underlying pathology is predicative identification; the sky is not always blue, and color is only one of its many predicates. In still other instances of even more severe pathology, neologisms represent either mere reversals of normal words or nonsense words masquerading as words with meanings.

Sentence Use

Whereas the single word carries with it the potential for a minor incomplete organization of thought, the sentence is an accomplished, major one. What is the nature of such an organization and of its failure in schizophrenia?

In a normal sentence (1) a series of potentially ambiguous words arranged in a certain temporal order is transformed into an increasingly meaningful structure as the sentence progresses; upon its completion all its parts (words) because of their then precise meaning and relatedness become the carrier of a comprehensible idea. Fusion—rather than diffusion and expansion—prevails. (2) Words or ideas belonging to different ideational categories or mental systems are excluded, and the appropriate mental set or frame of reference is apprehended and adhered to. (3) Relevancy is accomplished because meaningful configuration takes the place of random association, and elaboration rather than semantic caricature of thought prevails.

The net result of these three major criteria of a normal sentence or sum of sentences is that language now fulfills its social purpose of meaningful communication. The corresponding schizophrenic failures are asyndetic language, system shifting, and, if I may use my own descriptive term, "sham language."

Asyndesis. This characteristically schizophrenic thought disorder is more commonly known as scatter, or loosening of associations. Bleuler said, "The associations lose their continuity."[7] Such simple descriptions are, of course, useless for the understanding of the pathology. Suppose you would ask a normal person to construct a sentence around the three words "*child*," "*cry*," "*rain*." The three words are merely raw material or building blocks, and the resulting sentence should be an organized

construction and not a heap; an "integrate and not a conglomerate."[8]
Each of these three words will activate, to various degrees of awareness,
an extended cluster of images, ideas, related words, and even feelings.
From this potential source the normal mind selects some components
and eliminates all others. At the same time, it will fuse what it has
selected into an ideational organization in which relatedness based on
causality or *discordance* predominates. Mere enumeration or mere juxta-
position of words or short ideas is avoided. The selected words are
given precise meaning without desymbolization, metonymic distortion,
or semantic ambiguity. Intrusion or interpenetration of unconscious
derivates will not contaminate the antecedent material. Thus a normal
sentence may read, "The child cried, because it could not play in the
rain." But a schizophrenic with a minimal but noticeable degree of
asyndesis said, "The child cried, and then it rained."

I asked one of my patients to make a sentence around the words
"cat," "girl," "blood." She was a young woman of at least average intelligence and about to graduate from high school when the symptoms of
schizophrenia became evident. In her spontaneous language performance
she showed pressure of speech with overinclusion and resultant dilution
of relevance. She produced the following pseudosentence in response
to my request: "I am a girl. I saw a cat in the park. The cat had
blood on its tail." It will be noted that not a single causal relationship
has been constructed from the antecedent potential contained in the
three given words; instead, a mere enumeration of three isolated "mental
snapshots" emerged. She was unable to elaborate from the potential
of the words an event such as, "The girl had blood on her hand because
she had been scratched by a cat." Nonschizophrenics of limited intelligence will also quite often fail in the construction from given words
of sentences based on causal links. But they will, of course, not present
any signs of a schizophrenic thought and language disorder. In the
area of asyndetic language, they will not, for instance, introduce an
incomprehensible causality—as did the patient (reported by Cameron)
who completed the sentence, "The man fell on the street because . . ."
with the words, "of the first World War."[9] When I asked my patient
why she said that the blood was on the cat's tail, she replied, "I just
thought of it." She was unable to come up with any other explanation.
It is not at all inconceivable that "the bloody tail" represents a psychodynamic and "interpenetrating" derivative of an unconscious fantasy.

Asyndetic language can be noted both in the spontaneous productions
of patients and in their responses to specific questions. The lack of
fusion, the failure of selective elimination, and the general paucity of
causal links are, of course, more obvious in the severe degrees of thought
disorder. But even then most patients seem to comprehend and try

to answer a question, although with a disturbing lack of clarity and organization. Let me illustrate with an example. At the height of his illness a patient of Cameron's was asked to complete the following sentence, "My hair is fair because . . . ." He said, "Because of something else, because it is on my head; it comes from my mother."[10] It will be noted that the patient fails in two attempts to organize a normal causal relationship until he finally succeeds by saying, "It comes from my mother." My analysis of the nature of his failure suggests the following:

1. ". . . because of something else." The general idea of a causal relationship offered in the sentence is apparently apprehended, but the concept "cause" does not emerge. The phrase "because of something else" is a diffuse expanded generalization.

2. ". . . because it is on my head." The association "hair–head" derives from a cluster of related ideas. But, like in the positional Rorschach responses of schizophrenics, this *non sequitur* causal construction is determined by environmental rather than conceptual considerations.

System Shifting.   Precise and appropriate use of a word and syndetic fusion in the construction of sentences are relatively minor holistic organizations. One may consider them "subwholes." Beyond them there exist configurations, patterns, and *Gestalten* with an increasing and almost limitless number of parts but a constant and limited meaning of the whole. In these configurations, which Angyal calls "systems" and "arrangements of parts according to some unitary plan within a dimensional medium,"[11] each and every aspect of the part receives its meaning by and within the meaning of the whole. The schizophrenic fails in the apprehension of these systems, and—perhaps because of this failure—easily slips from one system into another. Bychowski[12] asked a patient, "Where is your husband?" The appropriate system to which this question addresses itself is spatial. Is he in the adjoining room, at work, out of town, abroad? In each instance his realistic physical-spatial whereabouts are the essence of the system. The patient replied, "He is on the wedding picture." The system "physical-real-alive-active" was not apprehended, and she slipped into the system "representational." System shifting in schizophrenics becomes evident in a variety of failures in tasks both verbal and nonverbal. Hanfmann reports on the performance of patients taking the Healy Picture Completion Test, concluding that "common to all schizophrenic solutions is the disregard of factors that make the picture represent a section of real space."[13] An inserted block symbolizes the situation without regard to the total configuration, or else psychological motivations which have no representation in the picture are imposed in violation of the uniformity and consistency of the meaning of the whole. In the verbal area I quote an example from my own observations. I asked a patient to classify human beings any way he saw fit. He said, "There are men, women, and homosexuals." Classification questions require awareness of and adherence to supra-ordinate wholes or systems. The patient failed to adhere to the system "sexual" with its anatomical, physiological, psychosexual, characterologi-cal, social, and cultural connotations, and slipped instead into the system "normal–abnormal" (albeit in connection with sexuality). The choice of the particular incongruous system was determined by psychodynamic forces but not the fact of its occurrence. No neurotic with identical psychodynamics would ever give such an answer. He may, of course, say the same thing in the course of free association; but in this case he would be fully aware of the fact that he is associating, not classifying. Storch, in discussing a different aspect of schizophrenia (namely, "mystic union") reports the case of a patient with ecstatic religious delusions, who referred to herself as "Mrs. Jesus."[14] This ludicrous combination of the name of the deity with an appelation indicating the civil status of a person—shifting from the system "divine" to one representing the most commonplace pedestrian arrangements—would be blasphemous if resorted to by anyone other than a schizophrenic. It is also a good example of a depolarization of ideational significances ordinarily per-ceived with especial awareness of their intrinsic polarity.

Sham Language. Elaboration of thought may cease, while its verbal counterpart may continue, like a caricature of its former healthy and meaningful relatedness. A total separation of thought and language has now occurred. I like the refer to this phenomenon as "sham language." In it we find irrelevance to a degree not seen in any other form of schizophrenic thought and language disorder. The point of view of the other person to whom language normally addresses itself is now totally ignored. Sham language may appear, as Bleuler noted, when a senseless compulsion to associate replaces thinking proper. Here is a classical example from one of his patients:

—He was a man with black eyes—there are also blue and gray eyes—snakes have green eyes—all people have eyes—there are some too who are blind—there are people who cannot hear—I know some who hear too much.[15]

It should be noted that not a single instance of asyndesis, metonymic blurring, system shifting, or desymbolization is found in this sample. The laws of association are preserved in sham language, in a fashion, because—as in flight of ideas—no attempt is made to organize ideas and thought. It is also of interest that in such cases of random association mere enumeration and irrelevant mentioning of opposites predominate. This kind of sham language seems closely related to "naming" and "touching" when patients simply name the objects seen or felt. Children of a certain age normally accompany their activities by verbalizing them in a manner which Piaget calls monologue or collective monologue.[16] But an adult schizophrenic as little relapses into "childhood" as a growing child recovers from "schizophrenia." Another variety of sham language leads to irrelevance when the meaning of the question has no bearing on the formulation of the answer.

Two examples from my recent experience come to mind. To my question, "What day is today?" the patient said, "Yesterday." Another patient was asked for the meaning of the proverb, "Do not cross a bridge before you come to it," and he said, "Don't do anything before it is done." Somewhat similarly, a patient in a study by Shimkunas *et al.,* responded to the proverb, "Don't swap horses while crossing a stream," with "Don't hate religion when you got your own."[17] Shimkunas designates this response as autistic. The introduction of the issue of "religion" is certainly suggestive of inappropriate and "interpenetrating" subjectivity; on the other hand, it would be of great interest to know whether the word "crossing" in the proverb may have been experienced by the patient *doubly,* in the sense of the semantic shift, and thus given rise to the idea of religion. The patient's response, as a whole, is a semantic mimicry of the syntax of the proverb, not an interpretation, and thus represents an instance of sham language. As we mentioned in an earlier chapter, Bleuler asked a patient what a cat was and received the reply that a cat was a mouse.[18] In all these instances a glaringly illogical answer is given—incidentally, in perfect syntax, because the questions are not perceived as or elaborated into a conceptual organization. Instead, they are reduced to a stimulus for an association masquerading as an answer that is based on quite irrelevant semantic pseudoconnections. In extreme cases of this kind not even such pseudoconnections are considered. Thus, to the question, "Why don't you work?" one patient said, "But I don't understand any French."[19] It seems that he realized that an explanation or apology was expected, and he gave one—irrelevant, random, asocial, and perfunctory—without even a shadow of an attempt at comprehension and elaboration of thought.

As a final example let us consider a patient who has for about ten years shown evidence of a mild schizophrenic process manifested mainly by pressure of speech, overinclusion, metonymic approximation, and generally asyndetic language. During occasional periods of stress she had suffered from short-lasting catatonic episodes. There was no evidence of secondary symptoms such as delusions or hallucinatory experiences. She was able to graduate from college and has been employed as a welfare worker for several years.

During a session which was by and large uneventful she spoke of some minor difficulties that she experienced recently in her work, and which she presented to me against the background of general unrest amongst welfare clients. Referring to the atmosphere within her department she used the phrase, "this stable chaos." In view of the obvious incongruity and incompatibility of these two terms I decided to question her about the meaning of this phrase, and the following exchange took place:

Q. Isn't that a contradiction? How can chaos be stable?
A. No, it isn't.
Q. What are you trying to describe by "chaos?"
A. All the rioting we had at the place, and the screaming, also there was destruction of property.
Q. Very well, I understand that. And what did you mean by "stable?"
A. By that I mean that we have *regular* hours, 9 to 5, and also that all the commotion was in the office, not in the street; I mean it was within *physical bounds*.
Q. So you wanted to tell me that the chaos existed within certain limits of time and place. Is that relevant?
A. It is relevant to me.
Q. Was it perhaps comforting to you that the chaos existed only between a limited number of hours, between nine and five?
A. No.
Q. Is it possible that you used these two words, "stable" and "chaos," because they are opposites?
A. Definitely.

The associations which the patient produced in elaborating on the idea "chaos" and "stable" may be considered the antecedent, preconscious, and diffuse material which the normal mind subjects to a largely unconscious process of screening and discriminating selection in order to exclude irrelevant content. In this the patient was unsuccessful because she included the idea of "regular hours" and "physical bounds" when she wanted to convey the chaotic conditions in her department. In addition, we must consider the word "stable" a poor (that is, a metonymic) choice. But was it really a choice? Was it in her power to discard it? Judging from her avowed preference for opposites we may consider the blurring of meaning a result of the associational tendency, in sham language, to resort to opposites. As to possible emotional or psychodynamic reasons for joining the idea of "chaos" with that of "stable," she denied my suggestion that she derived any comfort from the implications of "stability" in the presence of chaos.

If we look for the common denominator, *not* of the causes, *not* of the consequences, but of the *nature* of the formal thought and language pathology in dementia praecox, we may perhaps define it as follows:

1. The ability to experience and to use words as unequivocal conceptual symbols is impaired. The relationship between the word idea and the object idea that the word should represent is disturbed.

2. The ability to construct somewhat larger semantic configurations through selective and meaningful application of conceptual relationships is impaired. Thought becomes diluted as the volume of language increases.

3. The ability to apprehend and adhere to still larger semantic configurations—so-called systems—is impaired.

Rorschach Signs

The normal Rorschach response, like the normal organization of a semantic system, requires the creation of a frame of reference or a configurational system in which the whole determines (again by a process of selection and elimination) the appropriate and singular meaning of a potentially multivalent part or detail. I can only point to some of the many schizophrenic Rorschach signs in an attempt to demonstrate the fundamental similarity of the thought disorder in verbal and nonverbal performances.

Contamination. Two qualities of a blot detail, such as, Form and Color are given separate interpretations, which, however, do not remain separated; they are "neologistically" condensed, both in a semantic and in a Rorschach sense. The large green detail in Card 9 is first seen as a bear, and the color is then responded to as "grass." The contaminated response "grassbear" results. Another example is reported by Rorschach himself. The patient saw in Card 4 a detail which looked to him like a liver. The whole card appropriately reminded him of a heavy-set, portly man. His contaminated response was, "The liver of a solidly living politician."[20] Here we have a thought product with a grossly faulty organization. Two incompatible categories, "liver" and "politician," are condensed into one pseudosentence. Or, alternatively expressed, association takes the place of organization. Or, again differently stated, in terms of Gestalt, there is a typically schizophrenic reversal of figure and ground.

Position Responses. In this type of response a part or detail of the ink blot is perceived and interpreted not on the basis of its pertinent attributes of form or color or shading but solely on account of its spatial pseudosignificance. Thus any detail may be arbitrarily described as "a head" merely because it is on top, and another detail as "the thoughts of a man" because it is near a correctly perceived human head. The same fundamental incapacity which we see in the language area causes these positional responses. One may either say that the patient fails to apprehend or maintain the appropriate organizational set based primarily on the configuration of the ink blot and instead chooses or slips into the inappropriate and incongruous system of spatial dimensions. Or, alternatively, he resorts to reasoning by predicative identification with the identifying link being represented by the irrelevant fact of position, contiguity, or direction.

Whole Responses. There is an increase in the number of Whole responses with a decrease in their quality. Several factors other than contamination and positional responses account for this decrease in quality. For instance, confabulation—which is a Rorschach equivalent for overinclusion and asyndetic lack of causal links—is another reason. In the Rorschach test the qualities of the ink blot should be the basis for causal links between visual apperception and ideational correspondence, but not for capricious association of ideas. Other Whole responses are poor because they are platitudinous. This owes to the patient's inability to organize an ambiguous potential into a Gestalt with figures and ground; no figure emerges. Any card could be a "map" or "some sort of landscape." Such responses are perfunctory and reminiscent of sham language. They are sham interpretations.

I can mention only in passing that the same pathology of formal thought which we encounter in verbal performances shows itself in the failures of schizophrenics in such other nonverbal tests as the Vigotsky test and in Picture Completion tests.

COMPARISON OF ORGANIC AND SCHIZOPHRENIC THOUGHT DISORDER

The thought disorder in organic dementia is—to paraphrase Hughlings Jackson and Kurt Goldstein—more in the nature of an orderly retreat then a disorganized rout. Jackson's conception of dissolution as a reversal of evolution and Goldstein's emphasis on loss of abstract capacity with a concomitant emergence of concreteness clearly denote the character of a delamination of function, of a peeling-off process. In organic dementia voluntary and propositional thought and language performance gives way to a more automatic, passive, stimulus-bound response. Concept formation and conceptual discrimination are lost rather than pathologically altered or derailed. The lowering of the functional level in organicity is uniform and persistent, not variable and capricious as it is in schizophrenic dementia. While it is, of course, true that both types of patients fail in the area of thought and language, they fail in significantly different ways.

Where the schizophrenic creates new words to condense incompatible meanings, the organic cannot find the old words to name familiar objects.

Where the schizophrenic resorts to metonymic approximations only occasionally, the patient with verbal paraphasia fails persistently in the choice of the appropriate word.

Where the schizophrenic slips from one category or system of organization of thought into another, the brain-damaged patient perseverates; or he fails in the task of keeping several aspects of a given situation simultaneously in mind.

Where the schizophrenic slumps from the level of concept formation to that of mere association of unrelated ideas, the organic retreats from the higher level of abstraction to the next highest level of concreteness.

Where the schizophrenic overincludes because of his inability to select and exclude properly, the organic underincludes owing to his inability to mobilize and initiate properly.

Where schizophrenic communication fails in its inability, among other things, to maintain boundaries, communication in the organic fails by not even reaching normal boundaries.

THEORETICAL CONSIDERATIONS

Nobody, to my knowledge, has ever seriously suggested that the language pathology of aphasia was either motivated or represented attempts at restitution. But it has been suggested that the formal thought and language pathology in dementia praecox may spring from dynamic sources and aim at social goals—either by widening the gulf in communication for the sake of safety or by narrowing it through the supposedly magic and restitutive quality of autistic verbal idioms. The reason for this assumption may derive partly from the absence of demonstrable brain pathology and the presence (even abundance) of dynamic, personal material in schizophrenia. As to the first, the absence of demonstrable, gross brain pathology is very likely a result of the absence, so far, of methods to demonstrate such pathology. As to the second, I have asked myself the question why the presence or even abundance of most pressing and dynamically potent material in non-schizophrenic patients, if at all voiced, expresses itself through perfectly normal use of words and sentences. I submit that while psychodynamic factors *color* the thought and language pathology, they cannot *account* for it. Cameron's idea of "interpenetration of themes"[21] does full justice to this viewpoint. Psychodynamics account for ideational content but not for the manner in which such content is formally expressed. In my presentation I have deliberately avoided examples of schizophrenic thought and language, common as they are, in which the *breakthrough* of the primary process may tend to conceal the *breakdown* of the secondary process.

The phenomena which I have described have been compared to dreams. Freud said, "In schizophrenia words are subject to the same process as that which makes dream images out of dream thoughts."[22] One cannot deny the close resemblance between desymbolization and plastic representation; between metonymic distortion and displacement; between certain forms of neologisms and condensation. As to the phenomenon I called "semantic shift," I quote this passage by Freud: "The identity of the two [the squeezing out of a blackhead and an ejaculation from the penis], when expressed in *words*, not the resemblance of the objects designated, has dictated the substitution."[23] But might not the differences be more significant than the similarities? I am rather inclined to agree with Henri Ey that while the dream may well be the guardian of sleep it may also be its prisoner.[24] Could it not be possible to reconcile these two metaphorical inferences and say that the need to conceal the *content* avails itself of a particular form of concealment that is dictated, *like a somatic compliance*, by the very nature of the state of sleep? Thus, in the dream, unintelligibility may be both *intended* and *inflicted*. But can the same be said of the formal thought and language disorder in dementia praecox? Unlike the dream, there is no latent element of which schizophrenic dementia is the distorted, let alone disguised, manifestation. Unlike in the dream work and the mental mechanisms operating in waking life the psychic apparatus in schizophrenic dementia does not concern itself with attempts to obscure the truth. Instead, clarity, organization, and relevance of thought and language are obscured.

Slips of the tongue bear a formal but only superficial resemblance to neologisms and metonyms. They differ from both mainly because of their invariably dynamic origin. It is a common observation, both in patients and in persons not under analysis, that slips are aborted; the semantic expression of conflict succumbs to the censorship before the revealing word has been pronounced in its entirety. One of my patients whose brother is a homosexual said, "My bro—mother's breasts."

(Mother's breasts ⇄ brother's "mests"). But a metonymic word is never aborted. Because it lies within the conflict-free sphere of the ego there is no need and indeed no possibility for its being in any way affected by the censorship. Furthermore, a metonymic word cannot be rendered intelligible by free association to it as can a slip of the tongue. If we inquire into the reason for a metonym, patients without exception supply formal and never dynamic explanations. To return to my patient who confuses "half" and "part," this man will say, "This is a mistake on my behalf," or else, "This is a sign of lack of confidence on my behalf." The mere fact of the consistent use of this metonym precludes, in my opinion, a diagnosis of a slip. But the patient's own elaboration of the reason for his metonymic "choice" is even more convincing that we are dealing with a purely formal language disorder. He said, "One half is a part." The metonym is the result of a semantic shift that centers around "half."

Mosts slips of the tongue resemble neologistic combinations and condensations of words rather than metonymic substitutions. Neologisms, too, become intelligible by a formal and not by a psychodynamic analysis. As cited earlier in this book, one of my patients said, "I know my shortcomings and my longcomings." He knew that "longcomings" was his own creation. He explained, "I say longcomings because it is the opposite of shortcomings. If I had first said liabilities, I would have said assets." The word "short" in "shortcomings" was desymbolized by him from the figurative to the literal (physical) level. Continuing at the level of literalness, "longcomings" acquires for him a neologistic equivalence for "assets." A similar example is reported by Bleuler. His patient said, "As a child I was already an apartment."[25] She meant to convey the idea that she was a person "apart" from others, different from others.

The objection may be raised that the patients' explanations do not constitute free association, and that they are therefore dynamically invalid. This is a right conclusion based on wrong premises. For if semantic pathology is not caused by psychodynamic forces, it cannot be made intelligible by psychoanalytic methods. It has, furthermore, been my experience that free association to schizophrenic neologisms—while at times yielding psychodynamic material—has never supplied the explanation for the neologisms; very satisfactory explanations given by the patients have clearly demonstrated the existence of the well-known formal semantic and thought pathology.

Psychic determinism and its semantic manifestation in the form of dynamic coherence in free association are the proved foundation upon which psychoanalysis rests its undisputed claim to make the seemingly irrational rational. Free association appears to be irrational not because of any particular thought and language pathology but because of the temporary concealment of ideational and affective links; they represent, or attest to, the equivalence of temporal sequence and causality. Free association is rendered rational by, among other means, discovering these links. The formal thought and language disorder in schizophrenia—such as asyndesis, system shifting, and sham language—at first sight seems to resemble free association. It, too, is incoherent and not immediately intelligible. It, too, can be understood if we listen to the patient's explanations. But the area of understanding is predominantly a formal and not a dynamic dimension. In a social sense the initial unintelligibility in schizophrenia is permanent because even its explanation will never amount to a communication. A garbled message is quite different from a coded one. As Cameron has pointed out, asyndetic language is, among other things, characterized by a "paucity of causal links."[26] This paucity is real, not seeming; arid, not fertile; formal, not psychodynamic. In contrast to free association asyndetic language cannot be meaningfully projected against an existential temporal background of the patient's character structure and its fluctuating or stabilized dynamic currents and patterns. Further, the person who freely associates knows that he is intentionally and temporarily relinquishing the social function of language—not so the schizophrenic. There is no sign in ordinary (nonpoetic) free association of the schizophrenic semantic peculiarity; healthy words and healthy semantic units are produced. It is rightly stated that free association aims at avoiding goal-directed thought; it is equally obvious that there is lack of goal-directed thought in certain forms of schizophrenic dementia. But there is this significant difference: in free association goal direction is unconsciously shifted in the direction of dynamic relevance; in schizophrenia it is in every sense lost.

Formal thought and language pathology is not the result of an upsurge of psychodynamic content. Nor is this pathology the manifest, coded translation of latent psychodynamics. This does not mean that such pathology may not play some role in the emergence of dynamic material. I like to view this role as that of a *catalyst*, which facilitates a reaction but, in a sense, remains aloof. The formal phenomenon of predicative identification, for instance, is such a *catalytic event;* it is often placed in the service of delusional reasoning or leads the patient simply to draw false conclusions which are not motivated. Some of the formal pathology which I have described constitutes a catalytic event of a different kind. I will here give two illustrations from my own observations. In the first instance no latent element emerged; in the second the latent element jumped, so to speak, at the opportunity afforded by the catalytic event. The first patient, a man with a mild schizophrenic thought disorder, while speaking of fluctuations of his sexual desire, used the semineologistic terms "upshift" and "downshift." When I asked him to explain these words he said, "The sex drive is like driving a car; one shifts gears from high to low and back again." The formal mechanism of the double meaning of the word "drive" is the only—and, of course, purely verbal—link between sex and a car. It so happened that the patient did not go beyond this point. But had he done so, one might reasonably predict the emergence of dynamic sexual material in connection with a car or its driver, either in the form of a delusional idea or an apophanous delusional misinterpretation. The second patient, however, did go further. He was a young man who was admitted with what appeared to be an acute homosexual paranoid state with considerable thought and language pathology. I asked him for construction of a sentence using the words *"child," "cry," "rain,"* which I wrote out for him. As I handed him the paper I said, "Could you make a sentence around these three words?" He took the pencil and encircled the three words with an ellipse-like design, stating, "I am drawing a sentence around these words; and this is the mouth, but it is also sex." I suggest the following formal analysis: The desymbolization of the word "around" in my request to make a sentence around the words and also some element of system shifting from "making a sentence" to symbolically drawing one, resulted in the mouthlike design. This is the catalytic event which afforded the opportunity for the expression of a likely fellatio fantasy or a dynamically equivalent delusion.

Another example, reported by Bleuler, may serve as a further illustration of the fugitive and transitory interaction between (1) formal thought and language pathology and (2) psychodynamic, affective mental content. "A patient, about to tell of a walk she took with her family, began to enumerate the family members: 'Father, Son,' but she continued 'and the Holy Ghost,' and added even, 'the Holy Virgin,' showing that this familiar phrase threw her off completely."[27] In other words, she shifted from the system "relatives" or "things secular" to the system "Holy Family" or "things ecclesiastic." Nothing else is known to us about her psychopathology. Religious complexes were presumably sufficiently alerted by the idea of the mundane father and son; this sequence represents the "catalytic event." Had she merely persisted in nondynamic enumerative sham language, she would very likely have produced a series, such as, "father, son, daughter, mother, etc." Rapaport comments: "A psychoanalytic explanation would assume that in the subject's mind there is a connection between 'father, son,' and 'the Holy Ghost' other than their occurrence in the religious phrase . . . that the meaning for the patient of 'father, son' is . . . more consonant with 'Holy Ghost' than with, say, 'went for a walk.' "[28] This was certainly the case *at that moment.* We would not consider this verbal contamination to be an autistic phenomenon *unless* we knew that to the patient her father represented, or *also* represented, God.

Freud may have had something similar in mind when he quoted a delusion of a schizophrenic patient (reported to him by Tausk). This patient said that her eyes were twisted and added that this was so because her lover was an "eyetwister" (*Augenverdreher,* best rendered as "spellbinder"). But Freud called it a form of organ language, a hypochondriac trait.[29] He adds that "A hysteric would have convulsively rolled her eyes and would not have been able to give an explanation."[29] I think that in either case one is in such an instance dealing with identical dynamic factors. In the hysteric they constitute the latent element. In the schizophrenic patient of Tausk the catalytic event consists of the desymbolization of the metaphoric meaning of "eyetwister," which is experienced at the level of literalness. The statement is schizophrenic not because of the psychodynamic source but because of the semantic pathology—the catalytic event—which in schizophrenic dementia is always ready to serve.

In his book, *Schizophrenia,* F. J. Fish reminds us that Jaspers and European clinicians have in the past suggested the existence of two types of delusions. As we outlined previously, there are those that arise on the basis of an "understandable" precondition (delusion-like ideas); the delusional content is in harmony with the precondition. On the other hand, there are those "which cannot be understood" (true delusions or primary delusional experiences). It is pertinent to my hypothesis that in the former "the delusion-like idea can be understood as secondary to some other psychological change, such as, an endogenous or reactive emotional state . . ."[30] In other words, their source is clearly affective and thus psychodynamic, not *cognitive.* By contrast, the primary delusional experience, which such investigators consider pathognomonic for schizophrenia, is defined as the establishment of a reference without a cause. One form of the primary delusional experience is the delusional perception, in which "an abnormal significance, usually in the sense of self-reference, despite the absence of any emotional or logical reason, is attributed to the normal perception."[30] Nothing, of course, occurs without a cause. Implicit in this characterization of the phenomenon as an abnormal significance without a cause is the conclusion that these experiences by patients cannot be made intelligible in the light of their psychodynamic-affective psychopathology. Given the characteristic breakdown of the secondary process in dementia praecox, and bearing in mind the close relationship between the secondary process and the cognitive relatedness of the psyche to the outer world, incomprehensibility may be the result of a faulty interpretation of a perception that results from and is in accordance with the singular formal pathology of thought and language in schizophrenia. The latter may then either lead to the mere utterance of an incomprehensible idea or conclusion, or it may act as the catalytic event for the release of dynamic material in the form of a "reference without a cause." Fish cites the following example: This patient heard a floorboard squeak when one of his colleagues entered his office; looking down to the floor and seeing the linoleum he said to himself, "Lino, that means don't lie."[31] Apparently the first four letters in "linoleum" were experienced as desymbolized sounds leading to the idea "don't lie." ("Li-no" equals "no-lie"). But was this only an idea, without psychodynamic significance, squatting like a poor joke on a play of words? I know, of course, nothing about this patient, but it is not at all inconceivable, judging from the nature of the experience and the content of the association, that the formal language pathology has here, too, supplied the catalytic event for the release of dynamic content.

There exists an opinion that the peculiarities of language in the schizophrenic arise from his extreme need for a feeling of personal security, and that—so pressing is his state of desocialization—he avails himself of them, more or less knowingly, in the pursuit of security. His salvation might be achieved, in the words of Sullivan, "through verbal magic in the world of verbal entities,"[32] or, I may add, verbal realities. That would constitute intent, or at least purpose. Thought and language resembling what is seen in schizophrenia is indeed noted in various non-schizophrenic organismic states—such as childhood, the soliloquy with its total social immunity, the dialogue in the total absence of social anxiety during the proverbial seemingly magical semantic intimacy of lovers, and in the artistic representation of language. Despite all this, we must agree that the schizophrenic is neither a child nor an analysand, nor is he in intimate contact or a poet. He is a patient. It may be true that feelings of extreme security with one's fellow men *encourage* solipsistic expression, that artistic language *requires* it, and that children's language is largely *restricted* to it. But schizophrenic thought and language *suffer* from it. After all, schizophrenia is an illness. This brings to mind a conversation which took place between James Joyce and Carl Gustav Jung. Joyce's daughter Lucia was schizophrenic, and he brought her to Jung. It was unavoidable that the obvious similarities of Joyce's and Lucia's usage of language should come up for comparison. Jung used the inspired metaphor that while Joyce was going down to the bottom of the ocean like a diver, his daughter just fell in and drowned.

REFERENCES

1. N. Cameron. "Reasoning, Regression and Communication in Schizophrenia." *Psychological Monographs,* vol. 50, #1, 1938, pp. 1–34.
2. S. Arieti. *Interpretations of Schizophrenia.* New York, Brunner, 1955, p. 216.
3. A. M. Shimkunas, *et al.* "Schizophrenic Responses to the Proverbs Test: Abstract, Concrete or Autistic?" *Journal of Abnormal Psychology,* 1967, vol. 72, #2, pp. 128–133.
4. N. Cameron. "Experimental Analysis of Schizophrenic Thinking." *In:* J. S. Kasanin (ed.). *Language and Thought in Schizophrenia.* Berkeley, Univer. of California Press, 1944, pp. 50–64.
5. E. Bleuler. *Dementia Praecox or the Group of Schizophrenias.* New York, International Univer. Press, 1950, p. 20.
6. E. Bleuler. "Austistic Thinking." *In:* D. Rapaport. *Organization and Pathology of Thought: Selected Sources.* New York, Columbia Univer. Press, 1951, pp. 399–437.
7. E. Bleuler. *Op. cit.,*[5] p. 14.
8. N. Cameron. *Op. cit.*[1]
9. *Ibid.*
10. *Ibid.*
11. A. Angyal. "Disturbances of Thinking in Schizophrenia." *In:* J. S. Kasanin (ed.). *Op. cit.,*[4] pp. 115–123.
12. G. Bychowski. "Certain Problems of Schizophrenia in the Light of Cerebral Pathology." *Journal of Nervous and Mental Diseases,* vol. 81, 1935, pp. 280–298.
13. E. Hanfmann. "Thought Disturbances in Schizophrenia as Revealed by Performance in a Picture Completion Test." *Journal of Abnormal and Social Psychology,* #34, 1939, pp. 249–264.
14. A. Storch. "The Primitive Archaic Forms of Inner Experiences and Thought in Schizophrenia." *Nervous and Mental Disease Monograph,* Series #36, footnote, p. 75.
15. E. Bleuler. *Op. cit.,*[5] p. 17.
16. J. Piaget. *The Language and Thought of the Child.* New York, Harcourt Brace & World, 1932.
17. A. M. Shimkunas, *et al. Op. cit.,*[3] p. 130.
18. E. Bleuler. *Op. cit.,*[5] p. 27.
19. *Ibid.,* p. 22.
20. H. Rorschach. *Psychodiagnostics.* Berne, Huber, 1942, p. 38.
21. N. Cameron. *Op. cit.,*[4] p. 55.
22. S. Freud. "The Unconscious." *In: Collected Papers.* London, Hogarth, 1948, vol. 4. p. 131.
23. *Ibid.,* p. 133.
24. H. Ey. "Hughlings Jackson's Principles and the Organo-Dynamic Concept of Psychiatry." *American Journal of Psychiatry,* vol. 118, Feb. 1962, pp. 673–682.
25. E. Bleuler. *Op cit.*[5]
26. N. Cameron. *Op. cit.*[1]
27. E. Bleuler. "The Basic Symptoms of Schizophrenia." *In:* David Rapaport. *Organi-*

zation and Pathology of Thought: Selected Sources. New York, Columbia Univer. Press, 1951, p. 602.

28. D. Rapaport. *Op. cit.,*[27] footnote #49, p. 602.
29. S. Freud. *Op. cit.,*[22] p. 131.
30. F. J. Fish. *Schizophrenia.* Baltimore, Williams & Wilkins, 1962, pp. 29–30.
31. *Ibid.,* p. 32.
32. H. S. Sullivan. "The Language of Schizophrenia." *In:* J. S. Kasanin (ed.). *Op. cit.,*[11] pp. 4–16.

15

The Autistic Transformation
of the Personality
in Schizophrenia

The concept of autism embraces some of the most fundamental and consequential phenomena in psychopathology
and, indeed, in the mental life of man. This chapter is an attempt to
do justice to the magnitude of the issue and to meet the challenge
of presenting the material as an evolving and coherent construct. Quite
naturally we will first report and discuss what Bleuler himself had to
say about this subject, this "detachment from reality, together with the
relative and absolute predominance of the inner life . . . ,"[1] the pathological proportions of which he called *autism*. We will next examine
the nature of this "inner life" as a potential source of autism; this will
include consideration of the innate forces of affectivity and those inborn
primitive modes of apperception that emerge in our dreams and which
Freud called the primary process. At the same time it can be shown
that other aspects of man's inner life are not related to autism. The
next step is to demonstrate the impact of the pathological "preponderance of the inner life" upon the outer world of objects, upon ordinary
reality. It will then be seen that in all instances of autism the normal
state of polarization between self and nonself, between subjectivity and
objectivity, is unsettled by the former's imposing itself, in specific ways,
upon the latter. Instead of normal, interacting polarity we find a pathologically diffusing "osmotic depolarization" of inner life and outer world.
Finally, the relationship of autism to schizophrenia and to "nonschizophrenia," including various states of nonpathological apperceptive weakness, will be discussed.

The two main sources for an understanding of Bleuler's ideas about
autism are his monograph, *Dementia Praecox or the Group of Schizo-*

phrenias, and a lecture, "Autistic Thinking," which he delivered in the United States. It should be noted at the outset that Bleuler speaks of autism both as an abnormal psychosocial attitude—that is, as a detachment from reality and withdrawal into oneself—and as a special form of thinking which obeys its "own special laws."[2] He adds some descriptive comments regarding the peculiarities of these special laws of autistic thought, the deeper implications of which will be taken up later in this chapter: "Autistic thinking is directed by affective needs; the patient thinks in symbols, in analogies, in fragmentary concepts, in accidental connections."[3] Such autistic modes of thinking, Bleuler continues, are not only the source of the delusions but also of the crude offenses against logic and propriety, as well as all the other pathological symptoms. Concerning this autistic psychopathology of formal thought processes, Bleuler significantly noted that, "This purely intellectual aspect of autistic thinking has scarcely been studied. My presentation has an important gap in this respect which I cannot fill at this time."[4] The gap has been narrowed considerably since Bleuler made this honest admission. Bleuler was also aware of the possibility that the domain of autism could accommodate such diverse and nonschizophrenic phenomena as night dreams, day dreams, play activities, myths, and artistic representation. With regard to all these phenomena he chose to use the somewhat contradictory term "normal autistic thinking." We will attempt later to deal with the qualifications and discriminations which Bleuler's terminology in these areas requires.

Bleuler clearly recognized the essential unity of the autistic potential in man regardless of the ultimate character, quality, and appearance of the observable outcome. His broad and prescient view, which has been so thoroughly vindicated since he first expressed it in 1911, has nevertheless led to some measure of confusion and even criticism. How much could the term "autism" embrace without losing its validity and conceptual-psychological usefulness? Erling Dein says: "The difficulty with *Bleuler's* concept of autism is that he makes it too comprehensive."[5] But Bleuler clearly saw and contrasted with one another the pathological (schizophrenic) autism and other varieties of *subjectivity*—each of which for one reason or another failed to attain or maintain the polarity of interaction between the self and the object that is required from (and found in) the normal, adult, sophisticated human mentality. Those who succeeded Bleuler made their respective contributions within the general sphere of "self:nonself" relationships by focusing upon one or another variety of the concept's pitfalls or inadequacies. A new terminology was needed in each instance, depending from what angle one looked at the panorama of an essentially unitary phenomenon. Ethnopsychology speaks of diffuseness of organizations, of primitivation, and of magical notions of causality. In studying the mentality of the child, Piaget gave us the term "egocentrism," one aspect of which is "syncretism," the naive assumption "that objects or events *thought of together* belong together, in the absence of any reason to attribute time, space, or causal relationships to them."[6]

Although Bleuler recognized the "intellectual" aspects of autism in all their pathological distortions, he was strongly impressed by the role of affectivity in shaping the delusional content of the patients' thoughts and in permitting the existence of incompatible ideas and contradictions. He said that "to think of wishes as fulfilled is one of the main activities of autism."[7] Since reality is obviously the most powerful source of whatever is incompatible with or contradicts the delusional ideas of the schizophrenic, the patient withdraws from contact with the outer world in order to live within his unreal autistic world. To Bleuler, autism was essentially a way of life for the schizophrenic—determined and enforced by the pressure of his affective "complexes" and resulting in a malignant form of desocialization. Yet, astute observer that he was, Bleuler did not overlook the tenuously normal or the grossly pathological links with reality of which schizophrenics are capable. He observed that "normal material and trains of thought are . . . used side by side with the abnormal"[8] and, also, that autism may already exist to a pathological degree while the patient is still able to "show quite good contact with [his] environment with regard to indifferent, everyday affairs."[9] More significantly perhaps, Bleuler pointed out that autism was not exclusively a matter of withdrawing from and being indifferent to the outer world of objects, and that a relationship did exist at times, albeit a pathological one. He expressed it in these words: "Reality enters only in that it has supplied and still supplies the presentation-material which the autistic mechanisms use either as their point of departure or as their subject-matter."[10] It is to this last statement that we wish to give special attention. It contains beyond the point of mere implication the realization that there exists an inner and innate potential for autism, which under certain circumstances can produce a radical alteration in the relationship between "self" and "nonself," with pathological influences and distorting irradiations asserting themselves in either direction and in a manner not found in any other mental illness.

THE "INNER LIFE" AS A SOURCE OF AUTISM

We recall Bleuler's proposition that autism was characterized, in addition to several other important features, by the relative and absolute predominance of the "inner life." Our first task is to clarify the meaning, in the present context, of the concept "inner life." It has at times been suggested that "psychosis" is not created, but is *set free*. This is, of course, a generalization, but it does imply the specific notion of an inborn pathogenic potential. If this is true, such a pathogenic element must fulfill two requirements. It must be innate and primordial, and not the precipitate of the ordinary interactions of the psyche with the outer world of reality; it must always have been a component of the "inner life." The second requirement would be that this potentially autistic element is, because of its very nature, incapable of adequately preserving the required distance and existing differences between subjectivity and objectivity, and thus cannot effect the normal polarization between the inner and the outer world.

This whole issue of a hypothesized inherent potential for malignancy of the "inner life" is perhaps best introduced with the aid of an analogy. In the absence of any depolarization of the subject-object relationship— that is to say, normally—a perception, a word, a concept, an idea, or the need for interpretation and reasoning evokes "a unity occasioned by central objective ideas."[11] This process may be likened to the essentially unaltered reflection of a ray of light by a *mirror*. But our psychic apparatus contains also a built-in mechanism which can act upon that ray of light like a *prism*—diffusing, deflecting, decomposing, and dispersing it, widening its field but without giving it more clarity. In addition the "prism" will open the lid for *"colors"* to be set free, which otherwise would have remained concealed and contained, but which now erupt as a spectrum of *affective* and thus subjective forces. Considering the phenomena of the night dream, the day dream, and the mental features observed in children and primitive peoples who have not been exposed to the corrective experiences of an increasing polarization of the "inner life-outer world" interaction, we must conclude that this "prism quality" is part of our nature. It is not, in our waking state, a very prominent or disturbing part, and we as little know how it is malignantly set free in schizophrenic autism as why its controlled and benign counterpart emerges in myths, in wit, in rituals, and in the arts.

Returning now to psychological terminology we recognize that the innate sources of autism are partly represented by our affective endowment and partly by those primordial mental mechanisms which comprise the primary process. Bleuler had no doubt about the innate character of the autistic potential. He said that whereas "logical thinking in terms of memory-pictures must be learned from experience . . . autistic thinking follows inborn mechanisms."[12] He also thought that the phenomena of symbolism—particularly their universality and pronounced uniformity among individuals, races, and cultures—strongly supported the inborn nature of autistic forms of mentation. It can easily be shown that morbid and intense affects as well as mechanisms representing the primary process combine in the formation of autistic thoughts, beliefs, and behavior of schizophrenics. Bleuler rather strongly believed that the affective abnormality was the decisive source of autism, although he also observed that "many illogical connections . . . are not, or at least not directly, determined by complexes."[13] Similarly, Storch also stressed the primacy of affective pressures in the schizophrenic patient—adding that, given the affective psychopathology, "the archaic primitive thought forms are very useful foundations, because they alone possess the necessary elasticity to permit the erection of his tottering thought world . . . in keeping with the demands of his fitful humor and the moods of his vagrant imagination."[14] Any attempt to assign a primacy either to affectivity or to the primary process in schizophrenic autism creates very considerable difficulties. There are many nonschizophrenic psychotic patients who entertain delusions, but whose psychopathology (for reasons to be taken up later in this chapter) we do not designate as autism. On the other hand, the formal thought and language pathology of the schizophrenic, which we would not consider to be primarily a result of affective psychopathology, may become the trigger or "catalytic event" for psychodynamically determined behavior which would *then* have to be considered autistic. The following example, as reported by Werner, may serve as an illustration. This schizophrenic repudiated democracy because *Demokrat* (democrat) and *demütigen* (to abase) have a number of identical letters.[15] Each of the two operative words had first been desymbolized (*Dem* and *dem*) and through a further process of irrelevant predicative identification a diffusion and interchange of two concepts resulted. Considering the affective significance of feeling debased, it is easy to see how this autistic distortion may radically alter the relationship of the patient to anybody who is a democrat.

As far as the controversy of priorities is concerned, it may be said that schizophrenic autism is a particular and malignant form of subjectivity in which affectivity supplies mainly the motivation, and the mental mechanisms of the primary process the tools. Considering the power of affective needs and the astigmatic "prism qualities" of the primary process, it is not surprising that the schizophrenic can create innumerable expressions of autism and believe the most impossible ones. It is also true that even Bleuler had some difficulty with his own terminology, because he said: "Whether all affective thinking should be labeled autistic is a question I want to leave open. A positive answer to this question would imply that the concept of autistic thinking is broader than that of autism."[16] We would certainly agree that none of the many instances of affectively determined false beliefs and even delusions are representative of autism as long as the more malignant and clinically startling intrusions of the primary process are avoided or minimal. It would be naïve to assume, in this entire process, that sharp delineations are possible. It is not only a question of how much thinking is affectively directed but also how much it is affectively and/or otherwise deranged. Bleuler was well aware of the participation of the primary process in autism when he said: "Autism . . . equates concepts which have but a very unimportant objective component in common. It expresses ideas by most far-fetched symbols, . . . so that one thing will stand for another, giving rise to real displacements."[17]

Malignant Subjectivity

The following clinical examples will illustrate the respective participation of the two components of the "inner life" in the emergence of autism in schizophrenia. One prominent feature in schizophrenic autism is the reduction of a concept or an idea to the level of either literalness or pictorial representation. It is similar to the mechanism of plastic representation employed in the dream work. A schizophrenic was asked what a chair was. Picking up paper and pencil (but without, of course, having been told to *draw* a chair) he produced this design in lieu of the requested definition:

He then explained that this was a chair.[18] This is an unusual example of the schizophrenic's dedifferentiation of the normal word-thing polarity in that the letters of the word "chair" (by suitable spatial arrangement) were used at the same time to represent the thing "chair" pictorially. Werner quotes a schizophrenic as saying that "the single ideas are [now] much more picture-like than before."[19] Storch, who also stressed the fact that "the ideational formations in schizophrenics are much more completely saturated with perceptual elements than is the case in ordinary thought,"[20] tells of patients who spoke "of a heap of truth," or an "idea smaller than a flea." It is, of course, understood that such modes of expression are not meant by the patients to be metaphorical figures of speech; they are literal and pictorial reductions of ideas. Two more examples by the same author may be presented. Both patients were catatonic. The first patient performed rotating movements by passing his hand in a circular fashion around his navel. He said that he wished to make a hole in order to get out into the open.[21] In this instance the pictorial representation of the idea is provided by movement instead of by language, which is not surprising in catatonic schizophrenics. This patient's movement was as little a pantomime as the previous patients' statements were metaphors. First of all, the patient did not intend to communicate his desire "to escape" and it was in fact difficult to elicit the meaning of his movements. Furthermore, the incomprehensibly subjective manner of equating a circular movement with the idea of an "escape hatch" should be considered. Finally, the syncretic nature of the total situation must be pointed out. A geometrical configuration (circle) produced by movement is fused with the emotional meaning of the wish for the hole-through-which-to-get-out; the movement is centered around the navel, and although we do not have the patient's own confirmation of a symbolic significance of the choice of the location, our general knowledge of primitive symbolisms would certainly justify an investigation in the direction of, let us say, fantasies of rebirth. The second patient would creep under his bed and try with all his strength to raise it. He explained this act by stating that he wanted to raise the earth nearer to God.[22] He apparently considered himself to be the saviour of the world. Storch also tells us that the patient had expressed strong guilt feelings because of sodomistic transgressions during his youth. The literal and conatively pictorial expression of the idea of "elevation," which in this case can only mean spiritual elevation, is characteristically autistic. It may also be of interest to note that he chose the bed as the representative object. If we can assume, not unreasonably, that the sexual transgression took place in a bed, we see in the patient's act another illustration of condensation or syncretism in that objects and events "thought of" together "belong together."

One effect of the primary process on dream images consists of the selective (and therefore subjective) alterations of details in the representation of objects. There may be omissions, emphases, displacements, or totally incongruous additions. Similarly, autistic subjectivity, powerfully aided by morbid affective needs, may alter the significance of the physical aspects in the world of objects; they or parts of them are singled out and endowed with a pathological relevance in sharp contrast to their actual, objective insignificance. "There is a loss of the normal opposition of a closed, constant ego and a more or less stable and rigidly constructed objectivity."[23] Storch reports the case of a patient who was hit in the eye by a snowball, which caused some tearing; the patient thereupon stated that there was a great flood.[24] To him the flow of his tears became the equivalent of a cosmic catastrophe. Another patient, suffering from paranoid schizophrenia, became very disturbed when she noted the reflection of the neighborhood houses in the mirror of her washstand. She said "And everybody likes to have her house to herself!"[25] She attributed to the perfectly natural phenomenon of a mirror image the equivalence of the actual presence of the object (and the people connected with it) in her room. The paranoid suspiciousness of this patient caused her to single out an insignificant detail within her room—one to which a normal person would not pay any attention. In addition there had also occurred a total breakdown of the normal polarization between objective and subjective space. I once saw a patient who believed that a secret message was written in invisible ink between the lines of a letter which he had received. Not only did he reverse figure and ground by attributing more significance to the empty portions of the letter than to the written ones, but he was probably also aided in the choice of this particular displacement by the almost pictorial literalness with which he experienced the common metaphor of "reading between the lines." A somewhat similar situation prevailed in the case of another patient of mine who scrutinized the left side of every person he met for clues whether he could trust them; he once saw a man with a left-sided squint and promptly concluded that this person was a "crook." To this patient "left" was the equivalent for "wrong" because "right" was the opposite of both. This tendency of patients to decompose and dismember the object and to rearrange it in accordance with their autistic "inner-life" potential is particularly noticeable in Rorschach performances. This is not surprising because in the Rorschach test the object (ink blot) is by nature loosely constructed. Still, nonschizophrenics are not victimized by this inherent uncertainty of form and organization, and while they are supposed to project some measure of their subjectivity through their interpretations, there will be no gross violations of objectivity. By contrast, schizophrenics show—among other findings not relevant in the present context—poor accuracy in the perception of forms (low $F+\%$) for the following reasons: they may give undue significance to small, unusual, or otherwise perceptually irrelevant detail; they may interpret the whole blot in terms of a detail; or they may give completely autistic responses, with confabulations and contaminations.

Another area in which the malignant subjectivity of autism finds expression is in primitive causality. A great deal has been said about the schizophrenic's tendency toward magical thinking; effects are attributed, by magic, to impossible and incomprehensible causes. If impossible or irrelevant relationships become, respectively, possible or significant in the mind of the patients, we—*not they*—refer to this process as "magic." Affective pressures combine with the instrumentalities of the primary process to accomplish magical effects quite easily. Storch said that "the magic acts of our patients are for the most part performed involuntarily and without any clear understanding of their significance."[26] In other words, the patients do not see anything "magical" either in their acts or in their interpretations of causalities. Many magic movements are performed, particularly by catatonic schizophrenics, in the service of protection against delusional fears and beliefs. "Many patients bind cloths about their head to prevent the troublesome strange thoughts from entering."[27] The utterly ineffectual literalness of this act is not realized by the patient; on the contrary, he will strongly believe both in the effectiveness of the act as well as in the literalness of "thoughts entering from somewhere outside." His protective autistic intervention can neither be attributed to normal and shared symbolic understanding of its nature, nor to his ignorance as to the origin of thoughts. Such behavior is not to be equated with the apperceptive weakness of primitive peoples. If "the native of Somaliland places his foot on a turtle in order to make the sole of his feet as hard as the shell of the turtle"[28] he resorts to the same causality-of-action as our schizophrenic; but the Somali had never attained the degree of sophistication that had permitted the schizophrenic—before he became ill and in impersonal areas even during his illness—to comprehend causality in terms of the conceptual "why" instead of the literal, concrete, nearest-at-hand regressive "how." This is an example of autistic depolarization of relationships.

The following are further illustrations of primitive (schizophrenic) causality resulting in syncretic diffusion of "inner life" and the outer world of objects. One patient believed that people entered her body and "dispossessed her of her own power over that part of the body which they occupied . . . ."[29] This sounds like a delusional elaboration of somatic hallucinations in dementia praecox. The patient then added the following: "If one of them has not straight feet, I feel that my feet are bent."[29] This last statement merits further discussion. Let us suppose that a pregnant woman with a congenital clubfoot fears, or morbidly believes, that the child she is carrying in her womb will also have a clubfoot. She disregards the authoritative assurances of her physician that her fears or beliefs are unfounded. The crucial issue is contained in the meaning of the "also." In the example of the pregnant woman with the clubfoot (but without schizophrenia) we could say that the "also" would not be attributable to either transitivism or primitive (autistic) causality-of-contiguity. Transitivism is the belief of schizophrenics that other persons share, or know of, their morbid experiences; they hear the same voices, think the same thoughts as the patient does. The patient believes, for instance, that he has holes in his hands; therefore the nurse also has holes in her hands. Transitivism is generally considered to be a schizophrenic symptom; Bleuler conceded that it might also occur in nonschizophrenics, but only "when they are in a state of clouded consciousness."[30] In the transitivistic diffusion of ego boundaries the "osmotic depolarization" of self and nonself is extreme, so that attributes of one become automatically attributes of the other. Thus the patient who felt that her feet were bent because one of the persons who had entered her body did not have straight feet has regressed to the primitive transitivistic causality of contiguity; the transitivism in her case is somewhat unusual in that its direction is reversed, from the object to the self. But the fears or false belief of the pregnant woman with the clubfoot are clearly motivated, not transitivistic; perhaps she suffers from anxious anticipation, or unconscious guilt feelings ("The sins of the mother are visited upon the child"). Although she has literally another person in her body she resorts to the rationalization of heredity and not to the transitivistic causality of contiguity.

"Nearness at Hand."   In response to what must be primarily affective pressures the schizophrenic creates pseudorelationships of primitive causality by drawing syncretically upon the external environment—either the environment of actual proximity or that of pathological propinquity, of "nearness-at-hand." In this process paleological props and mechanisms belonging to the primary process play a prominent role and contribute to the "magical" quality of the phenomenon. The patient thinks that forces are effective at a distance. Within the present context, the difference between delusions of influence and nonschizophrenic paranoid delusions lies in the fact that in the latter one is dealing with a morbid and abnormally intense polarization of self and nonself; in the former there is a diffusion of forces between self and nonself—in either direction, a depolarization. This may be one of the reasons why delusions of influence are universally considered to be pathognomonic of schizophrenia. Storch reports and comments on a patient whose symptomatology is a good illustration of our present theme.[31] At one time the patient said that names went through her head and that she then felt as if she were connected with the persons to whom the names belonged. It seemed to her that she was always speaking with the voice of someone else; from this point on it would require only a short step for the patient to conclude that someone else is speaking for her—putting words, and thoughts, into her mouth and mind. She felt "magic power in objects streaming toward her. Everything seemed of increased significance. Behind everything was a meaning, and back of that still another . . . ."[31] She would see a wooden chair and was obliged to seat herself on it, even against her will. From a picture above her bed, depicting an insignificant landscape, "amazing" forces streamed down upon her; these powers were at once in the picture and in herself. Storch comments as follows: "The ego which had lost its consistency seemed to be drawn toward objects . . . and these objects were, it seemed, flooded with magic powers . . . ."[31] Another of his patients who often felt tired thought that "her power had been used by the peasants in their field work."[32] With regard to the schizophrenic primitivation of causality of the kind we have just described, it may be of interest to recall what Freud said about the representation of causation in the primary process of the dream work. If at all represented, says Freud, "*causation* is represented by succession"[33]—one dream image changing into another, or a prefatory dream being followed by the main dream. To equate axiomatically temporal succession with causality is, of course, incompatible with the secondary process. In some schizophrenics, as has been shown, causality may be autistically represented by spatial succession—that is to say, by distance.

Even time itself may be affected by the autistic process so that objective world time and subjective ego time are no longer coinciding or properly polarized. The experience of temporality may completely collapse.[34] Time experience, which is normally structured in terms of one's past, present, and future has now been diffused; this state may well be considered a form of "timelessness" such as prevails in the unconscious. Werner reports an observation on a schizophrenic who shot at the clock because time was his "worst enemy."[35] Werner calls this phenomenon a "materialization" of time. The action of this patient certainly combines the affective and cognitive aspects of the autistic process. The pictorial literalness of "shooting the clock" is a world apart from the metaphor or figurative phrase of "killing time." An equally wide gulf separates the schizophrenic autistic mentality from the use or comprehension of the metaphor.

There is one component of our "inner life" which, because of its very nature, cannot be considered as a potential source of autism (although the autistic process avails itself of its presence). We refer to the microcosmic deposit—e.g., in the form of memories—of our experiences in and with the outer world of objects, inanimate and animate. There can be no "osmotic depolarization" of self:nonself relationships without an antecedent integration and mastery of the nonself world of outer reality. Bleuler—the reader will recall—remarked: "Reality enters in autistic thinking only in that it has supplied and still supplies the presentation-material which the autistic mechanisms use either as their point of departure or as their subject matter."[36] He even said that he could not "conceive of autistic functions below a certain complexity of organization. Autism requires a complex memory."[37] He is, as we are, speaking of pathological autism in schizophrenia.

It seems almost superfluous to point out that the *innate* faculties and tools at the disposal of the conflict-free ego are not the source but rather the *target* of many features of the autistic process. But they are affected by autism in an entirely different manner from the way in which simple (organic) dementia undermines their effectiveness.

THE AUTISTIC TRANSFORMATION OF REALITY

Jaspers once said: "Things that are for the moment most self-evident are also the most enigmatic. Thus it is with Time, the Self and Reality."[38] When we speak of the grossly pathological autistic transformation of reality we must first make clear what kind or aspect of reality we have in mind. Much of reality is transcendent and unknowable; mankind as a whole, or various civilizations as groups, deal with this contingency with the aid of philosophical or religious subjectivity. There is nothing autistic in that. Another part of reality, while known to some, is not known or comprehensible to all; the latter may either ignore it or impart to it a false meaning as a result of ignorance. There is nothing autistic in that either. There is, however, one segment of reality the identity and meaning of which must be grasped and inter- preted with a sufficient degree of objectivity and comprehension by the adult, conscious mind of a person, lest such a person should be judged as suffering from psychopathology. That segment of reality is simply the every-day, tangible, and customary reality of perceptions, events, and relationships. It is the

awareness of the reality with which in practice we have to reckon and deal, to which we have to accommodate every moment. . . . Awareness of this reality pervades us all more or less clearly as a knowledge of the reality with which we are individually most concerned. This individual reality is embedded in a more general reality that has been structured . . . through the traditional culture in which we have . . . been educated. What is real for us in all this has many grades of certainty and usually we are not completely clear about it.[39]

It is of great importance to the entire theme and purpose of this presentation to delineate nonpathological or ordinary shortcomings in the comprehension of the meaning of practical reality from pathological ones, and among the latter category to isolate autistic from nonautistic pathological transformations.

If the concept of autism and autistic thinking is to retain its specific connotation in the psychopathology of schizophrenia, we must attempt to find cogent reasons for separating the autistic transformation of reality from other pathological processes that may also lead to impairment or loss of reality testing. If a patient has ideas of reference, if he believes that there is a plot directed against him, that his wife is unfaithful, that the policeman at the corner is observing his movements; or if a depressed patient believes that he will die of cancer because he had led a sinful life and that the minister's sermon on sin was deliberately chosen because of him, we would not in any of these instances describe these symptoms as "autistic," despite the fact that a pathological subjectivity had significantly altered the patients' interpretation of reality and thus the meaning of it to the patients. In the examples just mentioned it is clear that the transformation of reality resulted from the ascendancy of a purely affective subjectivity—that the patients judged perceptions, events, and causal relationships in conformity with their morbid emotions, but without participation of the primary process. The same may be said about ordinary day dreams and the false beliefs, anticipations, exaggerations, and some parapraxes of the neurotic patients. The imposition of affectivity *alone*—its subjective and innate nature notwithstanding—does not result in what we understand autism to represent. If it did, it would imply (to paraphrase Bleuler's previously quoted statement) that the concept of autistic thinking is broader than that of autism. Furthermore, purely affectively determined transformations of reality are usually "understandable." It is also questionable whether the employment of the primary process *alone*—again, its subjective and innate nature notwithstanding—should be included in the autistic process if affective-dynamic forces or motivations are absent. If this hypothesis is accepted the formal thought and language pathology of schizophrenia is distinct from autistic thinking. There is, as we have suggested, no doubt that the participation of the primary process in wit, myths, and artistic representation is nonautistic; however, the drawings of schizophrenics, falsely or colloquially referred to at times as "schizophrenic art," are representations of the autistic process.

Developmental Aspects. Although it would be obviously wrong to equate the autistic process either with the thinking of primitive peoples or of children, it may be useful to outline briefly the various stages in the maturation of human thought and comprehension of the meaning of practical reality as they evolve during childhood. In a chapter devoted to Piaget's theory of child language and thought, Vygotsky presents the essence of Piaget's ideas in these words:

According to Piaget, the bond uniting all the specific characteristics of child logic is the egocentrism of the child's thinking. To this core trait he relates all the other traits he found, such as intellectual realism, syncretism, and difficulty in understanding relations. He describes egocentrism as occupying an intermediate position, genetically, structurally, and functionally, between autistic and directed thought.[40]

The term "egocentrism," with all its various components, roughly corresponds to the concept of pathogenic subjectivity, in which we see the source of autism in the schizophrenic—the pathological predominance of the "inner life." One significant component of egocentricity is syncretism. The meaning of this term has been variously defined, and we have already quoted one such definition. Werner suggests the following version: "If several mental functions or phenomena, which would appear as distinct from each other in a mature state of consciousness, are merged without differentiation into one activity or into one phenomenon, we may speak of a syncretic function or phenomenon."[41] The name "syncretism" was actually introduced by Claparède to connote the tendency of children to merge the most diverse and even contradictory elements into one whole, image, relationship, or activity; the strength of affective needs as well as of some chance impressions and, above all, the lack of more matured and objective systems of understanding combine to make the child's *Weltanschauung* syncretic. The "incoherent coherence" (Blonski) which is the necessary consequence of the child's apperceptive weakness is also the clinical manifestation of that "regulatory inability" in schizophrenia, and especially in the disorder's characteristic feature which we call the autistic process. If the relatively few, stable, verified, discrete, and logically articulated objects and object relations of the outer world are being dismembered and reassembled by connections too subjective to be comprehensible, and too abundant to be contained within the limited and stringent possibilities and requirements of the secondary process, and if in addition characteristics belonging to one system of psychic organization determine the meaning of any aspect of reality in a language foreign to (and inherently incompatible with) its nature, the result will be, in Werner's words, "a loss of the normal opposition of a closed constant ego and a more or less stable and rigidly constructed objectivity. The milieu invades the ego and, on the other hand, the inner experience spreads outward into the world of things."[42] This is what Federn meant when he suggested that in schizophrenia there was a weakening not only of the ego but also of the ego boundary cathexis, with its ensuing autistically increased permeability. This is essentially also what we mean by the term "osmotic depolarization" between self and nonself, between part and whole, between the perception and its context, between the thought or wish and the event, between the word and the thing it connotes, and, ultimately, between one psychic system and another that will no longer be able to assert their extraterritorial immunity and independence.

CLINICAL ILLUSTRATIONS

It is quite likely that in a given case of advanced autistic transformation of reality the various areas and possibilities of depolarization find simultaneous modes of expression, some more and
others less prominently. Autism, in Minkowski's words, may be "rich"
or "poor." Thus no attempt will be made in the following presentation
toward systematically subdividing the phenomenon, although certain
characteristic features will be stressed.

One of the most far-reaching autistic forms of depolarization is the
loss of one's sense of identity and/or the delusion of being, becoming,
or having been transformed into someone else. The following account
represents the climax of a process of transformation into an exalted
personage, ultimately Christ, in a schizophrenic patient reported by
Storch.[43] This woman had strong guilt feelings because she had been
violated by her father when she was a child, and the affective need
for redemption or purification was intense. One morning, at breakfast,
she left her bread untouched. By chance her coffee cup tipped over
and the coffee spilled into her lap. At this she said: "Now it is all
out . . . the power of the wicked." With this she became Christ; Christ
had also used bread and wine to represent the spirit. She thought one
of the physicians would give her a "child of holiness." If this woman
had not been schizophrenic she might have chosen the nonautistic road
toward redemption and religious self-elevation by becoming a nun and
retreating into a convent. There she would *symbolically* have become
a "Bride of Christ." There she would have eaten her breakfast, like
everybody else, and during communion have shared in the *ritual* of
partaking in the Lord's Flesh and Blood through the *symbolism* of the
wine and the wafer. However, all these needs were autistically, syncretically, and delusionally satisfied by her in the manner described. The
bread and coffee are taken out of the context of an ordinary breakfast
and experienced as a sacrament; the coffee, merely by being a liquid,
is diffusely equated with wine; the spilling, an ordinary mishap, is dislodged from its position of insignificance and, under the affective pressure of the religious complex, drawn, as if by a magnet, into the domain
of an autistic symbolization. The "spilling into the lap" of coffee bears
only the most remote resemblance to the act of impregnation, yet it
sufficed to give her the idea that she had conceived a "child of holiness"
from the physician. In this relationship of partial identities or "participation," the autistic demolition and reconstruction of the world of objects
is quite transparent.

Bowers, in a paper entitled "Pathogenesis of Acute Schizophrenic Psy-

choses,"[44] gives a detailed account of the evolution of an autistic transformation in a young man, a medical student, whose illness began with
an intense fear (rapidly becoming a conviction) that he was seriously
ill—that he had a heart disease and that he was going to die. In order
to find confirmation for his delusion he first drew upon some of his
recollections as points of departure. "A friend had talked about a 'walkie
talkie,' and the thought occurred to me that I might be getting medicine . . . perhaps by radio."[44] The emerging delusion of influence is
here, as often, cast in the form of invisible and imperceptible emana-
tions; he knew, of course, that certain treatments are given by x-rays,
by radiation; but he did not claim that he had been exposed to x-rays.
Instead, by a process of diffusion of concepts, a radio set (walkie-talkie)
became the equivalent of an x-ray machine—in fact, the *word* "walkie-
talkie" became the *thing*. Then he heard someone talk about a one-way
plane ticket; "to me that meant a trip to Houston and a heart operation."[44] We see how an intensely cathected idea—in this case the fear
of fatal heart disease—can gather almost any conceivable perception,
memory, or event into its orbit by transforming the realistic, impersonal
context into an autistic syncretic one. The author adds that "a whole
series of interactions between the individual self and its altered perception of the world are required for the formation of delusional [autistic,
in this case] experience."[45]

I recently had the opportunity to make somewhat similar observations
in a patient who had shown distinct personality changes for the past
six months. She was a 22-year-old single woman who was hospitalized
because of a state of confusion with anxious anticipation of vague doom
and also because of increasing suspiciousness. One aunt has been hospitalized because of schizophrenia for about fifteen years. Her mother
had died several years ago and the patient lived with her father and
her older married brother. She had recently developed intense resentment and even frank paranoid ideas directed against her sister-in-law.
She also suspected that her father had made suggestive sexual advances
toward her. She related during our interview a number of "strange experiences and occurrences" that are relevant in the present context. She
had noticed "a stain of blood" on a wooden piece in the kitchen, which
upset her very much. She thought that it was her father's blood and
she took a rag "to wipe it off." She was not clear under what circumstances her father might have been bleeding, and she actually never
gave this question any attention. When I asked her whether she noticed
blood stains on the rag after she had used it, she was not sure whether
she had; this fact did not seem to matter to her at all. To my questions
as to how her father's blood got on the wooden piece she replied in
these words: "Perhaps because I had hurt his feelings." On that day

she also noticed that there was "a secret understanding" between her brother and herself and that he "transmitted messages" to her "by the way he put things on the table." For instance, while unpacking a small suitcase, he had placed its raised lid in such a position that the patient could not see her sister-in-law across the table; this indicated to the patient her brother's admission that her antagonism toward and differences with her sister-in-law could not be bridged. When clearing the table after dinner the brother left a knife on it; that meant that the patient had better protect herself against her sister-in-law. She did in fact carry a knife on her person from that moment on and until the time of her admission to the hospital. She then ruminated about having broken off a relationship with a young man six months ago and concluded that this event was also "somehow" willed by her brother.

This brief account illustrates how in the schizophrenic objects are selectively lifted out of their realistic and indifferent context and rearranged around a prevailing affective morbidity; how significant abstract ideas are experienced in the form of perceptual analogies; and how closely these regressive autistic mechanisms resemble the plastic representation of ideas in the dream. The tendency of the dream work to use "minor" elements for the representation of major issues is well known; these elements are chosen for their quality of literalness.

The tendency of schizophrenics to overreact to minor internal or external stimuli is also well known. They may do this in all psychic areas. Words and concepts erupt into irrelevant associational chains, significance is seen when none exists, and affectivity (powerfully aroused) will create meaning. The direction may be reversed so that suitably depolarized insignificances will arouse powerful emotions. It may well be that one is in actuality dealing with a circular process. With respect to this tendency to overreact, it seems that the normally containing negative feedback of reality-testing mechanisms is not available. Only by dealing with the existence and *resistance* of the external object can the ego mature toward attaining some mastery of the real world. The "resistance" of the external object—represented by its impersonal and physical identity, its separateness within a logically articulated context of other objects—is directed against the autistic affective-cognitive potential or temptation of the "inner world." The objects and persons in the outer world, of course, resist also our normal and enterprising wishes and needs to change the environment to our advantage; and they resist our efforts to understand the world of natural phenomena. The pursuit of this "supreme task of the ego," as Freud once called it, will, however, not lead to osmotic depolarization, although it may lead to failure or error. But if successful, it will result in a clearer, different, truer, and more adaptive polarization. It is not by chance that the laws of nature have been discovered by scientists instead of by poets.

AUTISM AND SCHIZOPHRENIA

Although Bleuler clearly stated that "schizophrenia is characterized by a very peculiar alteration of the relation between the patient's inner life and the external world"[46] and that autism was his term to designate the pathological predominance of that "inner life," the relationship of autism to schizophrenia and even the scope of the concept of autism are still unsettled questions and, occasionally, controversial issues amongst psychiatrists. In the preceding exposition I have been fully aware of the futility of attempting to deal with this subject with any claim of certainty, let alone finality. However, recognizing the desirability of making a contribution toward clarifying the problems under consideration, I have proposed a hypothesis that I believe could rest on the principal premises of Bleuler's definition. Taking these premises as points of departure I have expanded them in a way which would seem to reflect clinical observations.

Bleuler considered autism to be one of the fundamental symptoms of schizophrenia; at the same time he also speaks of "normal autism,"[47] referring, among other illogical modes of thinking, to such phenomena as fantasy, myths, children's plays, and a host of nonschizophrenic manifestations of loose thinking, which latter human foible he took pains to comment about in a monograph entitled *Autistic-Undisciplined Thinking*.[48] As a symptom of schizophrenia autism comprised in Bleuler's view detachment from reality in the sense of the patient's withdrawing his attention and interest from the outer world of objects; it included a specific psychopathology of thinking, many features of which are components of the primary process; it also entailed a way of life, of action, and of ideation that are all decisively determined by the patients' morbid affects (their "complexes"). Provided that the fact of the patient's withdrawal or "detachment" from the outer world—in whatever form and degree—includes the existence of those transformations of the world of objects and the self-concept, which we described as an "osmotic depolarization" between self and nonself, we would consider Bleuler's conception of pathological autism to represent a specific feature of dementia praecox. Schizophrenic autism is as little transient or episodic as is dementia praecox. Detachment from the outer world—even if prolonged and resulting from affective morbidity, as in nonschizophrenic depressions—does not, in principle, include the autistic transformation of the world of objects. In such instances the primitive cognitive modes of mentation, the primary processes, are not part of the psychopathology. Autism is, of course, not the only symptom of schizophrenia and we may expect that other signs of schizophrenia will be present as well. Dein, to whose constructive criticism of Bleuler's views on autism we have already briefly referred, nevertheless concludes that "autism stands out as the leading theme in the course of schizophrenias . . . autism has the function of unifying the schizophrenias into a group, and consequently it also demarcates them from other psychoses."[49] But the present writer could not associate himself with the rather surprising further statement by Dein in which he suggests that "autism should be understood as a statement on a person's relationship to other people, and that other psychopathological states as for instance thinking disturbances and unrealistic perceptions of the outside world should be kept outside the concept."[50] The concept of autism suggests to us such a profound and specific transformation of all aspects of the psyche that its existence and essence is not likely to remain restricted to one aspect of psychological functioning, including even one as significant as that of a person's relationship to other people.

We have given but a few of the myriad possible manifestations of schizophrenic autism in the spheres of perception, conation, ideation, self-image, reasoning, and beliefs. In this bewildering and teeming disparity and diversity of phenomena we have nevertheless attempted to search for, and perhaps to find, the unifying and thus clarifying common denominator.

AUTISM AND NONSCHIZOPHRENIA

Throughout this chapter we have supported the hypothesis that autism connotes a depolarization of the interactions between innate subjectivity and objective, tangible reality, and that this particular derangement of interaction is prompted by morbid affectivity, implemented by the primordial mechanism of the primary process, and manifested psychopathologically in schizophrenia. What then, one may ask, is the meaning of this current subheading? In this final section of this chapter we will present and discuss various psychological states, other than schizophrenia, in which mental and behavioral phenomena closely resembling autism occur. These organismic states will, of course, be principally distinct from schizophrenia.

The dream is an organismic state in which the autistic process presents itself in its most extreme form, both with respect to the affective motivation of the dream and the primary-process qualities of the dream work that are used in the transformation of the latent dream thoughts into their manifest representation. However, the state of sleep or profound reduction of consciousness in which dreams occur precludes any possibility of equating the autism of dreams with that of schizophrenia, in which condition there is no reduction of consciousness. The situation is somewhat different in the case of certain neurotic phenomena, particularly those of obsessional neurosis. Freud showed us that many formal aspects in the psychopathology of the neuroses have much in common with certain formal features of the dream, and we may therefore expect to find "autistic islands" in the former. The insular character of "autism" in certain psychoneurotic symptoms reflects what we have previously described as the breakthrough of the primary process, limited in degree and delimited in extent. The delimitation is clinically expressed in the ego-alien attitude which the patient with an obsessive neurosis presents toward his symptom. The mental mechanisms of isolation, displacement, or *pars pro toto* representation participate in the process of symptom formation, but repression and its "front-man," reaction formation, are probably the main psychodynamic reasons for the containment of whatever autistic features may be present in the form of the compact symptom. Thus, as is the case in all neurotic processes, there is no impairment (or depolarization) in the comprehension of ordinary reality. The isolated autistic element in obsessive neurosis reveals itself, for instance, in the subjective feeling these patients have about the "omnipotence" of thought, word, and ritualistic motor performances. A certain thought, a word spoken or heard, or a movement performed will bring on, or prevent, a dreaded event. The primitivation of causality inherent in these beliefs is clear from the lack of any logical connection between cause and effect. In addition, the implementation of autistic-magical causality is in this case, too, greatly aided by the inherent mobility, elasticity, and lack of stringencies of the primary process. As an illustration one could mention the common observations of magic and superstitions in compulsion neurosis. In his book *Totem and Taboo* Freud repeatedly pointed to the similarities in the mental life of primitive peoples and of obsessive-compulsive neurosis. In *A General Introduction to Psychoanalysis*[51] Freud records two examples of compulsive rituals that clearly show the "insular autism" in this nonschizophrenic condition. The first patient, a woman of 30 years, was compelled several times during each day to run into a room in her apartment, and stand before a table which was covered with a tablecloth. In the center of this tablecloth there was a "great mark," meaning a certain spot. After having taken up this position before the table she would summon her maid, give her a trivial order and dismiss her. The patient had, prior to analysis, not the slightest idea why she did all this. In the course of the analysis it was revealed that her husband had been impotent during the wedding night and that the patient had felt ashamed and humiliated over the fact that there had, therefore, been no blood stain on her bedsheet; this meant that the marriage had not been sexually consummated. In her compulsive ritualistic act she evidently, but unconsciously, attempted to undo or negate that fact, including her calling in a witness. The autistic element, prompted by an affective need, is represented in the equating of *any* stain on *any* piece of cloth or sheet with a stain of her blood, resulting from defloration by a potent husband. The displacement and the wish fulfillment of having secured a witness whose mere presence is to her tantamount to rendering a testimony, in conjunction with her total ignorance as to the real meaning of the entire ritual, appears to us indistinguishable from a dream representation of the same issue. The second case, which follows immediately in Freud's book, is too long to include here; but the reader of Freud's account will find in it the same elements of "insular autism," and in a much more elaborate form.[52]

We have already mentioned that the mentality of the child and of primitive peoples reveals certain traits which closely resemble the features of intermingling diffusion of subjective and objective qualities in autism. And yet, as Werner put it, "What a fundamental difference in the motives and meanings of primitive man's magical-mythical notion of the world and the daemonic concept of a psychotic!"[53] If our hypothesis of the innate potential for autism and autistic thinking is correct, it would seem to follow that one way to contain or overcome it presents itself in the opportunities and experiences of education—in the broadest meaning of this term—in the processes of socialization and of whatever is required for the development and strengthening of the reality ego and the secondary process. The anlage for this development has no doubt been supplied by nature; its growth is powerfully aided by the teachers and lessons of social living. Even primitive peoples, it is reported, will think and act nonautistically when the basic needs of survival are at stake; and whatever autistic or magical thoughts or notions they may entertain in connection with such needs and pursuits will not interfere with ultimate satisfaction. Primitive man is well adapted to his primitive society, whereas the schizophrenic is ill adapted in any society. Could we assume that in primitive man subcortical-cortical correlations are harmonious, even while his cortical equipment lacks in cultural (and evolutionary?) maturation and sophistication? But in the schizophrenic, subcortical-cortical correlations are deranged by disease—even while his cortical equipment had, prior to the onset of the illness, included a sophisticated cultural inheritance. This is true even if one makes allowances for the hazardous nature and degree of introversion in the so-called schizoid or premorbid personality structure. To primitive peoples many aspects of life appear mysterious for which civilized peoples have found, over the centuries, the rational and natural explanations. Therefore, primitive peoples treat such "mysteries" with the same affective and illogical subjectivity with which even civilized peoples approach whatever is still transcendent to them. In contrast to primitive man, or the child, the schizophrenic during the early phases of his autistic transformation still "knows better" and recalls the memory of his now fading capacity of "polarized" existence. As reported by Werner, one of Storch's patients said: "Reality, as it was formerly, no longer exists. Real life has suffered a decline."[54] Such patients complain of the insubstantiality of their beginning osmotic depolarization. Thus both in primitive man and in the child one is dealing with a state of apperceptive weakness that resembles many of the features of autism. The causes and the nature of this state are, of course, different in primitive man and in the child. The "apperceptive insufficiency" of the child is biological, not cultural; it is transitory and not permanent in the life of the individual. Metaphorically speaking, primitive man has not yet progressed from alchemy to chemistry; and a child's "autism" differs from that of the schizophrenic as a house being built differs from a demolished one.

In his book on wit, Freud has shown that the innate mechanisms of the primary process are used in the "wit work" as they are instrumental in the dream work that transforms the latent dream thoughts into the manifest dream. However, there are important differences. The purpose of the dream work is to *conceal;* the wit work avails itself of its roundabout techniques in order to *reveal,* in various ways, ideas, sentiments, or affects that would be socially offensive if they were directly expressed. There are, of course, many more psychological issues involved in the techniques and purposes of wit. Another difference between the dream work and the wit work lies in the fact that in the latter the mechanisms of the primary process are subordinate to, and in the service of, a superior intellectual and social accomplishment— especially in what one could for this very reason call "superior wit." One example taken from Freud's book may serve as an illustration: "a wealthy but elderly gentleman . . . showed his devotion to a young actress by many lavish gifts. Being a respectable girl, she took the first opportunity to discourage his attentions by telling him that her heart was already given to another man. 'I never aspired as high as that,' was his polite answer."[55] Freud considered this an example of "ambiguity" as a tool of the wit work. One may also point out that the word "high" in the gentleman's reply, while appearing to be metaphorical, was actually meant to be literal; what he aspired to was obviously "lower," both in terms of values and of anatomy. What he meant pictorially or literally he expressed conceptually and figuratively, but in the context of the joke the real intention can not be missed. Its direct formulation would not only be vulgar but would also undo the wit work. But it is in the area of artistic representation that the mutually enriching interaction between the primary and secondary process, in the service of emotional expression, is most striking and illuminating. Therefore, we will devote the next chapter to reflections on the differences between autistic and artistic representation.

Bleuler said that "a small degree of autism carried into life may be of some use."[56] The dilemma may be the difficulty of deciding upon a line and measure of proportions. Times may dictate priorities of either action, or contemplation and even play. No doubt we need men of action, but we contemplate at times with justifiable uneasiness the specter of the robot. No doubt we need men of vision, but there would be little chance of survival in a world of autistic visionaries.

REFERENCES

1. E. Bleuler. *Dementia Praecox or the Group of Schizophrenias.* New York, International Univer. Press, 1950, p. 63.
2. *Ibid.,* p. 67.
3. *Ibid.*
4. E. Bleuler. "Autistic Thinking." *In:* David Rapaport. *Organization and Pathology of Thought: Selected Sources.* New York, Columbia Univer. Press, 1951, p. 412.
5. E. Dein. "On the Concept of Autism." *Acta Psychologica Scandinavia,* 1966/42, Suppl. 191, p. 127.
6. H. B. English and A. C. English. *A Comprehensive Dictionary of Psychological and Psychoanalytical Terms.* New York, Longmans, Green, 1958, p. 540.
7. E. Bleuler. *Op. cit.,*[4] p. 436.
8. *Ibid.*
9. E. Bleuler. *Op. cit.,*[1] p. 65.
10. E. Bleuler. *Op. cit.,*[4] pp. 408–409.
11. H. Werner. *Comparative Psychology of Mental Development.* New York, International Univer. Press, 1948, p. 333.
12. E. Bleuler. *Op. cit.,*[4] p. 436.
13. *Ibid.,* p. 403.
14. A. Storch. *The Primitive Archaic Forms of Inner Experiences and Thought in Schizophrenia.* Nervous and Mental Disease Monograph Series, New York, 1924, p. 36.
15. H. Werner. *Op. cit.,*[11] p. 373.
16. E. Bleuler. *Op. cit.,*[4] p. 419.
17. *Ibid.,* p. 410.
18. C. Wolfman, M.D. Personal communication.

19. H. Werner. *Op. cit.*,[11] p. 331.
20. A. Storch. *Op. cit.*,[14] p. 9.
21. *Ibid.*, p. 2.
22. *Ibid.*, p. 86.
23. H. Werner. *Op. cit.*,[11] p. 368.
24. A. Storch. *Op. cit.*,[14] p. 80. (footnote)
25. *Ibid.*, p. 44.
26. *Ibid.*, p. 61.
27. *Ibid.*, p. 56.
28. *Ibid.*, p. 38.
29. *Ibid.*, p. 43.
30. E. Bleuler. *Op. cit.*,[1] p. 299.
31. A. Storch. *Op. cit.*,[14] p. 26 ff.
32. *Ibid.*, p. 45.
33. S. Freud. *The Interpretation of Dreams.* New York, The Modern Library (Random House), 1938, p. 344.
34. H. Werner. *Op. cit.*,[11] p. 189.
35. *Ibid.*, p. 190.
36. E. Bleuler. *Op. cit.*,[4] pp. 408–409.
37. *Ibid.*, p. 427.
38. K. Jaspers. "Delusions and Awareness of Reality." *International Journal of Psychiatry*, vol. 6, #1 1968, p. 25.
39. *Ibid.*, p. 26.
40. L. S. Vygotsky. *Thought and Language.* New York, Wiley, 1962, p. 11.
41. H. Werner.. *Op. cit.*,[11] p. 53.
42. *Ibid.*, p. 368.
43. A. Storch. *Op. cit.*,[14] p. 69.
44. M. B. Bowers, Jr. "Pathogenesis of Acute Schizophrenic Psychosis." *Archives of General Psychiatry*, vol. 19, #3, 1968, pp. 348–355.
45. *Ibid.*, p. 353.
46. E. Bleuler. *Op. cit.*,[1] p. 63.
47. E. Bleuler. *Op. cit.*,[4] p. 416.
48. E. Bleuler. *Das Autistisch-Undisziplinierte Denken.* Berlin, Springer, 1922.
49. E. Dein. *Op. cit.*,[5] p. 134.
50. *Ibid.*
51. S. Freud. *A General Introduction to Psychoanalysis.* New York, Liveright, 1935, pp. 231–232.
52. *Ibid.*, p. 234 ff.
53. H. Werner. *Op. cit.*,[11] p. 376.
54. *Ibid.*, p. 418.
55. S. Freud. *Wit and its Relation to the Unconscious.* New York, The Modern Library (Random House), New York, 1938, p. 652.
56. E. Bleuler. *Op. cit.*,[4] p. 435.

16

Artistic and Autistic
Representation

The late British neurologist Russel Brain[1] related a conversation between the painter Turner and an admiring lady. " 'I never saw a sunset like that, Mr. Turner,' said the lady looking at the canvas. 'Don't you wish you could, Madam?' replied Turner." We must therefore conclude that "a sunset plus Turner's lady questioner did not equal a sunset plus Turner." The two are a world apart. The sunset as an external object—that is, as a part of the physical world—was available to both Mr. Turner and his lady. But Turner's artistic contribution to the object (quite apart from his skill of execution)—a contribution which for the moment I should call his "inner world," and which his lady lacked—created the painting. Why is it true that a painting, but not a photograph, an original sculpture but not a cast, and a poem but not its propositional translation are artistic representations? What are the formal psychological aspects in the artist's contribution to an object, to sound, to language itself whereby he imposes upon them his inner world to achieve the artistic unification? Every piece of art is a message and thus there must be a sender and a receiver. There are psychological issues in all of these three areas. My presentation restricts itself to reflections about the psychological nature of the message.

As far as this alloy of an outer and an inner world is concerned, there exists a striking and perhaps not entirely unrelated analogy to artistic representation in the realm of the simple perception of sense data. The controversy between physiological realism and physiological idealism deals with the question of whether our perception of objects depends on our discovery and selection of sense data or on our creation of them through the activity of our brain. The physicist tells us that "red" is light of a certain wavelength. When it reaches the visual pathways the neurophysiologist tells us that the resulting nerve impulses are physically quite different from the wavelength of red light. The same applies to the transmission of soundwaves as electrical impulses in the auditory system. It thus follows that what is happening in the brain, not to mention in consciousness, when we see "red" is different from what is "red" in the world of objects. Indeed, the qualities of the nerve impulses in all sensory modalities (sight, hearing, touch, and smell) are very nearly alike, but not the resulting perceptions. The qualities of these are created by the corresponding cortical areas. As Lord Adrian[2] noted: "The quality of the sensation seems to depend on the path which the impulses must travel." It is therefore inevitable that every perception should contain subjective elements and that the perceptual "inner world" represents the physical outer world through a universal and quasibiological symbolism. The subjective contribution in simple perception consists of the decoding of coded nerve impulses, which, it is true, are derived ultimately from the physical qualities of the object.

In an attempt to draw the line between the objective and the subjective in perception, between the contribution of the outer world of objects and the inner world of the sensory cortex, Whitehead (cited by Brain)[3] said that "the bodies are perceived as with qualities which in fact are purely the offspring of the mind. Thus Nature gets credit which should in truth be reserved for ourselves."

Credit, however, is given to the artist for his subjective contribution in the representation of the object, of language, and of sound. Artistic representation reveals, to various degrees, features with which we are acquainted from our studies of the formal psychopathology of schizophrenia and our knowledge of the psychology of the unconscious and preconscious. Credit is given not to their presence but to their taming. It is the recurrent theme of the primary process in the service of the secondary process; of the primary process as a means to an end instead of an end in itself; of the employment in the service of a superior mental achievement of what in the area of psychopathology is an inferior tool; of a person dealing with his autism instead of his autism dealing with him; of a superior mind's indulging what a sick mind suffers from. For in every artistic creation two processes participate, to various degrees and in various proportions: inspiration, which is essentially regressive, and elaboration, which is essentially integrative.

The relative prevalence of these two psychic forces represents shifts in psychic levels and contributes significantly to what one may call *style*. An inspiration can inspire and communicate only if it is tamed and disciplined by a strong ego, that is to say, by hard work. Only then does "madness" emerge as what Plato called "creative madness." Supremacy of "inspiration"—maximal and uncontrolled as it is in the so-called artistic creations of the psychotic, and indeed in their thought disorders and use of language—is synonymous with autism; of itself it is uninspiring and of no communicative value.

Hughlings Jackson's concepts of propositional and emotional language may serve as an introduction to the psychology of artistic representation of language in the literary arts. I shall confine myself to oratory and poetry. I, for one, regret the decay (with one shining exception of recent days) of artistic oratory in our times—oratory which is superior in that its impact loses but little when it is read rather than heard. Oratory is somewhere between propositional and emotional language. It is not merely propositional because it arouses feelings; it is not entirely emotional because it also conveys thought. It differs from poetry not only in that it is, in its formal aspects, essentially prose, without rhyming, although not without cadence; more important, oratory addresses itself to, and inspires action and is thus not subject to what is known as the "aesthetic illusion." In other words, it lacks the "as if" or "make believe" quality of poetry and theatrical art. Winston Churchill—that unsurpassed master and unifier of thought, feeling, and action—was, of course, the shining exception to whom I have just referred.

I choose for the purpose of analysis a single sample of his oratory, both world-famous and, in retrospect, world-saving: "Never in the field of human conflict was so much owed by so many to so few." I ask you first of all to become aware of the almost poetic rhythm or cadence of this sentence. Rhythm is one of the several means of imparting feeling to language, and feeling is, of course, always a part of the subjective contribution in artistic representation. I happen to know that for reasons of cadence Churchill included the relatively insignificant words "in the field of human conflict." Note how much the sentence loses in emotional impact without these words: "Never was so much owed by so many to so few." However, the main artistic effect of the phrase owes to the particular use of the words "much," "many," and "few"—a surprising discrepancy between cause and effect, but a deceptive one. The deeper meaning is enhanced by the superficial contradiction! Finally, one notes the shift from the factual or propositional to the universal and emotional. A reversal of this shift would result in the following totally unartistic statement of fact: "Never, in any war, did some 40 million Englishmen owe their lives and national independence to only 1,800 fighter-plane pilots."

Some of the more obvious distinguishing features of the poetic modification of language, if compared with propositional speech and oratory, are rhythm, rhyming, and alliteration. We know from our studies of the use of language in schizophrenics that they have, or rather suffer from, a tendency to desymbolize the word—to reduce it from the level of connotation and denotation to that of verbalization. This regression to the phonetic aspect of the word, the clang, may even determine their associations. But whereas in the schizophrenic association based on word sound indicates the patient's inability to elaborate thought, the poet, while elaborating his thoughts, can at the same time afford the indulgence of rhyming and alliteration. Despite this superficial similarity, the word representation in the poem does not replace object representation.

Sound repetition as in rhyming, more conspicuous in end-rhyming than in internal rhyming or alliteration, as well as rhythm or meter, are psychological experiences rather akin to certain musical qualities; so is intonation when poetry is read. Nobody will doubt that the purpose of these devices is to evoke emotional overtones. Rhythm, in contrast to harmony and melody, is a relatively inferior tool in musical representation and communication of sound. I have often had the experience when thinking of a certain piece of music, while at the same time being exposed to interfering sounds, particularly another piece of music, that I was only able to become aware of the rhythmical pattern of the piece I was thinking about, while the more highly evolved sound representations (such as harmony, musical ambiguities, or the full impact of melody—the musical idea) were bleached or blotted out altogether. I see in this another confirmation of Jackson's law concerning the order of dissolution; the higher levels are more vulnerable than the lower ones. Applied to poetry, rhythm's quasimusical qualities are thus of a primitive nature.

AESTHETIC AMBIGUITY

When we choose a word in propositional speech, our aim is to restrict the meaning of the concept to the point of precision. The poet aims at the very opposite. He deliberately chooses a word in the service of a condensation of many and pertinent meanings. I would call this the poetic expansion of the concept. It is implied, a potential, that is aimed at the receiver of the artistic message. When the primary process—in the sense of a potential condensation of meaning—is applied to the word, the result is poetic ambiguity. The idea of the expansion of the concept was always recognized as one of the features of schizophrenic thought. But whereas the poet condenses multiple meanings into a word, the schizophrenic permits them to erupt from it. To the poet the word is a means toward a meaningful unification; to the schizophrenic it is a source of an irrelevant association. The aesthetic experience is immeasurably enriched by the multiplicity of meanings in the poetic use of language. Overdetermination and condensation, as well as the consequent ambiguity, are central to artistic representation of language. Aesthetic ambiguity in poetry is conjunctive and mutually reinforcing; it is integrative, not disjunctive, as is the mutually exclusive meaning of those dream elements which are represented by their opposites. In aesthetic ambiguity, the meanings of words, although multiple, are unified. It is a controlled regression in which the primary process, the inspiration, and the secondary process—the stringencies of the problem-solving task—cooperate. The multiplicity of meaning is covert and intended to be so. It is, as I said, a potential to which the receiver may react at various psychic levels and in a manner not necessarily identical with the experience of the creator. We agree with T. S. Eliot's statement, "A poem may mean very different things to different readers and all of these may be different from what the author thought." It is precisely this reliance on preconscious and unconscious clusters of related meanings in the listener—that is, undertones of words (to use Kubie's expression) in the listener—at which the poetic use of the word aims. The word is a symbol, not a code. And as a multivalent symbol, it is enriched, as indeed a single note in music is enriched by its overtones, not to mention other means in the service of aesthetic ambiguity. Freud noted that a certain flexibility of repression is required in artistic representation; this is the very opposite of what is required in the propositional and scientific use of language. In scientific creativity in general, stringencies are maximal; there is no room for ambiguity, no possibility of style, no theme upon which to improvise or create variations. And, incidentally, is it not also true (as Freud pointed out in *Wit and Its Relation to the Unconscious*) that in poetry one source of aesthetic pleasure derives from the economy of psychic energy that aesthetic ambiguity affords? It is the poem which is delightful, not its analysis. And what better way is there to destroy the humorous effect of the "wit work" than to undo it by subjecting it to a propositional autopsy?

Examples. Let us now consider one or two illustrations. Here is a poetic passage from the Bible: "because man goeth to his long home and the mourners go about the street." Is "long," which only seems to be inappropriate, a metonymic idiom as Cameron described it in schizophrenia? Is there a shifting of the frame of reference as Angyal described it in schizophrenia, a shift from the system "temporal" to the system "spatial"? Not at all! The word is appropriate, not metonymic. It is a meaningful condensation of two frames of reference, not a meaningless derailment from one system into another. The "long home"—the long shape of the grave—is an allusion to eternity.

Another sample of integrative poetic ambiguity was more elaborately analyzed (I should rather say "responded to") by Ernst Kris. It is a brief passage from T. S. Eliot's "Sweeney Among the Nightingales":

> Gloomy Orion and the Dog
> Are veiled; and hushed the shrunken seas;

Confining himself to the ambiguities in just the word "shrunken," Kris says:

Most directly, the reference is to the state of the tides, the moon having been mentioned in the previous stanza. But shrunken is also withered and old, and especially in the case of the seas, dried up; there is a suggestion that we are present at the end of the world. To shrink is to contract, huddle, cower; hence we find an attitude of fearful expectancy appropriate to impending death (the image of adulterous murder runs through the poem). To shrink is thus also to recoil in horror and detestation. Again the shrunken sea is at its most vulnerable. . . . And the vulnerability extends perhaps to the land on which the murderous action is to take place. . . . This brings us back to the literal reference to the tide. . . . the intermediate interpretations reinforcing the response to shrinkage.[4]

One may ask how valid these interpretations are; I think their validity lies in the fact that they are possible.

Application in Visual Art

It is obvious that the principles of artistic representation must apply to all art forms. In the visual arts the transformation of the object can be discussed with regard to means and goals. It is the artistic goal, aiming in various directions, that determines the means—carried to various distances from objective reality. An object may be artistically represented not merely for what it is but also in the service of expressing an idea which need not be at all inherent in the object as it appears in nature. In his "Creative Credo," Paul Klee says:

In former times artists represented things which were to be seen in the world, things which they liked to see. . . . Today the relativity of visible objects is made evident, testifying to the belief that that which is visible is merely an isolated example in relation to the totality of existence, and that most real truths lie hidden. . . . Art does not reproduce what we see. It makes us see.[5]

In the following discussion I shall not deal with the influence of personal or cultural dynamic forces on either content or style of artistic object representation. In what I may loosely call reality-oriented painting, the artistic modifications are relatively mild, permitting the object to remain intelligible. However, the object is nevertheless transformed by certain means and in the service of certain objectives. Simplifications, omissions, emphases, and color are some of the means; emotional values and quasiarchetypal universality of meaning are the goals. As Franz Alexander said, "The presentation of the universal, the timeless, the essential, has long been considered one of the main accomplishments of the artist."[6] In this process the object loses some of its physical identity, but it gains in symbolic meaning; it loses some of its cognitive qualities, but it gains in emotional significance; it loses some of its "thingness" or particularity, but it gains in the direction of "thinglessness" or universality. Photographic accuracy is sacrificed so that psychologically significant emphasis can emerge.

I have chosen as an illustration Stuck's famous painting of Beethoven, or rather of Beethoven's face. Artistically, but not realistically, the two are the same. Here is an omission, a *pars pro toto* representation in the service of emphasis and not of concealment. Stuck did not paint Beethoven's face to identify him, but to convey to us, in a highly condensed manner, all that is essential about the man, and perhaps, about a small but significant segment of humanity itself. Also, the actual Beethoven surely never looked like this; all the innumerable fleeting expressions of that actual person are for the candid camera and not for the artist to catch. Beethoven is painted with closed eyes to convey the idea of his perceptual, social, and spiritual detachment. You can not paint deafness; hence the displacement. Stuck did not *only* want to symbolize deafness; hence the aesthetic ambiguity of countenance. Here is the intense introversion and spiritual transfiguration of the late works of the master, of the *cavatina* and the *Agnus Dei* of the *Missa Solemnis*. All these feelings of the painter—and yours and mine—are condensed into a single feature: the closed eyes which are awake. There is only one color in this painting, namely, various shades of blue. To the degree to which artistic representation puts distance (for whatever purpose) between the object and itself, the color of the painting will be at variance with the natural color of the object. In extreme cases of so-called nonobjective art, color is the only aspect of the visual world which is represented. In this sense color, perhaps more than any other element in the visual world, arouses emotion. I think the color and shading in this picture create emotional responses which I would hesitate to put into words. They may be quite different in different people. I am reminded of color synaesthesia that some musicians experience in relation to the various keys. These color associations are constant; they correspond somehow to the emotional significance of the key and defy explanation.

In contemporary painting the artistic representation of the object may reach such degrees of derealization that the manifest work of art often fails to be intelligible, and its latent meaning can be arrived at only with the aid of the artist's secondary-process thoughts. Only then will it fulfill the requirements of an artistic message. It is in these instances that a differential diagnosis between nonobjective art and the pictorial creations of schizophrenics must be—and, I believe, can be—accomplished. While the common elements relating to the id, the rejection and demolition of the object, may appear very striking, the differences relating to the ego are decisive. I can therefore not quite agree with Franz Alexander's statement about the extremes of contemporary art, when he said, "they could not merely reject the external world . . . they had to repudiate a part of the self, that part which psychoanalysis calls the rational, conscious ego."[7] Intelligibility on sight alone may be equally reduced or impossible. But when the "art work" is undone and the latent art thoughts obtained, their meaning in real works of art will be found to be comprehensible, in the sense of Jaspers' *verstehende Psychologie,* and communicable. I would like to add that even at the level of the manifest creation there are usually significant differences: the stereotypes, glaring formal incongruities, and fragmentations of psychotic creations as contrasted with the distinctly harmonious and evenly patterned creations of even the most derealistic products of art. If it were not for these formal and ideational differences, the conception of artistic representation, at all psychic levels, as an interplay of the primary and secondary process would be invalid.

In 1930, Klee painted the picture which he called "Error on Green" (Fig. 1). The painting is not intelligible on sight; there is marked distortion, fragmentation, and condensation of the objects. Despite this, the first impression is one of harmony and balance. Klee gave us a few of his art thoughts. He says that the face is dominating at the center like an astral body; he speaks of the ladder that, like a bridge of thought, links the inside with the outside. He emphasizes how the head is in peripheral contact with a segment of a circle, a pointer to instability both in the bodily structure and on the spiritual level. He says, "This world of unreality is nevertheless plausible. It lies within the human sphere."[8] The theme of instability is convincingly and persistently expressed: the table stands on only two legs; a human leg is precariously placed at the very edge of the table; the ladder connects like a thin frail thread the table with the enormous head, which in turn is supported only by pinpoint contact by a body which it seems to dwarf and crush. Everything is quite tenuously maintained, like a house of cards. Obviously, many more details and art thoughts are missing in my brief reconstruction. But we do know about the issue of instability, the central

FIG. 1

position of the astral head, and we have the artist's title. What might be the nature of the "error"? And is there not a faint sadness around the mouth, and a tear? Does the error lie in the human illusion of omnipotence and invulnerability, and in man's restless wish not merely to discover but to alter the laws of nature, all of which is so cruelly denied by the eternal stability and indifference of the cosmos? I do not know whether this is the meaning of the painting, but from Klee's own words, it appears to me plausible—within the human sphere, emotionally significant, communicable, and deliberately artistically represented.

Pathologic Distortion

Figure 2, is the reproduction of a drawing made by a schizophrenic, I hope to show not only how the schizophrenic imposes the primary

FIG. 2

process upon the object representation (just as he imposes it upon words and language), but also why such products cannot be considered art. I chose this particular picture because the patient had revealed the thoughts which the picture expresses. These thoughts, I submit, are not "art thoughts"—that is, a rational equivalent of latent dream thoughts —but rather psychotic fantasies in a schizophrenic cast.

Perhaps we should first look at this drawing uninformed and record our general impression. That it is not immediately intelligible is not the crucial issue; neither is nonobjective art. It is my impression that there exists an unmistakable disharmony and incompatibility of pattern. A kind of system-shifting in object representation (reminiscent of equally incongruous shifts in the mental set in schizophrenic thinking) suggests a fragmentation of the secondary process.

These are some of the thoughts which the patient had when creating this drawing,[10] along with my comments: "At first the cobra stood in the air . . . and then came the leg and then the other leg was added." There is no intelligible connection between the cobra and the leg, except perhaps a similarity in shape and direction. This assumption seems to be confirmed by the parallel position of the second leg, which is contiguous with the horizontal portion of the cobra. It is somewhat reminiscent of verbal contiguity in schizophrenic language when sentences are replaced by a senseless enumeration of words. Then the patient said, "The second leg was formed out of a root." He associates this with *Ruebezahl,* a giant of German folklore. The literal translation (if one can call it such) of the name is "root" (*Ruebe*) and "pay" (*zahl*). It is designed to express the idea "repentance pays." It is easy to recognize the utterly arbitrary sequence "root-*Ruebezahl*-repentance pays," the desymbolization of the words, the birth (or rather the abortion) of an idea out of phonetic identities. No single element in the drawing reflects a part of a total conception. The patient continues, "On this second leg the face of my father-in-law appeared. Then it came out as a tree. . . . The hair formed the branches of the tree." Here we have a condensation of a face, a tree, the branches of a tree, and hair. In art, shapes as well as words have multiple meanings. But in the psychotic, multiple meanings do not represent relevant multiple aspects of a supraordinate unifying idea. In other words, they are not variations on a theme. The patient's final comment was: "One of the feet plants itself firmly against heaven; this means the fall into hell." This is a clear example of what Kris calls disjunctive ambiguity, of alternatives excluding and inhibiting each other. He further says that this type of ambiguity is especially suited to the expression of ambivalent attitudes. We know that schizophrenics, in their inability to elaborate thought, often produce associations merely because they are opposites.

Thus the schizophrenic—harkening back to Jung's comment about Joyce's daughter—drowns in the ocean of his autistic desocialization. But the artist, while he may at times starve and face other hazards— Taylor reports Spencer as having said "the activities we call play are united with aesthetic activities by the trait that neither subserves, in any direct way, the processes conducive to life"—nevertheless satisfies a psychobiological need in us which should not be underrated. As I am expected to remain "scientific," I will say that he achieves union between the primary and secondary process, that he puts each in the service of the other, and, in contrast to the schizophrenic, enhances communication in depth with his fellow man—in direct contrast to the schizophrenic! The autistic outpourings of the schizophrenic—whatever medium of expression, or rather of *leakage,* he may resort to, be it form, sound, or language—are as little true artistic creations as is the dream itself, and for the same reasons—formal similarities notwithstanding. This does not mean that either of these unmitigated examples of distortion is without meaning or intelligibility. But it does mean that they do not carry a message and can not be felt. Nor is the difference between artistic and autistic representation a matter of skill in execution; the dream work in this respect seems to be far superior to the primitive and crude ornaments found on the walls of caves of ancient races. One must not confuse distortion with art.

I conclude with this quotation from Joseph Beck: "Fantasy actually involves a creating of something totally new. . . . The schizophrenic's misconstructions take on fantastic form. But this is not fantasy. It is inaccuracy."[11] To this I may add that such efforts will remain a pathological performance because the patient can not produce latent art thoughts but only blatantly autistic ones.

REFERENCES

1. W. R. Brain. *Mind, Perception and Science.* Oxford, Blackwell Scientific Publications, 1951, p. 68.
2. Lord Adrian. *The Basis of Sensation.* London, 1938. Cited by Brain,[1] p. 6 ff.
3. W. R. Brain. *Some Reflections on Genius.* Philadelphia, Lippincott, 1960, p. 165.
4. E. Kris. *Psychoanalytic Explorations in Art.* New York, International Univer. Press, 1952, p. 249.
5. J. Spiller. *Paul Klee.* New York, Barnes & Noble, 1962, p. 12.
6. F. Alexander. "The Psychoanalyst Looks at Art." *In:* W. Phillips (ed.). *Art and Psychoanalysis,* New York, Criterion Books, 1957, p. 351.
7. *Ibid.,* p. 356.
8. J. Spiller. *Op. cit.,*[5] p. 80.
9. E. Kris. *Op. cit.,*[4] p. 100.
10. J. Taylor (ed.). *Selected Writings of John Hughlings Jackson.* New York, Basic Books, 1958, vol. 2, p. 360.
11. S. J. Beck. "Errors in Perception and Fantasy in Schizophrenia." *In:* J. S. Kasanin (ed.). *Language and Thought in Schizophrenia.* Berkeley, Univer. of California Press, 1946, p. 102.

17

Clinical Varieties of Schizophrenia

THE TYPICAL OR SYSTEMATIC SCHIZOPHRENIAS

The designation of "typical" or "systematic" schizophrenia, it will be recalled, denotes the sharply delineated end states of the several malignant, deteriorating, nuclear varieties of dementia praecox. The terminology in many instances has been introduced by Kleist and his pupils, notably Leonhard. Each variety, so they believe, is expressive of involvement of a distinct "psychic system." Four types are distinguished: the paranoid, the hebephrenic, the catatonic, and the confused form.

The Paranoid Form

Leonhard uses the term "paraphrenia" synonymously with "dementia praecox, paranoid type." The general features of the systematic paraphrenias include gradual onset, predominance of paranoid symptoms (such as certain delusions and hallucinations), and formal thought and language disorder in different degrees of severity. Catatonic or hebephrenic symptoms are extremely rare, and, in theory, should not be found at all. The following subforms have been isolated.

Phonemic Paraphrenia. In this variety auditory hallucinations of a certain character are the prominent feature. The voices concern themselves with whatever the patient may think at the moment—confirming it, contradicting it, or merely "reporting" it. The phonemes appear often in the form of a conversation between two or more persons. As their content follows so closely the thoughts of the patient it is not surprising that some of these patients also experience *Gedankenlautwerden*. The patients usually believe that the voices come from persons, near or far

284

away, perhaps over the radio, occasionally from within the body. Leon-hard states that in phonemic paraphrenia affectivity may be fairly well preserved for a considerable time: the patients tend to react with some measure of emotion to the voices, at least until the illness is far advanced. A formal thought and language pathology is present, but not very marked. As a result of the particular nature of the phonemes the patients believe that everybody knows what they are thinking. Leonhard con-siders this form to be the mildest variety among the systematic para-phrenias, largely because of the relatively limited degree of affective and intellectual deterioration.

Hypochondriacal Paraphrenia.   Fish, who is an outstanding proponent of the views of the Frankfurt school, states that "specific bodily hallu-cinations, specific hallucinatory voices, and a certain mood state must all occur for this sub-form to be diagnosed."[1] The somatic hallucinations are distinctly morose and eccentric; their paranoid nature is reflected in the secondary delusional elaborations by the patients, such as their being tortured, castrated, or abused. There is, of course, no possibility of confusing these phenomena with neurotic hypochondriacal sensations and ideas; nevertheless, it may be pointed out here that in the latter—circumstantiality of expression notwithstanding—bizarre descriptive ele-ments suggestive of participation of the primary process are lacking, and also that neurotic hypochondriasis concerns itself with fears of ill-ness, the "inner pole" of the symbolic process. The neurotic hypo-chondriacal patient does not attribute his bodily sensations and observa-tions to inimical outer sources. Auditory hallucinations in hypochondri-acal paraphrenia are incongruous with the patients' prevailing thoughts; they are usually disconnected short phrases which are felt as an in-trusion; this disparity between thoughts and phonemes is perhaps the reason that *Gedankenlautwerden* is not a common occurrence. Quite often the voices are attributed to apparatuses or machines which are placed far away, and delusions of influence are common. This observa-tion by a clinical psychiatrist coincides with the psychoanalytic view concerning the nature and meaning of the influencing machine, at least in principle. Fenichel, quoting Tausk, says that "the analysis of the frequent idea of being influenced by machines, which are supposedly used by the patient's persecutors, shows that these machines are replicas of the patient's own body."[2] We would also add that the intricate mys-teries of the internal organs are appropriately reflected by the usually arcane and complicated nature of the "influencing machine." The pa-tients tend to be greatly irritated by their hallucinations and are of a sullen disposition. There is a concomitant thought and language dis-order, with asyndetic and metonymic phenomena.

Incoherent Paraphrenia.   This variety is characterized by an almost continuous state of auditory hallucinations, marked disorder of thought and language organization, and very poor contact of the patient with his environment. The patients respond with anger or counterabuse to the voices. They pay little or no attention to the examiner. "The hallucinatory aversion and the continuous hallucinosis which cuts into all conversations occur in no other form of paraphrenia."[3] In addition they show marked affective and social deterioration, often to the point of incontinence.

Fantastic Paraphrenia.   The essence of this form of paraphrenia is the presence, in equal parts, of fantastic or incomprehensible visual hallucinations and somatopsychic delusional experiences. The visual hallucinations are described as "scenic" in nature, depicting grisly images of tortures, violence, or mass murder; auditory hallucinations, if at all present, play a subordinate role. The grotesque somatic delusions are probably elaborations of somatic hallucinations. Misidentification of persons and signs of formal thought disorder are noted. Occasionally, grandiose delusions are added to the clinical picture. The paranoid element is contained in the somatopsychic experiences and in the interpretation of the scenic hallucinations. Despite the abhorrent mental content the patients show, in time, progressive blunting of affect.

Confabulatory Paraphrenia.   This subform derived its designation from the fact that these patients produce, sooner or later, fantastic accounts of imaginary events in other, remote parts of the world or even in "other worlds" and on celestial bodies. Leonhard believes that these "confabulatory" accounts are derivatives, in a grossly distorted form, of memory images or of fantasy creations. These patients are quite capable of evaluating their present environment correctly on most occasions. At times, however, they complain that persons have suddenly changed. Minor changes in the appearance of a person whom they had seen the day before puzzle them. The essential similarity, on which recognition is normally based, is disregarded by them and, instead, irrelevant differences determine the misidentifications. Grandiose tendencies may, if present, contribute to the sensational quality of their confabulations. A formal thought disorder is also present. Pictorial representation of thought is common.

Expansive Paraphrenia.   The symptomatology is preeminently delusional, and in the later stages hallucinations are entirely absent. In contrast to the grandiosity described in some of the previous forms of paraphrenias the "expansive" paranoid schizophrenic conducts himself in accordance with his delusions of grandeur, displaying an arrogant, haughty, and condescending attitude. Depending on prevailing cultural or situational values and circumstances they claim to be in possession of privileged information such as secret and coded documents, or they intimate (or proclaim) their delusional accounts of acquaintance with important or leading personages. Their delusions are thus much less "fantastic" than those of other paraphrenic schizophrenics; in fact they tend to be monotonous. Again, as in all other paraphrenias, there is evidence of a formal thought disorder. The significance of this fact for the diagnosis of dementia praecox can hardly be overstated. It is because of the coexisting thought disorders and the resulting confusion that the expansive paraphrenic, believing himself at times to be a prophet or a world reformer, will never be able to create a movement of followers; conversely, none of the "successful" megalomaniacs in recent or distant times could have been a true schizophrenic, which may be considered as a poignant reminder of the difference between psychiatric and social malignancy.*

GENERAL COMMENTS: DIFFERENTIAL DIAGNOSIS

To repeat, the preceding descriptions of the various forms of paranoid schizophrenias (Leonhard's "paraphrenias") apply to the end states of the illness. Based on this hypothesis the clinical features of each subgroup are sufficiently distinct to permit a diagnosis not only of schizophrenia but also of the special form of its paranoid variety. The diagnostic problems are far more difficult either in the early stages of paranoid schizophrenia or in the case of psychotic states in which paranoid symptoms occur or dominate. There is, in fact, considerable confusion—both semantic and clinical—with respect to mental illnesses that are accompanied by paranoid beliefs, delusions, and attitudes. Fish, in a discussion and subsequent dismissal of the term "paranoid state," remarked that "the term 'paranoid state' is of as much value in psychiatry as the term 'dyspnoeic state' would be in general

---

* I am, of course, aware of the existence, both in the books of psychiatry and of history, of the so-called psychotic character. But my observations—derived from the study of both sources—have led me to believe that the successful paranoid and/or grandiose leaders suffered only from "primary delusions" which they were indeed capable of transforming into a kind of reality, at least among those who shared the same affective needs. What these leaders, reformers, and zealots (in contrast to the "true" schizophrenic) did *not* show and suffer were the "secondary delusions" and the breakdown of the secondary process. I realize that this entire issue is most insufficiently covered in these few sentences. Nevertheless, I feel strongly about the difference, in this context, between a "crank" and a "fanatic."

medicine. . . ."[4] It is, for instance, well known that paranoid symptoms may be present in nonschizophrenic depressions, in coarse brain disease (such as cerebral arteriosclerosis or senile dementia), in the paranoia vera of Kraepelin, and in those delusional-hallucinatory psychoses which Kraepelin, unhappily, called "paraphrenias" because in his view these patients were not sufficiently deteriorated to qualify for a diagnosis of dementia praecox, nor sufficiently lucid to lay claim to the rare disease entity of true paranoia.

Within the wide range of psychoses of a paranoid character two forms stand out in the sense that there is little or no difficulty as to diagnosis, and little or no controversy as to their nature. They are paranoid schizophrenia and true ("classical") paranoia. They may be said to stand at opposite poles of the spectrum of paranoid psychoses, because affective, cognitive, and social disintegration of the personality are maximal in the former and minimal in the latter. Concerning true paranoia, Fish quotes Kraepelin's characterization of it as "the insidious development of a permanent and unshakeable delusional system . . . , which is accompanied by perfect preservation of clear and orderly thinking, willing and acting."[5] As to the intermediate forms—the "paraphrenias" of Kraepelin, the "affect-laden paraphrenias" of Leonhard (see below), the *sensitive Beziehungswahn* (delusions of self-reference of the sensitive person) of Kretschmer, and the reversible paranoid reactions (including the schizophreniform or paranoid states of Langfeldt)—the issue seems to be reduced to the familiar but unresolved question of "differences in degree" or "differences in kind." It is the historic debate between the proponents of *gradualism* and those of *separatism*. From a pragmatic-clinical point of view we would restrict ourselves to the following suggestions. If a patient presents evidence of paranoid symptoms, our first task should be to search for decisive or pathognomonic signs of schizophrenia—by direct and indirect methods of examination, including the use of appropriate clinical psychological tests. The presence of such signs is not compatible with a purely affective disorder, although prominent disorders of affect are compatible with the early stages of a schizophrenic illness. Relative preservation of the affective, cognitive, and social faculties of the patient in the presence of a paranoid delusional element or system militates against schizophrenia. The age of the patient is not a reliable criterion, as paranoid schizophrenia as well as nonschizophrenic paranoid psychoses may for the first time occur in middle age. Examination for signs and symptoms of coarse brain disease will be of particular relevance in the elderly patient; but brain tumors and temporal-lobe epilepsy occur also in the younger age groups. Finally, if a patient recovers from a paranoid psychosis—with or without the presence of a plausible external provocation, but without any evidence of a Bleulerian "defect"—we may conclude that he does not suffer from dementia praecox. It may be harder to find a generally accepted terminology to designate the illness from which he has recovered.

The Hebephrenic Form

This type of schizophrenia, especially in its milder forms, is quite difficult to diagnose—largely because of the absence of dramatic and well-defined symptoms. Yet, hebephrenia is generally considered to be the most malignant and regressive form among the systematic schizophrenias. In the more advanced stages of this disease there is, however, an abundance of psychopathology. Certain general features of this variety of dementia praecox seem to stand out. The onset in almost all cases occurs between the age of 15 and 25 years, most often in the middle teens; as its name indicates, hebephrenia is the dementia praecox of puberty. The outstanding clinical feature is the profound and global deterioration, along with blunting and dehumanization, of the affective and social components of the personality. This emotional disintegration of the personality, with its occasional freakish and absurd spurts, has always been considered the hallmark of hebephrenia. As a distinguishing feature it ranks with the prominence of conative-motor abnormalities in catatonia, and of delusions of persecution and influence in paranoid schizophrenia. The early and profound withering of affectivity may account for the fact that intense or systematized delusions involving the psychosocial sphere are not found in hebephrenia, although fleeting and bizarre delusions —particularly of the somatic or hypochondriacal type—may occur. There is always evidence of a profound schizophrenic dementia. Acute and quite stormy emotional episodes do occur, either at the outset or during any time in the course of the process.

From a clinical-pragmatic point of view attempts to delineate subgroups, such as Leonhard proposed, are perhaps less significant than the realization that this malignant illness may in its "mild" form (or initially) be masked and pass unnoticed. Leonhard, of course, described end states when speaking of "silly," "eccentric," "shallow," and "autistic" hebephrenias. In his choice of adjectives he obviously wished to stress the respective prominent symptom, a difficult undertaking in the case of hebephrenia. To return to the question of the mild forms of hebephrenia, one may apply to such patients the statement which Bleuler included in his description of hebephrenia in its entirety, namely, "There are no specific symptoms for this group."[6] This writer believes that Bleuler's comment is far more appropriate to mild or early cases of schizophrenia simplex, which is not included in Leonhard's group of systematic schizophrenias but of which we will presently give a clinical account. Mild hebephrenics, in addition to the pathognomonic emotional blunting and psychosocial insufficiency, usually show some evidence of oddity in regard to appearance, social conduct, and ideation. Some like to discourse about esoteric subjects, using the most profound words to express their most inane "ideas," a situation which is at times spoken of as "pseudoprofundity." Others reveal their subtle hebephrenic mannerisms in ways which might suggest to the naïve or inexperienced observer expressions of "artistic" eccentricity. I recall such a patient. She was a young college student who was still able to maintain herself sufficiently both academically and socially. She preferred to sit on the floor during therapeutic sessions; she did this without any overt indication of either autistic motivation or ulterior intent. At times she would have a flower in her hair—but not in the manner of the happy "young maiden," but across the top of her ear in a way a stock clerk would carry his pencil. This patient once brought me the following "poem," which typifies the kind of expression common to this form of mild hebephrenia.

> I ask, why am I here and look (trees) around
> at (breezes) the things that I (birds) can see
> and my eyes (spring) search across (songs)
> the horizon as I search (children)
> for a purpose somewhere (sun)
> to life, and yet I (love) see nothing.

As a clinician, I took it for what it was; as one who enjoys poetry, I regret to admit that I was not impressed!

The concept of *simple schizophrenia* (schizophrenia simplex) was, as is well known, added by Bleuler to the original three major types of dementia praecox proposed by Kraepelin. Bleuler states explicitly that "we do not follow Kraepelin in including these patients in the hebephrenic group. . . ."[7] The characteristic feature of this type of dementia praecox is the absence of all Bleulerian accessory symptoms such as delusions, hallucinations, and catatonic features. Briefly, these patients begin to show, some time after puberty, progressive flattening of affect that is accompanied by gross formal thought and language pathology; as the disease process goes on there is increasing social incompetence and decline. Because of the paucity of the more explicit and bizarre schizophrenic symptoms the diagnosis may be quite difficult. The existence of simple schizophrenia may be almost concealed behind a facade of psychopathy, alcoholism, and, as Bleuler said, most commonly of apparent mental health. These patients' mentality tends to be barren rather than silly. The "psychopathic" features in the conduct of these patients are petty rather than vicious; they may become drifters and commit larceny and, if female, they are said to tend toward a life—or perhaps, a livelihood—of prostitution. They lack the cognitive and affective qualities usually required for the perpetration of more serious crimes. In view of the various indirect clinical expressions of simple schizophrenia, it is of the greatest importance to confirm the diagnosis if it is suspected. A thorough examination for formal thought disorder, including the administration of the Rorschach test, should, in conjunction with the patient's life history, enable us to diagnose simple schizophrenia.

The Catatonic Form

From the phenomenological point of view this form of dementia praecox may be described as having the most distinct and characteristic symptomatology among all schizophrenias. Catatonia expresses itself preeminently in the conative or psychomotor sphere. This aspect of the symptomatology requires a rather extensive presentation. Other but secondary features of catatonic schizophrenia include auditory hallucinations, delusions, formal thought disorder, and in many instances an acute onset either in the form of excitement with irrational activity or else of sudden cessation of activity and speech (mutism) that is at times preceded or replaced by severe retardation in these areas of motor behavior. A blank, staring facial expression, or rather the lack of any indication of expression through facial innervation, is almost pathognomonic.

It is difficult to find a principle by which to classify the many motor abnormalities of catatonia. Leonhard's classification of the catatonias, as reported by Fish, uses motor or psychomotor criteria (parakinetic, manneristic, proskinetic, negativistic, speech-prompt, and speech-inactive), but in a purely enumerative manner. Bleuler also thought "that the catatonic symptoms do not comprise a homogeneous group . . . [and] that we are lacking a unitary viewpoint for the genesis of all catatonic phenomena."[8] In view of this fact the following order of presentation of catatonic motor abnormalities is not based on biological or psychological principles but represents entirely a choice of convenience.

Negativism. It is a well-known fact that profound alterations of volition are found in catatonic schizophrenia, either in the form of "loss of volition," as in the phenomena of automatism, or, as an opposite trait, in negativism, an intensely exaggerated expression of "counter will." Catatonic negativism is entirely different from ordinary contrariness or lack of cooperation. It is a total and unqualified refusal, or rather inability, to do what is expected, requested, or necessary. In active negativism the patient will do the opposite of what he has been asked to do; if he was told to open his hands, he will close them tightly. Passive negativism connotes the tendency of some patients not to do what is expected of them, although no specific request has been made of them. Bleuler attributed negativism to a combination of causes such as a generally hostile attitude toward the world, a need to avoid any contact with reality which could, and very likely would, contradict autistic needs, and an inability to comprehend the meaning of surrounding events. The fact that negativism may be selectively directed toward certain persons of significance to the patient seems to support the participation of a psychological, complex-bound factor in its occurrence. Active negativism, as was already suggested by Bleuler, may represent the close relationship—albeit at the primitive level of the primary process—which exists between opposites. Catatonic negativism must be distinguished from the generally "negativistic" attitude of paranoid schizophrenics; their equally total lack of cooperation and responsiveness is usually expressed by them verbally, and in terms of their suspiciousness or delusions. They may, for instance, say that they refuse to answer any questions unless they have a lawyer with them to protect their rights, etc. The paranoid patient in general infers, through the mechanism of projected psychological causality, that everything which occurs and threatens him does so because of the will of another person. By contrast the catatonic resorts to the mechanism of introjected psychological causality; this concept, briefly stated, refers to the fact that a person establishes an illogical relationship between *any* act or expression of will by him and his responsibility for *any* consequences which may ensue. The prevailing mood of the patient determines whether the consequences will be feared or desired. In his book *Interpretation of Schizophrenia*, Arieti[9] has given a clear exposition, with clinical illustrations, of the relationship between introjected psychological causality and certain catatonic symptoms, particularly disturbances of volition, of which negativism is one variety. If the hypothesis of introjected psychological causality is applied to such expressions of negativism as spontaneous avoidance of action, resistance to action willed by another person, or even the phenomenon of a patient's responding to a requested act by doing the opposite (as if such a "catatonic ritual of undoing" could really relieve him of the sense of guilt and responsibility "of having done"), we would have a psychological explanation of catatonic negativism, and, as will be presently shown, also for its counterpart: catatonic automatic obedience. But even if this were so it would still be necessary to explain why the catatonic schizophrenic resorts to this particular method of dealing with his fear of committing himself to action and thus of assuming responsibility for these actions, and why he does not (or can not) make use of such mental mechanisms as protective ritualistic symbolization or any other psychological method of undoing as we see them used by patients suffering from obsessive-compulsive neuroses. I suppose that the reason lies in whatever constitutes the essence of schizophrenia. It may, however, be of interest to report in this connection that Arieti,[10] quoting Carothers, informs us that obsessional neuroses are "absent" in primitive and therefore highly ritualized cultures such as that of Kenya, but that the Kenyans have their regular quota of catatonic schizophrenia.

Catatonic ambitendency is a symptom which is somewhat related to the issue of negativism. It is easier to describe than to define it. A patient is offered a cigarette. He makes a grasping movement of his hand in the direction of the cigarette, but stops at midpoint. He is encouraged to go ahead and take the cigarette; he moves toward it, but the starting and stopping of the motor act—the back-and-forth movement of the hand—repeats itself. Ambitendency, as is implied by the term itself, combines elements of both negativism and suggestibility. It represents a much more profound disturbance than ordinary indecision as an expression of a conflict at the highest psychological level—such as compulsive doubting. The reason for this difference is that in ambitendency the commitment to an act—but not the significance of the act—determines the patient's behavior.

Although Bleuler describes catatonic *mutism* under the heading of "The Motor Symptoms," there are good reasons for including this phenomenon in our discussion of negativism. Speech is an especially significant motor act. It is revealing; it is an interpersonal communication; it consists of words. We are familiar with the pathological attitude, use, and experiences of the schizophrenic with respect to words. In the present context we may assume that the catatonic, among other possible operative factors, attaches an abnormal and dangerous significance to the utterance of words. Even normal people have had occasion to regret having said the wrong thing. If we extend the hypothesis of introjected psychological causality to the function of speech, we would conclude that catatonic mutism is the verbal counterpart of extreme passive negativism. But this is probably not the whole explanation. Bleuler, while also mentioning negativism as playing a role in mutism, stresses in addition such factors as the general lack of interest of these patients and their autistically determined desire to avoid any contact with the outer world. We find the most severe degrees of mutism in catatonic stupor; in less severe catatonic retardation of the conative functions there may be an occasional verbal expression by the patient. In nonschizophrenic depressive stupor the patient is not so much "mute" as he is extremely retarded in movement as well as in speech; depressive mutism has a quantitative rather than a qualitative connotation.

Automatic Obedience.   The catatonic motor phenomena collectively referred to as "automatic obedience" are in every sense the opposite of negativism. Several symptoms are included. Automatic obedience, as a separate sign, consists of the patient's carrying out any command given to him; such behavior is also known as "command automatism." Another example of catatonic passivity is *flexibilitas cerea* (waxy flexibility); the patient maintains any posture or position of his extremities which the examiner has actively induced, including absurd and quite uncomfortable ones. Waxy flexibility may be maintained for quite a few minutes and the patient relinquishes these induced postures slowly and often with an expression of puzzlement. *Mitgehen,* which may be translated as "going along with," is a form of excessive compliance in which the patient moves his entire body in response to the slightest finger-tip touch of the examiner; usually the patients move in the direction in which such a touch (one can hardly call it pressure) was applied. If, for instance, the examiner's finger touches the patient's head from behind, the patient may bend his head forward or even fall forward. As in the case of negativism, none of the phenomena of automatic obedience is in any way a result of muscular pathology, but rather it reflects fundamental attitudes, expressed in the conative sphere, and probably at various levels of impersonal-interpersonal integration. Even if the patient is instructed to resist the pressure he will nevertheless exhibit the symptom of *Mitgehen.* Echopraxia and echolalia are usually included among the features of catatonic automatisms. In echopraxia the patient repeats the actions, and in echolalia the words, of persons in his immediate environment. If either of these symptoms is present the patients do not seem to exercise any discrimination in their repetitive acts or words. There is no general agreement as to the cause or meaning of this phenomenon. Even Bleuler was not clear in his own mind as to the meaning of echopraxia and echolalia, although he considered psychological possibilities, such as a universal tendency to imitate perceptions, or a specifically catatonic manifestation of interpreting the examiner's acts or words as a command to imitate them. The fact that echopraxia and echolalia are, strictly speaking, repetitious performances, must not blind us to the recognition that they occur only in response to a stimulus; in this respect they differ from catatonic stereotypies; the latter occur independent of the examiner's words or acts. On the other hand, if one looks at echopraxia and echolalia outside the sphere of "automatic obedience," it is possible to envision another explanation, which was also considered by Bleuler. He suggests that echopraxia and echolalia may be understood in a similar manner as schizophrenic "naming" and "touching." The former consists in the patient's automatic naming of any object which he sees, the latter in feeling it with his hands. If one hypothesizes a combined affective and cognitive and even conative inability to relate *significantly* to the objects of the outer world, these four rudimentary methods of "object relationships" may represent the impoverishment to which the catatonic has been reduced. In this sense they may be considered to be restitutional in the manner in which many schizophrenic symptoms are interpreted by the psychoanalytic school of thought.

Mannerisms and Stereotypies.   These two behavioral abnormalities—which are so prominent in catatonic schizophrenia—will be described together, despite the fact that slight differences exist between them. Fish defines a mannerism in a way that Bleuler, and others, would consider to be rather circumscribed. Fish says: "A mannerism occurs when a normal goal-directed movement is carried out in an abnormal stilted manner and, although the purpose of such a movement can be understood by the observer, the manner of execution is abnormal."[11] Within this limited scope a mannerism would be diagnosed if a patient walked deliberately in a stilted, odd fashion, e.g., on his toes with one foot and on his heel with the other. Or else a patient may eat in a manneristic way, if "the spoon is held by its handle tip only or reversed."[12] Bleuler also defines mannerisms as "striking alternatives of ordinary activities,"[13] and he recognizes, of course, that the essence of the alteration lies in the artificiality and eccentricity of the performance, which has thus been reduced to a mere caricature of its normal counterpart. But Bleuler, in contrast to Fish, goes further by including also those mannerisms whose purpose can no longer be understood by the observer. Bleuler clearly states: "Most mannerisms have become entirely incomprehensible to us."[14] Stereotypies are spontaneous, repetitive, non-goal-directed, incomprehensible, and usually "compact" behavioral symptoms; they may occur in almost any conative sphere and we therefore observe stereotypies of movement, actions, posture, language, writing, and even (and particularly) drawing. One may perhaps say that the persistence of manneristic traits as a "style of conduct" may be contrasted with the intensely rigid repetitiveness of the various stereotypies. However, in a clinical sense, the similarities are more impressive than the differences. One noteworthy exception to this statement will be briefly mentioned later.

For purposes of illustration a few examples of stereotypies may be described. Most of them were chosen from Bleuler's observations. A spinster who had been in love with a shoemaker some 30 years before, imitated the movements of a shoemaker at work (sterotypy of movement). A patient lying on his back kept his head raised off the pillow for hours without evidence of muscular exhaustion; this characteristic

stereotypy of posture is known as the "psychological pillow." Another
patient constantly repeated the names of her children, or the names
of cities; there is no intent to communicate anything through words
in this form of stereotypy of words, which is known as "verbigeration."
Some patients produce stereotyped drawings, such as three-fingered
hands. In written stereotypies, letters, words, or sentences are endlessly
repeated. *Schnauzkrampf* (pursing of the mouth) is a pathognomonic
postural stereotypy in catatonia.

The origin and meaning of mannerisms is psychological; they are
caused neither by disease of the muscular nor the neurological apparatus.
Bleuler stated that mannerisms (and most stereotypies) "can be explained . . . on the basis of the persistent influence which [psychologi-
cal] complexes exert."[15] In this sense they may be considered as motor
caricatures of overdetermined ideas (Bleuler's "complexes"). Bleuler believed that such psychological explanations were by no means arbitrary—mainly because they were supplied by the patients themselves.
If we compare mild catatonic mannerisms with ordinary but highly personal and habitual modes of deportment, we can easily see that the
difference lies in the diversity of the state of normality as contrasted
with the exaggerated, incongruous, and monotonous repetitiousness of
the schizophrenic mannerisms or stereotypies. It is, however, true that
some of the obsessive-compulsive rituals of neurotic patients show the
same exaggerated, incongruous repetitiousness; here the essential difference lies in the fact that these patients, prior to analysis, have no knowledge whatsoever as to the origin and meaning of their rituals. This
point has been frequently made in the course of this book and does
not require elaboration here. Also, catatonics may, in many instances,
simplify and condense their mannerisms and stereotypes, as was emphasized by Bleuler; what originally was a verbigeration consisting of three
words may over the years be condensed into a single incomprehensible
neologism. Any such coarctation, semantic or otherwise, does not occur
in the case of repetitive obsessive-compulsive phenomena; it would,
in fact, be contrary to the express meaning and significance of detail.

In his presentation of the subject of catatonic stereotypies, Bleuler
makes a significant observation; this is the "noteworthy exception" to
which we have previously referred. He says: "we can prove that the
tendency to stereotypies occurs in schizophrenia also independent of
the complexes."[16] A word is accidentally snatched up and becomes a
verbigeration; another patient who had nodded his head in answer to
a question continues to nod for half an hour. With regard to these
extraneously provoked stereotypies, Bleuler says that these patients "demonstrate a perseveration similar to that seen in organic brain disease."[17]
By introducing the issue of organic perseveration in the context of cata-

tonic stereotyped behavior, Bleuler seems to include the possibility that we may indeed be dealing with two organismic states—one impersonal or formal and the other personal and pertaining to content. Thus whatever organic factors may be operative would account for the fact of perseverative repetitiousness, whereas the complexes give them their particular content and style. It is of interest to note that, in discussing catatonic symptoms as regressive phenomena, Fenichel makes this comment about catatonic abnormalities of motility: "They appear to be manifestations of the deeper layers of the motor apparatus, which, after the ego has disintegrated, have acquired a sort of *independent effectiveness*."[18] This conception seems to come very close to what Hughlings Jackson called the "independence of the lower levels" in organic dissolution.

The Confused Form

This variety of typical or systematic schizophrenias is not usually recognized as a subtype and on an equal level with the previous forms. It represents, as was already said, the view of Kleist that there exists a form of dementia praecox in which thought and speech disorders were so prominent as to justify the assumption of a specific major form of schizophrenia. Kleist did, of course, recognize that some psychopathology of the formal aspects of thought and language existed in every case of systematic schizophrenia. Kleist divides the confused types into two groups, depending on whether the *speech* or the *thought* processes are predominantly disturbed. The first group, called "schizaphasia," is characterized by the presence of paraphasic word abnormalities such as neologisms, metonymic approximations, or desymbolizations of words. In addition there is frequent use of secondary word formations and of so-called "stock-words" that are regular words but are used repetitively and often irrelevantly. One such patient—whom we mentioned in an earlier chapter—would refer to almost any object in terms of a "vessel;" a clock was called a "time vessel," and a book, presumably, a "word vessel." The schizaphasic group also shows evidence of general impoverishment of speech in the sense of a shrinkage that resembles agrammatism. The second group—which is "confused" in the area of formal thought processes or associations—manifests incoherence, alogia, and paralogia. The latter is an abnormality which seems to correspond to those formal thought disorders which we described by such terms as asyndetic thought, system-shifting, and sham language. In the confused forms of dementia praecox, delusional, hallucinatory, or catatonic symptoms are either absent or occur only occasionally. It appears likely that some patients who in the United States are designated as "chronic undifferentiated schizophrenia" belong in the category of confused forms, or would be included into it by Kleist.

THE ATYPICAL OR NONSYSTEMATIC SCHIZOPHRENIAS

The concept of "atypical" or "nonsystematic" schizophrenias was introduced by the Frankfurt school; Kleist used the former term, Leonhard the latter. Both authors meant to designate essentially the same group of psychoses, which, while closer to dementia praecox than to the purely affective psychoses, nevertheless differed from the former in some significant respects. The symptomatology in the atypical schizophrenias is more variable than in the systematic forms; signs tend to occur episodically rather than progressively and, perhaps for this reason, the personality is less subject to disintegration "at the core." The reader will find a good description of the atypical schizophrenias in Fish's publications, to which we have already referred. The terminology is complicated and confusing, but so are the so-called transitional psychoses; these are psychotic disorders which are neither clearly schizophrenic nor unequivocally manic-depressive and, again, terminology can not replace lack of clinical identity. There is one form of atypical schizophrenias that I believe should be described because of the diagnostic problems it poses and the relative frequency with which it occurs. This form is Leonhard's "affect-laden paraphrenia." As its name indicates, there is a great deal of affect associated with the delusions, which are both persecutory and grandiose. The bipolar nature of the delusional beliefs is matched by the emotional display of either suspiciousness and irritability or enthusiasm and arrogance, depending on the type of delusion which at the moment dominates the clinical picture. Auditory hallucinations accompany the paranoid phase, while visual and auditory hallucinations are said to occur during the grandiose episodes. The delusions are at all times strongly expressed and defended by the patient and any attempt to contradict them—by expressing doubt or by presenting evidence to the contrary—is vehemently scorned by the patient. Somatic delusions may also be present, and in advanced stages of the disease assume an increasingly bizarre character, associated with delusions of influence. But it is in the early stages, or in the less severe cases of affect-laden paraphrenia, that we at times encounter difficulties in differential diagnosis, particularly if grandiose symptoms are prominent. In that instance the condition may be confused with manic psychosis.

SPECIAL VARIETIES OF SCHIZOPHRENIA

Pseudoneurotic Schizophrenia

In their original 1949 publication on this syndrome, Hoch and Polatin[19] reported a number of patients who presented the clinical picture of a particularly severe and peculiarly compounded "pan-neurosis," but were inherently, in the opinion of the authors, schizophrenic. The assumed coexistence of neurosis and schizophrenia is reflected in the terminology which Hoch and Polatin suggested. The main clinical symptoms of this disorder consist of the intense and extensive features of the pan-neurosis. The patient experiences severe anxiety and depression and/or guilt ("pan-anxiety"). He may, either simultaneously or in short succession, show such diverse neurotic symptoms as phobias, conversions, obsessive-compulsive ruminations and rituals, as well as a polymorphously perverse sexuality. Several sexual perversions may be present. The term "pseudoneurotic" has, therefore, a twofold relevance. First, the patient's disease is not a neurosis, but a schizophrenic psychosis; and, although psychoneurotic symptoms are prominent, the presence of so many of them in the same patient at the same time runs counter to psychoanalytic theory concerning the neuroses. The concept of pseudoneurotic schizophrenia is somewhat controversial, although not so much so in the United States. Fish seems to repudiate this designation when he says that "it would appear that pseudoneurotic schizophrenia is, in fact, neurotic pseudoschizophrenia."[20] This writer suggests that the case histories, as presented by Hoch and Polatin, seem to render the terminological polemics unnecessary. The patients showed a clinical picture that, in our opinion, is both schizophrenic and neurotic—and even "a touch of schizophrenia" takes precedence over a "pan-neurosis." There was evidence of asyndetic language and of other formal thought and language disorders (Case 1 and 2); belief in thought magic (Case 1); *Gedankenlautwerden* (Case 3); regression to application of primitive, autistic causality, and depolarization between self and nonself body experience (Case 3); and tendency toward experiences of cosmic fusion (Case 5), which the authors interpreted as indicating that "the boundaries between the ego and the world are hazy."[21] In addition, the patients revealed a pathognomonic schizophrenic response on the Rorschach test, which confirmed the presence of a schizophrenic dementia. Under sodium amytal they expressed autistic ideation indistinguishable from "incomprehensible" delusions. Hoch and Polatin express the view, referring to their clinical material, that "none of the symptoms, which will be enumerated, is absolutely characteristic of schizophrenia."[22] It would, of course, be of great value to know whether any of these patients completely recovered from their schizophrenic symptoms.

There is another point of principle that should be considered in connection with pseudoneurotic schizophrenia. It is not unusual that schizophrenic patients—perhaps particularly in the early stages of their illness, before emotional blunting eliminates the need or capacity for neurotic symptom formation—will show signs and symptoms that we associate with our clinical concept of neurosis. They may also alloplastically act out and break the law. In that case, should we refer to them as having "pseudopsychopathic schizophrenia," as has been suggested? We do not think we should.

Mixed Psychoses

This concept addresses itself more to a problem than to the description of a specific psychiatric nosological entity. The problem is what to make of those forms of psychoses which present features of both schizophrenia and of manic-depressive psychosis. Features of the latter include pronounced affective psychopathology—usually a depression of phasic or cyclic course, with complete restitution of the personality after the psychosis has subsided. In the United States the term "schizoaffective" is often used to designate a form of schizophrenia in which a marked affective morbidity, either depression or elation, suggests a mixture of schizophrenia and affective functional psychosis. It is a generally accepted assumption that in the presence of decisive or first-rank schizophrenic symptoms, a seemingly "affective" disorder is, in fact, a schizophrenia. The reverse—namely, that a "seemingly" schizophrenic disorder subsequently reveals itself to be manic-depressive—is most unlikely to occur. Two types of "mixed psychosis" may be distinguished, depending on the trait of the manic-depressive syndrome that is added to an otherwise schizophreniform symptomatology. If the "trait" is purely affective, the term "schizoaffective" appears to be appropriate. If in such patients the depression is relieved by the administration of electroconvulsive therapy, the previously masked schizophrenic nature of the illness will become more evident. In the other type the manic-depressive trait is represented by the phasic course of the illness and, additionally, by complete recovery. These types of mixed psychoses, sometimes referred to as "degeneration psychoses," "marginal psychoses," or "cycloid psychoses," are (according to Leonhard, as quoted by Fish) "bipolar in that two extreme clinical pictures may occur,"[23] either alternatingly in the course of one attack or in pure form in different phases of the illness. Fish gives a brief account of the various cycloid psychoses, such as the motility psychosis of Kleist, the anxiety-elation psychosis, and the confusion psychosis.

Pfropf (Grafted) Schizophrenia

The German word *Pfropf* connotes the idea of being superimposed; it has been used in order to explain that schizophrenia may be *grafted onto* mental defect. Some instances of phasic and psychotic behavior—at times referred to as "psychosis with mental deficiency"—may be examples of *Pfropf* schizophrenia, particularly if the symptomatology is bizarre or if there are other signs which suggest a schizophrenic illness. It is an interesting question whether it does not require a certain minimum of intellectual power for certain schizophrenic symptoms—such as autistic depolarization or delusions of influence or systematized delusions of a paranoid character—to be possible. There may conceivably be a definite correlation between the degree of mental defect and the character of a psychotic decompensation which is temporarily superimposed upon the basic psychopathology. As will be presently shown, the clinical manifestations of infantile autism and of childhood schizophrenia show a very definite correlation to the age and inferentially to the intellectual level of the child.

Early Infantile Autism and Childhood Schizophrenia

Implicit in the formulation of the above subheading is the assumption that early infantile autism (Kanner) and childhood schizophrenia of older children, as well as a number of other severe abnormalities of ego development during childhood, are the expression of *one* basic disorder. Variations of clinical manifestations are assumed to be determined by the severity and the age of onset of the hypothesized basic disorder.

The concept of early infantile autism, first formulated by Leo Kanner, included the following major diagnostic criteria. First, these children show, from an early age onward, an inability or disinclination to relate to people—preeminently to the mother or her substitute; on the other hand, they exhibit an almost obsessional preoccupation with an attachment to inanimate objects, often in a manner which strikes us as stereotyped. Second, they do not develop and/or use language as a means of communication; their verbal productions contain characteristic peculiarities, such as echolalialike repetition of questions, often in the negative, and reversal of the personal pronoun. Third, the autistic child clearly desires to be left alone within his inanimate world of a few objects, showing considerable intolerance of intrusion into, or changes of, this world. Ornitz and Ritvo,[24] recently elaborated on the symptomatology of early infantile autism and suggested the existence of "sub-clusters" of symptoms, some of which may, in a given case, be more pronounced than others. We will mention only those symptoms which are not explicitly included in the foregoing brief characterization of this condition. In the perceptual sphere the following abnormalities have been noted by these authors: autistic children either overreact to sensory input or they disregard it under circumstances when a normal child would respond. Overreaction may manifest itself either by heightened awareness (characteristically of things that spin) or by irritability and signs of emotional rejection in case of sudden and intense sensory input. In the motor sphere various forms of "hand-flapping" and a decided but stereotyped preference for whirling or spinning body movements (vestibular preference?) are considered to be almost pathognomonic. Some autistic children exhibit odd manneristic gait, such as toe walking. Sudden lunging or darting movements for no apparent reason are noted. Finally, there are disturbances in the normal rate and sequence of ego development, pertaining essentially to the instrumentalities of the basic adaptive tools of the conflict-free ego sphere—such as development of locomotion, speech, and other basic skills. Thus one finds marked scattering in the scores of autistic infants on such tests as the Gesell.

Kanner's early infantile autism is only one of several designations of behavioral abnormalities in children that are severe enough to be considered "psychotic" and autistic enough to be considered "schizophrenic." The great variety, in the intensity and the specific features, of the symptomatology has quite naturally created problems—not so much of terminology, but of comprehension and of classification. Ornitz and Ritvo expose the terminological confusion in these words: "Within the decade since the syndrome of early infantile autism was first described by Kanner, terms such as childhood schizophrenia, atypical children, children with unusual sensitivities, and symbiotic psychosis were used to conceptualize similar, yet apparently distinctive clinical entities."[25]

Two issues present themselves. The first concerns itself with the question whether all forms and degrees of "childhood schizophrenias," under whatever terminology that may be described, can, or should, be conceptualized as the expression of one decisively responsible and explanatory underlying mechanism. Etiological considerations have, as one would expect, ranged from the purely biological to preeminently interpersonal factors. Kanner himself noted the frequency of "emotional refrigeration" to which, he thought, the autistic children were exposed by their aloof and overly intellectual parents; the concept of "symbiotic psychosis" clearly reflects an intensely abnormal mother-child relationship as a cause for infantile autism. Some writers have even raised the question whether the term "autism" could be properly applied to the mental state of an infant. What sense of reality, these critics say, can an infant or very young child possibly command the loss or distortion of which, in specific ways, is prerequisite to the presence of autism in the accepted Bleulerian meaning of that term? In other words, how can a state of depolarization occur at an age when "polarization" had in fact not yet taken place? Are we then, when infantile autism slips imperceptibly into childhood schizophrenia, dealing with a psychosis owing to a specific "agenesis"—a lag in maturation on a global basis involving all aspects of functioning, as L. Bender believes—or with a psychosis which has been "set free?" Proponents of the primarily organic etiological persuasion point to evidence of infantile autism at such an early age as to exclude any possible causative significance to interpersonal factors. Adherents of Melanie Klein would, of course, consider the age factor as being irrelevant to the issue. There are also many instances of emotional refrigeration, symbiotic mother-child relationship, institutionalism, and even of sensory deprivation to some degree without the child's succumbing to autism or to any other form of childhood schizophrenia. "Encephalopathy" in childhood schizophrenia has been advanced. Ornitz and Ritvo suggest that the decisive etiological or underlying factor lies within the child, not his environment, and they proposed that a basic inability to maintain "perceptual constancy" might be responsible.[24] "This mechanism involves the presence of states of hyperexcitation and inhibition that interfere with the normal capacity to maintain perceptual constancy."[26] Given this or any other primary brain dysfunction it would, of course, follow that the subsequent interpersonal or psychodynamic element plays its role in codetermining the severity and manifestations of the ultimate clinical picture.

This brings us to the second issue to which we should address ourselves, however briefly and tentatively. What might be the relationship between early infantile autism and "later" childhood schizophrenia? What is, in fact, the relationship of childhood schizophrenia to adult schizophrenia? There is certainly an enormous difference between an autistic infant whose earliest and then only symptom may be an unnatural "unwillingness" to be picked up by his mother and a 10-year-old schizophrenic child, let alone a 30-year-old paranoid schizophrenic, with his far more variegated and morbidly "sophisticated" symptomatology. There are cases on record, including the one mentioned by Ornitz and Ritvo,[27] in which the continuity of the psychosis can be traced from infancy to adulthood. But the symptomatology which such patients display in their later years, in the form of delusions, hallucinations, and autistic transformation of reality, also reflects the cognitive, affective, and conative experiences and acquisitions of their entire life. Thus childhood schizophrenia offers this challenge to the researcher, and to the theoretician as well: If there is a common and specific psychopathology, its evolution and correlative expression during a few but sociobiologically crowded years of ego maturation in childhood—however uneven, precocious, or stunted—might reveal its essential identity inductively through and despite its diversity.

REFERENCES

1. F. J. Fish. *Schizophrenia*. Baltimore, Williams & Wilkins, 1962, p. 69.
2. O. Fenichel. *The Psychoanalytic Theory of Neurosis*. New York, Norton, 1945, p. 430.
3. F. J. Fish. *Op. cit.*,[1] p. 71.
4. *Ibid.*, p. 77.
5. *Ibid.*, p. 83.
6. E. Bleuler. *Dementia Praecox or the Group of Schizophrenias*. New York, International Univer. Press, 1950, p. 234.
7. *Ibid.*, p. 235.
8. *Ibid.*, p. 442.
9. S. Arieti. *Interpretation of Schizophrenia*. New York, Robert Brunner, 1955, p. 222 ff.
10. *Ibid.*, p. 228.
11. F. J. Fish. *Op. cit.*,[1] p. 46.
12. E. Bleuler. *Op. cit.*,[6] p. 191.
13. *Ibid.*, p. 190, footnote.
14. *Ibid.*, p. 191.
15. *Ibid.*, p. 453.
16. *Ibid.*, p. 456.
17. *Ibid.*, p. 457.
18. O. Fenichel. *Op. cit.*,[2] p. 424.
19. P. Hoch and P. Polatin. "Pseudoneurotic Forms of Schizophrenia." *Psychiatric Quarterly*, vol. 23, 1949, p. 248.
20. F. J. Fish. *Op. cit.*,[1] p. 99.
21. P. Hoch and P. Polatin. *Op. cit.*,[19] p. 275.
22. *Ibid.*, p. 249.
23. F. J. Fish. *Op. cit.*,[1] p. 93.
24. E. M. Ornitz and E. R. Ritvo. "Perceptual Inconstancy in Early Infantile Autism." *Archives of General Psychiatry*, vol. 18, 1968, p. 76–98.
25. *Ibid.*, p. 76.
26. *Ibid.*, p. 89.
27. *Ibid.*, p. 78.

18

Depression and the Affective Transformation of the Personality

DEPRESSION AND ITS TERMINOLOGY

The need for clarifying the meaning of the term "depression" arises from several sources and reflects both a semantic and a clinical requirement. At what point or under what preconditions does a feeling of sadness or self-doubt—with or without a particular experiential provocation—become a clinically significant depression? Where does the pessimistic or cyclothymic personality end and the depressive illness begin? In other words, is there a merely quantitative difference between the "blues" and a depression, between a mood and an illness? The second reason for the need to clarify the meaning of "depression" derives from the fact that dysphoric affects may accompany many categories of mental illness that are themselves not depressions, such as schizophrenia and organic brain disease; in these conditions depressive episodes may occur and even dominate the clinical picture, at least in some patients. Furthermore, there is the question of what our principal conceptual model of depression is or ought to be; such considerations range from the extremes of purely psychoanalytic to purely biochemical views. Thus the psychoanalytical model views depression as the clinical manifestation of "unconscious hostility turned upon the self, the ego;" neurochemists focus upon "an imbalance of two biogenic amines in the central nervous system . . . norepinephrine and serotonin."[1] Finally, there exists the still-controversial issue of the nosologic specificity of depression as an illness *sui generis*, one that is caused by specific although not fully understood factors and that presents a characteristic and predictable symptomatology and course. This "disease concept" of

305

depression represents the original Kraepelinian definition of manic-depressive psychosis; it implies the assumption of an endogenous etiology, with strong hereditary loading; a cyclic course and other features underlining an essentially bipolar quality of the disease process; and a favorable outcome—that is, without intellectual deterioration. The "disease concept" of depression is still in competition with the "reaction type concept" of other clinicians, Meyerian or otherwise. One aspect and consequence of this divergence of views is distinguishing reactive-neurotic-exogenous depressions from autonomous-psychotic-endogenous types. This issue—its semantic and conceptual confusions and ambiguities notwithstanding—represents the very heart of present-day research and controversy in the broad and somewhat nebulous territory which we label "depression."

In this chapter the term "depression" is used to designate a specific category of psychopathology that is distinct from mood swings, grief, neurosis, schizophrenia, and mental disease resulting from coarse brain disease. I realize that, so far, this has been an essentially negative definition, and I also recognize the existence of unclear boundaries, admixtures, and a host of other unanswered questions. But there can be little doubt about the singular nature of the affective transformation of the personality which takes its place among the other major categories of mental illness—namely, the cognitive (organic), the schizophrenic, the paroxysmal (epileptic), and the functional (neurotic) groups.

THE CLINICAL MANIFESTATIONS OF DEPRESSION

The entire psychopathology of depression (and mania) can, in contrast to schizophrenia, be understood as a consequence or expression (in various psychological spheres) of the prevailing morbid affect. Thus, despite the presence of serious and impressive psychopathology, a certain *coherence* and *cohesion* of the personality is preserved even in severe depression. For this reason most authors accord a position of primacy to the affective rather than the cognitive distortion in their interpretation of depression. Even Aaron Beck, who takes the opposite view, admits that "in the moderate and severe depressions . . . there may be some argument as to which comes first: the cognition or the affect."[2] It is quite true that cognition and affectivity interact, one evoking or suppressing the other in a circular fashion; but I believe that a cognitive primacy is much more applicable to the interpretation of organic and schizophrenic dementia than of depression. With regard to the coherence and cohesion of the personality in depression, Lewis and Piotrowski observed: "In the manic-depressive patient the pathology consists of the fact that, for unknown reasons, the over-activity or underactivity is extreme, but the patient responds subjectively . . . in the same way as any other person experiencing similar extremes of energy output."[3]

A fairly severe depression can be diagnosed almost on sight from the appearance of the patient. The sad and painfully pensive facies, the dejection reflected in the sorrowful furrows of the face and the stooped posture, and the lack or marked reduction of spontaneity are pathognomonic. Hoch[4] introduced the term "benign stupor" as a designation for the state of extreme retardation that owes to depression in manic-depressive psychosis. There were, however, many instances of catatonic features in Hoch's series, such as negativism and catalepsy, and follow-up studies suggested that so many of these patients ultimately showed evidence of schizophrenia as to render the concept of benign stupor almost invalid. The retardation of depression is quite different from that of catatonia, both in principle and in its contextual manifestations. The patient's appearance in depression conveys the clear expression of sadness with which one can readily empathize and which is in marked contrast to the empty, far-away, and inscrutable stare of the catatonic. Retardation in depression is, of course, unaccompanied by the well-known psychomotor abnormalities associated with catatonia. Less severely depressed patients reveal the reduction of conative drive by the extreme slowness with which they move and speak. One gets the impression reminiscent of a slowly moving liquid of high viscosity. Even mildly depressed patients exhibit the cardinal symptom of conative retardation by the absence of normal gestures or facial modifications of expression that accompany normal speech. Such patients may deceive the inexperienced examiner; they may produce a perfunctory or resigned smile, but they have lost the capacity for experiencing mirth or humor. Crying spells are significant in those patients who did not easily cry when well; in our culture men must be included in this category. As the depression deepens the patient may notice that crying is no longer possible; the depression has become "dry," which is an unfavorable sign.

Negative Mental Content. The mental content of the depressed patient may be described, in its entirety, as "negative" in the sense of being anhedonic. Somewhat in contrast to the dysphoric affect of anxiety, the anhedonic quality of depression is poignantly reflected in what the patient *cannot* feel, do, or be. The theme or object of these anhedonic thoughts and feelings may be any major aspect of the patient's existence—such as his health, his wealth, or his worth. It may concern itself with his past as well as with his future. The degree of the depression determines not the choice of the theme but rather the malignancy of the negative view expressed by the patient. There may be a progression from pessimistic appraisal of a specific situation to anhedonic generalized exaggeration, falsification, and delusional distortion. Delusions of depressed patients have been aptly described as "nihilistic." Beck, who is a proponent of the primacy of cognition in the psychopathology of depression, suggests that "the disturbances in depression may be viewed in terms of the activation of a set of three major cognitive patterns. . . ."[5] He designates this primary triad in depression as "negative interpretation of experience," "negative view of self," and "negative expectations." A few clinical illustrations may be useful. The negative view that the depressed patient takes of himself indicates in one form or another a lowering of his self-esteem. He considers himself to be inadequate, particularly in those areas which in and because of his character structure are most vulnerable to shame. Shame is the feeling which accompanies actual or imagined failure to live up to the requirements of the ego-ideal. The patients tend to exaggerate the degree and the consequences of their deficiencies. They find confirmation for their low self-esteem not only in present situations but, as the depression progresses, also in inconsequential events of the past. Thus shame deepens into guilt; self-indictment becomes self-conviction; the tarnishing of the ego-ideal (which is one of the two components of the superego, the other being the conscience) is compounded by a corrosion of the ego itself; exaggeration gives way to delusional distortion. The patients then believe that they are responsible for any catastrophe, past or future; that they are the outcast of humanity—the ruin of their families and beyond redemption. Secondary delusions in which the environment is misinterpreted in accordance with the prevailing morbid affect and ideation appear to the patients as confirmation of the validity of their primary delusions of guilt. Such severely depressed patients may at times even hear voices which accuse and condemn them; however, only a small number (13 percent, according to Beck[6]) of patients with nonschizophrenic depressions experience hallucinations.

Hypochondriasis. Hypochondriacal features are very common in milder forms of depressions and in so-called depressive equivalents. This latter and somewhat controversial concept, introduced by Kennedy and Wiesel,[7] denotes a syndrome in which the depression is said to be "masked" by somatic complaints, sleep disturbances, and loss of weight, while the affective psychopathology is minimal or "concealed." This syndrome is not generally accepted as being a true equivalent of a depression, although it is said that these patients respond favorably to electric shock treatment. In severe depressions hypochondriacal preoccupation gives way to somatic delusions with a fairly characteristic content. The patients believe that parts of their internal organs are decaying, drying up, or obstructed. There appears to be a decided preference for delusional hypochondriacal beliefs involving the gastrointestinal tract. In contrast to the somatic delusions of schizophrenics, depressed patients do not attribute the cause or the source of their delusional observations to outside forces or other persons. Even when they believe that they are "poisoned," they do not accuse others of having poisoned them. The nihilistic element is quite transparent in these somatic delusions, all of which indicate to the patients approaching dissolution and death. The bizarre and incomprehensible element, as noted in many schizophrenic somatic delusions, is not usually found in depression.

Self-Negativism.   In order to round out the description of the "negative view of self" we must mention the patients' delusions of poverty. The presence—and indeed prominence—of this delusion can not in our view be explained by the fact that the patients live in a materialistic or affluent society in which material possessions determine what a person is "worth" and how worthy he is. Depressed patients, I submit, also believe that they are the world's worst sinners without living in a society of saints. It appears more likely that the depressed patient's delusional belief in his physical, moral, and financial ruin represents the ultimate depletion of those internal and external supplies which ordinarily sustain, in every sense, man in his mortality and social interdependence. Beck noted that this extreme state of hopelessness showed the highest correlation coefficient with suicide.

What Beck called the "negative interpretation of experience" coincides in its most severe forms with what we referred to as secondary delusions. A patient while riding on a subway train notices that the passenger next to him leaves the train at a station. The patient may see in this fact a confirmation of his belief that he is despised by others or that he is emitting a bad odor which drives people away, as if he were a leper. In less severe depressions there may be an expression of irritability or of feeling thwarted in the face of simple and insignificant obstacles or mishaps of ordinary everyday life. One of my patients broke into tears when his wife brought him a breakfast tray to his bed because he felt too guilty to accept "such undeserved kindness." It can easily be seen that practically any event or experience, significant or trivial, can be interpreted by the patient negatively and in accordance with the prevailing negative affect. It seems to me that the primacy of affect rather than of cognition can also explain the vast and morbid generalizations of depressed patients; they do not resort to the regressive mechanisms which characterize autistic thought and reasoning in the schizophrenic.

The attitude of "negative expectations" in depression reflects the psychopathology of the consciousness of the future in this condition. Whereas in anxious expectation the future is viewed as a possible and even likely source of psychological danger to the individual, the depressed patient experiences the future with the same affective morbidity with which he experiences the present and the past. In less severe cases the negative expectations of the patients may still, or temporarily, be reversible and responsive to reassuring and encouraging contact with the therapist, just as the anxious expectations of the neurotic patient are. Some clinicians consider this fact as an indication that the depression is "only neurotic" or "reactive."

Conative Defects.   Many clinical manifestations of depression may be considered to be abnormalities in the sphere of conation. They are therefore distinct from the anhedonic features. Retardation and agitation are comprehensive expressions, respectively, of the bipolar psychopathology of manic-depressive disease in general and of depression in particular. Diminution or paralysis of initiative are early and signal features in retarded depression; they are noted in regard to both simple and vital activities, such as taking food and attending to the need for elimination. But the patient may find it equally impossible to summon the initiative to carry on with ordinarily automatic activities such as brushing his teeth or taking a walk. He may feel that he can not "decide" on a course of action; however, the psychopathology does not seem to be the result of conflict, but rather of enfeeblement of conative impetus. The recognition of this incapacity often serves as a confirmation to the patient of his state of inadequacy and the hopelessness concerning his future. Thus he has to escape from activity and avoid responsibilities, and in this sense abdicate a large part of his former autonomy, all of which tends to lower his self-esteem even more. As his conative powers vanish his dependency on others increases. Clinicians with a psychoanalytic orientation, such as Abraham[8] and Rado,[9] considered these dependency needs as expressions of "oral regression." But this very dependency on others—usually on members of the family—reinforces the patient's conviction that he is a burden to his family and may thus substantially increase his feelings of guilt. By contrast, an "orally" regressed and anxiously dependent *neurotic* patient is very much comforted by having his dependency needs gratified. This fact represents a very significant difference.

Physical Signs.   Physical and autonomic nervous system manifestations of depression must also be mentioned. The regularity with which they are found seems to lend support to the role of autonomic and other physical abnormalities in the causation of depression. On the other hand, they have, as Beck pointed out, only a relatively low correlation with each other and with the clinically observable depth of the depression. Diminution or loss of appetite, both for food and for sexual activity, are frequently noted. Loss of weight is considered to be a sure indication of a rather severe depression and it appears that it can not be entirely accounted for as resulting from reduced intake of food. Sleep disturbances are characteristic, and are marked by early awakening. Many patients feel their depression most intensely when they wake up several hours before their usual time—an observation that is usually associated with so-called endogenous depressions. Constipation, frequent belching, and dryness of the mouth are also noted. In involutional depression (see below) vasomotor disturbances are considered to be the sole and direct clinical expression of endocrine (estrogenic) insufficiency.

It may be useful to conclude this descriptive account of the clinical manifestations of depression with a few remarks about the significant *absence* of certain symptoms in this disease. Although thinking is slow and problem-solving, such as calculations or similar abstract performances, is often faulty, there is no simple (organic) dementia. Whatever cognitive delays and failures are encountered appear to be the result of a conatively and affectively determined depletion of facilitating and motivating forces rather than the expression of a loss of the instrumentalities of the conflict-free ego. Nor is there any evidence of formal thought and language pathology of the kind noted in schizophrenia. The nihilistic delusions, despite their enormity in some instances, are comprehensible in the light of the affective morbidity from which they have sprung and of which they are an appropriate ideational representation. In other words, there is no breakthrough of the primary process.

THE CLASSIFICATION OF DEPRESSION

Although the clinical manifestations of depression are much more uniform than those of schizophrenia, most clinicians and researchers feel that there is sufficient evidence to recognize relevant distinctions. The entire history of the evolution of a nosology of depression, including present-day controversies, indicates the existence of a constant struggle about an essentially dichotomous concept of this disease—with some psychiatrists supporting and others minimizing the bipartite classification. This struggle has been (and is being) carried on in the area of etiology, clinical manifestations, prognosis, and treatment. Observations within any one of these areas have at times been used to make inferences with regard to another area—as, for instance, when the absence of discernable provocative experiences would be viewed as an indication of the "endogenous" cause and nature of the depression. If the depression was "endogenous" it was, by definition, "psychotic" in nature. Thus it would respond best to electroconvulsive treatment. These statements are not meant to be critical and it should be realized by the reader that they contain a great deal of factual truth. At the same time, all this points to the magnitude of the very difficult problem of classifying depression. It is indeed true, as was recently stated by Mendels and Cochrane, that "what we call depression is in fact a heterogeneous group of conditions when measured by such parameters as treatment response, hormonal assay, electrolyte balance, natural history and symptoms."[10] The real issue in all attempts to construct a nosologic conceptualization of depression lay in the question whether the disease was the expression of organic ("impersonal," "endogenous," "autonomous") or functional ("interpersonal," "exogenous," "reactive") events. Secondary inferences associated with the first contingency included the assumption of a "psychotic" state and the Jaspersian conception of "incomprehensibility." As to the second contingency it would follow that functional depressions were "neurotic" and "comprehensible," as Jaspers would say when defining "reactive disease" in general. Strict adherence to this dichotomy represents the view of the "separatists." The "relativists" would, of course, put the problem in a different form. They would wish to determine which and how many parameters in the case of a given patient support the participation of organic and functional factors in the evolution of the depression.

Kraepelinian Views. Kraepelin considered depression to be a phase of manic-depressive psychosis (the other phase being mania) and, as such, caused by internal, endogenous (organic) factors. Heredity and/or other biological abnormalities were the sole determining element in the occurrence of the disease. Depressions which resulted from external stresses were not included in the concept of manic-depressive psychosis and instead were relegated to the somewhat indistinct category that he called "psychopathies." Although Kraepelin used the term "exogenous" to include such external causes of mental disease as bacterial invasion or poisoning from without, this label is equated with "reactive" in contemporary classifications of depression. The terminological and conceptual confusion is further compounded by the fact that a so-called reactive depression is considered to be synonymous and identical with a "neurotic" depression and thus with an ultimately characterological and interpersonal issue. Also, the concept of a neurotic depression is in clear contrast to the concept of a psychotic depression; yet, as will be outlined later in this chapter, truly psychotic depressive syndromes have been reported as obvious "reactions" to particularly severe external stresses. Kraepelin himself had observed that even manic-depressive episodes may be triggered by experiential and clearly external stress—although he thought that they are usually independent of external influences. It was also stated by Kraepelin that the manic-depressive "psychoses" may at times be reduced in their clinical manifestations to very slight deviations of mood and affect and that there was not necessarily a sharp boundary between these rudimentary forms of the disease and the domain of personal predisposition. Yet the notion that an endogenous depression is "by definition" a psychosis, and thus a malignant process, persists—notwithstanding the fact that such an inference is mitigated by a number of observations. An endogenous depression, as a representation of a cyclic process, is inherently of limited duration; phenomenologically, the symptomatology may be less severe than in many cases of reactive depression; and in the great majority of patients there is an excellent chance of prompt and complete recovery from the attack with the aid of electroconvulsive therapy.

The assumed or factual existence of an involutional depressive syndrome is at times considered as evidence which would strongly support the biological and thus endogenous cause and nature of depression. Kraepelin had originally set the agitated depressions of middle life apart from the manic-depressive syndromes, but he dropped the distinction in the eighth edition of his textbook. Many contemporary psychiatrists doubt the usefulness and even the validity of a separate nosologic entity called "involutional psychotic reaction," depressive or otherwise. I would associate myself with them for several reasons. First, the occurrence of a mental illness at a certain (and ill-defined) time or period of life does not seem to be a sufficiently adequate basis to justify and sustain the construction of a nosologic identity. Authorities such as Novak[11] have pointed out that the only symptom directly related to the endocrine decline in menopausal women is vasomotor instability. Another objection to a concept of "involutional psychosis" derives from a still-existing tendency to include under this heading all psychotic reactions which are not clearly organic or schizophrenic, such as involutional melancholia, involutional paranoid reaction and, of course, involutional psychosis of the mixed type. Involutional melancholia is described, by those who adhere to this nosologic concept, as an agitated depression that is etiologically related to assumed biological and psychological changes occurring during that period of life and clinically characterized by severe insomnia, guilt feelings, hypochondriasis, and agitation rather than by retardation. The syndrome is considered likely to occur in persons who have strongly compulsive and perfectionistic character traits. Beck does not believe that a separate category of depression (namely, "involutional depression") is supported by carefully controlled research. Other authors, such as Rosenthal,[12] point to the lack of clinically acceptable research in the area of "involutional depression." One of Rosenthal's statements on this issue deserves to be quoted in full:

The question remaining, however, is whether involutional depression is a distinct syndrome with its own etiology, natural history and clinical picture, or whether it shades off continuously with milder menopausal neuroses on a vertical severity axis, and with other psychotic depressions on a horizontal descriptive axis.[13]

The basic classification of depressions has in effect remained dichotomous. Behind the terminological labels and combinations, namely, "endogenous-psychotic" versus "reactive-neurotic" hide etiological, phenomenological, therapeutic, and conceptual-theoretical issues. We will attempt to deal with some of them in the following paragraphs.

"Separatist" Views.   Reactive-neurotic depressions are, according to the "separatists," significantly different from the endogenous-psychotic group. In 1961, Kiloh and Ball[14] noted that persons with endogenous depressions made a significantly better response to the drug imipramine than did those in the so-called neurotic-reactive (exogenous) variety. The cluster of symptoms of those patients who responded positively "included items which many regard as characteristic of endogenous depression. . . ."[15] In a subsequent publication, Kiloh and Garside[16] reported their findings concerning 143 patients who had been selected because of the presence of "depression" and were subjected to a careful factor-analysis study which encompassed 35 clinical features. The authors' conclusions are as follows. Patients with neurotic depression show low genetic loading. The onset of the depression is closely related to external stress, not only in time but also in terms of a psychodynamically determined interaction and consequence. Thus the majority of patients with neurotic depressions, in contrast to those with endogenous ones, showed personality traits—prior to the onset of the depression— indicative of the neurotic character structure, with anxiety, obsessionality, hysterical features, and general emotional instability. The sedation threshold was significantly higher in patients with neurotic depression as compared with those suffering from the endogenous variety. Clinically, patients suffering from neurotic depression showed insomnia; worsening of the depression toward evening; little or no retardation; self-pity rather than self-accusation; and irritability and hypochondriasis. Nihilistic delusions were absent. It was also noted that the neurotic-reactive group did not respond as well to somatic therapy (electroconvulsive treatment or imipramine administration) as did the endogenous patients.

The separatist viewpoint has been maintained by many serious students of depression since the days of Kraepelin and up to this day, and while some novel terminological distinctions have been introduced over the years there has been little divergence with respect to the assignment of the respective clusters of symptoms to these two assumed groups. As early as 1920 Kurt Schneider[17] conceived the idea of a "vital depression" (*vitale Traurigkeit*) as the true expression of a truly endogenous and biologically determined illness. And as recently as 1960[18] and 1965[19] Pollitt proposed and sought to demonstrate the existence in "endogenous" depressions of a biological core and casting to which he gave the name of the "depressive functional shift." This somatic phenomenology, Pollitt's S type, is characterized, in his words, by "an alteration of biological rhythms, metabolism and autonomic balance," among other features, and it represents a syndrome "not seen collectively in any other illness." By contrast, the reactive-neurotic depressions show the presence of the J type constellation. J stands for "justified" and points to the assumed correlation between psychological stress and clinical response in the form of depression. If the clinical response is in this sense "justified," it would presumably also be "understandable" in Jaspersian terms. If Jaspers' criteria of "reactive disease" are applied to the concept of reactive-neurotic depression, the psychopathology becomes explainable and understandable in terms of the patients' character structure and the particular quality and poignancy of the precipitating stress. No such comprehensible correspondence would be found in the autonomous-endogenous depressions. The latter would thus have to be considered to be expressions of a "psychotic process" (Jaspers). While such a neat and engaging division will satisfy our need for clarity, it is to some degree voided by incongruities which emerge upon unbiased clinical scrutiny—at least in a substantial number of patients. Thus many patients suffering from endogenous (manic-depressive) depressions show prior to (or between) their attacks traits of the cyclothymic personality. In fact, cyclothymia has been described as "a miniature manic-depressive psychosis" in the *Psychiatric Dictionary* of Hinsie and Shatzky.[20] In such instances it would seem to this writer that we would be dealing with a Jaspersian "personality development" and not with a "psychotic process." Another instance of incongruity between theory and clinical experience is supplied by those patients who react with a clinically psychotic reaction to a particularly severe external stress; in such cases it appears difficult to maintain the implied correspondence of "reactive" and "neurotic." Beck and Valin[21] reported in 1953 a series of "psychotic" depressive reactions in soldiers who accidentally killed their buddies. These soldiers showed clear-cut psychotic symptoms such as delusions and hallucinations provoked by and centering around the signally traumatic event, and they recovered completely after administration of ECT and/or psychotherapy.

A More Unitary Concept. What do we really mean to stress or to identify by the use of the qualifying adjective "psychotic" in connection with depression? If the term "psychotic depression" is used synonymously with "endogenous depression," as is still customary, it would appear to this writer that such use is ill-suited and confusing because it fuses etiologic and descriptive concepts and dimensions. In contrast to schizophrenia there is no breakthrough of the primary process in depression, and reality testing is impaired only as a result of—and in proportion to—the ascendancy of the morbid affect. Therefore, it seems best to restrict the meaning of the connotation "psychotic" to quantitative issues. Many authorities, such as Paul Hoch and Mapother, espousing the "gradualists'" point of view, consider depression to be a single and unitary disorder in the etiology of which innate predisposition and external stress play their respective and complementary part. Differences in depth of the depression are considered to be merely quantitative and not qualitative expressions of the disease process. Thus Mapother states, as quoted by Beck: "The essence of an attack [of depression] is the clinical fact that the emotions for the time being have lost enduring relation to current experience and whatever their origin and intensity have achieved a sort of autonomy."[22] Mapother and other clinicians with a unitary view on the nature and phenomenology of depression consider that depressions are continuous along a spectrum of severity—that the most severe forms may justly be referred to as "psychotic" and that "the degree to which internal and external factors cooperate (in their genesis) is infinitely variable."[23] Paul Hoch, who also questions the essential independence of neurotic (exogenous) and psychotic (endogenous) depression, expresses his views about this issue in these words:

The dynamic manifestations, the orality, the super-ego structure, etc., are the same [in neurotic and psychotic depression] . . . If the patient had had some previous depressive attacks, he would probably be placed in the psychotic group; if not, he would be placed into the neurotic one. If the patient's depression is developed as a reaction to an outside precipitating factor, then he is often judged as having a neurotic depression . . . . Actually there is no difference between a so-called psychotic or a so-called neurotic depression. The difference is only a matter of degree.[24]

In our view the various "bipolar" aspects of depression and of manic-depressive disease at large are not incompatible with a broad unitary conception of depression (and mania). In contrast to the schizophrenias, depression is comprehensible as an expression of pathology of *one* "psychic system" only—namely, the superego, comprising both the ego-ideal and the conscience. We would say that the intensity of psycho-pathology within one system may be reflected in the clinical expressions and features of the disease in a sufficiently distinctive way to account for significant groupings and differences when the method of factor analysis is applied. And the greater the biological predisposition, the more readily will the psychological "causes and stresses" assume the role of precipitating events and, ultimately, of etiological rationalizations.

MANIA

It is not always realized that nobody doubts the endogenous nature of mania—its total unrelatedness to external causes, and its independence from characterological configurations. Fenichel states that "the depressive side of the manic-depressive phenomena . . . is understood analytically much better than is mania."[25]

The clinical manifestations of mania are almost entirely the reverse of what we see in depression. The only exceptions to this statement are the presence of insomnia and of flight of ideas in the manic episode. The manic does not consider his insomnia as a detriment or burden; on the contrary, he is likely to boast of the fact that he can survive and function splendidly on very little sleep. Flight of ideas connotes an associational abnormality and inferiority in which subordination of ideas to a significant and sustained goal idea is no longer possible. Instead, a leveling of ideas and associations takes place based on simple, irrelevant but recognizable links—such as clang, similarity, opposites, fleeting external perceptions, and similar well-trodden associational paths. It is likely that flight of ideas is an expression of the increased "mental tempo" and the decreased discriminatory capability of the manic patient. To use an analogy to "orality," he "wolfs" his environment without chewing and digesting it properly. Although flight of ideas may occur episodically in schizophrenia, it must be differentiated from schizophrenic incoherence that reflects formal thought and language pathology. None of the abnormalities described by the latter are really found in manic flight of ideas, which, despite its irrelevance and lack of communicative value, is usually "comprehensible" because of the recognizable links. Nor does the manic, in contrast to the schizophrenic, draw any conclusions from ideational sequences based on pathological links.

The remainder of the manic symptomatology may be briefly described in the approximate order of frequency of occurrence. The patient is hyperactive; he, much more than the grandiose schizophrenic, tends to carry out his expansive ideas by whatever means are available to him. The manic hyperactivity is affirmative, not anxious or desperate. In its extreme form it has been described by the term "delirious mania;" it may lead then to death from exhaustion. In less severe forms of the disease the patient shows pressure of speech, restless distractibility, and a euphoric drive to make contact with people, including strangers. He will attempt to draw them into his orbit of euphoria and hyperactivity, dazzle them with his at times infectious humor, and react with irritability or outright anger if he does not meet with the expected reciprocity. If he is delusional, he will show the presence of grandiose or religious-ecstatic delusions. There is heightened interest in sexual activity. Manic patients show an amazing tolerance of fatigue, which is in sharp contrast to the depressed patient.

Within the manic-depressive entity mania occupies one side of this bipolar syndrome. Theoretical formulations of mania along psychody-namic lines have either taken the form of reversing the specific mech-anisms hypothesized for depression or the manic attack is viewed as a "triumph" over the tyranny of the superego. Actually the manic attack is no triumph at all; being an illness, it is maladaptive. The real "triumph" over a tyrannical superego, as over any form of tyranny, aims at responsible ego autonomy and an accommodation within the psychic apparatus between what we owe ourselves and what we owe to others. No manic patient accomplishes this aim during or by his illness.

SOME THEORETICAL OBSERVATIONS

Despite the relative simplicity and coherence of the clinical phenomenology of depression there is considerable uncertainty and lively controversy surrounding the origin and essential nature of this disease, and of its "bipolar alternate," mania. The temptation to define depression within *one*—or one's own—theoretical framework and general psychiatric orientation is particularly great in the case of a condition which is as comprehensible and plausible as "depression." Lack-ing sufficient clinical and experimental verification some of these formu-lations have either been recognized as being somewhat less than final or else relegated to the domain of the history of the concept.

The reader will find accounts of the various attempts toward formu-lating the concept of depression in such excellent reference books as Bellak's *Manic-Depressive Psychosis and Allied Conditions*,[26] Arieti's chapter "Manic-Depressive Psychosis" in the *American Handbook of Psychiatry*,[27] and particularly in Beck's authoritative monograph *Depres-*

sion.[2] We will, therefore, confine ourselves to such comments as appear relevant to the scope and purpose of this presentation.

Etiology. One relevant problem appears to be the need to assign to biological as well as to psychodynamic and social factors the measure of etiological significance which these elements do have. This issue, although universal for depression, has to be settled individually for each patient. Biological explanations seem to find support in the following observations: heredity, especially in identical twins; prompt response of certain patients to somatic treatment, especially electroconvulsive therapy; the presence of autonomic nervous system-symptoms; the presence of other physical symptoms clearly not of a hysterical character; and the observation that manic-depressive attacks occur in patients otherwise free from significant psychopatholgy. Beck, after an exhaustive review of the biological studies of depression, concludes that "there is little, if any, solid knowledge of the specific biological substrate of depression."[28] Kraines'[29] conception of manic-depressive disease as a psychic response to a primarily diencephalic dysfunction raises the interesting question of how one should correlate neurophysiological and psychoanalytical formulations.

The classical psychoanalytical formulations of depression by Freud[30] and Abraham[8] are cast within the broad but rigid doctrine of metapsychology in general and of the libido theory in particular. "Orality" is given a prominent role in the psychodynamic exposition of depression; its prominence is reflected in the many and diverse assumed mechanisms and phenomena which it embraces and which constitute the psychoanalytic model of depression: introjection, external and internal narcissistic supplies, oral ambivalence, superego formation, oral aggression, and so on. Several of these original conceptualizations of depression have been challenged and modified by psychoanalysts who succeeded— but did not follow—Freud, such as Rado, Melanie Klein, Bibring, Jacobson, and others. It must be admitted that the classical psychoanalytical formulations, while theoretically coherent and even plausible, appear nevertheless remote when they are applied to an actual clinical situation. Too much has happened between the "oral phase" (and its vicissitudes in the course of the evolution of infantile sexuality) and the outbreak of the adult depression—even if one would concede the existence of a direct lineage of a spiritual dilemma, such as depression, from a visceral (oral) pathology. The assumption of such a continuity is expressed in a statement which Arieti made when he addressed himself to this particular issue in depression. He said that depression "is the evolutionary outcome at a human symbolic-interpersonal level of the biologic nociceptive pain."[31] And well it might be. Implicit in all this is, of course, the supreme task which confronts present-day psychiatry and occupies much of its research: namely, the neurophysiological and psychological exploration of psychiatric phenomena, such as depression. It is not only a question of the existence and inherently interrelated nature of these two dimensions; the issue also entails the alternatives and choices of therapy, somatic and psychological. Experience tells us from which end, in a given case, our therapeutic efforts will be most effective. At times, like tunnel builders, we dig from both ends. But there is as little therapeutic value in feeding a patient our psychodynamic formulations of his predicament as there is in telling him the chemical formula of an antidepressant pill.

Psychodynamics. All psychodynamic formulations of depression converge, one way or another, on a disturbance in the relationship between the ego and superego. The essential expression of this disturbance is a lowering of the patient's self-esteem. Fenichel states that "in the phenomenology of depression, a greater or lesser loss of self-esteem is in the foreground."[32] The superego may be viewed as a uniquely human and biosocial acquisition: phylogenetically as a potential or anlage, and ontogenetically as a precipitate of significant introjections that are derived from parents and their successors or substitutes. These introjects determine what ultimately evolves in our awareness as "right and good" or as "wrong and evil." The two components of the superego, the ego-ideal and the self-criticizing faculty, normally supply the ego with a set of values and goals the preservation and attainment of which determine our self-esteem. Each component accomplishes this end in its own way. The ego-ideal sets the goals the realization of which the individual experiences with a heightened sense of self-esteem, whereas the self-criticizing faculty acts as a guardian against anything which would tarnish the ego ideal. Normally, as Freud put it, the ego and superego pull in the same direction. The result is that, in this context, the normal person is "an idealist without illusions," and thus without depression. He has established a state of equality and mutual respect between ego and conscience, again without depression. The more excessive, unrealistic, and static the idealized image of self, the harsher the self-criticizing faculty, and the greater the dependence on external supplies to bolster self-esteem, the greater—from a psychodynamic point of view—will be the vulnerability of the ego to succumb to depression. We do not yet know whether, and, if so, to what degree, innate biological factors determine quantitative or qualitative elements within the superego structure, or the power of the ego to cope with superego forces. It may be well to recall that Freud did not think that "ego strength" was entirely the result of interpersonal influences and infusions.

There can be sadness without depression, as in grief and during the accomplishment of resignation. But there can not be depression without sadness. In grief there is a sense of loss, but no loss of self-esteem. The loss is also more likely to affect the "external supplies" while the "internal supplies" remain intact and inviolate. These internal supplies, as the term is used here, represent the inner resources upon which the ego may draw in case of a loss so as to protect its self-esteem and thus avoid depression. One of the protective devices is the ability of the ego to cathect (to use psychoanalytic jargon) alternative objects and objectives; another may be the capacity, in the case of loss or failure, to lower the goals but increase the efforts of pursuit. If the ego is equipped or otherwise supplied with these psychological anodynes and antidepressants, it may be possible to avoid a situation in which, to quote Freud, the loss of the object is transformed into a loss in the ego and in which "the shadow of the object . . . [will fall] upon the ego. . . ."[33] Goethe must have sensed the truth of this formulation when he said:

> Alles koenne man verlieren
> Wenn man bliebe was man ist*

Apart from psychodynamic theories of depression, there have also been some studies and reflections that were devoted to some of the formal aspects of this syndrome. When we stated earlier in this chapter that a certain coherence and cohesion of the personality is preserved in depression we referred to a phenomenological characteristic which has not remained unnoticed by other authors. Arieti remarks about "the relative simplicity of the formal mechanisms of manic-depressive psychosis in comparison to those of schizophrenia."[34] There is no autistic "osmotic depolarization" or formal thought and language pathology in depression. Arieti stresses the fact that the depressed patient shows a "tendency to accept, to internalize the interpersonal environment to a more pronounced degree than . . . the average person."[35] This tendency is a quantitative, not a qualitative departure from the norm. It is also restricted to the affective, not the cognitive aspects of the introject. "In the depressed person the cognitive component of the symbol . . . is not substituted by an autistic . . . symbol as in the schizophrenic and in some psychoneurotics. . . ."[36] It is the selective affective tonality

---

* All could safely be lost and surrendered
  If one would only remain what one is.—Au.

which imposes itself upon the object, the experience, the past and the future, and the self, without participation of the primary process. The transformation of the personality in the affective psychoses (as in organicity) is quantitative. Only in schizophrenia do we note a qualitative transformation of the personality and in a manner which we find so strange and incomprehensible. Even if we make allowances for the Jaspersian concept of the "physical psychotic process," as in frontal-lobe disease, I nevertheless believe that the aforementioned generalization is sound and clinically useful.

REFERENCES

1. H. E. Lehmann. "Clinical Perspectives on Antidepressant Therapy." *American Journal of Psychiatry, 124:* 15, 1968.

2. A. T. Beck. *Depression.* New York, Hoeber, 1967, p. 262.

3. N. D. K. Lewis and Z. A. Piotrowski. *In:* P. H. Hoch and J. Zubin (eds.). *Depression.* New York, Grune & Stratton, 1954, p. 27.

4. A. Hoch. *Benign Stupor: A Study of a New Manic-Depressive Reaction Type.* New York, Macmillan, 1921.

5. A. T. Beck. *Op. cit.,*[2] p. 255.

6. *Ibid.,* p. 39.

7. F. Kennedy and B. Wiesel. "The Clinical Nature of 'Manic-Depressive Equivalents' and the Treatment." *Transactions of the American Neuorological Association, 71:* 96–101, 1946.

8. K. Abraham. "Notes on the Psychoanalytic Investigation and Treatment of Manic-Depressive Insanity and Allied Conditions." *In: Selected Papers on Psychoanalysis.* New York, Basic Books, 1960, pp. 137–156.

9. S. Rado. "The Problem of Melancholia." *International Journal of Psychoanalysis, 9:* 420–438, 1928.

10. J. Mendels and C. Cochrane. "The Nosology of Depression: The Endogenous-Reactive Concept." *American Journal of Psychiatry, 124:* 1, 1968.

11. E. Novak. "The Management of the Menopause." *American Journal of Obstetrics and Gynecology, 40:* 589–595, 1940.

12. S. H. Rosenthal. "The Involutional Depressive Syndrome." *American Journal of Psychiatry, 124:* 21, 1968.

13. *Ibid.,* p. 32.

14. L. G. Kiloh and J. R. B. Ball. *British Medical Journal, 1:* 168, 1961.

15. L. G. Kiloh and R. F. Garside. "The Independence of Neurotic Depression and Endogenous Depression." *International Journal of Psychiatry, 1:* 448, 1965.

16. L. G. Kiloh and R. F. Garside. *British Medical Journal, 1:* 1225, 1962.

17. K. Schneider. "Die Schichtung des emotionellen Lebens und der Aufbau der Depressionszustaende." *Z. Ges. Neurol. Psychiat., 58:* 281, 1920.

18. J. Pollitt. "Depression and the Functional Shift." *Comprehensive Psychiatry, 1:* 381–390, 1960.

19. J. Pollitt. "Suggestions for a Physiological Classification of Depression." *British Journal of Psychiatry, 3:* 489–495, 1965.

20. L. E. Hinsie and J. Shatzky. *Psychiatric Dictionary.* London, Oxford Univer. Press, 1940, p. 131.

21. A. T. Beck and S. Valin. "Psychotic Depressive Reactions in Soldiers who Accidentally Killed their Buddies." *American Journal of Psychiatry, 110:* 347–353, 1953.

22. A. T. Beck. *Op. cit.,*[2] p. 66.

23. J. Mendels and C. Cochrane. *Op. cit.,*[10] p. 2.

24. P. H. Hoch and J. Zubin (eds.). *Current Problems in Psychiatric Diagnosis.* New York, Grune & Stratton, 1953, p. 49.

25. O. Fenichel. *The Psychoanalytic Theory of Neurosis.* New York, Norton, 1945, p. 407.

26. L. Bellak. *Manic-Depressive Psychosis and Allied Conditions.* New York, Grune & Stratton, 1952.

27. S. Arieti. "Manic-Depressive Psychosis." *In:* S. Arieti (ed.). *American Handbook of Psychiatry.* New York, Basic Books, 1959, vol. 1, pp. 419–454.

28. A. T. Beck. *Op. cit.,*[2] p. 152.

29. S. H. Kraines. *Mental Depressions and Their Treatment.* New York, Macmillan, 1957.

30. S. Freud. "Mourning and Melancholia." *In: Collected Papers.* London, Hogarth Press, 1948, vol. 4, pp. 152–170.

31. S. Arieti. *Op. cit.,*[27] p. 445.

32. O. Fenichel. *Op. cit.,*[25] p. 391.

33. S. Freud. *Op. cit.,*[30] p. 159.

34. S. Arieti. *Op. cit.,*[27] p. 445.

35. *Ibid.,* p. 444.

36. *Ibid.*

19

Toward a Comprehensive Psychiatric Diagnosis

"Toward" denotes a movement, a direction, a goal not yet attained, but also not yet abandoned. As any student of the history of medical psychology will readily see, every stage in the evolution of diagnostic, etiological, classificatory, and therapeutic conceptions reflected the then prevailing areas both of knowledge and ignorance, as well as the broader social and scientific attitudes. Against this background succeeding generations of observers of human behavior and particularly the professional medical observers attempted to find answers to those elementary questions "What is it?" "How did it come about?" "What am I going to do about it?" Nobody, with the exception of the great and thus few innovators, could deal with the problems of psychiatric (and medical) diagnosis ahead of his times. After mental illness was no longer viewed as the expression of a visitation by evil spirits and powers and had thus been elevated from a supernatural to a natural phenomenon the question "What is it?" was for some time dealt with, rather inadequately, by a reliance on a phenomenological approach that reflected insignificant variations among countless patients rather than significant correlations or systems of psychopathology. There was at that time also great reliance on the terminological label; there still is, at times. We need words, to be sure; but a pretense of semantic authority may render a real disservice to the reputation and merits of descriptive formulations. Ewen Cameron's counsel (quoted by Hoch and Zubin) may be repeated at this point: "back to better descriptions, less dynamics and more observation, clarify the causes, merge the schools, or, quite frankly, diminish the importance of the diagnosis by substituting simply a summarized statement of what has been found."[1] Thus we may assume that in our search toward a comprehensive diagnosis we are necessarily only at a certain point and level of ability and understanding.

The search for, and the diagnostic significance of, a presenting symptom or aspect of behavior is still valid and even prerequisite; but the shift, both in psychiatry and in the other sciences, from absolutism to relativism requires that we look at the phenomena, in *context*—whatever their nature or clinical prominence may be. "Context" in psychiatric diagnosis calls for a multidimensional view. One of these dimensions may be defined as the constellation of the totality of the presenting symptomatology; the significance of any *one* symptom (part) is code-termined by the configuration of the whole. Hallucinations are a case in point; their clinical significance and diagnostic relevance are largely determined by the patient's state of consciousness at the moment of their occurrence. Thus hallucinations in a state of clear consciousness, particularly auditory hallucinations, would strongly suggest a schizophrenic syndrome or a so-called hallucinosis; by contrast, hallucinations accompanied by cloudiness of consciousness suggest delirium, which, psychiatrically, is a benign hallucinatory state. Hallucinations as part of "dreamy states" in temporal-lobe epilepsy are paroxysmal, ego-alien, and accompanied by other signs of temporal-lobe disease.

As another illustration, the reader will recall the case of the schizophrenic patient who said that $1 + 1$ was "three" because "if two people get together they will have a baby." The miscalculation as such is of little diagnostic value; unless it be viewed in broad context it would not be possible to say more than that it is "wrong." The schizophrenic patient gave this "wrong" answer because of an autistic, parasymbolic derailment; a patient suffering from organic dementia or from feeble-mindedness might give this answer because of a reduction of cognitive capacity. As part of a Gerstmann syndrome the same "miscalculation" would be called "acalculia" and attributed to a lesion in a specific part of the parietal cortex. As an expression of the Ganser syndrome the "wrong answer" would be representative of the "syndrome of approximate answers," a form of "pseudodementia" of uncertain but functional origin.

Another dimension of context is longitudinal. This dimension comprises the issue of the evolution of the psychopathology rather than the question of its identity; it concerns itself with "becoming" rather than with "being." "Becoming" is a more complex process than a chronological account of the history of the present illness or the past history of the patient's life. The study of this process has been undertaken by the founders and proponents of the major theories of personality development in accordance with what to each of them seemed to be the most promising approach. The psychobiological view of Adolf Meyer holds that normal and abnormal personality development results from the interaction of the total personality with the total environment. The fact of the vicissitudes of the instinctual (especially the sexual) endowment of the human organism occupy the center and summit of Freud's theories of personality development, character formation, neuroses, and of the content pathology of the "functional psychoses." Recently, hereditary, constitutional, and other biological factors have taken their seat as permanent members in the process of "becoming." The *formal* aspects of a psychopathology—such as a delusion (including the evaluation of its malignancy), a hallucination, a phobia, and so on—can be moved to the level of a more comprehensive understanding only if the diagnosis of "becoming" adds relevance to the *content* of the delusion, hallucination, or phobia.

Finally, a comprehensive psychiatric diagnosis should also aim at a determination of the patient's capacity for and manner of interaction with others, both in social and psychotherapeutic situations. In this connection we must often give special thought and consideration to judging the patient's tendency or capacity to be dangerous and destructive—physically and otherwise—to himself and/or to others.

To sum up, the road toward a comprehensive psychiatric diagnosis poses a threefold problem. Psychopathology has to be comprehended and evaluated in the contexts of its phenomenological, developmental, and interactional dimensions. Each of these aspects is relevant, although in a given case one aspect may be more relevant than another. Each diagnostic dimension requires mastery of a technique and methodology uniquely its own. It has sometimes been said that the practice of psychiatry is not a science but an "art." It is, in fact, both. While its scientific aspects are obvious, its "artistic" counterpart is perhaps best explained in those psychological terms which we have applied in a previous chapter to the presumed nature of artistic representation of the object in general—namely, the participation of preconscious (and unconscious?) processes, but under the safe and disciplined control and guidance of the secondary process. In the specific area of the psychoanalyst's attitude toward the patient's free associations Freud ruled that "one's 'unconscious memory' is to be given full play."[2] A bad psychiatrist, to paraphrase T. S. Eliot, would be preconscious or "unconscious" when he ought to be conscious and conscious when he ought to be preconscious. Somewhere along the line of a reciprocal relationship of proportions must be the point reserved for the "ideal" psychiatrist and psychoanalyst.

THE PHENOMENOLOGICAL DIAGNOSIS

The scope of the phenomenological diagnosis includes the recognition of the presence and nature of the overt or easily educible symptomatology. It is, therefore, very likely that the phenomenological diagnosis will concern itself with the more conspicuous and thus often the more malignant abnormalities. Symptoms which are either inherently malignant or which have reached a certain stage of intensity are bound to be manifest in the patient's appearance, behavior, and verbal expressions. They are at or near the surface. They usually represent more directly the *formal* aspects of the psychopathology rather than the dynamic *content*. The latter, as will presently be shown, is much less accessible to direct observation and recognition.

In actual practice an experienced examiner will be able to recognize overt psychopathology at sight. The pathology may be expressly displayed or it may be suggested by the hints which the patients give us. It is the patients' total behavior—and not a prefabricated checklist of a possible inventory of symptoms—which should determine and direct the nature and course of the diagnostic interview. A competent mental examination is to a considerable degree responsive to the feedback from the patient's pathology. It is also necessary to follow through with a method of examination that is especially suited to the nature of the symptom that may be either obvious or merely suspected. In this way the diagnosis of the symptom is not only "nailed down" but is also rendered more valid and comprehensive. Depth and context are added to what otherwise would remain a mere notation of an abnormality.

Examples.   A few examples will illustrate this point.

A young man was referred to me because of "nervousness." No further information was given me before I saw him. He was a tall and ruddy 20-year-old who appeared to be in excellent physical condition. He had long hair, in the "hippie" fashion, but was well groomed. He greeted me with a grin, sat down and seemed to wait for me to open the conversation. He may have been embarrassed, I thought; many people "smile" when they actually feel anxious or socially uncomfortable. I asked him what his trouble was. He replied that for the past several months he had felt very self-conscious among strangers. Again he grinned, and I noticed that he turned his head and gave the room a sweeping glance. This was, I felt, the moment to investigate the exact nature and extent of his self-consciousness. It is of utmost importance in successfully reconstructing situational psychopathology to avoid the trap of exchanging generalizations and abstractions with the patient; instead, every effort should be made to recreate in the interview the situation to which a patient may refer in his account. I therefore asked him under what circumstances he had felt self-conscious: Had it been on the street, at work, or perhaps in the subway? He then told me that he had recently been riding in a bus and had noticed that a man looked at him "disapprovingly" because he (the patient) had looked at a girl's legs. At this point it seemed to me essential to determine whether the patient was describing an actual or an imaginary event. I therefore asked him where this man had been sitting and, also, whether the patient had noticed anything that would suggest to him that the man and the girl belonged together. No, he said, they did not belong together. I thought it rather unlikely, although not impossible, that a stranger would indicate disapproval of my patient's looking at the girl's legs. The apparent existence of an idea of reference had now to be clarified; it could develop that we may discover an even more malignant symptom than a mere or fleeting experience of projected psychological causality. I wanted to find out whether the patient was referring only to a "delusion-like idea" or to a "true delusion." So I explained to him that we can at times indeed conclude from the behavior or facial expressions of others what they feel or think at the moment. I gave him some examples. On the other hand, I continued, people may give "signs" of what they think and only those who know the signs will detect and understand them. He replied that the man had seemed to fuss with his eyeglasses and this observation indicated to the patient that the man "didn't want me to look." This conclusion appeared to me to be clearly autistic and I therefore proceeded to test the patient for the possible presence of a formal thought and language disorder. There had been no indication of such a disorder in his spontaneous productions. Nor did he reveal evidence of schizophrenic dementia on such tests as sentence completion, sentence construction, and explanation of similarities and differences. When I asked him what a "cat" was, he replied: "A four-legged feline animal." This definition seemed to be perhaps a trifle overinclusive. I asked him next what a "chair" was. He said: "This has also four legs, but I would not know its sex or gender." This statement is indicative of a semantic shift ("legs") and of interpenetration ("sex"); there is even a subtle tendency toward system-shifting—from "sex" to "gender." I now "fed" him an authentic schizophrenic statement, to test his judgment of it. I told him about the patient who had wrapped cloths around her head in order to prevent thoughts from entering her mind. My patient's response indicated that he did not in the least object to the absurd literalness of that patient's behavior and reasoning. Instead he commented: "She was probably *all wrapped-up* in her thoughts." He thus revealed the schizophrenic thought disorder by allowing the semantic shift around the concept "wrapped" to develop into the broader pathology of system shifting, from the literal into the figurative, thus actually reversing the direction of the first patient's derailment. Of course, he did not correct it by reversing it. The phenomenological diagnosis of a schizophrenic state had now been established. The previously noted affective display could now be more properly viewed as an expression of a schizophrenic affective abnormality, tending toward emotional inappropriateness, which called for an investigation of possible other schizophrenic symptoms and signs. The history of the evolution of the presenting symptoms and the determination of psychodynamic issues would be part of the developmental diagnosis.

Another illustrative example is that of a patient who was admitted to the psychiatric ward in a state of confusion. Physical and neurological examination at the time of admission was negative. He was a man of about 30 years of age. At bedside it was noted that he seemed to be talking to an imaginary—that is, a hallucinated—person. He was overheard saying such phrases as: "Come over here—Don't you say that to me—they are all running down this way—," etc. The content of what he said was ordinary enough, although it indicated that he was experiencing some sort of activity going on around him. He paid no attention to the examiner and was *at the moment* not in contact with his environment. The first diagnostic requirement in such a case, on the basis of the few observations described, is to determine whether one is dealing with a schizophrenic or a nonschizophrenic hallucinatory state. The latter contingency might be either a delirium or a toxic (?) hallucinosis. The first step toward this preliminary diagnosis would be to ascertain whether contact could be made with the patient and whether he was oriented about his temporal and physical surroundings. As soon as he was asked his name he turned his gaze toward the questioner and answered correctly. Fluctuations of consciousness and responsiveness—usually frequent and fugitive—are, of course, characteristic of delirium, but one would not yet know enough about this patient. Routine questions pertaining to orientation revealed that he was disoriented to time, and poorly oriented with regard to person and surroundings. This pattern of disorientation—as well as the nature of the substitutions which he produced in lieu of the correct facts—indicated that his misidentifications were the result of the cognitive insufficiency of delirium, and not of schizophrenic autistic distortion. Specifically, he thought that it was Sunday, that he wanted to go to church "like all these people here," but that "this man" told him that he, the patient, was "no good and would surely go to Hell." He believed himself to be on a prison ward of a hospital and asked the examiner whether he was the judge. If so, he, the patient, would beg him for mercy. Although the patient, when left to himself, would quickly lapse into the aforementioned state of hallucinatory confusion, he was able, when approached, to make some contact. In fact, he tended to cling to the physician. Confused and hallucinated schizophrenics are much more likely to be aloof, suspicious, negativistic, or assaultive, as the case may be. Also, their misidentifications tend to be bizarre as a result of the participation of the primary process in the perceptual and cognitive distortion. It is true that delirious patients, and particularly patients suffering from delirium tremens, have visual rather than auditory hallucinations; the former defects, however, are much more prominent during semidarkness, and the visions may in fact be illusions rather than hallucinations. This patient at the time of this examination was seen during daylight. When we asked the patient who all the other people in the beds were he replied that they may also be prisoners. (Max Levin has stressed the fact that delirious nonschizophrenic patients do not consider themselves in their delusions or environmental misidentifications "singled out as the solitary victims."[3] The element of self-reference that is so characteristic of schizophrenia is lacking.)

Subsequent investigation of this patient's history revealed that he had been previously on the prison ward of our hospital and that he had served a sentence for a misdemeanor. In the light of this information it is obvious that the patient showed the "familiar disorientation" (Max Levin) of delirium. At this point our phenomenological diagnosis was still confined to that of a *syndrome:* delirium. Additional diagnostic procedures, the details of which need not be discussed in this context, would be required to elicit the precise cause and nature of the toxic psychosis from which our patient suffered. It happened that he had a bromide delirium, which was confirmed by a toxic bromide level in the blood. At this point it may be instructive to introduce a hypothetical issue. A patient in a state of intoxication, such as our patient, may present a schizophreniform syndrome, presumably "set free" by toxicity in a "predisposed" person. In such a contingency the limitations of the phenomenological diagnosis, which is inherently partial and preliminary, and the need for further observation of the course of the illness are obvious.

Purposes and Techniques.   It can not be the objective of the phenomenological diagnosis to go beyond the recognition and delineation of the major psychopathological syndromes and thus the determination of the basic nosological entities. This first step toward a comprehensive diagnosis, no matter how expertly taken, will not advance the issue beyond that point. Nevertheless, the accurate and competent assessment of the presenting and readily educible state of the patient's psychopathology (the "mental status") has definite advantages; it is also the first stage for the subsequent stages toward optimal comprehension and therapy. Making a phenomenological diagnosis, impersonal as it may be, imparts some measure of identity to the patient; something has been defined in such terms as we ourselves and among ourselves understand. Furthermore, such a diagnosis also defines, by implication, the course the condition is likely to take and the treatment which promises best results. But even more important than that, the accurate and competent assessment of the presenting psychopathology will prevent the administration of wrong, ineffectual, and possibly harmful "therapy." A few examples may be mentioned as illustrations of this issue. It is, for instance, of great practical importance—as I recently pointed out as a discussant in a clinical neuropathological conference[4]—to differentiate between psychogenic retarded depression and organic apathy and unresponsiveness accompanying coarse brain disease. If the true nature of the latter is not recognized and the condition is thus wrongly diagnosed as, say, "involutional melancholia," the patient may not only get the wrong treatment (such as electroconvulsive therapy) but he would also be deprived of the *right* treatment that might save or help him; in any case, valuable time would be lost. In less dramatic situations failure to recognize the existence of a mild degree of schizophrenic affective blunting and conceptual blurring may lead to the application of psychotherapeutic techniques which are not only beyond the patient's affective and cognitive capabilities but which also, because of their "uncovering" methods and aims, may in fact do a great deal of harm. It may be said that our entire approach toward the developmental and interactional diagnosis—including the choice of therapy—is basically guided and determined by the results of the phenomenological assessment.

It is beyond the scope of this chapter to give a detailed exposition on the techniques of the phenomenological mental examination. But I believe that a few general principles may be worth mentioning. For their successful implementation the psychiatrist will have to draw on his store of information, on his "knowledge in depth," and on the feedback signals which he will receive from the patient. The relatively few but basic and major objectives of the initial diagnostic steps may be summed up as follows.

1. We want to determine whether or to what degree the patient is in contact with his environment; whether his general conduct is coherent and controlled.

2. We may either notice indications of or test for evidence of cognitive impairment suggestive of organic dementia or delirium.

3. We will either notice or test for evidence of a formal thought and language disorder suggestive of schizophrenic dementia.

4. We must evaluate the patient's affective participation and display.

5. We must try to elicit the presence, intensity, character, and degree of malignancy of the patient's false beliefs or delusions.

6. We will be alert to any indication of autistic "depolarization" in the patient's verbal and nonverbal expressions.

7. The clinical context may require investigation into the presence of perceptual disorders.

After the major areas of psychopathology have been determined and mapped out, a more detailed and specific method of examination (as dictated by the nature of the particular pathology under investigation) is usually required. This may include the administration of special clinical-psychological tests, such as the Rorschach test, the Thematic Apperception Test, the Bender-Gestalt test, Goldstein's various sorting tests, and others. I also believe that a routine electroencephalogram could profitably take its place alongside use of the routine chest x-ray in the practice of clinical psychiatry.

We have not included the psychopatholgy of character in our discussion of the phenomenological diagnosis for several reasons. It is, of course, true that character traits, both normal and neurotic, will be suggested even during the first contact with a patient; however, the phenomenology of character structure and character deformation is subtle, slight, ambiguous, and thus quite incomplete during the initial interview, even when undertaken by an experienced examiner. Character assessment requires the participation of the physician's "preconscious skills" and nonverbal tools in addition to his conscious knowledge of the facts and formulations of psychopathology. Furthermore, the character diagnosis appears to be more relevant to the discussion of the developmental and interactional diagnosis. But if an attempt is being made to get a limited but reliable view of a patient's character structure it is necessary that the examiner's approach meets the special requirements of such an undertaking. His questions should be constructed in such a way as to enable and even *force* the patient to respond with spontaneous elaborations rather than with a "yes" or "no." The examiner must also exercise his ability of transforming the abstract conceptualizations of psychopathology into "concrete" living experiences. Psychopathology, particularly in the character neuroses, reveals itself more convincingly in events than in words.

The following brief account of an examination which I conducted during a seminar may serve as an illustration.

The patient had been admitted to the psychiatric ward because of depression and suicidal rumination. He was a family man in his middle 50s. His business had recently lost money, through no fault of his. He felt ashamed that he could not provide for his wife and children. He indicated that he had spent much more money than he could really afford and that he was in fact in debt. The psychiatric resident pursued in his interrogation the line of "internalized aggression," trying to explain to the patient the reason for his depression. The patient, naturally, professed that he didn't hate anybody. At this point I intervened and asked the patient how many suits he owned. "Three," he replied. And how many dresses did his wife own? A pensive smile took possession of his face and he said: "About forty." I then asked him what his wife had given him for his last birthday and he said that he had received a new razor from her. And what had he given her for her last birthday? With obvious pride he told us that he had bought her a beautiful set of golden ear rings, which cost him several hundred dollars. Some of my younger colleagues found this method of examination rather unconventional, almost common; they also wondered why I had not given the patient an "interpretation" of his obvious "masochism." As to the first question, I pointed out that certain features of psychopathology are best elicited by recreating the reality and recollection of the events which represent them "live," so to speak; with regard to interpretation, I pointed both to the issue of timing, the initial tentativeness of psychodynamic formulations, and the possibility of a premature or wrong interpretation's doing either no good or perhaps actual harm. At this point I knew little about the patient's ego strength and the strength or weaknesses of his defenses. This patient, it seemed to me, was in no condition to be told that he "enjoyed suffering," which would mean nothing to him, or that he behaved like a doormat, which could only increase his self-contempt. Every experienced psychiatrist recognizes the importance of an accurate assessment of the patient's therapeutic tolerance. He may also agree that, in an example such as this, some nonverbal (and thus less traumatic) communication of all these likely contingencies may have reached the patient if he was ready and strong enough to receive it.

THE DEVELOPMENTAL DIAGNOSIS

The developmental diagnosis aims at a better and more comprehensive understanding of the presenting psychopathology by viewing it in the context of its origin and subsequent development. Generally speaking, a temporal dimension is added that links phenomenology or "being" with "evolving" or "becoming." This temporal dimension adds continuity to our efforts to make the psychiatric diagnosis more meaningful and intelligible. The developmental "diagnosis" or appraisal will thus concern itself with issues which constitute, or are part of, the "history of the present illness," the patient's past life history, and the etiology (or rather the array of interacting causative and contributory factors) that led to the presenting psychopathology.

The scope of the question "How did it come about?" still far exceeds our ability to supply definitive answers. Psychoanalysis, which addressed itself preeminently to this question, concerned itself only with *one* area of psychopathology—namely, the abnormal personality development as seen in the neuroses, all its other major discoveries or speculative applications notwithstanding. The entire psychoanalytic literature fundamentally deals with the factual coherence and continuity of psychopathology; the presenting psychopathology is intelligible in terms of past predispositions, life experiences, and defensive adaptations or failures. This conception is indeed true for many, but not for all, forms of psychopathology. The writer therefore suggests that the problem of the developmental diagnosis could be presented, following Jaspers' hypothesis, by stressing two major ways of "becoming" ill. The first possibility—which Jaspers called "personality development" and which is the main theme of psychoanalytic theory and practice—is represented by the understandable progression of personality or character deformations, interspersed, in times of crisis, with either accentuations or more isolated symptoms, all of which are reversible. There is no real break in the personality in this contingency; the patient may indeed get worse, but he will not become "different." In the case of the second possibility, however, which (as Fish reports) Jaspers called the "psychic process" and the "physical psychotic process," "a new development . . . begins at a definite point in time."[5] This decisive turning point in the patient's psychological status signals an entirely new direction in the evolution of psychopathology from which there is, so it is assumed, no return to the former self.

In Terms of Personality Development

In the neuroses the "history of the present illness" is largely contained in the history of the patient's early (and, indeed, entire) life. Recent developments, if at all relevant, may perhaps affect the intensity of the symptoms but not their essence. Since neurosis—even in its disabling and symptomatic (hysterical or obsessive-compulsive) forms, is the manifestation of a coherent albeit pathological development—the recent history and psychopathology can not be expected to represent more than another variation on the original theme. Character, despite its relative stability and stubborn solidification, does not readily reveal itself in the verbal traffic of the initial interview. We speak of character as the sum total of essentially psychodynamic ego modifications that are brought about as a result of the interaction of the individual with significant persons in his environment. The character structure, both normal and pathological, is predominantly of interpersonal or social origin and its manifestations are consequently also largely interactional. Character manifestations, to a perceptive or professional observer, are quite predictable. Pathological character traits, in contrast to symptoms, represent more permanent, less conspicuous, and more ego-syntonic expressions and attempts at resolution of conflict.

Just as psychoanalysis started with the study and treatment of the neurotic *symptom*—that strange child of unconscious, conflicting imperatives—and turned its gaze and efforts much later to the more prosaic, predictable, and permanent features of the personality structure, so does the clinical diagnosis usually succeed much earlier and easier in defining and identifying the symptom than in unraveling the identity, interrelationships, and developmental aspects of the character pathology. During our contact with the patient the developmental element inherent in the character diagnosis is doubly represented, so to speak. The evolution of the character diagnosis is first traced from the account which the patient gives us of his past life experiences, from childhood to the present; from the nature of his present symptoms; and from other indications in his behavior, both gross and subtle. At this early stage the character diagnosis is largely descriptive, although aimed at becoming dynamic, and largely tentative, although aimed toward becoming definitive. The further evolution of the character diagnosis coincides with the initiation and progression of psychotherapy, particularly psychoanalytic therapy. As the sources and areas of information given to us by the patient increase, and also as the patient reacts (through the transference) to the psychiatrist in accordance with his neurotic character structure, we will increasingly note the evolving patterns as well as the remedial modifications within his ego, if therapy is successful. Then the character diagnosis is largely dynamic and becomes more and more definitive.

As this is not a text on the techniques and principles of psychoanalytic "diagnosis in depth," our presentation of these issues will remain brief. We mean only to set forth and suggest some principles, within the broader context of this chapter. For the same reason, extensive clinical illustrations are omitted. When listening to the gradually unfolding mental content of a patient in therapy, the experienced psychiatrist will soon recognize the existence and prominence of certain psychological issues and patterns. He will designate them in accordance with his theory of personality development and neurotic deviation. The leading theme of the neurosis becomes clearer—with regard to its origins, its manifestations, and its consequences in the life of the patient. It is far more important to diagnose the *Leitmotif* of the character psychopathology than to get lost in or enamored of the pursuit of a fragmentary detail (such as a slip of the tongue, a symptomatic act, or a dream element).

In this connection I should like to mention another possible source of error in the pursuit of the developmental diagnosis and illustrate this contingency with a well-documented case history. This particular case, in addition, serves as a suitable link to the immediately following description of the "physical psychotic process." The error to which I refer consists of making a characterological diagnosis without sufficient evidence of supporting characterological development, compounded by failure to recognize the existence of a "new development."

A 15-year-old girl began to vomit, about once a day, immediately after having lost a class presidential election. This started about 6 months before her admission to the hospital. She lost weight and it was noted that she staggered when she walked, "but without ataxia of an organic or abasic nature." The history further contained a reference to episodes of depression and of "a pressure in the head." No striking abnormalities were noted on physical or neurological examination, at that time. She was referred for psychiatric treatment in the course of which "it soon became apparent that there was a marked degree of sexual stimulation at home . . . . Whenever the mother went on a trip she substituted for the mother, cooking the father's meals and sleeping with him (in the same room). During such occasions she frequently wore only a pajama top . . . sleeping arrangements were quite sexually stimulating to all concerned." The only neurological sign noted on admission (for observation for gastric disease) was nystagmus, both horizontal and circular. Waxy flexibility was also recorded. On the morning following admission the patient was found dead. I quote the following observations from my discussion of the case. "The comments in the clinical history pertaining to sex that 'the sleeping arrangements were quite stimulating to all concerned' is . . . an understandable but not proven interpretation. Who said that he or she suffered from, enjoyed, or was indifferent to, these arrangements? . . . sexual secrecy can 'understandably' be as traumatic as can be seductiveness. However, in this case we have to confront the more serious problem of a differential diagnosis between organicity and psychogenicity. . . . Almost all of her symptoms, *in isolation*, could understandably be of emotional origin: vomiting, shortness of breath, fainting, psychogenic blindness, apparent episodic lowering of the level of consciousness, cataplectic states, hysterical disorders of gait. The only exception appears to be the presence of nystagmus. I submit that it is contrary to our conception of hysteria to have more than *one* conversion symptom. . . . Thus the multiplicity and perhaps also the pattern of the symptoms, much more than their nature seem to militate against a diagnosis of hysteria." Later in the discussion I said: "I am, however, concerned over the combination of vomiting, gait disturbance, nystagmus and episodes of flaccidity without loss of consciousness. I would want a thorough investigation of the archicerebellum and the midline cerebellar structures above and below it . . . . This is the direction in which I would proceed." Autopsy disclosed a large medulloblastoma arising from the midline cerebellar structures. A constructively critical reviewer of this case would have to conclude that the psychological interpretation, such as it was, had been imposed upon, instead of derived from, the history of the patient's present and final illness.[6]

In Terms of the Physical Psychotic Process

Significant alterations of brain function resulting from physical processes—whether they are brought about by structural, metabolic, or paroxysmal (epileptic) disease—result in corresponding alterations in the mental life of the patient of such a nature as to clearly indicate the Jaspersian conception of a new development which can be traced to a definite point in time. The particular nature of this physical process will determine whether the change is transient, as in delirium or in epileptic psychopathology, or permanent, as is the case in the various forms of dementia and other coarse brain disease. In all such instances the "history of the present illness" will clearly reveal that a decisive break in the familiar behavior and general mental condition of the patient has occurred, either gradually and subtly or more suddenly and dramatically, and that the patient's present state of mind is irreconcilable with the features of his premorbid personality. Fish, paraphrasing Jaspers, states that "there is an indiscriminate irregularity of the symptoms and course of the illness. All the phenomena succeed one another in an underivable confusion. . . ."[7] Thus the goal of the developmental diagnosis in such patients is best achieved by trying to ascertain, step by step and with great accuracy, the identity and *sequence* of the symptomatology and to establish the existence of that substantial transmutation which is inherent in the physical psychotic process.

As an example of the principle, one may say that the so-called "psychic seizures" among the epilepsies—such as temporal-lobe seizures and epileptic twilight states—represent the essence of the "physical psychotic state" most completely and instructively. At a certain point in time coincident with the onset of the paroxysm, a radical alteration in the patient's behavior (twilight state) or mental experiences (dreamy state) takes place. In neither instance can any comprehensible link be detected between the psychopathology and the patient's previous and usual mental make-up. The premorbid (preictal) personality is fully restored upon cessation of the epileptic discharge. In actual clinical practice it is of great diagnostic significance to elicit and verify the suddenness, the episodic character, and the sequence of the usually impressive symptomatology. Also, it is both of practical and theoretical interest to realize, as Jackson stressed, that patients suffering from epileptic twilight states can not be held responsible or accountable for whatever antisocial or criminal acts they may commit in the course of their attacks. They are not *motivated.* This fact alone is convincing evidence for the existence, in these patients, of a "physical psychotic process."

In cases of frontal-lobe disease, either from general paresis or tumor, the developmental history is equally representative of the physical psychotic process. There may be a history of personality changes too subtle to be clinically impressive but too painfully embarrassing to have been overlooked by the family. It is well known how often the family of such patients tell us that they can simply no longer recognize "the same person" in the patient. Alternatively, the transmutation of the personality in these patients may take place more suddenly, such as when they suffer short lapses of alertness with fugitive confusion, transient aphasia or monoplegia, or a convulsive seizure (the first of its kind in their life).

In contrast to the "psychic process," which will be described next, the physical psychotic process may be transient, or permanent and irreversible.

In Terms of the Psychic Process

Karl Jaspers,[8] in a paper on delusional jealousy, hypothesized in 1910 the existence of an irreversible and "nonunderstandable" psychic transformation in certain patients with paranoid symptoms. The presenting psychopathology in such cases, Jaspers thought, could not be comprehended or explained in terms of the patients' premorbid personality structure, either as a natural development or as an accentuation caused by external adaptive stress. It was also assumed that coarse brain disease was absent. Fish comments that "Jaspers did not say that the psychic process was synonymous with schizophrenia, although in a later work he pointed out that in a large number of cases where there was a process, the psychological changes of schizophrenia were present."[9]

I have throughout this book stressed the inherently incomprehensible character of the schizophrenic psychopathology and thus, implicitly, its unrelatedness to the premorbid personality structure as well as its irreconcilability with the functioning of the secondary process. But I must confess that the introduction of the concept of the psychic process creates problems as well as it seems to solve others. There is, of course, little doubt that a carefully taken developmental "history of the present illness" in patients suffering from either the process-type or the episodic variety of schizophrenia will reveal significant psychological and behavioral abnormalities wholly inconsistent with their previous and familiar personality and conduct. The reader will recall our saying that a neurosis will decompensate into a more severe neurosis but not into a schizophrenia. But no matter how sound a principle may appear and how readily it may be embraced, clinical experience teaches us often enough that the so-called exceptions are, more likely, representations of still-unknown facts and that we can only hope that we will some day learn to recognize these facts as part of a larger rule. In the specific instance of schizophrenia, the hypothesis of the "psychic process" has to be reconciled with the concept of the schizoid personality; allowances have to be made for the existence of the reversible "schizophreniform psychoses"; the existence of the so-called symptomatic schizophrenias accompanying coarse or epileptic brain disease may tend to lessen the credibility of a too-rigid distinction between the "psychic process" and the "physical psychotic process." Nevertheless, it is my belief that, if all relevant elements of a comprehensive diagnosis are taken into consideration, the "new development" of the schizophrenic psychopathology—incomprehensible both with regard to phenomenology and personality development—constitutes a most useful and reliable diagnostic observation and prognostic guide.

In the area of nonschizophrenia, the hypothesis of the psychic process finds expression in our attempts to differentiate paranoia vera from episodic paranoid "states." Cyclic or phasic psychoses of whatever variety do not conform with Jaspers' definition of the psychic process, even if we must admit that these disorders, while they last, fundamentally alter the patient's behavior and mental experiences.

THE INTERACTIONAL DIAGNOSIS

Phenomenological and developmental features converge in providing us with the data upon which we base our determination of the patient's capacity for and quality of contact—that is, psychosocial interaction. The need for interactional appraisal is constant, regardless of whether we see a patient once or for several years. The accuracy of the psychosocial assessment contributes not only to making the clinical diagnosis more precise but also to the proper choice in the selection of the strategy and tactics of therapy. Like all the other aspects which enter into the making of a comprehensive psychiatric diagnosis, the interactional diagnosis helps us to answer the question "What am I going to do about it?" And very often, particularly in psychoanalytic therapy, it represents the problem about which something has to be done.

Extreme degrees of interactional psychopathology are, of course, found in the major psychiatric disorders (the psychoses). There may be instances of clouding of consciousness, catatonic mutism, cognitive insufficiency, paranoid negativism, schizophrenic incoherence of thought and language, or severe agitation or retardation owing to depression. In such instances there will be no difficulty in recognizing the presence and nature of the interactional pathology. The more severe or malignant the interactional incapacity or distortion, the more will the strategy of therapy shift from psychological or interactional to physical or "impersonal" therapy—from the appeal to the person to the appeal to the soma.

In psychoanalytic treatment—which is the most sophisticated, the most demanding, and (I believe) the most significantly interactional of all psychotherapies—the recognition and interpretation of, as well as the reaction to, the interactional display on the part of the patient occupies most of the therapist's attention and makes the greatest claims to his professional efforts and skills. Freud, it will be recalled, defined psychoanalysis as that form of psychotherapy which makes use of resistances and transference; both phenomena are intensely interactional and the direct expression of the "therapeutic confrontation." To do justice to the magnitude and ramifications of this issue would require a very substantial text on the techniques of psychoanalytic therapy and is quite beyond the scope of this chapter. I may, however, mention briefly some of the major areas of relevance of the interactional diagnosis in the field and course of psychotherapy.

In addition to the issues of resistances and transferences we may consider the interactional manifestations of the character structure and the neurosis itself; the patient's interactional responses to our interpretations and therapeutic interventions; and the interactional manifestations of progress in therapy. In regard to the latter a few comments may be useful. Desirable modifications in the behavior of the patient toward others, including the therapist, may be noted in different ways. Previously predominant neurotic trends may show signs of having abated or they may be reversed. A previously neurotically compliant patient may show signs of standing up for his rights, appropriately, and interrupt or contradict the psychiatrist, without meaning or giving offense. Some of his transcendent false beliefs show evidence of having given way to more realistic appraisals; the neurotic *image* of the therapist dissolves and is replaced by the *person* who, in the newly acquired outlook of the patient, is neither demolished nor vulgarized. In his relations to the psychiatrist the patient realizes, more and more, that he has neither to fear nor to expect as much from the physician (and his equivalent representations) as was assumed and displayed at the beginning of therapy.

PROBLEMS BEYOND TODAY

It may be fitting to conclude this chapter by raising a few related but controversial issues and accepting the challenge of meeting them. Our diagnostic potential—both in the field of phenomenology and of evolution of personality and of psychopathology—is quite considerable. As far as therapy is concerned, our theories are ample and thoughtful, ranging from the most sophisticated to the most pragmatic approaches. Our tools and methods are attuned to the particular character and exigencies of the problems with which we are confronted in our daily work. Our successes and failures are well within general medical expectations and statistics. Intuition and research will no doubt add new dimensions and new knowledge. And yet! What is our goal— what should be our goal in medical psychology? What are the limits of our power and the boundaries of our competence and responsibility? Should they be reconsidered and revised?

There is no particular problem in defining and pursuing any of these goals and issues in the areas of major psychopathology, such as the schizophrenias, the organic syndromes, or the affective psychoses. In all of these conditions the abnormalities are obvious, genuine and, ultimately, biological. The organismic fiber is diseased, the need for repair is evident, and the goals, methods, and possibilities for our intervention are coincident with the pursuits of rational science. A somewhat different situation presents itself in the case of the neuroses and of other states of, let us say, subjective discomfort and discontent—many of which disorders seem to be related to objective indications of psychosocial failures and limitations.

In his book *Civilization and its Discontents* Freud[10] raised the issue of social origins and contributions in the sphere of human unhappiness and human neurosis. He dealt with this subject in terms of his times and his theories. Both have since changed. But the issue has not only remained, but it has perhaps also grown more *sinister*. Freud saw in the "social neuroses" an analogy to the human variety, and although he cautioned us against equating one with the other he expressed the hope that "to analytic dissection of these social neuroses therapeutic recommendations might follow which could claim a great practical interest."[11] But this hope is quickly dampened, "since no one possesses power to compel the community to adopt the therapy."[12] Some fifteen years before Hiroshima Freud thought that men "could now very easily exterminate one another to the last man."[13] And he abstained from making judgments or urgent recommendations, declaring his impartiality, claiming that he really knew very little about these things (!), and invoking at the end of the book "eternal Eros" to come to the rescue of mankind. I am inclined to believe that he would have accepted Thanatos with similar detachment and resignation!

But our problems, as we view them in these concluding paragraphs, are not only those of being threatened by self-imposed death, but also by self-imposed life. Evolution, at the human level, has largely ceased to be biological. Instead, it has become psychosocial—and its most pressing problems are ecological consequences. Profound alterations of living have been let loose with the explosive expansion of technology, communication, and the sheer numbers of mouths which must breathe and eat. I shall be careful so as not to overstate the issue. Nor am I unaware of the potential for human growth and fulfillment which modern society still offers and of which many people have been quite capable of taking fullest advantage. But some of the questions which are being anxiously asked are these: Are some aspects of the environment which we have created beyond the capacity of human adaptation? Are other aspects of our way of life contrary to the biological needs of the human mind? Do we need speed or repose? Can the conquest of outer space fill the void of "inner space" within humanity? Are the subtle acids of faulty metabolism to be matched and augmented by the invisible poisons of industrial wastes? Is our psychic apparatus, already engaged in the task of protecting consciousness from the return of the repressed and the setting free of the primitive, sufficiently armed against the rising din and the ceaseless rush of perceptual assault which modern man created and invited?

Environmental-preventive medicine has always accepted the responsibility, and proved its competence, to deal with certain tangible health hazards inherent in or introduced into our physical surroundings. The psychiatrist, as a scientific medical professional man, has the competence and responsibility to address himself to all those man-made cultural and environmental forces which threaten man's adaptive reserves, emotional needs, and soul-sustaining values. A psychiatrist in his lifetime will diagnose and treat a handful of psychiatric casualties. But is there not a bitter irony in treating the wounds of battle if it could be within our power to prevent them from being inflicted?

REFERENCES

1. P. H. Hoch and J. Zubin, (eds.). *Current Problems in Psychiatric Diagnosis.* New York, Grune & Stratton, 1953, p. 42.
2. S. Freud. *Collected Papers.* London, Hogarth Press, 1948, vol. 2, pp. 324–325.
3. M. Levin. "Toxic Psychoses." *In:* S. Arieti (ed.). *American Handbook of Psychiatry.* New York, Basic Books, 1959, vol. 2, p. 1223.
4. "Clinical Neuropathological Conference." *Diseases of the Nervous System,* vol. 30, #1, January 1969, p. 58 ff.
5. F. J. Fish. *Schizophrenia.* Baltimore, Williams & Wilkins, 1962, p. 85.
6. "Clinical Neuropathological Conference." *Diseases of the Nervous System,* vol. 24, #12, December 1963, pp. 758–762.
7. F. J. Fish. *Op. cit.,*[5] p. 85.
8. K. Jaspers. "Eifersuchtswahn. Ein Beitrag zur Frage 'Entwicklung einer Persoenlichkeit oder Prozess.'" Zeitschrift f.d Gesamte Neurologic und Psychiatrie, vol. 1, 1910, p. 567.
9. F. J. Fish. *Op. cit.,*[5] p. 84.
10. S. Freud. *Civilization and its Discontents.* London, Hogarth Press, 1946.
11. *Ibid.,* p. 141.
12. *Ibid.,* p. 142.
13. *Ibid.,* p. 144.

Index

Footnotes are indicated by *n* following the page number.